Brussels

Derek Blyth and Rory Watson

Prentice Hall Travel

New York • London • Toronto • Sydney • Tokyo • Singapore

THE AMERICAN EXPRESS ® TRAVEL GUIDES

Published in the United States by
Prentice Hall General Reference
A division of Simon & Schuster, Inc.
15 Columbus Circle
New York, NY 10023

PRENTICE HALL and colophon are
registered trademarks of
Simon & Schuster, Inc.

First published in the United
Kingdom by Mitchell Beazley
International Ltd, Michelin House
81 Fulham Road, London SW3 6RB

Edited, designed and produced by
Castle House Press, Llantrisant
Mid Glamorgan CF7 8EU, Wales

Library of Congress Catalog Card
Number 92-082887
ISBN 0-671-84933-6

The editors thank Neil Hanson and
Alex Taylor of Lovell Johns, David
Haslam, Hilary Bird, Sally Darlington,
Anne Evans, Melanie Gould, Anna
Holmes, Muriel and Alf Jackson, and
Andrea Thomas for their assistance
during the preparation of this edition.

FOR THE SERIES:
Series Editor:
  David Townsend Jones
Map Editor: David Haslam
Indexer: Hilary Bird
Gazetteer: Anne Evans
Cover design: Roger Walton Studio

FOR THIS EDITION:
Edited on desktop by:
  Eileen Townsend Jones
Illustrators:
  Sylvia Hughes-Williams,
  David Evans
Art editor: Eileen Townsend Jones
Cover photo: Joyce Photographics/
  Colorific

FOR MITCHELL BEAZLEY:
Art Director: Tim Foster
Managing Editor: Alison Starling
Production: Matthew Batchelor

PRODUCTION CREDITS:
Maps by Lovell Johns, Oxford,
  England
Metro and tram map by TCS,
  Aldershot, England
Typeset in Garamond and
  News Gothic
Desktop layout in Ventura
  Publisher
Linotronic output by
  Tradespools Limited, Frome,
  England

Contents

How to use this book   6
Key to symbols; Information for readers   7
About the authors   8

Introduction — A tale of two cities   11

Culture, history and background

Landmarks in Brussels' history   15
A Belgian who's who   20
The international institutions   26
The European Community locations   27
The people   30
The language question   30
The architecture of Brussels   32
Five centuries of Belgian painting   38

Basic information

Before you go   44
   44: Documents required; Insurance; Money. **45:** Customs.
   46: Tax refunds; Belgian National Tourist Offices. **47:** Getting
   there. **48:** Clothes; General Delivery.
Getting around   48
   48: From airport to city; From stations to city. **49:** Public
   transport; Tickets. **50:** Metro; Trams. **51:** Buses; Taxis;
   Driving. **52:** Car rental. **53:** Bicycles; Trains; On foot.
On-the-spot information   53
   53: Time zones. **54:** Climate; Public holidays; Banks and
   currency exchange. **55:** Shopping and rush hours; Post,
   telephone, fax. **57:** Public lavatories; Electricity; Laws and
   regulations; Etiquette; Tipping. **58:** Disabled visitors;
   Publications. **59:** Museums; Brussels for free.
Useful addresses   59
   59: Tourist information. **60:** Post offices; Telephone services;
   Bus, taxi and walking tours; Airlines; Ferry companies.
   61: Coaches; Bookstores; Worship; Embassies.
Business in Brussels   62
   62: Business services; Translation agencies. **63:** Couriers.

Emergency information   64

64: Emergency services; Medical/dental problems; Pharmacies; Automobile accidents/breakdowns. **65:** Help line; Lost passport/travelers checks/cards/property; Emergency phrases.

Planning your visit

When to go	66
The Brussels calendar	69
Where to go	72

Sightseeing

Introduction	75
Sights classified by area	76-77
Walks and tram rides	78
Sightseeing themes	90
Museums	94
Landmark buildings	120
Ecclesiastical buildings	125
Streetscapes and neighborhoods	130
Off the beaten track	138
Parks and open spaces	143
Excursions	150

Where to stay

Making your choice	154
Hotels classified by area	158
Brussels' hotels A to Z	158
Apartment hotels	163

Eating and drinking

Dining out in Brussels	164
Restaurants and cafés classified by area	166
Brussels' restaurants A to Z	167
Eating in the European Quarter	172
Belgian beers	175
Cafés	176
Cafés A to Z	177

Entertainments   *by Lucy Walker*

Brussels by night	180
Performing arts	180
Nightlife	185

Shopping *by Lucy Walker*

Where to go 191
What to buy 193
   International clothing sizes chart 194

Recreation

Brussels for children 205
Spectator sports 208
Participant sports 209

Words and phrases

A brief guide to French 213

Index 217
List of street names 226
International conversion formulae at back of book

Maps

Belgium 14
The European Quarter 73
Area: The Lower Town 79
Area: The Upper Town 82
Area: Ixelles 85
Area: Forêt de Soignes 87
Grand'Place 133

Key to main map pages 229
Brussels Environs Maps **1** and **2**
Brussels City Maps **3** to **6**

Tram and metro systems at back of book

How to use this book

Few guidelines are needed to understand how this book works:

- For the general organization of the book, see CONTENTS on the pages preceding this one.
- Wherever appropriate, chapters and sections are arranged alphabetically, with headings appearing in **CAPITALS.**
- Often these headings are followed by location and practical information printed in *italics.*
- As you turn the pages, you will find subject headers, similar to those used in telephone directories, printed in CAPITALS in the top corner of each page.
- If you still cannot find what you need, check in the comprehensive and exhaustively cross-referenced INDEX at the back of the book.
- Following the index, a LIST OF STREET NAMES provides map references for all roads and streets mentioned in the book that are located within the areas covered by the main city maps.

CROSS-REFERENCES
These are printed in SMALL CAPITALS, referring you to other sections or alphabetical entries in the book. Care has been taken to ensure that such cross-references are self-explanatory. Often, page references are also given, although their excessive use would be intrusive and ugly.

FLOORS
We use the European convention in this book: "ground floor" means the floor at ground level (called by Americans the "first floor").

AUTHORS' ACKNOWLEDGMENTS

The authors would like to thank the following for their help and advice: Val Jacobs, Danielle Larivière, Etienne Meurice, Barney Trench, and last but not least, that invaluable Brussels institution, *The Bulletin.*

Key to symbols

- ☎ Telephone
- [Fx] Facsimile (fax)
- ★ Recommended sight
- *i* Tourist information
- ⇐ Parking
- 🏛 Building of architectural interest
- [☉] Free entrance
- [☒] Entrance fee payable
- *Ƙ* Guided tour
- ☕ Cafeteria
- ♣ Special interest for children
- 📷 Photography forbidden
- ✎ Hotel
- ⌂ Simple hotel
- 🏨 Luxury hotel
- ☐ Cheap
- ☐ Inexpensive
- ☐ Moderately priced
- ☐ Expensive
- ☐ Very expensive
- [AE] American Express
- [◆] Diners Club
- [◐] MasterCard/Eurocard
- [VISA] Visa

- ⊞ Air conditioning
- ☐ Secure garage
- ☺ Quiet hotel
- ✿ Garden
- ≪ Good view
- ♦ Elevator
- 🐕 Dogs not allowed
- ☐ TV in each room
- ☎ Telephone in each room
- ≋ Swimming pool
- ♨ Sauna
- ⚐ Golf
- ♔ Gym/fitness facilities
- 🖥 Business center
- ♟ Conference facilities
- ▤ Mini-bar
- ☗ Bar
- ☰ Restaurant
- ♣ Good value (in its class)
- ♨ Simple restaurant
- ☖ Luxury restaurant
- ☰ Good wines
- ☻ Open-air dining
- ♪ Live music

7

About the authors

Born in Scotland, **Derek Blyth** is a European writer, translator and journalist. He has lived in the Low Countries since 1980 and has written several travel books including *Flemish Cities Explored* and two titles in this series, *American Express Amsterdam, Rotterdam & The Hague* and *American Express Berlin*. Madly fond of Brussels and Belgium, he currently writes for *The Bulletin* magazine in Brussels and can occasionally be found drinking a *Bière Blanche* at Café Cirio or buying mushrooms at the Place du Châtelain market.

Derek Blyth's fellow-Scot **Rory Watson** has been Brussels bureau chief of *The European* since December 1990, having previously worked as a journalist in Brussels from 1976 to 1984. Before joining *The European* he worked for nine years for *The Scotsman,* both as European correspondent and London Editor. He has traveled widely in Western Europe.

Lucy Walker, Brussels correspondent of *The European,* contributed the chapters on SHOPPING and ENTERTAINMENTS, and some sections of BASIC INFORMATION. Food writer, critic and long-time Brussels resident **Midge Shirley** contributed the restaurant entries outside the European Quarter in EATING AND DRINKING.

A message from the series editor

In designing *American Express Brussels* we aimed to make this brand-new edition simple and instinctive to use, like all its sister volumes in our new, larger paperback format.

The hallmarks of the relaunched series are clear, classic typography, confidence in fine travel writing for its own sake, and faith in our readers' innate intelligence to find their way around the books without heavy-handed signposting by editors.

Readers with anything less than 20:20 vision will doubtless also enjoy the larger, clearer type, and can now dispense with the mythical magnifying glasses we never issued free with the old pocket guide series.

Months of concentrated work by the authors and our editors have gone into ensuring that this edition is as accurate and up to date as possible as it goes to press. But time and change are forever the enemies, and in between editions we very much appreciate it when our readers advise us of changes that they discover.

As ever, I am indebted to the many readers who wrote during the preparation of this book. We strive to tailor the series to the very distinctive tastes and requirements of our sophisticated international readership, and your feedback is therefore extremely valuable.

Send your comments to me at Mitchell Beazley International Ltd, Michelin House, 81 Fulham Road, London SW3 6RB; or, in the US, c/o American Express Travel Guides, Prentice Hall Travel, 15 Columbus Circle, New York, NY 10023.

David Townsend Jones

Brussels

A tale of two cities

Brussels is a much misunderstood city. For some it is merely the center of an expanding and soulless European Community bureaucracy whose tentacles reach from the Atlantic to the Urals. Others imagine the Belgian capital's geographical location to provide a heady cocktail of Parisian grandeur and bohemian Amsterdam. Both are misjudgments, ignoring the city's own discreet style, evolved over the centuries at this meeting point between the Latin and Germanic cultures.

Brussels has had more than its fair share of war and occupation during the past 1,000 years. The Burgundians, Austrians, Spaniards, French, Dutch and Germans have all ruled the city at some time. Some occupiers left more of a mark than others, bequeathing an impressive architectural legacy. But, at the very least, reminders of each can be seen in the names of local streets, buildings, cafés and monuments. The city has an equally rich history as a refuge, or temporary shelter, for a host of literary, artistic and political figures, Karl Marx being perhaps the most famous.

As the 20th century draws to a close, the attractions of Brussels for foreigners are no less strong. A quarter of the city's one million inhabitants is non-Belgian, making it one of the most cosmopolitan centers in the world. Their ranks include unskilled immigrants from North Africa and Turkey, well-heeled businessmen from around the globe, diplomats from the twelve European Community (EC) countries and farther afield and, latterly, visitors from the former Communist countries of Eastern Europe seeking to carve out a new life. The result is a heady mixture of culture, cuisine and customs.

Brussels had to work hard to gain its reputation as the capital, or at least the heart, of Europe. Some would say, too hard. The headlong pursuit of the future in the 1960s and '70s saw the wanton destruction of large swathes of the city, as tree-lined streets and imposing bourgeois town houses were sacrificed on the altar of property developers' love for modern office blocks.

Conservation groups are now fighting back, with some success, although the battle is far from won. But they are taking heart from the view of Charles Piqué, effectively the Prime Minister of Brussels, who maintains: "There is nothing more important for the future of a city than its history and its soul."

With the city's own government keen to nurture civic pride, more pains are now being taken to ensure an ordered expansion of the EC institutions. These have mushroomed since the European Commission and the Council of Ministers were located in Brussels in 1958. Never mind that officially the European Commission is only "provisionally" in Brussels, as governments remain unable to agree a permanent address for the European institution. Few believe it will ever leave.

This is a bewildering polyglot world centered around the rond-point Schuman. EC jargon and at least a dozen languages can be heard, but French and, increasingly, English are the main means of communication. The various EC institutions in Brussels employ 15,000 civil servants. But the very presence of these European law-shapers has encouraged 1,400 international non-governmental organizations, more than 100 embassies, several thousand lobbyists and almost 600 journalists to base their operations in Brussels.

Farther out toward Zaventem airport are the headquarters of the North Atlantic Treaty Organization, which moved to the Belgian capital in 1967 when former French President Général de Gaulle encouraged it to leave France. Late in 1992, another defense body, the Western European Union, also decided to move from its London base to the Belgian capital.

And as if this international diversity were not enough for one city, some 2,000 multinational companies have established a presence in or around Brussels, and the city now boasts the world's fourth largest conference industry.

It is to Brussels' credit that it has coped with such an influx of nationalities and backgrounds. There has, to be sure, been some friction as local inhabitants complained about rising rents and pressure on services. But the outbursts have been isolated, and the city is still one of the safest in Europe.

THE PEOPLE'S BRUSSELS
Alongside this international community is another Brussels, whose French- and Dutch-speaking inhabitants lead their own lives, politely oblivious to the foreigners in their midst. It is a world where food and beer are important — two commodities which go a long way toward bridging cultural divides and preventing Belgium and Europe's capital from being a tale of two cities.

Brussels' cuisine is yet further proof of the meeting between Latin and Germanic cultures. Belgium's neighbors from Germany, the Netherlands and even France regularly cross the border to eat in Brussels, where the cooking is a healthy mixture of French style with German-sized portions.

The city is a treasure trove for beer, Belgium's national drink. Almost 600 different kinds of beer are brewed in the country. They range from the familiar *pils* to the more exotic strawberry- and cherry-flavored brews and the dark, rich beers made by Trappist monks. Savoring one of the many brands in a comfortable café breaks down most national barriers.

Brussels offers others delights for residents and visitors alike. It enjoys a feast of architectural styles. In the Grand'Place, the city has one of Europe's finest town squares, described by the playwright Jean Cocteau as "the richest theater in the world." The imposing arch at the Cinquantenaire Park, commemorating the 75th anniversary of Belgium's existence, is Brussels' answer to Berlin's Brandenburg Gate. The city launched the Art Nouveau style that swept Northern Europe around the turn of the century, and some fine examples of that glory still remain.

Then there is the greenery. Brussels is blessed with numerous parks and open green spaces. They range from the Bois de la Cambre, where British regiments played cricket on the eve of the battle of Waterloo, to the Neoclassical Parc de Bruxelles and the undulating Parc de Woluwé where strollers, runners, children and dogs all mingle on the 71-hectare site created by Leopold II. On the city's doorstep is the Forêt de Soignes with its magnificent expanse of oak and beech trees.

The city enjoys its pageantry and takes seriously its traditions, history and folklore. The highlight is the colorful *Ommegang* each summer, which goes back 600 years. But there are scores of smaller carnivals and historical re-enactments throughout the year, many organized individually by the 19 communes.

Brussels, like Belgium itself, has always seemed to have a certain difficulty in projecting its image abroad. This is not surprising given the country's place between its historically more powerful French, German and Dutch neighbors and the confusion that foreigners frequently display when confronted with an official bilingual (and in Belgium's case, a trilingual) society.

Perhaps for that reason Brussels conjures up different images. For some its reputation rests on the Grand'Place or the Berlaymont. For others it lies in its Art Nouveau or its opera. For a further group the capital's fame springs from its small Manneken Pis fountain and the huge Atomium. But all are there to be savored.

Understandably, the city has changed over the years. But some values, as visitors will readily discover, remain constant. Writing of his experiences during a visit over 70 years ago, Scotland's former chief law officer, Lord Alness, recalled fond impressions of "the magnitude of the city, of the attractiveness of its shops, of the excellence of its hotels and restaurants, and of the all-round moderation of its prices." He also admitted alarm at the speed of Brussels taxis. But not even the atrocious weather, with "rain as continuous and pitiless as any Scottish variety," could dampen his spirits and enthusiasm for the city.

Those comments are as pertinent today, with the possible additional lament about ever-rising prices. They are a sturdy tribute to the ability of the city and its inhabitants to adapt to change without losing sight of life's basic essentials.

Brussels is a city that somewhat shyly reveals its many charms, almost imperceptibly working its seduction. Many are the long-term residents who first made acquaintance with the city as casual visitors and yet will now readily admit they fell under its spell.

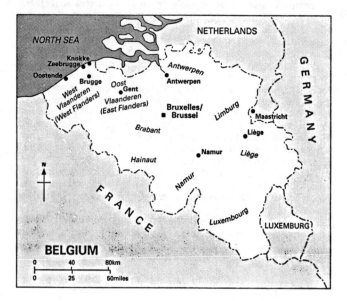

NORTH SEA

NETHERLANDS

GERMANY

Knokke
Zeebrugge
Oostende
Brugge
West
Vlaanderen
(West Flanders)
Oost
Vlaanderen
(East Flanders)
Gent

Antwerpen
Antwerpen

Bruxelles/
Brussel

Limburg

Maastricht

Liège

Brabant

Namur

Liège

N

Hainaut

Namur

FRANCE

Luxembourg

LUXEMBURG

BELGIUM

| 0 | 40 | 80km |
| 0 | 25 | 50miles |

Culture, history and background

Landmarks in Brussels' history

Excavations have unearthed evidence of neolithic sites dating as far back as **2250BC** in the Brussels suburbs of Schaerbeek, Boitsfort and Uccle, and of Roman villas from the **first** and **second centuries AD**. But the earliest reference to Brussels does not come until much later **(695)**, when St Géry, bishop of Cambrai and Arras, falls ill at the settlement then known as Brosella. It then takes almost four centuries before a recognized settlement begins to emerge.

979: Charles of France builds a fort on the island of Saint-Géry in the Senne river and moves to *Bruocsella* (*bruoc* meaning marsh and *sella,* dwelling) from Cambrai. Nine hundred years later, a market — Les Halles Saint-Géry — is built on the same site.

THE FEUDAL PERIOD

Brussels is not only a strategic, defensive post: it is also growing as an administrative and commercial center, with craftsmen and traders setting up their businesses around the early fortress.

In **1010**, Abbé Otbert of Gembloux describes the town as a port on the increasingly important trade route between Bruges and Cologne.

The area passes into the ownership of the counts of Louvain and dukes of Brabant. In **1047**, Lambert II completes construction of the Duke's palace of Coudenberg. By **1100** Brussels has its first fortified wall, some 4km ($2\frac{1}{2}$ miles) long and up to 10m (33 feet) high (the only remains to be seen today are at Anneessens Tower and on boulevard de l'Empereur).

By **1194**, when the English King, Richard the Lionheart, passes through, Brussels has most of the characteristics of a town: six churches, two markets, infirmaries and a network of streets. In the **12thC**, its population climbs to 30,000, and soon trade expands, with wine coming from Cologne, Beaune, La Rochelle and Greece, while Brussels' own wealth is built on wool and linen. Brussels cloth is sold in Paris, Douai, Avignon, the Tyrol, Florence and Cyprus.

1229: Henri I, Duke of Brabant, publishes the first Brussels charter, setting out punishments for crimes such as harboring criminals or using false measures, and guaranteeing protection for citizens and private property.

1276: Fire destroys more than one third of the town's buildings.

1303: Brussels' craftsmen, led by the weavers and fullers, rebel against the patrician bourgeoisie who hold all privileges. After an initial victory which wins them some rights, they are defeated by the army of Jean II, Duke of Brabant, at the battle of Vilvoorde.

1377: Second fortified town wall, 8km (5 miles) long with seven gates, is completed to protect the expanding population. It is to act as the Brussels perimeter until the beginning of the 19thC, when it is dismantled and turned into pleasant squares and public thoroughfares (known as the Inner Ring). The only remains are the Porte de Hal, which survive because it was used as a prison until 1824.

THE BURGUNDIANS

Between **1384** and **1477**, four dukes of Burgundy — Philip the Bold, John the Fearless, Philip the Good and Charles the Bold — rule Brussels and succeed in expanding the empire of the ambitious House of Burgundy.

1402: Construction of the town hall begins.

1430: Philip the Good takes possession of Brabant and makes Brussels, rather than Dijon, his main residence. The city is capital of the Low Countries, and the arts flourish with the 15thC school of Flemish painters of Jan van Eyck, Roger van der Weyden, Hans Memling and Dirk Bouts. Brussels' famous cloth industry goes into decline, partly through English competition, but is replaced by a flourishing tapestry industry. Philip the Good is also dubbed *Conditor Belgii,* the founder of Belgium.

1482: Death of Mary of Burgundy, Philip the Good's granddaughter, who had come to the throne and married Maximilian of Austria five years earlier. Brussels passes under the rule of the Hapsburgs.

HAPSBURGS

Maximilian rules as regent until his and Mary's son, Philip the Fair, takes up the reins of power of the Low Countries in **1494**. Two years later this first national prince to be born and bred on Belgian soil marries Jeanne of Aragon and Castile, and the future of the Low Countries becomes tied to the House of Spain.

1515: Charles V, their son, begins his rule of the Low Countries, nine years after the death of his father. The following year he becomes King of Spain and later of Naples, Sardinia, Sicily and of Spanish territories in the New World. In **1519** he is crowned Emperor of Germany. Under Charles V the Low Countries prosper economically and culturally. Brussels benefits more than any other town from the centralization imposed on the large Hapsburg territories.

It is during Charles V's reign that Erasmus stays at Anderlecht (**1521**), Brussels is proclaimed capital of the Spanish Netherlands (**1531**) and work starts on the 28-km (18-mile) Willebroek canal, which for 400 years will provide Brussels with vital access to the sea, boosting the city's economic life after the river Senne has silted up. The city is now also the center of the largest private postal system in Europe, with the Princes of Tour et Tassis running a messenger service for Charles V.

SPANISH RULE

1555: Charles V abdicates in favor of his son Philip II of Spain. It is a time of religious wars, and the new Spanish King is determined to defend the Catholic faith. In **1567** he sends the Duke of Alba to be the new governor of the Low Countries, and Spanish repression starts in earnest.

1568: The Counts Egmont and Hoorn, powerful symbols of Brussels' opposition to Spain, are publicly executed on the Grand'Place in front of the Maison du Roi. The Inquisition is brought to Brussels and 8,000 death sentences are passed. Spanish repression sparks off a revolt as Brussels supports the Calvinist cause of William of Orange, who in **1581** abolishes Catholicism. Philip II retaliates by sending a powerful army under Alexander Farnese, who accepts the surrender of Brussels in **1585**, after a lengthy siege has brought famine to the city.

In **1598**, shortly before his death, Philip II entrusts the independent kingdom of the Spanish Netherlands to his daughter, Archduchess Isabella, and her husband, Archduke Albrecht of Austria. Over the next 40 years there is a brief period of recovery as the economy and culture of Brussels prosper. But the gradual stagnation and decadence of the Spanish Hapsburgs throughout the 17thC not only slow the city's advance, but also lead to a new round of European wars.

1695: Louis XIV's French army under Marshal de Villeroy bombards Brussels for two days in retaliation for Dutch and English attacks on French Channel ports. They destroy 4,000 houses, 16 churches and much of the Grand'Place, although the town hall is miraculously spared. It takes a year to clear the rubble, but within four years, the Grand'Place, including its sumptuous houses of the nine main guilds, is completely rebuilt and becomes one of Europe's most magnificent squares.

AUSTRIAN RULE

With the end of the Spanish war of succession and the Treaty of Utrecht (**1713**), Brussels and the Low Countries pass into the hands of the Hapsburgs of Austria, who replace their Spanish cousins. The transfer of ownership leads to initial unrest between the inhabitants of Brussels and their new ruler, Charles VI, culminating in the beheading of the guild leader François Anneessens (**1719**).

But gradually, under the successive Austrian sovereigns — Charles VI (**1711-40**), Maria-Theresa (**1740-80**) and Joseph II (**1780-90**) — there is an upsurge in prosperity, even if Belgian privileges are restricted. This period of 18thC Austrian rule fuels a real surge in Brussels' urban development, with the construction of new squares like the place des Martyrs and place Royale and the completion of the Royal Palace at Laeken (**1784**). By the eve of the French Revolution, one third of the city has been completely replanned.

But as elsewhere in Europe, the French Revolution of **1789** sparks off rebellion in Brabant against the unpopular reforms of Joseph II, which had upset both the privileged and the working classes. Austrian troops are driven out of Brussels, and the United Belgian States are proclaimed in January **1790**. The success is short-lived, with Austrian troops retaking the capital before they in their turn are ousted by the revolutionary French.

FRENCH RULE

From **1794** to **1814** Brussels is under French control. The initial impact is far from beneficial. Museums and libraries are sacked, and equipment and able-bodied men are requisitioned for the army. But later, monetary stability encourages economic recovery. French rule also brings with it the Napoleonic code, French constitution and Concordat with Rome.

Napoleon Bonaparte visits the city twice (**1803** and **1810**) and lays the foundations for today's wide boulevards when he orders the city's old ramparts to be destroyed.

1815: One of the turning points in history, with the defeat of Napoleon after a closely-fought battle by British and Prussian forces at Waterloo, just outside Brussels. Belgians fight on both sides.

THE KINGDOM OF THE LOW COUNTRIES

With Napoleon's defeat, the Congress of Vienna (**1815**) creates the new kingdom of The Netherlands, largely to preserve the balance of power in Europe. Brussels and The Hague become the kingdom's twin capitals. The king, William of Orange, divides his time between each. His rule brings a brief period of stability to Brussels again, allowing the arts, education, industry and trade to flourish. But his clampdown on the press, widespread promotion of Dutch language and nationals, at a time when the bourgeoisie speaks French, and the introduction of other unpopular measures, combine to provoke another revolt.

INDEPENDENCE

1830: Revolutions sweep through Europe. There is a double irony about the revolt in Brussels on August 25. It occurs on William of Orange's 58th birthday and begins at the Théâtre de la Monnaie, built during his reign just 13 years earlier. Inspired by Daniel Auber's opera *La Muette de Portici*, which lauds the patriotism of Neapolitans against their Spanish masters, the mainly young bourgeois audience takes to the streets. After several weeks of riots and skirmishes with Dutch troops, a provisional government proclaims independence on October 4.

1831: The conference of London in January recognizes Belgian independence, and on July 21, Leopold of Saxe-Coburg Gotha, uncle of the future British monarch Queen Victoria, takes the constitutional oath as the first king of the Belgians.

With independence, the way is clear for the development of Brussels, and of Belgium. Brussels has grown to 100,000 inhabitants. The Free University of Brussels is created (**1834**), the Royal Library established (**1837**) and ten years later sees the inauguration of the Galeries Saint-Hubert — the first covered gallery in Europe.

1835: Leopold I opens the first public railway on the continent of Europe, from Brussels to Malines. George Stephenson, the Englishman whose workshops built the engines and who had invented the first train ten years earlier, is present.

1847: Karl Marx, who had fled to Brussels from Paris, and Friedrich Engels complete their landmark work, *The Communist Manifesto*. When

Leopold I dies in **1865** he is succeeded by his son Leopold II, whose passion is to make the small country of Belgium a great nation, through colonial conquests and the development of Brussels and Antwerp.

His attention is fixed on the wide open spaces of Africa, and in **1879** he instructs the Victorian explorer Henry Stanley to explore the Congo. Six years later, this tract of land the size of Western Europe, with its riches of ivory and rubber, becomes Leopold II's personal property, rather than that of Belgium, when he declares himself Sovereign of the Independent State of the Congo. Only in **1908** does the colony revert to Belgium.

During his reign, Brussels continues to become an ever more elegant city with the construction of the Brussels Conservatory (**1872**), the Palais des Beaux-Arts (**1876**), the Palais de Justice (**1883**), the opening of the first cinema (**1896**) and the flourishing of Art Nouveau architecture.

1880: On the 50th anniversary of Belgian independence, Brussels hosts the International Exposition in the Cinquantenaire Park. From **1870-1910**, the population of the city grows from 250,000 to 800,000.

1909: Leopold II dies and is succeeded by his nephew, Albert I, who, as the war clouds gather, is soon preparing his country's defenses with a law on compulsory military service (**1913**).

1914: Brussels is occupied by advancing German troops on August 20th as World War I breaks out. The city remains under German occupation until November **1918**, provoking acts of defiance from the local population such as the first clandestine appearance of *La Libre Belgique,* a newspaper encouraging Belgian patriotism.

After the war, King Albert, one of Belgium's most popular monarchs after his spirited defense against the German army, uses his personal prestige to bring in political and social reforms. In **1919** universal suffrage is introduced (although it will not apply fully to women until **1949**), the 8-hour working day is adopted, and university education in Dutch begins.

1934: Albert I, a keen mountaineer, dies in a climbing accident and is succeeded by his son, Leopold III. Brussels soon faces its second German invasion in three decades.

1940: The city is bombed by German aircraft on May 10, occupied eight days later and only liberated by allied troops on September 3, **1944**.

The end of war sparks off a constitutional crisis in Belgium, with the country split over Leopold III's decision to remain under German occupation. The division lasts until **1950**, when Leopold III abdicates in favor of his son, King Baudouin, who comes to the throne the following year.

THE POSTWAR PERIOD

The postwar period is marked by Brussels' determination to place itself firmly on the European, and international, map.

1958: Brussels becomes the provisional seat of the European institutions — the European Commission and the Council of Ministers — with the creation of Euratom and of the six-member European Economic Community. At the International Exposition at the Heysel, 51 countries participate in the 6-month event, which draws 41.5 million visitors. With hopes high of the contribution of science to mankind's well-being, the event's symbol is the giant Atomium.

1960: Brussels hosts a month-long conference on the future of the Belgian Congo. The new state becomes independent on June 30, but the transition is far from smooth and many Belgians flee the Congo.

1960: Maurice Béjart establishes the Ballet of the 20thC company in Brussels. **1963**: After growing unrest by Flemish demonstrators, new language laws are passed, decreeing that the 19 communes of Brussels are officially bilingual. **1967**: A horrific fire destroys the Innovation department store in rue Neuve: 251 people are killed and 62 injured. A year later, new legislation is in force on workplace safety.

1967: The North Atlantic Treaty Organization moves to Brussels from France, a year after French withdrawal from the military wing of Nato.

1967: The executive bodies of the EEC, Euratom and The European Coal and Steel Community merge, creating one Community. **1970**: Completion of the European Commission's Berlaymont headquarters, begun 3 years earlier. The Dutch-language section of Brussels Free University leaves to create a separate University.

1973: Denmark, Ireland and the United Kingdom join the EEC, bringing membership up to nine.

1976: Brussels opens its metro system, 113 years after London, 100 years after Budapest and 76 years after Paris, whose own system was constructed by a Belgian, Edouard Empain.

1979: Brussels celebrates its millennium. **1981**: Greece joins the EEC. **1986**: Spain and Portugal join the EEC, bringing membership to 12.

1990/1991: Belgium celebrates King Baudouin's 60th birthday, 40 years of his rule and 160 years of Belgian independence.

1993: Brussels is at the heart of the European Community's single market as the final trade barriers between the 12 member countries and their 345 million inhabitants are dismantled.

A Belgian who's who

Ignorant quippers suggest that it is impossible to name five famous Belgians. Equally galling for stoical Belgians (Georges Simenon's urbane detective Maigret, for example), is to be presumed to be French.

Many are surprised to learn that the Club Méditerrannée, so popular with the French, was founded by a Belgian, or that pop singers Johnny Hallyday and Plastic Bertrand and comedian Raymond Devos are not French after all. A large number of Belgians have contributed to the development of their country, their capital and to the wider world.

Yet there are also occasions when, at least initially, it has been thought prudent to gloss over a Belgian identity. One of the acknowledged pillars of the French language is the book *Le Bon Usage*, written by Belgian school teacher Maurice Grévisse. In 1947, the French author, André Gide, commenting on the work, wrote: "*Le Bon Usage* never leaves my desk." He did not mention Maurice Grévisse's nationality, fearing that his French compatriots would ignore the book if they knew the truth.

Belgium, and in particular Brussels, has, over the years, served as a haven for many fleeing persecution. Writers, politicians and free thinkers, some famous, others not, have been grateful for the city's warm embrace. Among their number are Polish officers who took shelter after the failure of their 1830 revolt against the Czar; Prince Metternich when chased out of Vienna in 1848; and French citizens who, like Victor Hugo, opposed Napoleon III in 1851 or who 19 years later had manned the barricades. At one point in the 1850s the single commune of Saint Josse had 165 political exiles. More recently the tide has included refugees from the Russian revolution, Jews from the Germany of the 1930s and latterly many Eastern Europeans keen to make a new life in the West.

Many poets and writers have also spent time in the city. They include the French poets Paul Verlaine and Arthur Rimbaud. Originally friends, they quarreled so violently that the former shot the latter, injuring him with a pistol he had bought in the Galeries Saint-Hubert. He spent two years in the prison of Mons for his crime.

Not every visitor over the years has appreciated the city's charms. The French poet, Gérard de Nerval, who came on frequent trips between 1836 and 1852, bemoaned the absence of a river. "What sort of capital is it where you cannot drown yourself?" he lamented. Voltaire, who stayed twice, was particularly critical of the town "where the devil has sent me." He attacked the ignorance, boredom and indifference of its inhabitants. "Neither the arts nor pleasure are to be found in Brussels," he complained. It should be said that a number of superficial visitors still share that view.

The memory of many of these inhabitants and visitors, including even Voltaire, lives on in the names of streets, squares and metro stations dotted around the city. What follows is a selection of celebrated names associated with the city.

Anneessens, François
A chairmaker and leader of one of the city's guilds; he was executed in 1719 for heading a revolt against tyrannical Austrian rule.

Bouillon, Godefroid de
Leader of the first crusade in 1100 and uncrowned King of Jerusalem; now to be seen on horseback in the middle of place Royale.

Brel, Jacques
He became famous in France, but the singer, actor, film director and poet never forgot his Belgian roots. Born in 1933 into a middle-class Brussels family living in rue du Diamant in Schaerbeek, he went into the family's packaging business, married young and had three daughters before devoting himself to music and recording more than 200 songs. He died in 1978.

Brontë, Charlotte
In 1842, at the age of 26, the celebrated English writer came to Brussels with her sister Emily, to learn French. She returned later as an English teacher and captured the spirit of the Brussels of the 1840s — much of which has now disappeared — in her novels *Villette* and *The Professor.*

Byron, Lord George Gordon
He stayed at 51 rue Ducale in 1816. Like many British authors and visitors, he came to visit the battlefield of Waterloo. He is rumored to

have used his walking stick to knock the nose off one of the statues in the Parc de Bruxelles. The poet had to leave town hurriedly when he could not afford to pay for the coach he had ordered to be made.

Cavell, Edith

An English nurse from Norfolk who came to Brussels as a governess to improve her French and later ran a nurses' training school. During World War I, she helped French and British soldiers escape the German occupation. Arrested in August 1915, she was executed at the age of 49 by a six-man squad on October 12 at the former Tir National, now the Enclos des Fusillés, where visitors may pay tribute to war victims. Her sacrifice is commemorated by a gravestone in this poignant enclave.

Claudel, Paul

The celebrated author ended his diplomatic career as French ambassador to Belgium, arriving in 1933 at the age of 65 and leaving two years later.

David, Jacques-Louis

Born in Paris in 1748, he rose to become Napoleon's official painter. He fled from France in 1816 after the emperor's defeat, and lived in Brussels (in what is now rue Leopold) until his death, influencing a generation of Belgian painters.

Empain, Edouard

Born in 1852, the son of a Hainaut schoolteacher, he trained as an engineer and constructed railways in Belgium and Northern France before turning to Egypt, Spain, Russia and China. Among his most important achievements was the building of the Paris Métro, which opened in 1900. He also created his own bank, Banque Empain, to encourage new industries. He died in 1929.

Erasmus, Desiderius

Although he was born in Rotterdam in 1467 and died in Basel in 1536, he spent some time in 1521, while he was advisor to Charles V, in what is now the Brussels suburb of Anderlecht.

Hankar, Paul

Born in 1859 the son of a stone mason, Hankar's studies and lengthy apprenticeship in Brussels made him a master of wrought iron; examples of his work can be seen in the Petit Sablon. He ventured into architecture in the 1880s, at about the same time as Victor Horta, during a period when Brussels was expanding and architects were in great demand.

Hepburn, Audrey

The famous actress was born in Brussels in 1929, while her Scottish father, Joseph Hepburn, and Dutch baroness mother, Ella Van Heemstra, were living in rue Keyenveld at #48. When war broke out in 1939, the family fled to Britain.

Horta, Victor

Born in Ghent on January 6, 1861, this son of a shoemaker of Italian origin was destined to become one of Belgium's most famous architects. After studies in Paris, he returned to Brussels and, from 1893, began to make his name as he designed a series of striking avant-garde houses. Among the most impressive is the Hôtel Solvay on avenue Louise and his own house in rue Américaine. He was also responsible for the Palais des Beaux-Arts and the Gare Centrale. Made a baron by King Albert in recognition of his work, he died in 1947.

Hugo, Victor

The French author spent several periods in Brussels between 1837 and 1871. It was here that he worked on *Les Misérables*. His son Charles married in the city in 1865 and it was in Brussels that the death of his wife, Adèle, occurred six years later. While widely respected in literary circles, he was nicknamed "the rat" by others for his avarice and refusal to give any money to the children who looked after his horses. Nor was he popular for suggesting that Belgium was the country in the world "where the houses are the cleanest and the women the dirtiest, as the filth off what was washed spread to the washerwomen." He redressed the balance somewhat by describing the city's town hall as "a jewel comparable to the spire of Chartres."

Magritte, René

Although born in Charleroi in 1898, the Surrealist painter spent most of his working life in Brussels, after a brief spell in Paris. He died in 1967.

Marx, Karl

Expelled from France, the author of *Das Kapital* arrived in Brussels on February 9, 1845 at the age of 31 with his wife, Maria, and their one-year-old daughter, Jeanne. Constantly under the watchful eye of the police, he changed lodgings several times. One of his favorite meeting places on Sundays and Wednesdays with like-minded friends was the first floor of Le Cygne in the Grand'Place, where the Belgian Workers Party was founded in 1885. Now it is one of the city's best restaurants. It was in Brussels that he collaborated with Engels to produce in 1847 *The Communist Manifesto*. He was expelled from the city in 1848.

Max, Adolphe

A liberal politician, he was one of Brussels' most popular and effective mayors, administering the city for 30 years until his death at the age of 70 in 1939. As the city's mayor during World War I, he had constantly stood up to the occupying German Forces — a defiance that led to his imprisonment for four years.

Metternich, Prince Clemens Lothar Wenzel

Chancellor of the Austro-Hungarian empire for more than 30 years, he resigned from the post in 1848 and a year later came to Brussels to live in what is now the town hall of Saint-Josse. It was while he was in Brussels that he wrote much of his *Memoirs.*

Petit, Gabrielle

Born in Tournai in 1893, she worked for the allies, and operated an escape route to The Netherlands from German-occupied Belgium during World War I. She distributed the clandestine *Libre Belgique* newspaper, founded in 1915, even putting copies through the letterbox of the German Governor General. Arrested several times, she was eventually sentenced to death and shot on April 1, 1916.

Prigogine, Ilya

A naturalized Belgian who left his native Russia when he was 10, he received the Nobel Prize for chemistry in 1977 at the age of 60, for his work at the University of Brussels.

Reiff, Gaston

Born just outside Brussels at Braine-l'Alleud on February 24, 1921, he was destined to become Belgium's first Olympic track gold medalist when he won the 5,000 meters at the 1948 London Olympic Games, beating the legendary Czech, Emil Zatopek, among others. He so dominated Belgian running that in 1951 he held every national record from the 1,000 meters to the 10,000 meters. He died in 1992.

Rémy, George

Known the world over as Hergé, the creator of Tintin the boy reporter and his dog Snowy, Rémy was born in 1907 and spent all his life in Brussels. Although little traveled himself, he carefully researched his hero's adventures around the world. Along with Simenon and Brel, he is one of the three most widely known Belgians. Former French President Général de Gaulle once said: "My only international rival is Tintin." The uncrowned king of comic strips died on March 4, 1983.

Sax, Adolphe

Born in Dinant in 1814, the young Sax worked in his father's workshop making flutes and clarinets. In 1840 he invented the saxophone and the following year submitted nine inventions to the Brussels Industrial Exhibition. He was prevented from receiving the gold medal when the president said: "Sax is too young. We would have nothing to give him next year." After overcoming initial hostility, he succeeded in persuading French army musicians to play the saxophone. In 1857 the Paris Conservatoire opened saxophone classes. He died in 1894.

Solvay, Ernest

Born in 1838, Ernest Solvay was Belgium's answer to Rockefeller. He and his brother Alfred succeeded in making sodium bicarbonate, an essential ingredient in 19thC glass and textiles, on an industrial scale. By 1900 there were scores of factories around the world using their techniques. Deeply interested in science, he organized from 1911 onward gatherings that brought together, often for the first time, people like Einstein, Madame Curie, Rutherford, Plack and de Broglie. He died in 1922.

Spaak, Paul-Henri

Born in Brussels in 1899, he became Belgium's best-known international statesman. A former Foreign and Prime Minister, he was elected first president of the UN General Assembly in 1946 and later served as secretary general of the North Atlantic Treaty Organization for four years. He signed the Treaties of Paris and Rome — the cornerstones of the European Community — on behalf of Belgium. He was a leading figure in forcing the abdication of Leopold III in 1950 for his conduct during World War II. He died in 1972.

Thielemans, Jean (Toots)

Born in Brussels in 1922, he achieved fame, particularly in the US, for his harmonica playing.

Vesalius, Andreas

Born in Brussels in 1514, he is credited as the father of anatomy. In

1543 he published his *De Humani Corporis Fabrica,* whose detailed woodcuts shed new light on the human body. Before his death in 1564, he acted as Philip II's court physician.

Wynants, Pierre
Born in 1939, he is widely considered to be the best chef in Belgium, and his Brussels restaurant COMME CHEZ SOI is one of the country's culinary pinnacles.

Yourcenar, Marguerite
Born Marguerite de Crayencour in Brussels in 1903, the poet and writer became the first woman elected to the male-dominated Académie Française in its 350-year history.

The gentleman, after looking towards me once or twice, politely accosted me in very good English — I remember I wished to God that I could speak French as well; his fluency and correct pronunciation impressed me for the first time with a due notion of the cosmopolitan character of the capital I was in; it was my first experience of that skill in living languages, I afterwards found to be so general in Brussels.
(William Crimsworth at breakfast on his first morning in Brussels — Charlotte Brontë's *The Professor,* 1845)

The international institutions

The presence of the European Community's institutions has been the greatest single social and economic influence in Brussels' recent development, transforming a previously provincial European town into a symbol of Europe's collective future.

The change in the nature of the city has been clear to see. The expansion of the EC in the last 35 years from six to twelve members has led many more nationalities to put down roots in Brussels. For some in the diplomatic service the stay may be for just three to four years, while for others working in the EC institutions or elsewhere it may be for life.

That expansion has also led to a change in the organization's identity, as more issues are handled at a European level. The original three bodies, the European Atomic Energy Community (EAEC), the European Coal and Steel Community (ECSC) and the better-known European Economic Community (EEC) have gradually merged, and, since the late 1980s, have been collectively known as the European Community (EC).

The growth of the EC's responsibilities has acted as a magnet, pulling people to Brussels not only from the twelve EC countries, but from around the globe. There is hardly a government in the world that does not have an embassy or some listening post in the city. Indeed, some have three embassies: one accredited to Belgium, another to the EC and a third to the North Atlantic Treaty Organization. Only New York has a greater number of diplomatic missions and diplomats.

Of Brussels' one-million population, 120,000 non-Belgians are directly involved in the EC, international organizations and multinational business. A 1992 study for the Brussels Region revealed the following breakdown: 15,000 EC officials (out of a total EC staff Europe-wide of 24,000); 120 diplomatic delegations; 1,400 international non-governmental organizations; more than 450 international companies; 31 foreign banks; 37 offices representing international finance; almost 600 foreign journalists (the second largest press corps after Washington); and at least 20 European and international schools.

The overall economic impact of the EC's presence generated 120 billion BF in 1991, of which 96 billion BF stayed in Belgium. It also created jobs for 46,000 people (seven percent of the city's total employment), of whom at least half are Belgian. The economic benefits are even greater if the business given to hotels, restaurants, shops, translators, secretaries, childminders, security and maintenance firms, taxis, removal companies, express courier services and others are included.

Clearly, the EC is big business, and the city is understandably determined to project the European image to continue attracting international organizations and companies. Among the most recent to decide to move to Brussels are the London-based secretariat of the European defense organization, the Western European Union, and the European Free Trade Association, which is transferring part of its staff from Geneva. They join the North Atlantic Treaty Organization, the transatlantic defense body based in Brussels for more than 25 years, and Eurocontrol, the air safety organization.

As if this concentration of international interest were not enough, Brussels ranks fourth in the world league as an international conference city, behind Paris, London and Geneva.

That Belgium should be the home for so many international bodies is not surprising. Apart from its central location in Northern Europe, the country has, since 1948, been linked with Luxemburg and the Netherlands in an economic union (Benelux), a useful forerunner of the European Community.

But the arrival of such an influx of generally wealthy foreigners has not been without friction and disappointment. For many, moving to a new city with its unaccustomed ways and practices can be a harrowing experience. From another perspective, some of the city's long-term inhabitants complain of rents and house prices soaring and of having to move farther and farther out to find affordable accommodation. Other inhabitants complain about relentless urban development as offices devour once proud houses and tree-lined streets become motorways. But shop keepers, landlords, restaurants, taxi drivers and other service industries have welcomed the latest waves of foreigners.

The presence of so many non-Belgians has great political significance in communes like Overijse and Tervuren on the edge of Brussels. In the former there live 4,500 non-Belgian Europeans and almost 50 nationalities. If, as has been suggested under EC law, they should have the right to vote in local and European elections, their presence could tilt the balance (since most foreigners tend to speak French rather than Dutch) and boost local francophone politicians to the detriment of their Flemish rivals.

To help smooth the path of these new relationships, the Brussels Region has established a new Brussels-Europe Liaison office with a staff of almost a dozen to handle any problem that EC officials or people associated with the EC might have. In its first six months it dealt with more than 500 inquiries. (This service is not open to the private sector.)

In addition, a regular dialogue has been established between senior officials of the international organizations and the Brussels' authorities to try and iron out any problems at an early stage.

The European Community locations

For most of the world, the one concrete symbol of the "European Community" is the Berlaymont, the distinctive 13-story glass-and-concrete, star-shaped building that for more than 20 years graced television news reports of EC events.

The Berlaymont, however, was only ever the headquarters of one institution, the **European Commission**, and not of the European Community itself. The other institutions, such as the **European Parliament** and the **Council of Ministers**, have their own separate offices.

Built in the late 1960s on the site of a former convent, the construction is now, somewhat ironically, empty. Its 3,000 occupants moved out at the end of 1991 when leaking asbestos made it a health and fire hazard. The Belgian government, which owns the building, decided against its demolition, and have kept the basic structure, partly for its symbolism and partly because it is considered to be a good example of 1960s Belgian architecture. The interior is to be renovated and refurbished by 1997.

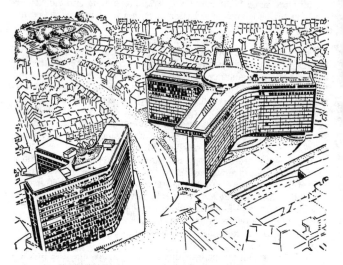

The **Berlaymont** *(right)* and **Charlemagne** *(left)* buildings

The Berlaymont's former occupants have been rehoused in a dozen new offices around the city with the strategic core of key personnel revolving around the 17 European Commissioners now working from the Breydel building in avenue d'Auderghem, just a stone's throw away from their previous desks.

One practical consequence of the move is that European Commission staff now work in more than 40 offices around Brussels. Most of these are clustered around rue de la Loi, rue Belliard and rond-point Schuman (named after the French Foreign Minister Robert Schuman, whose famous declaration on May 9, 1950 launched European integration). But some are as far away as Evere, near to Nato, and others at Beaulieu, near to the start of the motorway to Namur. So it is essential to have the correct address. If you are in any doubt, call one of the telephone numbers on the next page.

The European Commission is not the only institution to be involved in new premises. As any casual visitor can see, the area around rond-point Schuman and the Gare Leopold is one massive building site and has been for several years.

The **Council of Ministers**, which provides the setting for meetings of government ministers and officials, is building itself new headquarters in front of the Berlaymont, just opposite its current premises. These are expected to be ready in 1995 and will cater to 2,500 officials and offer conference facilities for up to 3,500 people.

The third EC institution in Brussels, the **European Parliament**, is also expanding. While the week-long monthly plenary sessions are held in the French city of Strasbourg, the meetings of the Parliament's political groups and committees generally take place in Brussels. The Belgian capital, in the face of French opposition, is also fighting hard to host more parliamentary activities.

This ambition is matched by property expansion. The parliament has taken possession of several buildings along rue Belliard and in 1992 signed a 20-year deal to rent, and ultimately own, part of a prestigious new conference center at Gare Leopold. The building is so high it can be seen from miles around.

This relentless construction is a clear sign that the European Community, despite its ups and downs and rumors of a move to Bonn, is here in Brussels to stay. Indeed, it is preparing to welcome into the fold later this decade such new member countries as Austria, Sweden and Finland.

It is not possible to visit the buildings of the various European Institutions without prior arrangement, and then usually only in a group. But it is worthwhile spending some time walking in the rond-point Schuman area, to gain an understanding of how, from just one small building overlooking the nearby Cinquantenaire Park, the EC has increased its territory in only 25 years.

USEFUL BUSINESS ADDRESSES AND TELEPHONE NUMBERS
- **American Chamber of Commerce**   av. des Arts 50, B-1040 ☎(02)513.67.70 or 513.68.92
- **British Chamber of Commerce**   rue Joseph II 30, B-1040 ☎(02)219.07.88
- **Bureau de Liaison Bruxelles-Europe**   av. d'Auderghem 63, B-1040 ☎(02)280.00.80
- **Chambre de Commerce et d'Industrie de Bruxelles**   av. Louise 500, B-1050 ☎(02)648.50.02
- **Commission of the European Communities**   rue de la Loi 200, B-1049 (address for mailing purposes only) ☎(02)235-11.11 or 299.11.11
- **Council of Ministers**   rue de la Loi 270, B-1040 ☎(02)234.61.11
- **Economic and Social Committee**   rue Ravenstein 2, B-1000 ☎(02)519.90.11
- **Eurochambres** (Association of European Chambers of Commerce and Industry)   rue Archimède 5, B-1040 ☎(02)231.07.15
- **European Parliament**   rue Belliard 97-113, B-1047 ☎(02)284.21.11
- **Info Point Europe**   rond-point Schuman 12, B-1049 ☎(02)236.55.55
- **North Atlantic Treaty Organization**   Nato, B-1110 (mailing address) ☎(02)728.41.11

The people

About one million people live in the 19 self-governing communes that make up Brussels. More than a quarter of these inhabitants (270,000) are non-Belgian. The figure is almost certainly higher, given that there are a number of illegal immigrants as well as many who have not registered their presence in the city with the local commune.

The city maintains its traditional role as a home for exiles and refugees. In 1991, 15,000 people requested political asylum in Belgium, with an upsurge in demands from Yugoslavs and Zairois but a decrease from Turks and Poles. These recent arrivals joined well-established communities of North Africans and Turks, while the most recent wave of immigrants has brought Eastern Europeans in increasing numbers. It is not unusual for Brussels inhabitants to have a Polish cleaning lady, whose family remains at home in her native country, or a Bulgarian carpenter.

Like many large cities, Brussels is a city of commuters. Of the 650,000 people who work in the Belgian capital every day, just under half (300,000) commute daily, some two-thirds of them from Flanders.

The change in nationalities is not the only recent development to determine the present face of Brussels. On June 18, 1989, the city of Brussels became one of Belgium's three regions (the others being Flanders and Wallonia) in its own right, with its own government, when elections were held to the 75-strong legislative council. The event marked the culmination of a 20-year battle to create the Region of Brussels-Capital. Written into the Belgian constitution since 1970, the status had been either ignored or suspended until 1989.

The development means that there are at least three tiers of authority in Brussels: at the lowest level, the commune; next the government of the region; and finally the Belgian government itself. In essence, the regions have mainly socio-economic powers over unemployment, the local economy, environment, water, infrastructure, housing, traffic and the preservation of monuments and historical buildings.

Interestingly, Brussels has its own minister for external affairs in the Regional government. The post involves fostering the city's national and international interests, defending its European interests and promoting Brussels abroad. There is now a widespread belief that, since it has had its own government, civic pride has strengthened and more initiatives have been taken to enhance Brussels' claim to be the capital of Europe.

The language question

The traveler in Belgium may not appreciate that Braine-le-Comte and 's-Gravenbrakel are one and the same place, or that Brussels is officially bilingual. In fact, three different languages are spoken in Belgium. The 5 million Walloons in the south are French-speaking, the 5.5 million Flemings speak Dutch, and a small community in the eastern Ardennes has German as its first language.

The language frontier dividing French Belgium from Dutch Belgium crosses the country from E to W a few kilometers S of Brussels. Bitter political rows often flare up between the Walloons and the Flemings. One solution to the feuding has been the creation of a bilingual Brussels.

Every street or official building in Brussels has both a French and Dutch name. You will see signs for Grand'Place and Grote Markt, Gare Centrale and Centraal Station, avenue Louise and Louizalaan. In the pursuit of bilingualism, bizarre compromises have sometimes been invented, such as the signs at taxi stands that read *taxis/taxi's*, or the lazy running together of the two names as in *rue Leopoldstraat*. Many receptionists answer the phone with a bilingual *bonjour/dag*, although some international organizations duck the issue by speaking English.

The language frontier has its roots in the collapse of the Roman Empire. The region now known as Flanders was invaded by Salic Franks who spoke Dutch, a Germanic language. The Romanized Franks, who spoke French, fled to the safety of the forests of Wallonia. The Forêt de Soignes marked the frontier between two languages and two cultures.

Situated to the N of the language frontier, Brussels was once a Dutch-speaking city. But in the Middle Ages the ruling Dukes of Burgundy imported French language and culture. The aristocracy of the Upper Town spoke French, while Dutch remained the language of the Lower Town. Hence the Dutch names you will observe on many guild houses on Grand'Place.

French gradually gained ground in the 18thC and 19thC. The decline of Dutch accelerated during the French occupation, when all the street names in Brussels were translated from Dutch into French, not always accurately. The Belgian revolt of 1830 was led by French-speakers who rejected the Dutch king as their ruler. The new Belgian state was French-speaking. The Flemings were forced to learn French in order to gain employment in administration or the professions. The domination by Wallonia was reinforced by the industrial revolution in southern Belgium, which gave that region superior economic influence.

The Flemings have fought to resist French domination since the late 19thC — a case boosted by the recent economic upswing in Flanders, while the fortunes of Wallonian coal mines and steelworks plunged. One result is that Brussels is no longer purely French-speaking, and Dutch is increasingly to be heard in the street. Both language communities have flourishing cultural centers, theater groups, universities and bookstores.

The traveler in Brussels is rarely affected by the language question. Employees in post offices, banks and hotels will normally speak both languages, albeit sometimes with a grimace. Brussels is now such a cosmopolitan city that English is almost always adequate for getting by in hotels, restaurants and shops.

But tread more warily when you venture outside the city. Brussels occupies a bilingual enclave in Dutch-speaking Flanders. The Flemish villages around the city are keen to preserve their hard-won gains. They see their linguistic purity increasingly threatened by high-earning European civil servants based in Brussels, who can outbid them in the housing market. The traveler can usually manage by speaking English in Brussels and Flanders, although French may be useful in Wallonia.

The architecture of Brussels

A first-time visitor to Brussels is likely to be struck by the architectural chaos of the city. As your taxi emerges from a four-lane tunnel, you might catch a glimpse of a skyscraper towering above a 19thC mansion, or a rotting Baroque house next door to a petrol station.

Brussels has had scant regard for urban planning, and its rulers seem still to prefer the splendid spectacle of a single monument to the seamless preservation of the urban fabric. The result is a city of grandiose buildings standing in splendid isolation — the twin-towered Cathedral and the glittering Baroque gables of the Grand'-Place; the awesome bulk of the Palais de Justice or the shiny futurism of the Atomium. Elsewhere, old buildings are left to rot and ugly billboards multiply in a sad process that has given birth to the term "Brusselization." A great deal of bad architecture remains, dating from the boom years of the 1960s and '70s, although the relatively new Brussels

Hôtel de Ville

Region authority has begun tentatively to improve the city's image by projects such as the restoration of the Place des Martyrs.

THE MEDIEVAL PERIOD *(13th–14thC)*

Brussels is a city with ancient origins, although its oldest buildings date from the Middle Ages. The medieval architecture of Brussels was initially based on the High Gothic style of northern France, which featured pointed arches and flying buttresses. Cathedrals such as Amiens provided the model for the **Cathédrale Saint-Michel** in Brussels. During the 15thC, the architecture of Brabant and Flanders blossomed into an exceptionally ornate style known as Flamboyant Gothic or Late Gothic. Churches and town halls were built in this style throughout the Burgundian Netherlands. The **Église Notre-Dame du Sablon** is the best example of the style in Brussels.

LATE GOTHIC *(15thC)*

The elaborate Late Gothic style was likewise applied to town halls throughout the Burgundian Netherlands. The 15thC **Hôtel de Ville** in Brussels is an exceptional Late Gothic building, with its proliferation of statues, and lace-like spire designed by Jan van Ruysbroeck.

The Late Gothic buildings of Brabant provided a perfect setting for the great processions staged by the Burgundians, such as the annual *Ommegang* and the meetings of the Order of the Golden Fleece. The architects employed a particular type of Brabant sandstone which was almost white in its pristine state. The frail stone unfortunately turns rapidly black in the polluted city air. The recent restoration of the Cathédrale Saint-Michel and the Église de la Chapelle shows the stone as it appeared in the 15thC, while the blackened exterior of the Église Notre-Dame du Sablon reveals the sad effects of pollution.

RENAISSANCE AND BAROQUE *(16th–17thC)*

Mechelen and Antwerp boast grand Renaissance palaces, but almost nothing survives in Brussels from the Renaissance age, except for a few isolated houses, the most famous of which is the **Maison d'Erasme**.

Brussels does, however, have some magnificent 17thC buildings designed in a flamboyant Flemish Baroque style. Reflecting the confidence of Counter-Reformation Catholicism, Flemish Baroque was largely inspired by the Antwerp architecture of Pieter Paul Rubens. The guild houses on **Grand'Place** (pictured on page 131) were rebuilt after the 1695 bombardment in a bombastic Baroque style, although the facades retained the elongated proportions of Gothic architecture. Many of the damaged churches in the Lower Town were also rebuilt in Flemish Baroque, including **Notre-Dame de Finistère** and **Notre-Dame du Bon Secours**.

THE NEOCLASSICAL PERIOD *(18th–19thC)*

Brussels was under Austrian rule for most of the 18thC, and the buildings during this period were designed in a modest and harmonious Neoclassical style. The rationalism of the 18thC is reflected in the cool symmetry of the **place des Martyrs** and the **Palais de Charles de Lorraine**. The fire that burned down the old Ducal palace in 1731 helped to clear the way for the creation of the Guimard Quarter in the Upper Town. Planned by Barnabé Guimard in the 1770s, this quarter was developed as a harmonious unity combining place Royale, the Parc de Bruxelles and the Palais de la Nation.

The urban harmony of Brussels was largely destroyed following Belgian independence in 1830. Extravagant buildings were erected in an effort to give Brussels the allure of a cosmopolitan capital. One of the first improvements was the construction by Jean-Pierre Cluysenaar in 1847 of the vast glass-roofed **Galeries Saint-Hubert**. Several other arcades were built in the Lower Town, including the **Galerie Bortier** by Cluysenaar, the passage du Nord and the now dilapidated Galerie du Commerce.

ECLECTICISM — THE REIGN OF LEOPOLD II *(1865–1909)*

Many grandiose buildings date from the reign of King Leopold II, who used the vast wealth generated by the Congo to fund magnificent public buildings and town planning schemes. The period had no style to call its own, drawing instead on diverse historical motifs to create a vigorous Eclecticism. Leopold II's crowning achievement was the construction of the overbearing **Palais de Justice** by Joseph Poelaert. Several streets in the Marolles were destroyed to make way for the monstrous edifice, larger than St Peter's in Rome, and designed to evoke the temples of the Pharaohs. The word *architek* (architect) subsequently entered Marolles dialect as a term of abuse.

Triumphal arch and **Musées du Cinquantenaire**

The age of Leopold saw buildings constructed in diverse historical styles. The stately Neoclassical **Museum of Central Africa** at Tervuren, opened in 1910, was modeled on the Petit Palais in Paris, while the triumphal arch in the **Parc du Cinquantenaire**, flanked by sweeping colonnades that link up to large museums, bears a striking resemblance to the Brandenburg Gate in Berlin. The eclecticism of the age is reflected in the extraordinary parade of architectural styles to be seen in the 19thC residential streets of Ixelles, Saint-Gilles and Schaerbeek, ranging from turreted Neo-Gothic to the most fanciful Art Nouveau.

The city witnessed an industrial boom in the late 19thC, leading to the construction of innovative buildings that used glass and iron. Several relics of the industrial age have been preserved, including the **Abattoirs d'Anderlecht** (1890), and the **Halles de Schaerbeek** (1901), but perhaps the most impressive buildings from this period are the bulging iron-and-glass **Serres Royales** (Royal Greenhouses), built by Alphonse Balat in 1870-79. Leopold II later boosted the cosmopolitan image of Brussels by purchasing a Chinese pavilion and a Japanese pagoda displayed at the 1900 World Exposition in Paris.

Not everyone in Brussels supported Leopold's theories of urban development. Burgomaster Charles Buls fought hard in the late 19thC to preserve picturesque corners of the old Flemish town. He saved Grand'Place and halted the demolition of several medieval city towers. A memorial to Buls on rue du Marché aux Herbes shows some of the buildings spared because of his efforts.

ART NOUVEAU *(late 19th–early 20thC)*

Brussels was briefly at the forefront of architectural innovation in the 1890s. Leopold II remained on the throne throughout the heady days of Belgian Art Nouveau, although he took scarcely any heed of the radical new style, preferring to live amid the trappings of traditional Baroque and Classical architecture.

Art Nouveau architecture was launched in Brussels in 1893 when Victor Horta designed the revolutionary Hôtel Tassel for a Belgian industrialist, and Paul Hankar built an equally innovative house for his own use a few blocks away. Horta had worked under Alphonse Balat, the architect of the Serres Royales and the Musées Royaux des Beaux-Arts. He learned from Balat the techniques for building in glass and iron, but invented new organic forms for balconies and staircases. His swirling ironwork and sinuous masonry can be admired at the **Musée Horta**, the former Magasins Waucquez department store (now the **Centre Belge de la Bande Dessinée**), the **Hôtel Solvay** and the **Hôtel Van Eetvelde**.

Maison de St-Cyr

Following the lead given by Horta and Paul Hankar, other architects designed flamboyant residences and elegant department stores, using wrought iron and costly wood in a way that still seems almost fantastic. One fine surviving example is the **Maison de Saint-Cyr** in square Ambiorix. Built by Gustave Strauven in 1896, it shows an even more flamboyant interpretation of Art Nouveau, with its scintillating display of ironwork on the balconies and roof.

Horta and other architects in the Art Nouveau style were until recently virtually ignored in Brussels, and many of their finest houses and department stores were torn down in the 1960s and 1970s. The demolition of Horta's Maison du Peuple sparked off worldwide protests, leading to the Belgian authorities adopting a more judicious policy.

Follow WALK 3 (page 84) to discover a few of the fortunate Art Nouveau buildings to have survived Brusselization.

ART DECO *(1920s)*
The explosive energy of Art Nouveau was followed by a cooling-off period in the 1920s when Art Deco was in vogue. Even Horta abandoned Art Nouveau in favor of a chilly Art Deco in his later works, such as **Gare Centrale** and the **Palais des Beaux-Arts**.

Brussels still has some spectacular Art Deco apartment blocks, including the huge 1925 **Résidence Palace**, which incorporates a swimming pool and theater, and the 1928 **Palais de la Folle Chanson** *(rond-point de l'Etoile 2)*. The impressive 1930 **Palais du Centenaire** — a major exhibition center on the northern edge of the city — is a dramatic example of geometric Art Deco style, with terraced tiers surmounted by statues.

POSTWAR *(1945–present)*
The most extraordinary building in Brussels is the **Atomium**, built for the 1958 World Exposition. Modeled on a crystal of iron, the 102-meter-high (335-foot) steel structure consists of nine separate spheres linked by spherical columns.

A rash of office blocks appeared in Brussels in the 1960s, including the **Sabena building** next to Gare Centrale and the cruciform **Berlaymont** building, seat of the European Communities (pictured on page 28). The office boom, fueled by the growth of the European Communities, led to several ill-advised projects, including the huge Manhattan office complex near the Gare du Nord, which was abandoned when office demand slumped, leaving several skyscrapers stranded amid urban wasteland.

The **Manhattan Quarter** is at last being completed, to give Brussels a major new business node, while the quarter around the Gare du Midi is being redeveloped in connection with the new high-speed train (TGV) station. Further massive construction projects are currently to be seen around rond-point Schuman and the Gare Leopold, as the EC gradually expands.

Several recent buildings in Brussels are worth a glance, such as André Jacqmain's twin office blocks at **place Stéphanie**, which hark back to the Art Deco style, and the careful restoration of a former 19thC hotel on avenue Louise to form the centerpiece of the **Conrad Hotel**. Civic pride is currently growing as Brussels Region gradually improves the quality of the built environment to make the city a worthy capital of Europe.

Five centuries of Belgian painting

Belgium is not particularly famed for its artists, yet a remarkable number of paintings in galleries all over the world come from this region of Europe. A visitor to Brussels can easily visit the places associated with artists such as Jan van Eyck, Roger van der Weyden, Pieter Paul Rubens and René Magritte.

Many Belgian paintings have been exported abroad or taken as war booty, but there are still exceptional collections in the main art galleries of Brussels, Bruges, Antwerp and Ghent. Some of the old churches in Belgium still have masterpieces hanging in the chapels, and countless small museums contain notable works.

The art galleries in Belgium are generally uncrowded, and some of the smaller collections are utterly deserted in winter. A painting that would draw crowds in Paris or New York is often ignored in Belgium, and the museum visitor often has the rare opportunity of being utterly alone with a work such as Bruegel's *Fall of Icarus* in the MUSÉE D'ART ANCIEN or Magritte's *Empire of Lights* in the MUSÉE D'ART MODERNE.

EARLY FLEMISH PAINTING

The oldest paintings in Belgian galleries were produced by the Early Flemish artists (sometimes called the Flemish Primitives) in the 15thC. The Dukes of Burgundy, such as Philip the Good and Charles the Bold, admired the precise craftsmanship of Flemish painters, sculptors and woodworkers. They supported a flourishing artistic community in the great Flemish cities of Bruges, Ghent and Brussels. The studios of Flanders produced works that were exported throughout medieval Europe, profoundly influencing the development of painting in Germany, the Netherlands, France and Italy.

The precious fabrics and costly interiors of the Burgundian Netherlands are reflected in the paintings of **Robert Campin** (c.1380-1444). Little is known of Campin, except that he worked in Tournai from about 1406. Identified as the Master of Flémalle and the Master of Mérode, Campin invented the Early Flemish technique of painting townscapes through open windows. An *Annunciation* by Campin hangs in the MUSÉE D'ART ANCIEN in Brussels.

The brothers **Jan van Eyck** (c.1390-1441) and **Hubert van Eyck** (died 1426) pioneered revolutionary new techniques of oil painting, enabling them to depict jewels and fabrics with an astonishing realism. Born in Maaseik, the brothers were tempted to Flanders by lucrative commissions from the Burgundian court. Little is known of Hubert, although a tombstone bearing his name was discovered a few years ago in Ghent. Jan van Eyck worked for Count John of Holland in The Hague from 1422-24, before moving to Bruges as the court painter of Philip the Good. Their single greatest work is the *Altarpiece of the Mystic Lamb* which hangs in Ghent Cathedral. Other important paintings by Jan van Eyck can be seen in the Groeningemuseum in Bruges and the Museum voor Schone Kunsten in Antwerp. The art of the Van Eycks profoundly influenced Italian artists such as Antonello da Messina.

Roger van der Weyden (Rogier de la Pasture in French, c.1400-64) is another shadowy Flemish artist. He was apprenticed to Roger Campin in 1427-32, and worked in Brussels from 1435-49. He was town painter of Brussels, but many of the works commissioned by the city were destroyed in the 1695 bombardment. Van der Weyden's compositions are fluid and dramatic compared to those of the Van Eyck brothers, and he painted several remarkable portraits of Burgundian nobles dressed in black: two fine examples in this style hang in the MUSÉE D'ART ANCIEN in Brussels.

Petrus Christus (c.1400-72) probably studied in Bruges under Jan van Eyck. His religious compositions are in the tradition of Van Eyck, although Christus often achieved a notably softer, more sensual tone in his portraits.

Dirk Bouts (c.1415-75) worked mainly in Leuven, where he painted large works for the town hall and St Pieterskerk. Influenced by the Van Eyck brothers and Van der Weyden, he developed a cool realism in his large paintings, although his smaller portraits have greater warmth. Go to the MUSÉE D'ART ANCIEN to see Bouts' impressive double painting of *Justice,* commissioned for the town hall in Leuven.

A member of the Ghent guild of artists, **Hugo van der Goes** (c. 1440-82) painted remarkable works despite bouts of deep depression. He became a lay member of the ABBAYE DU ROUGE-CLOÎTRE in about 1474, but continued to paint until the year before he died. His greatest work is the Portinari Altarpiece in Florence, which influenced Ghirlandaio. In Belgium, there are works by Van der Goes in the MUSÉE D'ART ANCIEN and the Groeningemuseum in Bruges.

Born in Seligenstadt near Frankfurt-am-Main, **Hans Memling** (c.1433-94) traveled to Brussels to train in Van der Weyden's workshop. He later moved to Bruges, where he became a highly successful painter. Memling was not an innovator, and often repeated the same theme in different paintings, but his idealized figures and gentle, rolling landscapes appealed immensely to foreign merchants based in Bruges. Many of his paintings were shipped to Italy and England in the 15thC, but the St Janshospitaal in Bruges still owns several of Memling's greatest works, including the remarkable *Reliquary of Saint Ursula.*

Named after the Dutch town of 's-Hertogenbosch where he mainly worked, **Hieronymus Bosch** (c.1450-1516) developed an extraordinary style of painting that featured bizarre beasts and fantastic landscapes. These enigmatic and often erotic works appealed immensely to 16thC Spanish collectors, including Philip II, and some of Bosch's greatest works are now in Madrid and Lisbon. The MUSÉE D'ART ANCIEN owns a strange *Crucifixion* by Bosch.

Gerard David (c.1460-1523) was born in Oudewater in the Netherlands. He moved to Bruges in the 1480s, and eventually succeeded Memling as the foremost painter in the city. His style was soft and sensual, although he could, when called upon, produce terrifying pictures, such as the double panel of *Justice* for the Bruges town hall (now in the Groeningemuseum). There are other paintings by David in the MUSÉE D'ART ANCIEN in Brussels.

FLEMISH RENAISSANCE ART

The Flemish Renaissance flourished under the Emperor Charles V, when Flanders was briefly the commercial center of the vast Spanish Hapsburg Empire. Born in Leuven, **Quentin Metsys** (1465/6-1530) moved to Antwerp in 1491, where he became the city's leading Renaissance painter. Metsys received numerous commissions for altarpieces and portraits from the city's rich merchants. Influenced by Raphael and Leonardo da Vinci, Metsys represents the beginnings of the Flemish Renaissance. Some of his greatest works remain in Antwerp at the Museum voor Schone Kunsten; other examples are in the MUSÉE D'ART ANCIEN in Brussels.

The **Antwerp Mannerists**, such as **Jan Mostaert** and **Jan Gossaert**, flourished in early 16thC Antwerp. They produced religious paintings featuring figures dressed in elaborate costumes, amid heavily-decorated Renaissance architecture. Scenes of the Adoration of the Magi particularly appealed to the Antwerp artists because of the opportunities they offered for extravagant costumes and jewel-encrusted objects.

Pieter Bruegel the Elder (c.1525-1569) grew up in Renaissance Antwerp, where he discovered the eccentric works of Bosch. Details of his life are vague, but he worked for a time in Hieronymus Cock's printshop in Antwerp, where he produced drawings in the style of Hieronymus Bosch.

Bruegel was admitted to the Antwerp painters' guild in 1551 and traveled to Italy at about the same time. He moved in 1563 to the Marolles district of Brussels, where he married the daughter of Pieter Coecke van Aelst, an Antwerp painter. Bruegel made frequent trips to the villages of the Pajottenland, w of Brussels, to paint his famous scenes of peasant weddings and winter landscapes.

His works are suffused with human warmth and compassion, even when they deal with harrowing subjects such as the *Massacre of the Innocents*. Some 40 paintings by Bruegel survive worldwide, of which one remains in Antwerp and five in Brussels. Bruegel was buried in the ÉGLISE NOTRE-DAME DE LA CHAPELLE in Brussels. The house where he probably lived is still standing in rue Haute, but plans to turn it into a museum have repeatedly come to nothing.

Several of Bruegel's descendants became painters, including his son, **Pieter Bruegel the Younger** (1564-c.1638), who slavishly copied his father's works. He earned the nickname "Hell Bruegel" because of his obsession with his father's more macabre works. His brother **Jan Bruegel** (1568-1625), known for his fastidious still lifes with flowers, was dubbed "Velvet Bruegel."

FLEMISH BAROQUE PAINTING

Flemish artists such as Rubens and Van Dyck filled the 17thC palaces and churches of Europe with gigantic paintings expressing the confidence of the Catholic Counter-Reformation.

Born in Siegen in Germany, **Pieter Paul Rubens** (1577-1640) moved to Antwerp when he was ten, after the death of his father. He later spent eight years in Italy, where he discovered the art of Titian and Caravaggio, before settling permanently in Antwerp. Much admired by the Archdukes Albrecht and Isabella, Rubens was soon overloaded with commissions to paint giant altarpieces and more intimate portraits. He also designed scenery for triumphal processions and built his own sumptuous Baroque home in Antwerp.

In addition to this prodigious artistic output, Rubens was frequently sent on diplomatic missions to England, Spain and France. His international contacts led to major commissions to paint Baroque ceilings in London, Paris and Madrid. Some of Rubens' most memorable works are intimate sketches of his children, or his two wives, Isabella Brant and Hélène Fourment. Troubled with rheumatism in his right hand toward the end of his life, Rubens retired to Steen castle near Elewijt, where he began to paint landscapes.

The art of Rubens had an enormous influence on later painters, including Watteau, Delacroix, Reynolds, Gainsborough and Constable, although his reputation had now faded somewhat. The MUSÉE D'ART ANCIEN in Brussels has a large Rubens collection, but his style can best be appreciated in Antwerp. Go to Rubens's Baroque house, now a museum, to witness the grandeur of the studio and garden. Seek out the artist's tomb in the Sint Jacobskerk, and gaze at the altarpieces in the Museum voor Schone Kunsten.

ROMANTICISM AND IMPRESSIONISM

The 18thC marked a low ebb in Belgian art, but painting gradually revived in the 19thC, under the influence of French Romanticism and Impressionism. Inspired by Rubens and Michelangelo, **Antoine Wiertz** (1806-65) labored on heroic paintings representing Classical themes or grim social misery. He might have been forgotten if he had not forced the Belgian government to preserve his former home as a museum. Go to the WIERTZ MUSEUM to discover some of the largest paintings ever produced.

Belgian art began to be noticed abroad in the 1880s, after twenty Belgian artists and sculptors, led by Octave Maus, formed a group known as **Les XX**, or **Les Vingt** (The Twenty). From 1883-93 they organized controversial annual exhibitions which launched the careers of several Post-Impressionists including Van Gogh, Cézanne and Toulouse-Lautrec. Disapproved of by conventional Belgians, they nevertheless won the support of several leading Belgian industrialists, including Solvay, Tassel and Hannon. The MUSÉE D'IXELLES owns a sizeable collection of Les XX paintings donated by Octave Maus.

The eccentric **James Ensor** (1860-1949) was a founder of Les XX. Born in Ostend, Ensor originally painted domestic interiors in a dark Impressionist style. His palette changed dramatically in about 1883, when he began using vivid colors to depict Carnival parades and seascapes. Ensor's new style proved too radical for Les XX, who rejected his *Christ's Entry into Brussels,* painted in 1889. Ensor had to wait until the 1920s for recognition in Belgium.

A room at the MUSÉE D'ART ANCIEN is devoted to Ensor's works, and his home in Ostend is now a museum.

THE LATEM PAINTERS

A group of Belgian artists settled in the village of Sint-Martens-Latem on the River Leie in the early 20thC. They sought to enjoy the simple life of the Flemish peasant, painting rural scenes in dark earthy browns and golds. Two separate groups coalesced in the village. The **First Latem Group** was formed around 1900 by Gustave van de Woestijne, Albert Servaes and Valerius de Saedeleer.

The more influential **Second Latem Group** was founded in about 1910 by **Gustave De Smet** (1877-1943) and Fritz **Van den Berghe** (1883-1939). During World War I, both artists were exiled in the Netherlands, where they fell under the spell of German Expressionism. De Smet and Van den Berghe returned to Latem after the war, where they were joined in 1918 by **Constant Permeke** (1886-1952). Permeke had lived in Ostend from 1912-14, painting the local fishermen. Wounded in the siege of Antwerp in 1914, he was taken to convalesce in Britain, where he discovered Expressionism.

In 1930, Permeke built himself a house called *De Vier Winden* (The Four Winds) at Jabbeke, w of Bruges. The house is now a museum of his paintings and sculptures.

BELGIAN SURREALISM

Surrealism began in Paris in the 1920s, when artists began to explore dreams and the subconscious. The ideas seeped across the frontier into Belgium, where they were enthusiastically taken up by Magritte and Delvaux.

René Magritte (1898-1967) developed a vivid Surrealist style following his chance discovery in 1924 of a reproduction of a Giorgio de Chirico painting. Magritte's fame grew in Belgium after World War II, and he was commissioned to produce a series of Surrealist murals for the casino at Knokke.

A room at the MUSÉE D'ART MODERNE in Brussels is filled with paintings from Magritte's private collection. His giant mural, titled *Les Barricades Mystérieuses,* can be seen in a hall in the Palais des Congrès.

Paul Delvaux (born 1897) was schooled in the strict Classical techniques of the Académie Royale des Beaux-Arts in Brussels. His early works were inspired by De Smet and Permeke, but in the 1930s he fell under the influence of Magritte and Chirico. He was obsessed from an early period with the rural railway stations on the edge of the Forêt de Soignes, the old trams of Brussels, and the ominously empty streets of the Quartier Leopold after dark. In such settings, Delvaux created an edgy atmosphere of fear mingled with erotic desire through the juxtaposition of inscrutable female nudes and old trams.

In recognition of his love of public transport, Delvaux was commissioned to paint the mural *Our Old Brussels Trams* at Bourse metro station. The railway station at the new university town of Louvain-la-Neuve has several full-size reproductions of Delvaux paintings. Several of his greatest works now hang in the Delvaux Museum at the coastal village of Sint-Idesbald, while others occupy a room at the MUSÉE D'ART MODERNE in Brussels.

COBRA

The postwar art group called Cobra flourished in Northern Europe from 1948-51, taking its name from the initial letters of Copenhagen, Brussels and Amsterdam. Inspired by German and Flemish Expressionism, Cobra artists painted abstract works with vibrant colors and childlike forms. The MUSÉE D'ART MODERNE has a collection of works by Cobra members such as **Pierre Alechinsky** (born 1927) of Belgium and **Asger Jorn** of Denmark (1914-73).

CURRENT TRENDS

Contemporary Belgian art remains individualistic and quirky, as can be seen in the rooms devoted to recent art at the MUSÉE D'ART MODERNE. A noticeable trend in recent years has been to break out of the straitjacket of the art gallery, as in the *Chambres d'Amis* show in 1986 in Ghent, where modern art was exhibited in private houses. Several prominent Belgian artists were invited to create works for the Brussels metro (see OFF THE BEATEN TRACK, page 142), while others produced unique installations for the bedrooms in the New Siru Hotel (see WHERE TO STAY, page 161).

Basic information

Before you go

DOCUMENTS REQUIRED

EC citizens must carry at all times a passport or national identity card. US citizens need a passport. For stays exceeding 3 months, all foreigners must obtain an identity card from the local commune.

Car drivers must be able to show a national driver's license and a vehicle registration certificate. Non-Belgian cars must have a national identity plate.

TRAVEL AND MEDICAL INSURANCE

It is advisable to take out an insurance policy covering loss of deposits paid to airlines, hotels, tour operators, etc., and emergency costs, such as special tickets home, as well as a medical insurance policy.

Free medical treatment is available in an emergency from a doctor, pharmacist or hospital, to visitors from EC countries. Travelers from the UK should obtain **form E111** from a post office before leaving, to prove their entitlement. It is still advisable to take insurance cover for all other emergency expenses incurred. All other nationals should take out comprehensive travel and medical insurance. Travelers from the US should always consult their own insurance company before going abroad.

The **IAMAT** (International Association for Medical Assistance to Travelers) is a nonprofit organization that has a directory of English-speaking doctors who will call, for a fixed fee. There are member hospitals and clinics throughout the world, including two in Brussels. Membership is free, and other benefits include information on health risks overseas. For further information write to **IAMAT** headquarters in the US or in Europe *(417 Center St., Lewiston, NY 14092, USA, or 57 Voirets, 1212 Grand-Lancy, Genève, Switzerland).*

MONEY

The **Belgian franc** (**BF**, also seen as **FB** or simply **F**) is the basic unit. There are 0.5 BF, 1 BF, 5 BF, 20 BF and 50 BF coins, and banknotes of 100 BF, 500 BF, 1,000 BF and 5,000 BF. The possibility of introducing other denomination notes — 200 BF, 2,000 BF and 10,000 BF — is being studied. There are no restrictions in Belgium on the import or export of currency.

For over 60 years Belgium and Luxemburg have operated a monetary union, and coins and banknotes from one country circulate widely in the other. Coins from Luxemburg present no problems, but occasional difficulties arise in using its banknotes in Belgium. However, these can easily be exchanged for equal-value Belgian notes at banks.

Increasingly, a number of shops in Brussels, particularly those with close links to the European Community (EC), give prices in both Belgian francs and **European Currency Units (ECU)**. This is more a gesture of support for an eventual single EC currency than a practical measure, since ECU coins and banknotes do not exist in Belgium.

Travelers checks issued by all major companies and, for Europeans, Eurocheques, are widely accepted. **It is important to note separately the serial numbers of your checks and the telephone number to call in case of loss.** Specialist travelers check companies such as American Express *(see page 55 for details)* provide extensive local refund facilities through their own offices or agents.

Currency may be changed and travelers checks and Eurocheques cashed at all banks, and at bureaux de change in Zaventem Airport, mainline rail stations and various locations in Brussels. Most bureaux de change remain open until 7pm, but those at the Gare du Nord *(map 4 A5* ☎ *(02)218.39.14)* and the Gare du Midi *(map 5 G1* ☎ *(02)521.12.84)* are open every day of the week until 11pm. Some hotels will also handle foreign currency.

American Express also has a **MoneyGram®** money transfer service that makes it possible to wire money worldwide in just minutes, from any American Express Travel Service Office. This service is available to all customers and is not limited to American Express Card holders.

Major **charge and credit cards** such as American Express, Diners Club, Access and Visa are widely accepted in stores and hotels throughout Brussels.

CUSTOMS

Following a special agreement reached in 1991, travelers within the European Community will continue to be eligible to make duty-free purchases until the end of June 1999. After that date, duty- and tax-free shopping will be restricted to travelers arriving in and leaving the EC.

An EC agreement has increased personal allowances of duty-free drinks and tobacco. With effect from January 1, 1993, everyone aged over 17 will be entitled to import 60 liters of champagne or 90 liters of table wine, 110 liters of beer, 10 liters of spirits or 20 liters of fortified wine, plus 800 cigarettes or one kilo of rolling tobacco into another EC member country, provided they can prove they are **for personal use only**.

The duty-free limits for people entering Belgium from a non-EC country such as the US are far lower: 2 liters of table wine and one liter of spirits, or 2 liters of sparkling wine; 200 cigarettes or 250 grams of rolling tobacco; and 50 grams of perfume.

At the time of writing the duty-free import allowance for all other goods (perfume, electrical goods and gifts bought tax-free) was still ECU 45 (about £32 or $55) in all EC countries, although there is pressure from industry to increase this amount.

Remember, import restrictions are different outside the EC. Find out from your local Customs and Excise office before you leave, or from the **Belgian Tourist Office** *(rue du Marché aux Herbes 61, B-1000, Bruxelles* ☎ *(02)512.30.30, map 3 E3).*

Apart from such obvious exceptions as drugs, endangered plants and animals, and ivory, there are no restrictions on what may be brought into Belgium for personal use. It is advisable to carry receipts for any expensive items (such as electrical goods, computers or luxury clothing).

There are no restrictions on what may be taken out of the country, and no special licence is required, for example, to export antiques.

VAT REFUNDS

Visitors are exempt from paying Value Added Tax (**TVA** or **BTW**) on purchases above a certain amount, on completion of a simple form and presentation of a passport at the time of purchase. As this is currently 19.5% of the bill, it is well worth the trouble. For EC residents, this facility can only be used on individual items that cost more than BF 25,500. For non-EC residents, conditions are more generous, with a minimum spend of BF 5,000 per store.

However, to validate the refund, which will be paid to you at your home address, or through a charge or credit card refund, you must present the paperwork and goods at a checkpoint before the passport control before leaving the country.

You will need to keep the receipt for the items purchased, and obtain a tax-free shopping form from the store. At customs, you will need to supply your name, home address and passport number, and show the documentation, and sometimes even purchases. Remember to pack them somewhere accessible. If everything is in order, the papers will be stamped and can then be presented for the requisite refund.

At Brussels Zaventem airport, the office is clearly marked, to the left of passport control in the departure hall. Visitors leaving the country by road can present the papers at a major border crossing.

Travelers by rail may have difficulty, as there are few, if any, customs officers on trains to neighboring countries, making it harder to get the official stamp necessary for the refund to take place. In such cases, it is possible to have the papers stamped by Dutch, Luxemburg or French customs, or, alternatively, at the Belgian consulate in the destination country. Papers should then be sent to: **Lieutenance des Douanes**, Gare du Midi, B-1070 Bruxelles.

BELGIAN NATIONAL TOURIST OFFICES

Belgium   Office Belge du Tourisme, rue du Marché aux Herbes 61, B-1000 Bruxelles, map **3E3** ☎(02)512.30.30. Provides information on all parts of Belgium.
T.I.B./Tourist Information Brussels   Hôtel de Ville, Grand'Place, B-1000 Brussels, map **3E3** ☎(02)513.89.40. Brussels runs its own separate tourist service, which offers more detailed information on the city.
United Kingdom   Belgian Tourist Office, Premier House, 2, Gayton Rd., Harrow, Middlesex HA1 2XU ☎(081) 861 3300.

USA   Belgian Tourist Office, 745 5th Ave., New York NY 10151
☎(212) 758-8130.
Belgian Tourist Reservation   Boulevard Anspach 111, B-1000
Brussels *(map 3 D3)*. Reserve here, for no charge, a hotel room
anywhere in Belgium *(* ☎ *(02)513.74.84* Fx *(02)513.92.77).*

GETTING THERE

• **By air**   Brussels' **Zaventem Airport** *(map 2 B5)* is located 15km (9
miles) NE of the city. The ever-expanding airport handles international
flights operated by the Belgian national airline **Sabena** and other major
carriers. For 24-hour information ☎(02)722.31.11.

• **By train**   The introduction of high-speed trains such as the French
TGV *(Train de Grande Vitesse)* is set to revolutionize rail travel on
mainland Europe. Belgian railways are currently constructing a new
TGV terminal at the Brussels Gare du Midi. Once the station opens
(scheduled for late 1994), rail journey times to Brussels will be dramatically reduced. The journey time from Paris should be cut to 75 minutes.
The completion of the Channel Tunnel link in 1994 will reduce the
journey time from London to Brussels to 3 hours, although the completion date for this still seems unreliable. Other TGV services are planned
to link Brussels with Amsterdam (1 hour) and Cologne (1 hour).

Even before TGV services begin, Brussels can easily be reached by
direct train from Amsterdam (3 hours), Cologne (3 hours) and Paris (3
hours). Direct international trains also link Brussels to Luxemburg ($2\frac{1}{2}$
hours) and Strasbourg (5 hours), carrying mainly European politicians,
journalists and secretaries. The Strasbourg trains stop at the Gare Schuman and the Gare Leopold for the European Community Quarter.

• **By sea**   The main sea route from the UK is the **Dover to Oostende**
crossing, run by **P&O Ferries** *(reservations in UK* ☎ *(071) 233 6480).*
There is a regular service up to 6 times a day. The crossing takes 4
hours. Those without cars are sometimes tempted to pay a supplement
for the **Jetfoil** service operated by the **Dover-Oostende Line** *(same
UK* ☎ *as P&O Ferries),* which cuts the journey to 100 minutes. The
journey can be pleasant if the sea is calm, but the service is apt to be
canceled due to gales or mechanical problems. Passengers are then
switched to the next available ferry.

Hardy northern Britons often book the **Hull to Zeebrugge** ferry,
operated by **North Sea Ferries** *(* ☎ *(0482) 77177).* The night crossing
takes 14 hours.

For details of the ferry companies' Belgian offices, see USEFUL ADDRESSES
on pages 60-61.

Car drivers to Belgium increasingly use the short **Dover to Calais**
ferry crossing (90 minutes), where stylish, comfortable new ships such
as the *Fantasia* or *Fiesta* have been introduced by the **Sealink Stena
Line** *(* ☎ *(0233) 647047)* to compete with the Channel Tunnel. Allow 3
hours to drive to Brussels from Calais.

Hoverspeed *(* ☎ *(0304) 240241)* offer the fastest crossing, by hovercraft from **Dover to Calais** (35 minutes). Coaches using this route depart
from London's Victoria Coach Station for Brussels, Bruges and Antwerp.

Renowned for comfort, **Sally Line** *(☎ (0843) 595522)* crosses from **Ramsgate to Dunkirk** in $2\frac{1}{2}$ hours.

CLOTHES

It is advisable to carry a raincoat and umbrella, even in summer, as protection against the changeable weather. Flat, comfortable shoes are recommended as a means of combating hours of walking across the uneven cobbles.

Belgian dress sense is relatively conservative. For business occasions, men are expected to wear a tie for meetings, although a suit is less common than a smart jacket and trousers. Women generally wear skirts and suits for business.

See also CLIMATE on page 54.

GENERAL DELIVERY (POSTE RESTANTE)

Letters to be collected should be marked *poste restante* and addressed to **Bureau de Poste**, Centre Monnaie, B-1000 Bruxelles. The post office *(☎ (02)219.38.60, map 3 D3)* is located on the first floor of the shopping complex at place de la Monnaie (metro to de Brouckère).

American Express *(write to: Client Mail, American Express Travel Service, pl. Louise 2, B-1050 Bruxelles ☎ (02)512.17.40)* provides the same service for its customers.

Getting around

FROM THE AIRPORT TO THE CITY

A regular **rail shuttle** runs from the airport to the city, stopping at Gare du Nord and Gare Centrale only. Trains are rather antiquated, but they are rarely delayed, whereas taxis can sometimes be held up by traffic jams. See GETTING FROM THE STATIONS TO THE CITY (below) to decide on the best station to use.

When it comes to catching the train back to the airport, ignore the signs at Gare Centrale pointing to the airport train as they do not always indicate the correct departure platform. Look instead at the electronic departure board or the official timetables in the station hall.

Only taxis registered in Zaventem are permitted to pick up passengers outside the arrivals hall, although you can sometimes save money by taking a Brussels-registered taxi from outside the departures hall.

GETTING FROM THE STATIONS TO THE CITY

Most trains stop at the three mainline rail stations in Brussels. The **Gare du Nord** *(map 4 A5)* is a large modern station convenient for hotels on place Rogier and Boulevard Adolphe Max. The station is located directly above a major underground public transport interchange. Trams 52, 55, 58, 62, 81 and 90 stop in the underground station.

Gare Centrale *(map 4 E4)* is reasonably user-friendly although a little gloomy. It was designed by Victor Horta, but it has none of the elegance of his earlier Art Nouveau buildings. Walk down the hill from the station to reach Grand'Place in a few minutes, or take the exit signposted Galerie Ravenstein to get to the museums around place Royale. Gare Centrale is linked to a metro station, with direct trains running to Schuman (5 minutes), and to the Brussels Exhibition Centre (20 minutes). Note that international trains to Paris do not stop at Gare Centrale.

The **Gare du Midi** *(map 5 G1)* is in turmoil pending the completion of the new TGV station, and will best be avoided until late 1994. The station is served by the metro and trams 52, 55, 58, 62, 81 and 90.

Gare Quartier Leopold *(map 1 C3)* is a small station within walking distance of the European Parliament on rue Belliard. **Gare Schuman** *(map 1 C3)* is 5 minutes' walk from the main EC buildings. Trains to Luxemburg and Strasbourg stop at both Quartier Leopold and Schuman, as well as the three mainline stations.

Weary travelers are apt to complain at the absence of both baggage trolleys and porters at Brussels' rail stations. Buy a wheeled suitcase to avoid back strain.

PUBLIC TRANSPORT

The Italians and Greeks who have settled in Brussels view the public transport system as a model of efficiency, whereas the Germans and the Dutch are more scornful. The Brussels network may appear confusing and often outdated, but it has a good safety record and relatively low crime rate, though you should obviously still watch your wallet or purse in crowded vehicles. Disabled travelers and parents with baby buggies will encounter exasperating problems such as narrow tram doors and inaccessible metro platforms.

Brussels has an integrated system of metro, trams and buses run by the public transport authority **Stib**. Most Stib buses and trams are painted a distinctive blue-and-yellow livery. Most routes are served from about 5.30am-midnight, but schedules are drastically cut after 6pm and on weekends. Some routes do not operate at all in the evenings and on Sundays. Network maps and route timetables are posted in the metro and at tram and bus halts.

Our transportation map at the back of the book covers most of the tram and metro network in a way that is designed to be user-friendly. You can also pick up a free map showing routes at the Stib offices at the Gare du Midi, Porte de Namur and Rogier metro stations.

The public relations department *(Galerie de la Toison d'Or 20, 6th floor ☎ (02)515.30.64, map 6 G4)* will provide a free computer print-out of any route you need.

Public Transport Weekend, in early October, allows everyone limitless travel on virtually the entire public transport network. You buy a single ticket costing a nominal sum and travel as you please on trains, trams and buses throughout Belgium.

TICKETS

A ticket for a one-way (single) journey *(carte à un voyage)* can be bought in metro stations, and from the bus or tram driver. The ticket is valid on all public transport for one hour from the time stamped. The only limitation is that you may not go back on the same route using one ticket.

A cheaper option is to buy a multi-journey ticket. Tickets for 5 journeys *(carte de 5 voyages)* are sold on buses and trams, but the best value is the 10-journey ticket *(carte de 10 voyages)* sold at metro stations, rail stations in Brussels, and in newsagents (newsdealers) displaying a Stib sticker. The *carte 24 heures* gives unlimited travel on the city public transport network. All tickets except the *carte à un voyage* must be clipped in one of the red machines in the metro stations, or in the orange machines on buses and trams. Keep the card dry or it will not work.

Multi-journey tickets are valid throughout the Stib network for one hour, except on the sections marked on the back of the card. They include the rural part of the tram 44 route from Quatre Bras to Tervuren; those going out to Tervuren must buy a *carte à un voyage* from the driver. It is always worth asking the driver for help if you are confused. Otherwise, you run the risk of being embarrassed by Stib's plain-clothes inspectors.

Children under 6 years old travel free.

METRO

The city is proud of its metro system, with its fast, clean and safe trains. They provide rapid access to some, but not all, of the outer suburbs. Metro stations (identified by a white **M** on a blue background) are spacious. Many stations are decorated with specially commissioned works of art, ranging from abstract sculpture to Surrealist paintings (see page 142).

The metro has two main routes. **Line 1** follows a half loop around the outer boulevards, from Gare du Midi to Simonis, with stops at place Louise (for avenue Louise) and Rogier (for rue Neuve). **Line 2** crosses the city, with stops at place de Brouckère, Gare Centrale (for Grand'Place), Schuman (for the EC quarter) and Mérode (for the Cinquantenaire museums). Take care to get on the right train if you are heading to the outer suburbs, as line 2 splits at either end.

TRAMS

Trams are a slower way of getting around town, but they let you see something of the sights. Brussels has rather old-fashioned stock with narrow doors. Newcomers are sometimes baffled by the doors, which are opened by pressing a thin green strip between the two doors. To request the tram to stop, press the black button. A light will come on above the door. Note that the button marked "stop" is for use in an emergency only.

Among the most useful trams are the 92, 93 and 94, which run through the upper town past the Parc de Bruxelles, the palace, the Musée des Beaux-Arts and the Sablon. Tram 94 is popular with Sunday hikers as it terminates close to the Forêt de Soignes. But the most spectacular tram ride is on tram 44, which runs through the forest to the Africa museum at Tervuren. The routes of trams 44 and 94 are described as excursions on pages 88-90.

BUSES

Buses within Brussels are convenient for reaching many suburban destinations. They tend to provide faster links than trams.

Country buses will get you to the sights around the city including Waterloo battlefield, Beersel castle and Grimbergen abbey, although the services can be minimal. You need to know whether your destination lies in Flemish Brabant or French Brabant. Places in Flemish Brabant are served by **De Lijn** buses (☎ *078.11.37.73, toll-free),* which leave from the underground terminus at the Gare du Nord. Destinations in French Brabant are served by **T.E.C.** buses (☎ *(02)287.29.11)* departing from place Rouppe.

TAXIS

Being a major international business and diplomatic center, Brussels has a plentiful supply of taxis 24 hours a day. These can be hailed at a number of taxi stands in the center of town or from the EC area around rond-point Schuman. They can also be ordered by telephone. The standard of driving and knowledge of Brussels displayed by its taxi drivers varies considerably. Be prepared to help navigate if your destination is away from normal tourist and business routes.

All taxis have meters and the fare shown includes taxes and tips. Some firms offer a discount for the round trip between Brussels and the airport. Taxis at the airport bearing a square sticker of a white airplane on an orange background give the reduced round-trip fare between the airport and Brussels. The offer is valid for two months.

Should you have a complaint, note the taxi's license number, the color and model of the vehicle, and contact the **Service des Transports (Taxis)** *(Bloc Lendi, Manhattan Centre, av. du Boulevard 21, B-1210 Bruxelles* ☎ *(02)219.72.80, map 4 B4).*

Some widely used companies are:

- **Taxi Verts**   ☎(02)349.49.49
- **A.T.R.**   ☎(02)242.22.22
- **Autolux**   ☎(02)512.31.23
- **Taxis Orange**   ☎(02)513.62.00

See also TAXI TOURS on page 60.

GETTING AROUND BY CAR

Cars once ruled supreme in most of Brussels, where until recently traffic jams were almost unheard of. An extensive system of highways and tunnels, the oldest of which date from the 1958 International Exposition, generally enables drivers to travel easily and quickly through and around the city. But a sharp increase in traffic, extensive road repairs and more frequent demonstrations (whether by Europe's many minorities seeking international recognition or by striking Belgian teachers) can now cause unexpected delays.

For the newcomer, driving in Brussels is difficult. Many Belgians drive fast, but not always skillfully. A compulsory practical driving test was only introduced in Belgium in 1977. The city must also have one of the most cosmopolitan groups of car owners in the world, judging from the license plates, which range from the distinctive blue "EUR" of an EC official and official CD plates to the latest arrivals from Scandinavia and Eastern Europe. Many are also adjusting to driving in Brussels for the first time.

Belgium continues to practice *priorité à droite*, a convention designed to help the flow of traffic and requiring drivers to yield to vehicles coming from their right. In some cases, as on main streets and larger traffic circles, this practice is being phased out, although this has not yet changed the behavior of some drivers. If in doubt, be prepared to yield and, to be safe, do not expect other drivers always to yield to you.

There are two other cardinal **rules** for safe driving in Brussels. By law you must always give way to a tram, whether it is coming from the left or the right. Never park in front of a private garage. If you do so, you may come back to find your car towed away. Usually, but not always, the garage will display the license number of the resident vehicle.

There are **other rules** to keep in mind. The maximum permitted level of alcohol is 0.5 grams per liter of blood. If a breathalyser test is positive, a driver's license is taken away for at least six hours. Seat belts must be worn at all times. The only exceptions are for pregnant women and if serious medical reasons dictate otherwise. Children under the age of 12 must sit in the back unless there is no space available. It is compulsory to carry a red warning triangle in the vehicle.

Speed limits are changed from time to time. In general the maximum speed permitted in built-up areas is 50km (30 miles) per hour. On motorways it is 120km (75 miles) per hour and on other roads 90km (55 miles) per hour.

Parking in Brussels is relatively easy (compared to other major cities), although the center can sometimes be very crowded. Parking meters take 5 BF and 20 BF coins, and there are many underground garages.

Lead-free **gasoline** is on sale at most filling stations. Look for *Essence sans plomb* or *Loodvrij*.

RENTING A CAR

Most major international car rental firms have branches at Zaventem airport and in the city. Payment by charge/credit cards avoids the need for a large cash deposit. A current driver's license is required, and the minimum age is normally 18.

For car rental firms in Brussels consult the *Pages d'Or* (Yellow Pages) of the telephone directory under the heading *Location d'autos*. Some of the main names are:

- **Avis**   Av. des Communautés 5 ☎(02)724.04.11, open 8am-6pm; Hilton Hotel ☎(02)513.10.51, open 8am-8pm; Airport ☎(02)720.09.44, open 6.30am-11.30pm.
- **Budget**   Av. Louise 327 ☎(02)646.51.30, open Mon-Fri 8.30am-6pm, Sat 9am-noon; airport ☎(02)720.80.50, open 6.30am-11.30pm.
- **Hertz**   Blvd. Maurice Lemonnier 8 ☎(02)513.28.86, open Mon-Fri 7.30am-8.30pm, Sat 8am-4pm, Sun 8am-1pm; airport ☎(02)720.60.44, open 6.30am-11.30pm. International telephone reservations ☎(02)735.40.50.

GETTING AROUND BY BICYCLE

Getting onto a bicycle in Brussels makes Russian roulette seem a relatively safe pastime. Car drivers are generally too occupied in conversation or phone calls to take any heed of cyclists. Bad driving habits are made even worse by inadequate lane markings and pot-holed roads, making cycling in Brussels an abysmal experience. Until the situation improves, it is sensible not to cycle within the city limits.

Immediately you cross the line into Flemish Brabant, however, the roads are thick with enthusiastic cyclists, but even here you must watch out for the occasional lone madman.

GETTING AROUND BY TRAIN

The rail network within Belgium varies from efficient to antiquated. The fastest trains are **intercity services (ICs)**, which provide a frequent international service linking major Belgian cities with Randstad Holland, Paris, Luxemburg, Strasbourg and Cologne. Fast **inter-regional trains (IR)** run between major Belgian cities, while trains marked **L** putter nostalgically along rural routes.

Good services radiate from Brussels to the main cities of Belgium, including Ghent (30 minutes), Bruges (1 hour), Antwerp (30 minutes), Liège (1 hour) and Namur (30 minutes). Several towns on the Belgian coast are reached by direct trains, including fashionable Knokke-Het Zoute (1 hour 20 minutes).

For information on all aspects of rail services ☎(02)219.26.40.

Special reduced-rate fares apply on weekends, for trips to stations in the Ardennes or on the coast. The B-Tourrail ticket is valid for unlimited rail travel in Belgium on any 5 out of 17 days. The Benelux-Tourrail is a similar ticket valid throughout Belgium, the Netherlands and Luxemburg.

GETTING AROUND ON FOOT

Many of the sidewalks in Brussels are in a neglected state, with potholes and loose paving stones a constant hazard. To make matters worse, local car drivers are unwilling to cede priority to pedestrians on crossings, so that you must be always wary of the traffic. Yet Brussels is a relatively compact city for walking, and you can sometimes find quiet routes through parks or along back streets.

See our street maps in the back of this book. If you need to cover a wider-than-normal radius, buy the Falkplan of Brussels.

On-the-spot information

TIME ZONES

Belgium falls in the same time zone as most Western European countries, being 1 hour ahead of Greenwich Mean Time in the winter and 2 hours ahead in the summer. In winter, clocks are turned back in Belgium a few weeks before the UK, and for a brief period the time is harmonized on both sides of the English Channel.

For US visitors, Belgium is 6 hours ahead of Eastern Standard Time and 7-9 hours ahead of the other US time zones.

CLIMATE

The best times to visit Brussels are April and May, when the city is awash with pink and white spring blossom, and September to October, when the many trees and shrubs in and around the capital take on the colors of fall. The weather is variable throughout the year; the sky is often overcast and rain is a fairly frequent occurrence. Winters are rarely harsh, and while the temperature may fall below zero, there is usually little snow in the city. Average temperatures: summer 16°C (60°F), winter 3°C (37°F).

PUBLIC HOLIDAYS

January 1; *Pâques* (Easter Sunday) and *Lundi de Pâques* (Easter Monday); Labor Day, May 1; Ascension (6th Thursday after Easter); *Pentecôte* (Whit Sunday, 7th Sunday after Easter) and *Lundi de Pentecôte* (Whit Monday); *Fête Nationale* (National Holiday), July 21; *Assomption* (Assumption), August 15; *Toussaint* (All Saints' Day), November 1; Armistice, November 11; *Noël* (Christmas Day), December 25.

The European Community institutions do not count Armistice as a holiday, but they have their own holiday on May 9, in honor of the declaration made on that day in 1950 by former French Foreign Minister, Robert Schuman, one of the driving forces behind the creation of the European Community.

It is worth noting that many Belgians and EC officials will often take a Friday or Monday off as well, if a public holiday falls on a Thursday or a Tuesday. This practice is known as *faire le pont* (building a bridge).

BANKS AND CURRENCY EXCHANGE

Most banks are open from 9am-4pm Monday to Friday. Currency transactions are dealt with at the counter marked *change/wissel.*

There are some late-opening facilities. All central branches of the **Kredietbank** stay open until 5.15pm on Friday but are closed on Saturday. Consult the telephone directory for branch addresses. Some suburban branches of the **Générale de Banque/Generale Bank** remain open until 6pm on Friday, but none in the city center. The most central bank operating on Saturday is the **Générale de Banque/Generale Bank** near the Bascule shopping center *(chaussée de Waterloo 659a, B-1060);* it is open from 9.15am-12.15pm.

Banks in the arrivals hall at Zaventem airport are open longer, usually from 8am-9pm, seven days a week. The **Générale de Banque/Generale Bank** (☎ *(02)720.16.82)* at the airport is open from 7am to 9.45pm seven days a week.

Bureaux de change are open longer and later, and many hotels will change cash and travelers checks, although the rates are less favorable than in the banks. Many hotels and some of the shops around the Grand'Place will let you pay in any of the major foreign currencies.

The city is well supplied with hole-in-the-wall cashpoint machines, many of which take the most common plastic cards. Two which take American Express, Mastercard, Eurocard, Visa and Eurocheque cards, can be found at the **Kredietbank** in Grand'Place *(#17, map 3 E3)* and at the **Credit Communal de Belgique/Gemeentekrediet van Belgie** *(av. Louise 20, map 6 H4).*

There are two **American Express Travel Service** offices where cash can also be obtained *(pl. Louise 2, B-1050 ☎ (02)512.17.40, map 6 G4 and blvd. Souverain 100, B-1070 ☎ (02)676.25.25, both open Mon-Fri 9am-5pm, Sat 9am-noon).*

SHOPPING HOURS

The main shops usually open between 9.15am and 10am and stay open until 6 or 6.30 pm. In busy shopping areas like the Rue Neuve, many shops stay open until 8pm on Fridays. The big supermarkets such as GB and Delhaize are open from 9am to 8pm Monday to Thursday and Saturday, and there is late-night shopping until 9pm on Friday.

Most shops except bakers, florists and a few newsagents (newsdealers) are closed on Sunday. Small local Turkish and Moroccan-owned shops selling groceries are open on Sunday and late during the week. There are a few night shops in downtown Brussels selling drinks, confectionery and snacks.

During the four weeks running up to Christmas, shops are open later during the week and are also open on Sunday.

RUSH HOURS

The rush hours are from 8-9am, noon-2pm and 4-6pm, and the metro, trams and buses are all crowded at these times. Traffic in the street generally moves slowly, and the metro is the only reliable means of getting around. The rush hours are especially chaotic when it rains heavily.

POST, TELEPHONE AND FAX SERVICES

Post offices are open from 9am to 5pm, Monday to Friday. The post office on the first floor of the **Centre Monnaie/Muntcentrum** *(above de Brouckère metro station, B-1000 ☎ (02)219.38.60, map 3 D3)* sells stamps until 6pm Monday to Thursday and until 7 pm on Friday. It is open from 9am to noon on Saturday. The main post office is open 24 hours, seven days a week and is located at the **Gare du Midi/Zuid Station** *(av. Fosny 48a, B-1000 ☎ (02)538.40.00, map 5 G1).* Local post offices are listed in the telephone directory under *Postes.*

When **calling Brussels**, the code from within Belgium is **02**, followed by a seven-digit local number. From outside Belgium, dial the international access code (**011** from the US and **010** from the UK), then the code **32** for Belgium followed by **2** for Brussels.

- **Brussels from the UK**   ☎010.32.2+number
- **Brussels from the US**   ☎011.32.2+number

Public telephones (marked *téléphone/telefoon*) are located in main streets, metro stations and some cafés. They take 5 BF and 20 BF coins. The minimum charge is 10 BF, although you sometimes find they will only accept 20 BF coins. More common now are cardphones which use a prepaid phonecard (*Telecard*®). These are available from local shops, newsagents and post offices *(poste/posterijen)* at a cost of 200 BF for 20 units or 1,000 BF for 105 units.

International calls can be made direct from any public phone booth displaying a band around the top representing the 12 European Community flags.

International calls from Brussels should be preceded by **00** and the country code (**US = 1, UK = 44, Ireland = 353**), then the telephone number minus any initial 0 digit in the area code. On some of the few remaining older telephones, wait for a second tone after the 00.

Toll-free numbers within Belgium always begin with **078.11**.

Charges for international calls are at the same tariff whatever the time of day or night. There is a cheap rate for domestic calls from 6.30pm to 8am, and all day on Saturdays, Sundays and public holidays.

Collect/reverse charge calls can be placed direct to the operator in some countries abroad:

- **US via AT&T** (AT&T Direct Service) ☎11.00.10
- **US via MCI** (MCI Call USA) ☎11.00.12
- **UK** ☎11.00.44
- **Canada** ☎11.00.12
- **Australia** ☎11.00.61
- **New Zealand** ☎11.00.64

Operator services are divided into French-speaking services (where the number starts with a **13**) and Dutch-speaking services (the number starts with a **12**). Both usually speak English.

- **Directory inquiries** ☎1307 or 1207
- **International directory inquiries** ☎1304 or 1204
- **Information on international dialing codes or charges** ☎1324 or 1224

Operator services are divided by region:

- **Brussels** ☎1380 or 1280
- **Elsewhere in Belgium** ☎1329 or 1229
- **International** ☎1324 or 1224

If you are looking for a number in the telephone directory, it helps to know the address. The book is divided into sections, with Brussels at the front followed by the outer suburbs (like Waterloo) at the back. Entries are listed alphabetically in each section.

For business and service listings, consult the English-language index in the Yellow Pages *(Pages d'Or/Gouden Gids)*.

Urgent documents can be sent by **fax** from the 24-hour post office at the **Gare du Midi/Zuid Station** *(av. Fosny 48a, B-1000, map 5 G1)*. Larger hotels will sometimes send faxes for nonresidents.

Telegrams can also be sent by telephone (☎ *1325 for the French-speaking operator or* ☎ *1225 for a Dutch-speaking one)*.

You can make a telephone call or send a telegram *(télégramme/tele-graaf)* between 8am and 10pm from the **RTT** (Régie des Telegraphes et des Telephones/Regie van Telegrafie en Telefonie) center *(blvd. de l'Impératrice 17, B-1000, map 4 E4)*.

PUBLIC LAVATORIES (REST ROOMS)

Every cafe has a bathroom that you can use without having to order a drink. You should tip the attendant 10 BF or 15 BF, or leave it in the saucer by the door. Rest rooms are found at all main line rail stations, although they are not common in the metro. There is one at de Brouckère metro station in the downtown shopping area.

Men are luckier — there are a number of old-fashioned open-air *pissoirs,* including one against the wall of the Sainte-Catherine church in the fish market area.

ELECTRIC CURRENT

The electric current is 220V. Sockets are the standard mainland Europe 2-prong type. Adaptors are sold at major airports.

LAWS AND REGULATIONS

Belgium is a meeting of cultures. Belgians are not as zealous as Germanic nations in fully respecting the letter of the law, but nor do they have the cheerful disregard of some Latins. But on one item they do insist — you must be able to prove your identity at any time. Always carry your passport with you if you do not have a Belgian identity card; the police sometimes carry out spot checks. You will also need it for such matters as collecting a registered letter from the post office or for entering EC or government buildings.

It is forbidden to hitchhike on Belgian motorways.

For laws connected with driving, refer to GETTING AROUND BY CAR on pages 51-2.

ETIQUETTE

It is normal to shake hands when you meet someone in Belgium. It is usual for women to kiss male and female friends and acquaintances on the cheek, usually three times in formal situations, but it can be twice between friends. Unfortunately, there are no fixed rules on which side to start. Men do not normally embrace unless they are relations. Say *bonjour* and *au revoir* when you enter and leave a shop. Be sure to say *excusez-moi* if you happen to bump into someone or accidentally tread on their foot.

Invitations to dinner are common. It is polite to arrive 15 minutes after the time specified, but not much later. It is considered impolite to arrive at the invited time. Take a gift of flowers or chocolates for the hostess. It is good manners to send a short handwritten "thank you" note the next day. For business meetings, err on the side of caution and arrive on time or five minutes early.

TIPPING

Taxi drivers do not normally receive a tip, as this is included in the fare. But it is customary to give a little extra if the driver has come to fetch you from your office or restaurant or performed any other small service. In **cinemas and theaters**, give usherettes 20 BF per person in exchange for the program they give you — their main source of income.

In **hotels**, service is included in the bill, but after a lengthy stay it is customary to leave a tip for the chambermaid. In **restaurants**, Value-Added Tax and service are included in the bill, and tips are not normally left except to indicate particular satisfaction. A cloakroom attendant will expect between 20 BF to 50 BF per person. At the **hairdresser**, if service is not included, leave a tip of between 10 and 20 percent. In **public lavatories**, a cleaning attendant is often present at the exit. Leave 10 BF or 15 BF.

DISABLED VISITORS

Brussels is an obstacle course for even the bravest disabled visitor. Many streets, particularly in the center, are cobbled, and the sidewalks are often in an alarming state of disrepair. Public transport is almost totally inaccessible for someone in a wheelchair.

A brochure of special information for disabled visitors may be obtained by writing to the **Minister for Social Affairs and Health** *(rue Belliard 7, B-1040)*. The **Belgian Tourist Office** *(rue du Marché aux Herbes 61, B-1000* ☎ *(02)512.30.30, map 3 E3)* can also offer helpful information.

In the US, for further information and details of tour operators specializing in tours for handicapped people, write to the **Travel Information Service**, Moss Rehabilitation Hospital *(12th St. and Tabor Rd., Philadelphia, Pa. 19141)* or to **Mobility International USA** *(PO Box 3551, Eugene, Or. 97403)*.

In Britain, you should consult **RADAR** *(25 Mortimer St., London W1N 8AB* ☎ *(071) 637-5400)*.

LOCAL AND FOREIGN-LANGUAGE PUBLICATIONS

Brussels' central location and the presence of so many foreigners in the city have increasingly encouraged newsdealers to stock a wide range of foreign-language publications. Nearly all the main European newspapers are available on the day of publication, some, like the British newspapers, from very early on.

The most comprehensive English-language publication covering Brussels' events is *The Bulletin*, a weekly that appears on Thursdays with extensive local news and reviews and details of forthcoming events.

Both *Le Soir* and *La Libre Belgique* have wide-ranging arts/entertainment supplements that appear on Wednesdays with information on attractions in Brussels and throughout Belgium. *Kiosque Bruxelles*, a handy weekly publication that can fit into a pocket or handbag, also lists, in French, a wide range of cultural events in Brussels, set out in useful chronological order.

Visitors can also enjoy a wide range of television in Brussels. Belgium has one of the widest linguistic ranges of cable television in the world, providing at least 25 channels from Britain, France, Germany, Italy, Luxemburg, the Netherlands, Spain and the United States (CNN) as well as local channels, one of which is devoted specifically to Brussels history, folklore and news.

See page 61 for a list of shops selling good travel guides.

MUSEUMS

Museums in Belgium tend to take Monday as a rest day. The normal opening hours are Tuesday to Sunday 10am-5pm. Some museums close for one hour at lunch, and all but the most benign institutions like to clear visitors out at least 10 minutes before closing time.

You may be expected to leave coats, bags, cameras and umbrellas in the cloakroom (*garderobe*). Normally no charge is requested for this service.

Many of the major museums in Brussels are open free of charge (see BRUSSELS FOR FREE below). There are sometimes collecting boxes to encourage voluntary contributions, but no attempt is made to embarrass people into paying.

BRUSSELS FOR FREE

A trip to Brussels need not be expensive if the obvious traps are avoided, such as business hotels and expensive restaurants. You can find fairly cheap hotels if need be, and eat well in the neighborhood restaurants of the MAROLLES. The pricey areas to be avoided include the Sablon and the streets around the EC neighborhood.

One of the blessings of Brussels is that some of the greatest museums are free. You can see the Bruegels at the MUSÉE D'ART ANCIEN and the Magrittes in the MUSÉE D'ART MODERNE without paying a franc. The sprawling collection of antiquities at the MUSÉE D'ART ET D'HISTOIRE is likewise free, as is the adjoining MUSÉE DE L'ARMÉE. The TOUR JAPONAISE, the MUSÉE BELLEVUE and the MUSÉE WIERTZ are among the other free museums.

Many buildings throughout Belgium open on Heritage Day (see THE BRUSSELS CALENDAR on page 70).

The GALERIES SAINT-HUBERT originally charged visitors to marvel at the glittering 19thC shops, but the arcade is now one of the free sights in the city. The CATHÉDRALE SAINT-MICHEL and the many parish churches cost nothing to visit, though you might want to donate a few francs to help maintain the fabric or feed the local poor.

Free concerts are often staged in the PARC DE BRUXELLES in the summer months. The cheapest entertainment after dark is found in the jazz cafés, where you can hang around for the price of a *bière blanche*.

Useful addresses

TOURIST INFORMATION

The **Office Belge du Tourisme** *(rue du Marché aux Herbes 61, B-1000 Bruxelles* ☎ *(02)512.30.30, map 3 E3)* provides information on all parts of **Belgium**.

Brussels runs its own separate tourist service, which can offer more detailed information on the city. The office of **Tourist Information Brussels (T.I.B.)** is located at the Hôtel de Ville *(Grand'Place, B-1000* ☎ *(02)513.89.40, map 3 E3).*

MAIN POST OFFICES
At **Gare du Midi/Zuid Station**   av. Fosny 48a, B-1000
☎(02)538.40.00, map **5G1**.
Centre Monnaie/Muntcentrum   above de Brouckère metro
station, place de Brouckère, B-1000 ☎(02)219.38.60, map **3D3**.

TELEPHONE SERVICES
Speaking clock (in French)   ☎1300

BUS TOUR OPERATORS
Arau   rue du Midi 2 ☎(02)513.47.61, map **3E3**. Vigorous tours led
by radical architects and planners, who point out showpiece buildings
and damned quarters. Arau runs regular tours in English covering
Brussels 1900, Thirties Brussels and *Alternative Brussels*. Dates are
listed in *The Bulletin* and, more fully, in the Wednesday supplement of
Le Soir under *Visites Guidées*.
Arcadia   ☎(02)643.02.26. Sunday coach tours on Brussels art and
history given by experts.
Brussels City Tours   rue de la Colline 8 ☎(02)513.77.44. Map
3E3. The lazy way to see the sights, with commentary on headphones
available in eight languages.

TAXI TOURS
Taxi drivers identified by a **Taxi-Tour** badge provide guided tours of
the city. The tour costs the standard taxi rate. Call any taxi company
and ask for a Taxi-Tour driver. See TAXIS on page 51.

WALKING TOURS
Babbelbus   ☎(02)673.18.35. Off-beat walking tours of the sights
and the secrets.

AIRLINES
Air UK   ☎(02)507.70.52. Flights from London (Stansted).
American Airlines   ☎(02)508.77.00. Flights from New York
(Kennedy) and Chicago (O'Hare).
British Airways   ☎(02)725.30.00. Flights from London
(Heathrow).
British Midland   ☎(02)772.94.00. Flights from London
(Heathrow) and Birmingham.
Sabena   ☎(02)511.90.30. The Belgian national airline, with a
substantial international route network.

SEA-CROSSING OPERATORS
The **British Tourist Authority** av. Louise 306, B-1050
☎(02)646.35.10, off map **6I5**; stocks ferry brochures and makes
reservations on services to the UK
Hoverspeed   rue Antoine Dansaert 101 ☎(02)513.93.40, map
3D3
North Sea Ferries   Zeebrugge ☎(050)54.34.30

Ligne Oostende-Dover (Dover-Oostende Line) place Madou 1
☎(02)219.55.55, map **4D6**
Sealink Stena Line rue de la Montagne 52 ☎(02)513.41.05, map
4E4

COACH SERVICES
Europabus ☎(02)217.00.25. Daily services to Paris, London,
Amsterdam and Cologne.

ENGLISH-LANGUAGE BOOKSTORES
W H Smith blvd. Adolphe Max 71-75, B-1000 ☎(02)219.50.34,
map **4C4**.
House of Paperbacks chaussée de Waterloo 23, B-1180
☎(02)343.11.22, off map **5I2**.
The Strathmore Bookshop rue Saint Lambert 110, B-1200
☎(02)771.92.00, map **2C4**.
European Bookshop rue de la Loi 24, B-1040 ☎(02)231.04.35,
off map **6E6**.

PLACES OF WORSHIP
The cathedral and parish churches in Brussels are Catholic, but most
other religions have regular services. For a full list, look in the tele-
phone directory under *Églises*.
American Protestant Church Kattenberg 19 ☎(02)673.05.81,
map **2D4**.
Anglican rue Capitaine Crespel 29 ☎(02)511.71.83, map **6G4**.
Catholic St Nicolas, rue de Tabora 6 ☎(02)511.27.15, map **3D3**.
Mass in English on Sundays at 10am.
Church of Scotland chaussée de Vleurgat 181 ☎(02)649.02.19,
map **1C3**.
Quakers square Ambiorix 50 ☎(02)230.49.35, map **1C3**.
Synagogue rue de la Régence 32 ☎(02)512.43.34, map **5G4**.

EMBASSIES
Most countries maintain an embassy and consulate in Brussels. The
offices are listed in the phone book under *ambassades*.
Canada av. de Tervuren 2 ☎(02)735.60.40, map **2C4**.
Ireland rue du Luxembourg 19 ☎(02)513.66.33, map **6F6**.
Japan av. des Arts 58 ☎(02)513.92.00, map **6E6**.
United Kingdom rue d'Arlon 85 ☎(02)287.62.11, off map **6F6**.
United States boulevard du Régent 27 ☎(02)513.38.30, map **6E6**.

Business in Brussels

Brussels caters well to itinerant businessmen and businesswomen. There is a fair selection of **serviced offices** for rent by the month, week or day, with **secretarial** and **translation services** attached. Most also offer a separate message-taking service, which is useful if you travel a lot. These offices serve the city's two main international business districts: the area between rue de la Loi and rue Belliard, where the European Community institutions are clustered, and avenue Louise, home to law firms, accountants and the Brussels headquarters of many international businesses.

The **telephone** operator can arrange conference calls for three or more people, in Belgium or abroad (☎ *1314 (French-speaking) or* ☎ *1214 (Dutch-speaking).* For other services, and information on **fax** and **postal services**, see pages 55-6.

It is worth noting that new business facilities are expected to spring up in the area around the Gare du Midi, in preparation for the high-speed rail terminal that is being built there. Addresses include:

In the EC area:
Regus   Trèves Centre, rue de Trèves 45, B-1040 ☎(02)238.77.11

On avenue Louise:
Acte   av. Louise 304, B-1050 ☎(02)640.24.85, off map 6I5
Axeurope   av. Louise 212, B-1050 ☎(02)645.59.11, off map 6I5
Bureau Service AAA   rue Souveraine 97, B-1050 ☎(02)506.45.11, map 1C3
Business Communication International   av. Louise 480, B-1050 ☎(02)645.12.11, off map 6I5
Regus   place Stéphanie, av. Louise 65, boîte 11, B-1050 ☎(02)535.77.11, map 6H4
HQ Services & Offices   av. Louise 149, B-1050 ☎(02)533.16.11, off map 6I5
NCI Business Center   av. Louise 149, B-1050 ☎(02)535.75.11, off map 6I5
Wordforce   av. Louise 207, boîte 14, B-1050 ☎(02)649.60.43, off map 6I5

TRANSLATION AGENCIES
Brussels also has a wealth of translation agencies for dealing with officialdom and business. Some of the following can also arrange interpreters for meetings or conferences.
Berlitz   av. des Arts 36, B-1040 ☎(02)513.92.74, map 6F5
CBG   av. Albert 137, B-1060 ☎(02)345.75.68, map 1D3
Idioma   rue de Genève 4, boîte 33, B-1140 ☎(02)215.71.30, map 2B4
Lexitech   chaussée Saint-Pierre 119, B-1040 ☎(02)640.03.85, map 1C3
Lu's Paragraph   rue de Spa 61, B-1040 ☎(02)230.30.01, map 1C3
Singer   Centre Rogier, 20th floor, boîte 362, B-1210 ☎(02)217.37.91

W.S.T.T.B.C.   av. Charles Quint 124, boîte 14, B-1040
☎(02)465.91.62, map **1B2**

COURIER SERVICES
For keeping in touch with home, most of the major courier services are
represented in Brussels.
DHL   Kosterstraat 210, B-1831 Diegem ☎720.95.00, map **2B4**
Eurocolis   rue Picard 130, B-1210 ☎(02)425.38.01, map **1B3**
Federal Express   Brussels National Airport, Building 2, B-1930
Zaventem ☎(toll-free)078.11.35.55, map **2B5**
Free Lance Express   Woluwélaan 6-10, B-1931 Diegem
☎(02)725.00.50, map **2B4**
New Poney Express   Leuvensteenweg 571, B-1932 Zaventem
☎(02)725.19.00, map **2B5**
TNT Express Worldwide   Leuvensteenweg 46-50, B-1932
Zaventem ☎(02)070.23.36.33, map **2B5**

Emergency information

EMERGENCY SERVICES
Coins are not needed for emergency calls from public telephones.
Police   ☎101
Ambulance   ☎100
Fire   ☎100

MEDICAL AND DENTAL EMERGENCIES
Doctors' emergency service (24 hours)   ☎(02)479.18.18
Private medical service (24 hours)   ☎(02)648.80.00
Dentists' emergency service (9pm-7am Monday to Saturday; 7am
Saturday to 7am Monday)   ☎(02)426.10.26 or 428.58.88
Anti-poison center   ☎(02)345.45.45
Burns center   ☎(02)268.62.00

24-HOUR PHARMACY
Pharmacies are open during normal shopping hours. A list of addresses
of those open at night and outside normal hours is placed in the
window of most pharmacies and in Belgian newspapers. For security
reasons, the telephone numbers of duty pharmacists are not published.

AUTOMOBILE ACCIDENTS
*   Do not admit liability or incriminate yourself.
*   Ask any witness(es) to stay and give a statement.
*   Contact the police.
*   Exchange names, addresses, car details and insurance company
    details with any other drivers involved.
*   Give a statement to the police, who will compile a report
    acceptable to insurance companies.

CAR BREAKDOWNS
*   Put on flashing hazard warning lights and place a warning
    triangle 50m (55 yards) behind the car.
*   Call the police *(☎ 101)* or one of the following automobile
    organizations, who provide services to their members, but may be
    able to help for a membership fee paid on the spot.

Royal Automobile Club de Belgique   rue d'Arlon 53, B-1040
☎(02)287.09.11-12, off map **6**F6.
Service S.O.S. Dépannage   ☎(02)287.09.00
Service "Touring Secours"   ☎(02)233.22.22
Touring Club de Belgique   rue de la Loi 44, B-1040
☎(02)233.22.11, map **6**E6.

HELP LINE
English-speaking Samaritan service ☎(02)648.40.14

LOST PASSPORT
Contact the local police and your consulate immediately. Consular addresses are on page 61.

LOST TRAVELERS CHECKS/CHARGE/CREDIT CARDS
Notify the local police immediately, then follow the instructions provided with your travelers checks, or contact the issuing company.
- **American Express** ☎(02)676.21.21 (lost card) ☎078.11.76.32 (toll-free — lost travelers checks)
- **Diners Club** ☎(02)515.97.13
- **Eurocheque** ☎(02)352.51.51
- **MasterCard/Eurocard** ☎(02)741.66.12
- **Visa** ☎(02)535.28.25

If stranded with no money, contact your consulate (see page 61) or **American Express** *(☎(02)676.21.21)*.

LOST PROPERTY
For goods lost on the **metro, bus or tram**, contact the **Lost property office** *(av. de la Toison d'Or 15, B-1000 Brussels ☎(02)515.23.94, map 6 G4)*.

For property lost in a **taxi**, go to the police station nearest to your point of departure.

For property lost elsewhere, contact the local police station or **Brussels Central Police Station** *(rue du Marché-au-Charbon 30, B-1000 ☎(02)517.96.75, map 3 E3)*.

At **Zaventem airport**, contact the lost property office *(Régie des Voies Aériennes, 1st floor Visitor's Hall ☎(02)722.39.40)*.

EMERGENCY PHRASES
Help! *Au secours!*
There has been an accident. *Il y a eu un accident.*
Where is the nearest telephone/hospital? *Où se trouve le téléphone/ l'hôpital le plus proche?*
Call an ambulance! *Téléphonez une ambulance!*
Call the police! *La police, s'il vous plaît.*

Planning
your visit

When to go

Brussels has a climate similar to London and Paris, with mild winters, cool summers and the possibility of rain throughout the year. Riotous Carnival celebrations in late February to early March symbolically herald the beginning of spring, although the air continues to feel chilly until Easter at least. By late April you may begin to notice a drop in the number of elderly ladies wrapped in thick furs.

The narrow streets of Bruges tend to become choked with tourists in spring, but Brussels remains fairly quiet. You may notice Grand'Place mobbed with German and Dutch tourists during the Easter weekend or on one of the public holidays in May, but most of the city remains uncrowded throughout the summer months.

July and August, when Belgians are inclined to take their vacation, are pleasantly soporific in Brussels. The traffic becomes noticeably calmer, offices are half empty, and many restaurants and shops close for a few weeks. Yet Brussels is never as dead as Paris in high summer. Look out for posters announcing orchestral concerts in the BOIS DE LA CAMBRE or puppet shows in the Parc de Bruxelles.

Children begin to troop back to school in early September. Brussels often looks its best in the mellow golden light of autumn. Take a tram out to TERVUREN on a sunny day (see TRAM RIDES, page 89) to see the woods tinted with vivid golds and reds. Or join the locals in the forest on a Sunday afternoon hike. Check out the menus outside the traditional Belgian restaurants for autumn specialities such as pheasant or wild boar.

The dark days of winter begin in November, but Brussels becomes one of the more cheerful northern European cities during December. The Christmas period extends from St Nicholas' Eve (December 5) to Epiphany (January 6). Fir trees and Christmas decorations enliven the city, and the Sablon and Grand'Place look particularly festive.

Planning when to visit Brussels may be dictated by pleasure or business needs. Either way, consult THE BRUSSELS CALENDAR on page 69, to gain a better idea of what to aim to see, or what times to avoid.

STRATEGIES FOR A SUNDAY
The center of Brussels is quiet on Sundays apart from a few people ambling to Grand'Place to look at the bird market. Cinema fanatics rouse themselves on Sunday mornings for the 10am screening at Acropole Prestige *(av. de la Toison d'Or 8, map 6 G4* ☎ *(02)511.43.28,*

metro to Namur), which combines coffee and fresh croissants with a cult film.

Several markets get going in the early morning, including a sprawling food market near the Gare du Midi and an antique market on the Sablon. By noon, the markets are beginning to close down, and the locals head home for lunch clutching a roast chicken and a fruit tart. Many restaurants are closed on Sunday, but there are plenty of places to eat in the Îlot Sacré or at place Sainte-Catherine. Those who have not dozed off after lunch head for the BOIS DE LA CAMBRE or the forest for a brisk stroll.

STRATEGIES FOR RAINY DAYS

Brussels is blessed with a labyrinth of covered arcades where you can shop on rainy days without ending up soaked to the skin. The grand 19thC arcades in the Lower Town are for strolling, rather than buying (see GALERIES SAINT-HUBERT, page 122, and GALERIE BORTIER, page 121; also page 192). The best shops for clothes are located in the modern arcades in the Upper Town (see SHOPPING, page 195).

Museums offer an obvious refuge from the rain, but on Mondays, when they are closed, you might be tempted to go to an afternoon screening of a movie (see NIGHTLIFE on page 185).

A WEEKEND IN BRUSSELS

A number of hotels offer special weekend rates that are well worth snapping up. The amount of money you can save might make for quite a special weekend, especially if you choose to spend the proceeds of the discounts on a good meal or a trip to the cinema.

SATURDAY

- Spend the morning looking at GRAND'PLACE and the GALERIES SAINT-HUBERT.
- Try **Le Falstaff** for lunch, or, if it is impossibly crowded, one of the fish restaurants on place Sainte-Catherine.
- Take the metro to the MUSÉE D'ART ET D'HISTOIRE in the afternoon to look at the unjustly neglected collection of Flemish tapestries and retables, not to mention the extraordinary Classical art.
- If time allows, cross the square to the MUSÉE DE L'ARMÉE, to find out about the many battles fought on Belgian soil.
- Return to place de Brouckère by metro for a drink at the **Café Métropole**, and eat, if fish is your favorite dish, at one of the restaurants on the nearby place Sainte-Catherine.

After dinner, walk to the Grand'Place to look at the floodlit buildings, and wander into the GALERIES SAINT-HUBERT, where the street musicians tend to play classical music.

SUNDAY

- Visit the MUSÉE D'ART ANCIEN in the morning, to look at the Flemish Primitives or the 19thC Belgian Impressionists, or, alternatively, the MUSÉE INSTRUMENTAL, with its exceptional collection of old musical instruments.
- Then have lunch in the vicinity of the place du Grand Sablon.
- Wander into the stately PARC DE BRUXELLES, with its fountains and

statues, and then look at the florid Gothic architecture of the CATHÉ-DRALE SAINT-MICHEL.

- Descend to the Lower Town to buy chocolates to take home. Enjoy a last drink at **Mokafé** in the Galeries Saint-Hubert before the homeward journey.

AN ART NOUVEAU WEEKEND

Pick a hotel in the heart of the Art Nouveau quarter such as the MANOS or the REMBRANDT.

SATURDAY

- Visit the MUSÉE HORTA, located in the exquisite Art Nouveau home of the architect Victor Horta.
- In the afternoon, follow WALK 3 (page 84) around the grand turn-of-the-century mansions in Ixelles.
- At the end of the walk, turn right up rue Vilain XIV. Pick up tram 93 or 94 on avenue Louise to go back to town.
- Get off at the Sainte-Marie stop and go to the sumptuous restaurant **De Ultieme Hallucinatie** *(rue Royale 316, see page 179),* which is located in a fine Art Nouveau house designed by Paul Hamesse.

SUNDAY

- Take tram 92, 93 or 94 to place Royale to look at the Art Nouveau Old England department store (now the MUSÉE INSTRUMENTAL).
- Visit the CENTRE BELGE DE LA BANDE DESSINÉE, situated in the sole surviving Art Nouveau department store designed by Victor Horta.
- Have lunch, or a snack, at **Le Falstaff** *(rue Henri Maus 17-23)* in an environment that is a luxurious blend of Art Nouveau and Art Deco.

A WEEKEND OF BELGIAN ART

Brussels has several distinguished collections of ancient and modern Belgian painting and decorative arts. The most appropriate place to sleep would be in a room adorned with the work of a modern Belgian artist, at the somewhat eccentric NEW SIRU (see HOTELS A TO Z on page 161).

SATURDAY

- Go to the MUSÉE D'ART ANCIEN in the morning to look at the paintings by Van der Weyden, Bruegel, Rubens and Ensor.
- Spend the afternoon in the rooms of the adjacent MUSÉE D'ART MODERNE looking at the Surrealism of Delvaux and Magritte, or the French and Belgian Impressionists.

SUNDAY

- Go to the MUSÉE D'ART ET D'HISTOIRE to explore the quiet rooms of European decorative arts.
- Take the metro to look at works by Belgian artists in several metro stations, or, if you prefer your art in more conventional locations, explore some of the commercial art galleries on the place du Grand Sablon, rue Ravenstein or avenue Louise.

The Brussels calendar

The tourist office is the best source of information on current events, but the following list provides some of the highlights of the Brussels calendar.

JANUARY
• The **International Brussels Film Festival** (early January) is a brave attempt to re-create the glamor of Cannes on the windswept Mont des Arts. Major French films dominate the program, with a few US and British premieres plus the occasional offbeat discovery.

FEBRUARY
The gloomy days of February are mercifully enlivened by several regular events. • Delve in the vast Brussels **International Book Fair** (late February) to find out what's new in French literature and cartoon books. • Or go to the **Festival du Dessin Animé** (Festival of Animated Film, late February/early March), for the latest cartoon feature films, Disney classics for children and workshops for professionals. Most films are in French or Dutch, but the occasional animated film is screened in English.

APRIL
• The exotic **Royal Greenhouses at Laeken** are open to the public for just a few days each year (late April/early May). Extraordinary African plants thrive in daring 19thC iron-and-glass structures. Expect to swelter in the tropical heat.

MAY
• The **Jazz Rally** (late May) is a wacky event in which some 60 far-flung cafés host jazz concerts over a long weekend. Old London buses run a shuttle service between the different venues (free to those who have bought a badge). Hunt down the best sounds at Grand'Place, the Bourse, the Sablon and place Fernand Cocq. • The **Queen Elisabeth International Music Competition** takes place every year and is held in the Palais des Beaux-Arts. • The **Brussels Run**, over a 20-km (12-mile) circuit, takes place usually on the last weekend in May.

JUNE
• **Anniversary of the Battle of Waterloo** (June 16), fought 18km (11 miles) s of Brussels in 1815. Mock armies converge on Waterloo every 5 years to commemorate the rout of Napoleon. The next is due to happen in 1995. • Brussels' *Ommegang* (late June/early July) is one of Europe's most lavish pageants. Dating from the 14thC, the costumed parade was staged in its most spectacular version in 1549 for the benefit of Charles V and his son Philip. The modern event attempts faithfully to re-create the 1549 *Ommegang* with a vast parade of flag wavers, trumpeters, stilt walkers and giant figures enacting a game of chess. The nobles on horseback are often genuine Belgian aristocrats

descended from the 16thC participants. Reserve — if you can — a grandstand seat on Grand'Place for the spectacular evening show, or join the crowds earlier in the day on the place du Grand Sablon.

JULY
• **Brosella Festival** (mid-July) provides a weekend of Celtic folk and Mid-Atlantic jazz in an open-air amphitheater under the Atomium. Features a free fest for kids. • **Belgian National Day** (July 21); the Belgian army struts in front of the Palais du Roi, and fireworks explode in the evening.

• The **Foire du Midi**, a raucous annual funfair, takes place along the boulevards near the Gare du Midi. • The **Palais du Roi opens to visitors** (late July to mid-September). Visitors must wait patiently in long lines for a chance to shuffle through the royal residence built by Leopold II. The rooms are grand and glittering, but are now sadly empty of family mementoes.

AUGUST
• **Planting the Meyboom** (August 9). A run-down corner of the old town is animated every year by the planting of the Meyboom. The ceremony has continued almost without interruption since 1213. Giant effigies and brass bands assemble in Grand'Place at 3.30pm, and a team of locals then hauls the 10m-long (11-yard) tree trunk through the streets to the spot where it is ceremonially planted at about 5pm (at the corner of rue des Sables and rue du Marais, not far from the CENTRE BELGE DE LA BANDE DESSINÉE). The old town becomes briefly Bruegelian as people celebrate late into the night. • Every year or two (check with Tourist Office), a vast **floral tapestry** is created on the cobblestones of Grand'Place (mid-August), featuring over half a million Belgian begonias.

SEPTEMBER
• **Festival of Flanders** (September to October). Concert halls, churches and castles throughout Flanders stage performances of modern and classical music. • **Heritage Day** (mid-September). Historic buildings throughout Belgium admit the public for just one day each year. An opportunity to peer inside private castles, artist's studios, Art Nouveau homes, theaters and even barracks. Look out for the flag decorated with the EC ring of stars, which marks the buildings that are open free of charge. Expect long lines outside the landmark monuments. • The **Brussels Marathon** involves thousands of runners, one weekend early in September. • **Brabant Kermis** (mid-September): a weekend event on Grand'Place, with traditional Brabant folk music, and stalls selling beer and food.

• The **Bruegel Festival** (mid-September) is a weekend of Bruegelian fun in the Marolles quarter, where Pieter the Elder lived until his death in 1669. Most of the action happens between the PORTE DE HAL and the ÉGLISE NOTRE-DAME DE LA CHAPELLE. • **Europalia** (mid-September to December, every 2 years, in odd years) is a sprawling event to celebrate the culture of a particular country. Expect major art exhibitions, contemporary dance, concerts in castles, conferences and cuisine.

OCTOBER

• **Public Transport Weekend** (early October) lets everyone loose on virtually the entire public transport network. You buy a single ticket costing a nominal sum and travel as you please on trains, trams and buses throughout Belgium. Special events are staged at museums and castles, but the crowds are often daunting. • **Belga Jazz Festival** (late October to early November) features international jazz stars at several major venues in Brussels.

NOVEMBER

• On **All Saints' Day** (November 1), Belgians flock to cemeteries to lay flowers on relatives' graves.

DECEMBER

• **St Nicholas' Eve** (December 5) and **St Nicholas' Day** (December 6), when children are given presents from St Nicholas. Look in the shop windows at the traditional *speculoos* (gingerbread biscuits) and marzipan molded in the shape of fruit. • **Christmas decorations** throughout the city (December 6 to January 6). Grand'Place is lavishly decorated with lights, fir trees from the Ardennes and a mock nativity scene complete with live sheep. Potent Christmas beers are served in the best cafés. • **European Christmas Market** (mid-December) on the elegant place du Grand Sablon. The square is crammed for one weekend with dozens of illuminated Christmas stalls selling traditional Scandinavian tree decorations and Belgian crafts. Drink a glass of German *Glühwein* (mulled wine) and tot up the number of languages you can hear.

   • **Christmas Day** (December 25). Belgian families celebrate Christmas with expensive delicacies such as lobster and *boudin de Noël* (white pudding). Restaurants traditionally offer solid *Menus de Noël* around Christmas. • On **New Year's Eve** (December 31), restaurants end the year by offering lengthy *Menus de la Saint-Sylvestre*. Crowds gather in the PARC DU CINQUANTENAIRE for a fireworks display at midnight.

Where to go

Brussels is a sprawling city with a remarkable diversity of urban quarters. Travelers new to the city tend to spend most of their time around Grand'Place, though some of the most interesting museums and parks are located in the outlying suburbs. Distances are often too great to cover on foot, and a rudimentary grasp of the public transport system is necessary to get the most out of a visit.

The **old city** (or "Pentagon") lies within a ring of 19thC boulevards known as the *Petite Ceinture* (inner ring). This area is divided into the *Bas de la Ville* (Lower Town), and the *Haut de la Ville* (Upper Town). Boulevard de l'Empereur and boulevard de l'Impératrice mark the division between the Lower and Upper Towns.

Brussels Region is divided into 19 different communes, including Brussels commune (roughly the area enclosed by the inner boulevards). The communes are often based on old villages swallowed by urban expansion. Each commune has a town hall and a local shopping quarter. Some have old churches, attractive squares and local museums.

The diversity of the 19 communes forms one of the most engaging features of Brussels. The communes to the s and e of the old town tend to have a French character, whereas those to the n and w are apt to be more Flemish. Almost every quarter of the city has a good park or a noteworthy restaurant.

Maps of Brussels can be found on the following pages:
- **European Quarter**: see opposite
- **Grand'Place**: page 133
- **Brussels Environs**: maps **1** & **2** at the end of the book
- **City Center, Lower and Upper Town**: maps **3**, **4**, **5** & **6** at the end of the book

ORIENTATION

Travelers can only discover the real Brussels by delving into the neglected quarters in the suburbs. The following list gives a brief impression of the special features to look out for in the 19 communes. For more detailed information, see STREETSCAPES AND NEIGHBORHOODS (page 130) and PARKS AND OPEN SPACES (page 143).

BRUSSELS *(maps 3, 4, 5 & 6, city center).* Brussels commune mainly covers the Lower Town and the Upper Town, though it extends beyond the Pentagon to include the European Quarter, avenue Louise, Heysel and Laeken. The population of Brussels commune is governed from the spectacular Gothic Hôtel de Ville on Grand'Place.

BRUSSELS/AVENUE LOUISE *(map 6 G4-I5, s of the city center).* A 19thC artery lined with a visually jarring mixture of 19thC town houses, Art Deco apartment blocks, and a few skyscrapers, leading to the Bois de la Cambre.

BRUSSELS/EUROPEAN QUARTER *(map 1 C3, e of the city center).* A rather forbidding district of large offices and busy streets. The Berlaymont building once provided a focus for the European Communities. Although empty, it provides a landmark in the European quarter. The nearby Parc du Cinquantenaire is dominated by several important museums.

BRUSSELS/HEYSEL *(map 1 B3, N edge of the city)*. A sprawling entertainment and business complex next to the Atomium, comprising the Brussels Exhibition Centre, the Heysel soccer stadium, Kinépolis and Mini Europe.

BRUSSELS/LAEKEN *(map 1 B3, N of the city)*. Dominated by the royal palace, Laeken, a wealthy residential commune, is dotted with curiosities built by Leopold II, including a Japanese pagoda and a Chinese pavilion.

BRUSSELS/LOWER TOWN *(maps 3 & 5, W of city center)*. The oldest quarter of the city, with intriguing cobbled streets leading to spectacular sights such as Grand'Place, the Galeries Saint-Hubert and the Cathédrale Saint-Michel. Many of the old markets have gone, but you will still find a local ambience on the place du Jeu de Balle or the place Sainte-Catherine. What nightlife remains takes place around place de Brouckère.

BRUSSELS/UPPER TOWN *(maps 4 & 6, E of city center)*. A formal 18thC quarter where the parliament and the royal palace are located, with straight streets leading to grand 19thC buildings such as the Musée des Beaux-Arts and the Palais de Justice. The square du Grand Sablon is the most elegant area.

ANDERLECHT *(map 1 C1-2, W edge of the city)*. A 19thC industrial quarter with traces of the old Brabant town surviving around the Maison d'Erasme and the church of Saint-Guidon. A vast market takes place at the Abattoir each Sunday.

EVERE *(map 2 B4, NE edge of the city).* The offices of Nato are in Evere, not far from the Cimetière de Bruxelles, resting place of some of the soldiers killed at Waterloo.

IXELLES *(map 1 C3, SE of the city center).* A fascinating commune dotted with 19thC Art Nouveau mansions, Art Deco apartment blocks and secluded parks. The elegant town hall stands on place Fernand Cocq, while local markets happen on place Flagey and the chic place du Châtelain. The boulevards and arcades between place Louise and Porte de Namur have some of the best shops in town. A cluster of big cinemas keeps this area throbbing after dark.

SAINT-GILLES *(map 1 C3, SW of the city center).* Lively and cosmopolitan, Saint-Gilles has handsome Art Nouveau houses and romantic parks. The low rents attract young artists and craftsmen. The overbearing 19thC town hall stands on place Van Meenen, but the Parvis Saint-Gilles is where you find the local market.

SAINT-JOSSE-TEN-NOODE *(map 1 C3, N of the city center).* At times crowded and grimy, Saint-Josse nevertheless has a few attractive features such as the former botanical gardens. The town hall is tucked away in the former home of the violinist Charles de Bériot, while the local market is squeezed onto place Madou.

SCHAERBEEK *(map 1 B3, NE of the city center).* Once an elegant 19thC quarter, Schaerbeek still has grand 19thC streets and good parks, though some areas are rather forlorn.

UCCLE *(map 1 D3, S of the city center).* A mixture of grand boulevards and modest neighborhoods, with attractive parks and a fascinating cemetery. Place Brugmann is the most fashionable square, but place de Saint-Job has a convivial local ambience.

WATERMAEL-BOITSFORT *(map 2 D4, S edge of the city).* A romantic, leafy neighborhood on the edge of the Forêt de Soignes, with rambling 19thC villas and 20thC garden cities.

WOLUWÉ-SAINT-LAMBERT and **WOLUWÉ-SAINT-PIERRE** *(map 2 C4, E of the city center).* Leafy communes with handsome 20thC villas favored by European civil servants.

Sightseeing

Introduction

The sights of Brussels tend to be scattered around a fairly extensive urban area. Many visitors make the mistake of confining their visit to the old town, and so miss some of the more exciting and unusual sights in the outlying districts, such as the museums in the CINQUANTEN-AIRE complex and the suburban parks.

USEFUL TO KNOW

Most museums in Brussels are closed on a Monday. The Royal Museums (Musées Royaux) are normally open free of charge, except occasionally when special exhibitions occupy the building. It hardly needs to be said that donations are welcome, although the staff are never so impolite as to bully one into contributing.

The opening times given below were correct at the time of going to press, but they may well change as museums struggle to cut their costs. Be prepared for small museums closing on weekends, while larger ones may sometimes shut off certain departments. Some museums may be willing to admit visitors to a closed-off department if they are given advance notice. Telephone the museum directly, to avoid the disappointment of a wasted journey.

For the footsore, or those who seek a moment's respite from the din of Brussels' traffic, a few quiet spots in which to rest and recover are mentioned in INTERLUDES on page 91. If the desire to see the city from above is overwhelming, select one of the spots mentioned in VIEWPOINTS on page 93. For those who have come to Brussels in search of the unexpected or bizarre, turn to page 90 for CURIOSITIES.

LOCATING THE SIGHTSEEING ENTRIES IN THIS CHAPTER

The sights of Brussels have been divided up into seven different sections: **sightseeing themes, museums, landmark buildings, ecclesiastical buildings, streetscapes and neighborhoods,** "**off the beaten track,**" and **parks and open spaces**. Each section is arranged alphabetically. Use the INDEX whenever the appropriate category is not immediately obvious.

For those with time to spare, some **excursions** in the environs of Brussels are briefly described on pages 150-3, while the suggested **walks and tram rides** (pages 78-90) will provide a number of other ways to see both Brussels and its environs.

Sights classified by area

SPECIAL FEATURES
COVERING ALL AREAS
Cartoons
Curiosities
Interludes
Metro stations
Statues
Viewpoints

LOWER TOWN
Bourse
Brasserie Wielemans
Cathédrale Saint-Michel ★ 🏛
Centre Belge de la Bande
Dessinée ★ 🏛 ❉
Église Notre-Dame de la
 Chapelle
Église Notre-Dame de
 Finistère
Église Saint-Nicolas
Galerie Bortier
Galeries Saint-Hubert ★ 🏛
Grand'Place ★ 🏛
Historium ❉
Hôtel de Ville ★ 🏛
Ilôt Sacré
Maison de la Bellone
Manneken-Pis
Marolles
Medieval Wall
Musée de la Brasserie
Musée Communal
Musée du Costume et
 de la Dentelle

Musée des Égouts
Place des Martyrs 🏛
Place Sainte-Catherine
Place Saint-Géry
Porte de Hal
Théâtre Toone

UPPER TOWN
Avenue Louise
Bibliothèque Royale
Centre Culturel le Botanique
 🏛
Chapelle de Nassau
Église Notre-Dame du Sablon
 ★ 🏛
Hôtel Charlier
Jardin Botanique
Mont des Arts
Musée d'Art Ancien ★
Musée d'Art Moderne ★
Musée Bellevue
Musée du Cinéma
Musée Instrumental 🏛
Musée des Postes et
 Télécommunications
Musées Royaux des Beaux-
 Arts ★
Palais de Justice 🏛
Palais du Roi
Parc de Bruxelles ★ ❉
Parc d'Egmont
Place du Grand Sablon
Place Royale 🏛
Square du Petit Sablon ★

A few lesser sights do not appear under their own headings but are included within other entries. If you cannot find them readily in the text, look them up in the INDEX.

If you wish to plan your days geographically, see the LIST OF SIGHTS above and right. Brussels divides into three natural areas for sightseeing; the **Lower Town**, the **Upper Town** and the **Outer Districts**.

The **Lower Town** is the old quarter around the HÔTEL DE VILLE and the BOURSE. This area lends itself well to idle strolling and window shopping. The **Upper Town** is the 19thC quarter, built on the hill to the s of the

OUTER DISTRICTS
Abbaye de la Cambre
Abbaye du Rouge-Cloître
Atomium ◁€
Autoworld
Basilique du Sacré-Coeur
Bibliotheca Wittockiana
Bois de la Cambre ★ ✿
Bruparck ✿
Cimetière de Bruxelles
Cimetière de Laeken
Cinquantenaire Museums
Église Saint-Denis
Enclos des Fusillés
Espace Photographique
    Contretype ▥
Fondation pour l'Architecture
Forêt de Soignes
Geografisch Arboretum te
    Tervuren
Koninklijk Museum voor
    Middenafrika ★
Maison Erasme
Mini Europe ✿
Musée David et Alice van
    Buuren
Musée Communal d'Ixelles
Musée de la Gueuze
Musée Horta ★ ▥
Musée de l'Institut Royal des
    Sciences Naturelles ✿

Musée Constantin
    Meunier
Musée Royal de l'Armée et
    d'Histoire Militaire
Musées Royaux d'Art et
    d'Histoire ★
Musée du Transport Urbain
    Bruxellois
Musée Wiertz
Parc de Wolvendael
Parc Tenbosch ✿
Parc du Cinquantenaire
Parc Duden
Parc Josaphat
Parc Leopold
Parc Tournay-Solvay
Parc de Woluwé
Park van Tervuren
Pavillon Chinois
Sentier du Chemin de
    Fer
Square Marie-Louise
Tour Japonaise

EXCURSIONS
Brussels environs
Grimbergen
Kasteel van Beersel
Pajottenland
Tervuren
Waterloo

Lower Town. It is a formal district, with the PALAIS ROYAL and Parliament forming focal points. The **Outer Districts** section covers the urban area beyond the ring of boulevards. It includes the European Quarter and many of the city's parks.

EXPLAINING OUR TYPE STYLES
Bold type is generally employed to indicate points of outstanding interest. Entries given without addresses and opening times are often described more fully elsewhere: check the **cross-references**, which are in SMALL CAPITALS.

In this chapter, look for the ★ symbol against the outstanding, not-to-be-missed sights. The ▥ symbol indicates buildings of great architectural interest. Places of special interest for children (✿) and outstanding view (◁€) are also indicated.

For a full explanation of all the symbols, see page 7.

Walks and tram rides

Certain areas of Brussels are ideal for strolling through, even if the occasional hazardous road has to be crossed. The old lanes of the Lower Town (WALK 1) contain many hidden delights, the Upper Town (WALK 2) offers spacious parks and elegance, and the prosperous streets leading off avenue Louise are dotted with florid Art Nouveau buildings (WALK 3).

The great Forêt de Soignes to the s provides vast tracts of beech woods for rambles (WALK 4). A lazy alternative would be to take a leisurely tram ride. There are two suggested tram journeys — either a trip to Boitsfort or a ride through the forest to TERVUREN.

WALK 1: THE LOWER TOWN
See maps 3 & 4 and map opposite. Allow 2hrs.
The Lower Town has been bombed by the French and battered by developers, yet still retains pockets of architectural grandeur and urban conviviality. The walk described here is designed to guide the inquiring visitor to notable features that tend to be overlooked by suburbanites and tourists alike. This quarter is at its best on working days.

Begin with a coffee on GRAND'PLACE. Leave the square to the left of the Hôtel de Ville by the narrow rue Charles Buls. Superstitious visitors pause in the arcade underneath the Maison de l'Étoile *(#8)*, to rub the arm of the recumbent statue of the 14thC military leader Everard 't Serclaes as a defense against ill health. Others press on straight ahead, to join the steady stream of tourists pouring along rue de l'Étuve to look at the MANNEKEN PIS. The route is lined with cramped tourist shops selling kitsch souvenirs in dubious taste. The real statue (on the corner of rue du Chêne) may appear rather dull by comparison, unless you happen to arrive during one of the regular unveiling ceremonies, when the Manneken appears dressed in the costume of a local society or celebrity.

Go right down rue des Grands Carmes to reach an undiscovered old quarter dotted with dusty haberdashers' shops and lively Spanish cafés. On rue du Marché au Charbon, turn left, pausing to admire the fashionable café in the corner building, **Au Soleil** *(# 86)*. Once a 19thC tailor's shop with handsome glass advertising signs, it has been sensitively restored.

Go briefly into the Baroque pilgrimage church of **Notre-Dame du Bon Secours** to gaze up at the lofty dome. Turn right after the church down rue du Jardin des Olives, and left to reach place Fontainas. Crossing the road, continue down rue de la Grande-Île to reach the oldest quarter of Brussels.

The impressive Baroque exterior of **Notre-Dame aux Riches Claires** stands as a reminder of better times in this sadly decayed neighborhood. The city is currently searching for the elusive formula that will revitalize this historic quarter, but so far with only limited success. You can spot tentative signs of gentrification around PLACE SAINT-GÉRY, such as the prim cobbled courtyard beside an exposed stretch of the River Senne. To see this, you need to go through the gate at #23.

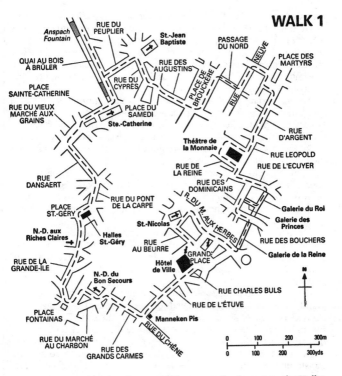

But the story of the handsome 19thC meat market known as the Halles Saint-Géry is more discouraging. The iron-and-glass structure was restored to create a complex similar to London's Covent Garden, but it closed down after a few years. The future of the market is again uncertain, although it may reopen one day.

Now walk down rue du Pont de la Carpe, cross the road and turn left along **rue Dansaert**. This street has recently become chic, thanks to a few daring boutiques that sell bold fashions in bare brick interiors. If food is on your mind by now, dive into **Le Pain Quotidien** *(#16)*. Sit at the big farmhouse table to eat a rye bread sandwich or a hunk of heavy chocolate cake.

Now turn right down **rue du Vieux Marché aux Grains**, a shady square with a rather provincial feel. Go past the shops selling cheese and flowers to reach PLACE SAINTE-CATHERINE. A moldering 19thC church designed by Joseph Poelaert (before he exhausted himself building the PALAIS DE JUSTICE) looms over the square. All that remains of its Baroque predecessor is a nearby solitary 17thC tower.

A few market stalls on the square provide a dwindling local population with Flemish potatoes and Spanish oranges. You might be tempted to investigate the stall that sells Breton oysters and Muscadet by the glass.

Go down the left side of the church and turn left along **quai au Bois à Brûler**. The windswept square alongside was once a harbor where boats unloaded fish, wood and bricks. The harbor has gone, but the fish merchants are still based on the former quays as a memento of the past. The immediate neighborhood abounds in serious fish restaurants serving lobster or Ostend sole.

An ornamental pond at the end of the square surrounds a massive fountain commemorating Burgomaster Anspach, whose main claim to fame was to put the River Senne underground. The **Anspach fountain** is a spectacular sight on the rare days when water cascades down its mock rocks and gushes from a monster's gaping jaws. Once you have admired the fountain, return along the quai au Bois à Brûler.

Turn left before the end of the street down rue du Peuplier, for a spectacular view of the theatrical facade of the Baroque **Église Saint-Jean Baptiste**. This church once belonged to the religious community of Beguines. The brick houses occupied by the religious women have sadly been left to rot.

Leave the square along rue du Ciprès, cross the place du Samedi and follow rue des Augustins to get to **place de Brouckère**. Cross the square and turn left. The glittering 19thC opulence of the **Café Métropole** *(part of the Hôtel Métropole, place de Brouckère 31)* may prove too tempting to resist.

Beyond the Hôtel Métropole, turn right into the **passage du Nord**, a grand 19thC arcade decorated with ornate lamps and dusty statues. It leads to rue Neuve, a busy pedestrianized shopping street. Turn left, then first right to find the elusive PLACE DES MARTYRS. This Neoclassical relic of the Austrian Period was once shamefully dilapidated, but restoration work began in the spring of 1992. Pause on a bench to admire the transformation, or meditate on the monument in the middle of the square, which commemorates the dead of the Belgian Revolt.

The 1830 Revolt began in the nearby Brussels opera house, the THÉÂTRE DE LA MONNAIE. To reach the "Monnaie," as it is known locally, leave the square along rue d'Argent, continue along rue Leopold and turn right down rue des Princes. The Monnaie now stages daring and dazzling modern ballets.

Go up rue de la Reine, next to the theater, and turn right again along rue Leopold. The French Neoclassical painter Jacques-Louis David died in 1825 in the Classical building at #5. Turn left up rue de l'Ecuyer and then right into the magnificent **Galerie du Roi**, one of three arcades forming the GALERIES SAINT-HUBERT. Stop for an espresso coffee at **Mokafé** *(Galerie du Roi 9)*, then turn right down the **Galerie des Princes** to browse in **Tropismes** bookstore *(#11)*.

At the end of the gallery, turn left along rue des Dominicains, then left up rue des Bouchers. The cobbled lane runs through a genial old quarter packed with restaurants. It can be fun to amble among the dripping-wet displays of cod and lobster (or rabbit and pheasant during the hunting season), but the ÎLOT SACRÉ, as it is called, is not the best area in Brussels for serious eating. But you might try **Chez Vincent** *(rue des Dominicains*

8) for steaks, or **Aux Armes de Bruxelles** *(rue des Bouchers 13)* for *waterzooi.*

Head back up rue des Bouchers and turn right into the **Galerie de la Reine**. Stroll past the marble-fronted shops to reach rue du Marché aux Herbes. Turn right down this old merchant street, noticing the frail ironwork on a former 19thC glass store *(#47)*. Make your theater reservations at the tourist office *(#61)*, then continue down the street, glancing into the semi-secret lane on the right known as the **impasse Saint-Nicolas** *(#12)*, which leads to the old tavern **Au Bon Vieux Temps**. Another lane takes you to the intimate Flemish tavern **A l'Imaige Nostre-Dame** *(#8)*.

Turn left at the ÉGLISE SAINT-NICOLAS, the merchants' church, almost hidden by the old houses built against its walls. Enter the w porch and go through the right-hand door. The stone wall that you almost hit your head against is a last vestige of the original Romanesque church. Enjoy the shadowy interior with its sensual mixture of Baroque gilt and candle wax, then turn left up rue au Beurre to return to Grand'Place.

WALK 2: THE UPPER TOWN

See maps 3, 4, 5 & 6 and map overleaf. Allow 2hrs.

The Upper Town was created in the 18thC as a stately quarter elevated above the overcrowded old town. It is now mainly a business district, but hints of calm elegance persist in the parks and Sablon quarter.

Begin the walk with a leisurely coffee in one of the cafés on Grand'Place. Leave the square by rue de la Colline. Stop to inspect the Tintin souvenirs in the shop at #13. Go up rue de la Montagne and pause at the top of the street to admire the twin towers of the CATHÉDRALE SAINT-MICHEL. Cross the boulevard and go up rue du Bois Sauvage, left of the cathedral. Like many curious street names in Brussels, rue du Bois Sauvage, or "Wild Wood Street," is a mistranslation of a Dutch name (Wout de Wilde is the name of a person). Look out for the turreted 17thC town house *(#15)* at the back of the choir. Go into the echoing cathedral by the s portal (on place Sainte-Gudule) to admire the Brabant Gothic architecture.

On leaving, go up rue de la Chancellerie, then rue des 12 Apôtres and rue Ravenstein, where Marie-Puck Broodthaers runs the off-beat Galerie des Beaux-Arts *(#20)*. Expect to be amused or amazed by Surrealist constructions with whimsical titles. The owner is the daughter of the Belgian Surrealist Marcel Broodthaers. Make a note to go one day to the Broodthaers room at the MUSÉE D'ART MODERNE to see the source of her often zany notions about art.

Cross the road at the Galerie Ravenstein. The PALAIS DES BEAUX-ARTS opposite stands on the site of the boarding house where Charlotte Brontë stayed in 1842-43. Go up rue Baron Horta to the MUSÉE DU CINÉMA entrance. Check the program posted outside to find out about rare films or eclectic festivals that might be worth catching. Put a coin in the slot machine for a current program, and reserve well ahead if you seriously want to catch a particular movie.

WALK 2

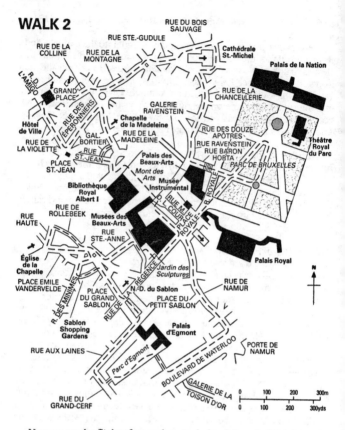

Now go up the flight of steps that rise behind the splashing fountain, to reach the Upper Town by the most attractive route. Cross the road and enter the PARC DE BRUXELLES. Wander as you please in the park, or take the following route.

Go straight ahead to the round pond surrounded by curious statue-heads sitting atop their square supports. Look to the right to catch a glimpse of the PALAIS DU ROI, then turn left along the main alley to reach an octagonal pond overlooked by statues of Greek goddesses and heroes. The Classical building facing you is the **Palais de la Nation**, or parliament building. To your right, half hidden by trees, stands the Théâtre Royal du Parc. Turn around and take the diagonal alley leading from the pond to PLACE ROYALE. The vast dome you see in the distance belongs to the PALAIS DE JUSTICE.

On leaving the park by the corner gate, cross rue Royale and turn left to reach **place Royale**. You need to be on the same side of the square as the church with the Classical pediment. Go through the Classical arch to the right of the church and follow the steep, winding **rue de Namur**, past shops selling frilly English dresses or sleek Italian skirts.

On reaching the Porte de Namur, turn right along **boulevard de Waterloo**. Before the road tunnels were built in the 1950s, this was an elegant tree-lined avenue. It has been brutalized beyond recognition, yet the avenue remains a fashionable shopping quarter. The smart names in European fashion occupy the few surviving town houses on the boulevard. Less expensive boutiques sell smart clothes and shoes in the Galerie de la Toison d'Or and the Galerie Louise opposite.

An old cobbled lane leads right from the avenue into the tranquil PARC D'EGMONT. Overlooking the park is the Palais d'Egmont, which is often the setting for EC conferences. Turn left and follow the winding path to reach rue du Grand Cerf. Turn right, then right again along rue aux Laines, lined with grandiose 19thC town houses built for lawyers and doctors.

You will see a park on the left, the PLACE DU PETIT SABLON. Go through the iron gate and descend the steps, past 19thC statues of eminent Flemings and Walloons. The Tour et Tassis family, who founded Europe's first postal service in the 16thC, once owned a palace to the left of the park. The building has gone, but the Baroque family chapel survives in the 15thC church opposite. Go into NOTRE-DAME DU SABLON to admire the marble memorials and stained glass.

Now walk down the left side of the PLACE DU GRAND SABLON, where the city's exclusive antique dealers display elegant French *escritoires* and 19thC Belgian paintings. Turn into the **Sablon Shopping Gardens** *(#36)* to look in the upmarket art galleries. Leave along the passage on the right of the courtyard. On rue des Minimes, turn right, past more antique shops displaying battered rocking horses and Belgian Impressionist landscapes.

Go right down Petite rue des Minimes, past a dusty brick post office. The MUSÉE DES POSTES ET TÉLÉCOMMUNICATIONS is up a flight of stairs in this old building. Back on place du Grand Sablon, turn left down the hill, cross the road and continue down rue Joseph Stevens, where shops sell engravings and antique glass. Pause on place Emile Vandervelde to look at the lugubrious office block *(#11)* put up on the site of Horta's famous Maison du Peuple.

The ÉGLISE DE LA CHAPELLE stands at the bottom of the hill. Look inside if the door is open, to find the memorial to Pieter Bruegel the Elder, who is buried here. Now turn right along rue Haute and right up the cobbled rue de Rollebeek. Glance in the antique shop windows at dented fairground horses and busts of forgotten Belgians.

Back on the Sablon, go up the left side of the square, stopping to admire the chocolates and cakes in the window of **Wittamer** *(place du Grand Sablon 12)*. A left turn down rue Sainte-Anne brings you to the **Archives Générales du Royaume**. Check the poster outside for interesting exhibitions of ancient books or prints from the national archives.

Now go through the passage and up the stone steps straight ahead to reach the unexpected **Jardin des Sculptures** *(open 10am-5pm)*. Sit on a bench to admire the eleven bronze statues on the side wall of the MUSÉES ROYAUX DES BEAUX-ARTS.

Once on rue de la Régence, turn left, past the giant statues flanking the entrance of the MUSÉE D'ART ANCIEN. Back on place Royale, turn left down rue du Musée. Look through the gap in the buildings on the right to admire the frail Art Nouveau ironwork on the MUSÉE INSTRUMENTAL, which was formerly a department store. Continue down the hill to the normally deserted 18thC courtyard facing the former Palais de Charles de Lorraine. Peer through the stone balustrade for an unexpected view of the sunken courtyard of the MUSÉE D'ART MODERNE.

Now turn right past a statue of Charles of Lorraine to reach rue Montagne de la Cour. Pause to admire the mock Gothic facade of the 19thC Pharmacie Delacre, designed by Paul Saintenoy in Neo-Gothic style. You can still see decorated tiles with the words *Pharmacie Anglaise* (English Chemist) and a scene at the top of the gable modeled on a 15thC Flemish miniature.

Turn left to reach the top of the MONT DES ARTS. Look for the spire of the HÔTEL DE VILLE and the green domes of the BASILIQUE DU SACRÉ-COEUR in the distance. Go down the steps on the right to discover the CHAPELLE DE NASSAU, now part of the BIBLIOTHÈQUE ROYALE ALBERT I. Look out for posters outside the library announcing exhibitions in the chapel. Cross the boulevard at the bottom of the steps and go down rue Saint-Jean. Turn right into the GALERIE BORTIER *(#17)*, a forgotten 19thC arcade immersed in a sad sepia light.

Walk through the arcade and turn left down rue de la Madeleine, past the **Chapelle de la Madeleine**. Turn left into **rue des Éperonniers** and squeeze past the parked cars to look at the quaint little shops specializing in tin toys *(#4)*, dollhouses *(#12)* and books on cinema *(#14)*. Browse in Plazier *(#50)* for wistful postcards of Laeken cemetery or quirky works by Belgian cartoonists.

At **place Saint-Jean**, pause to look at the statue of Gabrielle Petit, a Belgian resistance heroine shot by the Germans in 1916. Go right down rue de la Violette to reach rue de l'Amigo. Walk along the right side of the street to see two small fountains on the back wall of the HÔTEL DE VILLE. Turn right through the gateway to discover two splendid fountains in the courtyard of the town hall.

Return to Grand'Place through the Gothic portal.

WALK 3: ART NOUVEAU IN IXELLES
See map opposite. Allow 2hrs.

Brussels was one of the foremost centers of Art Nouveau architecture at the turn of the century. The distinctive style was launched in Brussels in 1893 with the construction of two houses in Ixelles, designed by Victor Horta and Paul Hankar. Local architects were commissioned to design flamboyant residences for industrialists or elegant department stores along the boulevards. They used wrought iron and costly wood to create escapist fantasies.

Many of the finest Art Nouveau buildings in Brussels have been

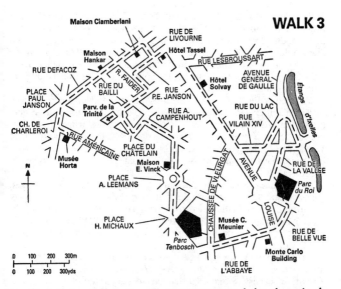

WALK 3

demolished, but the streets off AVENUE LOUISE and the chaussée de Charleroi are still dotted with architectural delights. This walk takes you past some noteworthy buildings, including the two original houses dating from 1893.

Begin with a visit to the MUSÉE HORTA. Leaving the museum, turn left along rue Américaine. On chaussée de Charleroi, turn right to place Paul Janson, then right again along rue Defacqz, where Paul Hankar built himself an Art Nouveau dwelling and studio in 1893 *(#71)*. The **Maison Hankar** struck a new architectural note with its florid ironwork, sgraffito tiles designed by Adolphe Crespin, and artful blend of stone and brick.

During his brief career, Hankar worked mainly in the immediate neighborhood. He designed two other buildings in rue Defacqz, the most impressive of which was the **Maison Ciamberlani** *(#48)*, built in 1897 for a melancholy Symbolist painter. The frescoes under the eaves were designed by Ciamberlani himself, though a century of air pollution has eroded the finer details. The adjacent house *(#50)* was designed by Hankar one year later for the landscape painter René Janssens, but a subsequent owner has effaced much of the artistry.

Continue down rue Defacqz and go right down rue de Livourne, then left along rue Paul-Emile Janson to look at the **Hôtel Tassel** *(#6)*, designed by Victor Horta in the same watershed year as the Maison Hankar. The facade is spotlit at night, but it was the interior, and particularly the staircase, that altered the direction of European architecture. Sadly, unless you can invent some legitimate excuse to visit the Venezuelan embassy based there, you have little chance of seeing the sinuous wrought iron and delicate murals that lie hidden within.

Turn around and walk the length of rue Paul-Emile Janson. Hankar designed the **Maison José Ciamberlani** *(#23-25)* in 1900, though it has been modified since. Stop at the end of the street to view the sgraffito tiles on the house designed by Albert Roosenboom in 1900 *(rue Faider 83)*. Now turn left along rue Faider and right on rue du Bailli. Go to **Passiflore** *(Parvis de la Trinité 6)* for coffee and cakes in a flamboyant Oriental setting.

Turn left at the church down rue de l'Amazone and left again on place du Châtelain. This intimate leafy square looks its best during the weekly market on Wednesday afternoon. Go right down rue Armand Campenhout and right on rue Washington, past the Art Nouveau **Maison Émile Vinck** *(#85)*, designed in 1903-6 by Victor Horta. Gustave Strauven designed an Art Nouveau house at the late date of 1911 farther down the street *(#127)*.

On reaching place Henri Michaux, turn left into the PARC TENBOSCH. Take the path through the middle of the park, looking out for the colony of parrots that nest in the trees on the right. Leave the park and turn right on chaussée de Vleurgat. Go first left down rue de l'Abbaye. The MUSÉE CONSTANTIN MEUNIER on the left *(#59)* has an impressive collection of 19thC sculpture and painting.

At the end of the street, pause to look at the curious peeling facade of the Monte Carlo building opposite *(#413)*. The panels under the roof show four successive buildings that have occupied the site.

Cross AVENUE LOUISE and go down **rue de Belle Vue**. Ernest Blérot built five Art Nouveau houses in this street in the 1890s. Stop to admire the convoluted iron balconies and faded murals *(#42-46 and #30-32)*.

Turn left up rue du Monastère and go into the **Parc du Roi**, following the path that curves around the statue of Leopold II. Leave the park at the opposite corner and turn right down **rue de la Vallée**, a quietly fashionable street that plunges down to the Étangs d'Ixelles. Ernest Blérot designed the two Art Nouveau houses at #40 and #31.

Turn right down **rue Vilain XIV** to discover other examples of Blérot's style dating from 1902 *(#9 and #11)*. Admire the iron balconies twisted like tendrils of ivy, and the fluid lines of the stonework. Like a painter, Blérot has signed his artwork with a flourishing signature carved on a stone set in the wall.

The most spectacular Blérot house is nearby, overlooking the Étangs d'Ixelles. Go to the bottom of the street and turn left along avenue Général de Gaulle to find the house *(#39)*, with its Art Nouveau ironwork running rampant on balconies and staircases.

Now walk on and turn left up **rue du Lac**. Stop to admire the house designed by Léon Delune for a glass craftsman *(#6)*, with its flamboyant stained glass windows. Climb the street and turn right up rue Vilain XIV to reach AVENUE LOUISE. Pick up tram 93 or 94 to return to the center, or pause first at **Nihoul** *(#300)* for coffee and cakes. The best restaurants nearby for an inexpensive lunch are located on rue Lesbroussart or around place du Châtelain. To reach the restaurants on foot, walk down avenue Louise, pausing to admire the **Hôtel Solvay** *(#224)*, built by Victor Horta for a Belgian industrialist in 1894-98.

WALK 4: THE FORÊT DE SOIGNES

See map below. Allow 2-3hrs or whole day. See also FORÊT DE SOIGNES on page 145.

The vast forest to the s and E provides an easy escape route from the city. Several city trams and buses run out to the forest's edge and, equipped with a good map, you can easily plan a short stroll or a one-day hike. The following route provides a taste of the pleasures of the Forêt de Soignes.

Take tram 94 to Boitsfort station, reading the route described on pages 88-9. Cross the chaussée de la Hulpe at the traffic lights and go down the cobbled chemin des Silex, which runs past the melancholy ruins of a

WALK 4

Forêt de Soignes

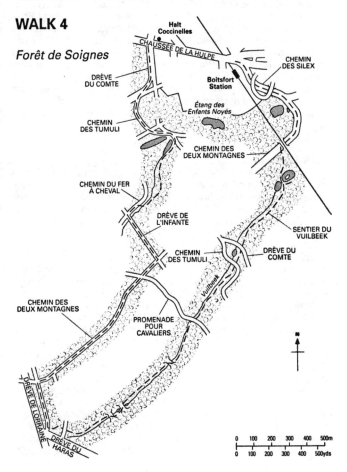

19thC castle in the grounds of the PARC TOURNAY-SOLVAY. After plunging through a tunnel, you come out at a house with a faded inscription. It was one of several 19thC *laiteries* where the fashionable once flocked to drink a wholesome glass of milk.

Now walk up the **chemin des Deux Montagnes,** past misty lakes where the smell of woodsmoke drifts across the fields. Go under the railway line and turn left immediately down the **sentier du Vuilbeek**. Follow the path down to two ponds and continue along the valley of the Vuilbeek. You eventually come to the drève du Haras, where you should turn right. Turn right again where the road joins the drève de Lorraine and then return to the woods on the chemin des Deux Montagnes.

Turn left on the drève de l'Infante and descend to the valley. Once across the stream, turn immediately right along the chemin du Fer à Cheval and after about ten minutes turn right down a path that leads to two ponds, one of them called the Étang des Enfants Noyés. The name in French means Lake of the Drowned Children, but derives not from any dreadful accident but a mistranslation of the original Dutch name *(Verdronken Kinderen,* meaning "the children of Verdronken").

At the end of the ponds, turn left up chemin des Tumuli. Follow the road to the edge of the forest and pick up tram 94 at Coccinelles halt on chaussée de la Hulpe, to return to place Louise, the Sablon or place Royale.

TRAM RIDES

The antiquated Brussels trams are not for people in a hurry, but at uncrowded times of the day they offer an inexpensive means of observing the town. When planning a route, try to avoid the rush hour, and be sure to have a valid ticket (see page 49 for an explanation of the ticket system, and metro and tram map at back of book).

Tram 94 to place Wiener
Allow 2hrs for the round trip.
The route of tram 94 from Botanique to place Wiener provides a glimpse of the elegant quarters of the Upper Town as it passes through the communes of Brussels, Ixelles and Watermael-Boitsfort.

Board tram 94 in the direction of Wiener at the Botanique halt. If a seat is available, sit on the side on which the doors open.

Look right at the first stop after Botanique to glimpse the Colonne du Congrès, erected in 1850-59 to commemorate the 1830 congress that led to the enactment of the Belgian constitution. As the tram goes down rue Royale, look left at the florist *(#13),* situated in an Art Nouveau shop designed by Paul Hankar.

After the next stop, look left to see the formal PARC DE BRUXELLES, followed by the PALAIS DU ROI. From the tram stop at PLACE ROYALE, you get a panoramic view of the Lower Town to the right, including the spire of the HÔTEL DE VILLE on Grand'Place. As the tram moves off, you pass the MUSÉE D'ART MODERNE (a white Neoclassical building) and the MUSÉE D'ART ANCIEN (a monumental front with columns and statues), both on the right.

The tram stops next at the PLACE DU GRAND SABLON, where on the right is the blackened Late Gothic ÉGLISE NOTRE-DAME DU SABLON. Before the tram moves off, glimpse, on the left, the intimate park on the PLACE DU PETIT SABLON. As the tram screeches round the corner at the end of rue de la Régence, perhaps ringing its bell to warn an inattentive driver of its approach, notice the massive proportions of the PALAIS DE JUSTICE on the right.

The tram stops at place Louise. Look left to see the elegant shops on avenue de la Toison d'Or. It continues down AVENUE LOUISE along a bottleneck that is often jammed with traffic, giving you ample time to admire the elegant boutiques on either side of the street.

Avenue Louise opens out beyond place Stéphanie, and the tram sways as it picks up speed, passing an untidy pluralism of architectural styles —anything from demure 19thC town houses to glass-walled skyscrapers. Look out for two Art Nouveau houses on the left by Horta *(#224 and #346).* Look right to see the Monte Carlo office building with its fake peeling facade *(#413),* then left to see the spire of the ABBAYE DE LA CAMBRE poking above the trees.

Get off at the next stop (Legrand) to go walking in the BOIS DE LA CAMBRE or, if you are enjoying the ride, continue to the terminus. After turning left, the tram comes to the **rond-point de l'Étoile**. Look left to see the **Palais de la Folle Chanson**, a spectacular Art Deco apartment block built in 1928.

The tram soon turns up avenue Adolphe Buyl, passing the campus of the Université Libre de Bruxelles on the right. After the stop named Brésil, look left to see a whitewashed Brabant farmhouse converted into a puppet theater (see **Le Perruchet** under BRUSSELS FOR CHILDREN on page 207).

As the tram turns left onto the chaussée de la Hulpe, you glimpse the hippodrome on the right. The terminus is at place Wiener. Leave the tram and cross the road. Go up rue de la Vénerie and rue Middelbourg, then follow the chemin des Silex to reach the Forêt de Soignes.

Take tram 94 back to the city center or, for a change of scene, pick up bus 95 on the square to return to place Royale, the Sablon or the Bourse.

Tram 44 to Tervuren

Allow 2hrs for the round trip, or a whole day if you spend time in Tervuren.
Tram 44 takes you through the beech forest, and the route terminates near the Central Africa Museum in Tervuren. The ride makes an idyllic excursion at any time of the year, but particularly in the fall when the trees have turned vivid shades of red and gold. The antiquated tram that runs in the summer from the Musée du Transport Urbain Bruxellois follows the same route.

Get on tram 44 at the underground terminus at Montgomery (reached by metro, or tram 23, 81 or 90). Once above ground, the tram runs along a broad boulevard created by Leopold II to provide access to the museum at Tervuren. After the first stop (named Père Damien), look right for a glimpse of the **Palais Stoclet**, which was built in 1905 by the Austrian architect Josef Hoffman in the sober style of the Wiener Werkstätte.

At the next stop, look right to see the rolling lawns of the PARC DE WOLUWÉ. Look left at the next stop to see the MUSÉE DU TRANSPORT URBAIN BRUXELLOIS. The tram continues down the leafy avenue, past embassies and offices, and soon plunges into the forest. The stop named Quatre Bras marks the limit of bilingual Brussels. Here you enter Flanders region, and the signs are in Dutch only.

The tram terminates at an elegant 19thC station on the edge of the village. A short walk down the road straight ahead is the impressive KONINKLIJK MUSEUM VOOR MIDDENAFRIKA.

See also TERVUREN in EXCURSIONS on page 152.

Sightseeing themes

There is more to visiting a city than just checking off a list of sights. For a chance to experience the "real" flavor of Brussels, refer to OFF THE BEATEN TRACK on pages 138-143, and dip into the brief "themed" sections on the following pages:

CARTOONS   STATUES, including
CURIOSITIES   MANNEKEN PIS
INTERLUDES   VIEWPOINTS ◄€

CARTOONS

Fans of Tintin and other Belgian comic strip characters flock to Brussels to visit the CENTRE BELGE DE LA BANDE DESSINÉE. The museum shop is packed with comic books and quirky souvenirs. Devotees can hunt down elusive volumes in the many cartoon shops on the chaussée de Wavre, such as **La Bande des Six Nez** (#179) or **Bédéscope** (#167). Tintin T-shirts and comics are sold at **La Boutique de Tintin** (rue de la Colline 13).

Take the metro out to **Stockel station** to see a huge frieze decorated with characters from Hergé cartoons. The Bar Dessiné at the **SAS Royal Hotel** is decorated with Belgian cartoon memorabilia.

CURIOSITIES

Brussels is often disparaged as a dull city, yet the diligent traveler will find many curious and bizarre sights in unexpected quarters.

The old city is dotted with unusual **fountains**, of which the MANNEKEN PIS is the most famous although hardly the most spectacular. Look out for the little bronze fountains in the Lower Town, decorated with figures from Bruegel paintings. The fountain on rue de Rollebeek features characters from Bruegel's *Battle Between Carnival and Lent,* while another, on place de la Vieille Halle aux Blés, is based on figures in Bruegel's *Harvest.*

There are countless bizarre **sculptures** dotted throughout the city, such as the medieval capital in the arcade of the HÔTEL DE VILLE, showing several men shoveling chairs, and the little-known **Monument du**

Pigeon Soldat *(square des Blindés, map 3 C2)* commemorating carrier pigeons killed in World War I.

The **art galleries** in Brussels contain many bizarre works, notably the strange landscape paintings containing hidden faces in the MUSÉE D'ART ANCIEN (room #34). The MUSÉE WIERTZ has an offbeat if morbid appeal, and the rooms devoted to Delvaux, Magritte and Broodthaers at the MUSÉE D'ART MODERNE take you into the bizarre world of Belgian Surrealism. Marie-Puck Broodthaers, the daughter of Marcel Broodthaers, organizes engagingly eccentric art exhibitions in the **Galerie des Beaux-Arts** *(rue Ravenstein 20-22, map 4 E4)*.

The large-scale destruction of the city has left some strange **urban features**, such as the ancient flight of steps beside the Hôtel Ravenstein, which are a last vestige of the medieval Escalier des Juifs, and the CHAPELLE DE NASSAU embedded in the National Library.

Nearby, on rue de la Madeleine, you will see a Baroque fragment rescued from the demolished Chapelle Sainte-Anne, which has been tacked onto the N side of the 15thC **Chapelle de la Madeleine** to form a small side chapel.

The city has several **unusual buildings**, including the futuristic ATOMIUM and the exotic TOUR JAPONAISE. Take the metro to Alma to explore the strange buildings of Lucien Krol designed in 1974, composed of patchworks of stone, brick and concrete. Follow the signs to the place du Campanile to discover a mock Italian village square, or take one of the meandering paths signposted "Hôpital Saint-Luc" *(in av. E. Mounier)* to discover a reconstructed 18thC wooden windmill *(which turns most Saturdays)*.

The **street names** in Brussels are often rather quirky. The rue d'Une Personne *(opposite rue des Bouchers 28, map 4 E4-D4)*, for example, owes its name to its narrowness. Many of the oddest names arose in the 19thC, when the Napoleonic occupying army mistranslated old Dutch names into French. The rue de la Fiancée (Bride Street) and the rue du Bois Sauvage (Wild Wood Street) arose from translators' wild errors. The fanciful French names have now been translated into Dutch, while the original street names have vanished from the maps.

Travelers who want to spend the night in an unusual setting should consider the **hotel** NEW SIRU (see HOTELS A TO Z), where each room contains a unique contemporary Belgian work of art.

INTERLUDES

Brussels is not a particularly exhausting city, but you may sometimes need a quiet retreat from the traffic. Some of the city squares provide a moment of tranquility, such as GRAND'PLACE and PLACE DES MARTYRS. Brussels is blessed with numerous parks, ranging in style from the rambling to the regimented.

The PARC DE BRUXELLES makes a convenient interlude during a tour of the vast MUSÉES ROYAUX DES BEAUX-ARTS, while the semi-secret PARC D'EGMONT is a quiet retreat from the shopping arcades in the Upper Town.

Those looking for a green space in the Lower Town will find benches set amid the ponds and hedges of the JARDIN BOTANIQUE *(an entrance is hidden behind the Palace Hotel, off place Rogier).* Anyone who needs to unwind between EC meetings should head down the hill to the PARC LEOPOLD, while those who seek a refuge from avenue Louise should look for a shady corner in the gardens of the ABBAYE DE LA CAMBRE (see ECCLESIASTICAL BUILDINGS, page 126)

The Catholic churches of Brussels are normally open throughout the day. You can escape from the frantic crush on rue Neuve by ducking into NOTRE-DAME DE FINISTÈRE. The quietest retreat near Grand'Place is the ÉGLISE SAINT-NICOLAS, while the ÉGLISE NOTRE-DAME DU SABLON offers a cool place to pause on the Sablon.

Cafés in the center of town are generally crowded, except in the early morning. The brasseries at the CENTRE BELGE DE LA BANDE DESSINÉE and the CENTRE CULTUREL LE BOTANIQUE are among the most peaceful places for a coffee. When the sun shines, you can sit on a café terrace on Grand'Place or the Sablon, but perhaps the most romantic terrace is on the shady and secluded **place de la Liberté**, where four converging streets are named after the freedoms guaranteed by the Belgian constitution.

STATUES

The public spaces of Brussels are densely populated with statues representing dukes, kings, nymphs, musicians, painters, gods and generals. The most famous sight in Brussels is the little statue of the MANNEKEN PIS, depicting a boy urinating.

The buildings on GRAND'PLACE are mobbed by symbolic statues, and the 19thC arcades such as the GALERIES SAINT-HUBERT have a resident population of dusty, demure female statues. The PLACE DU PETIT SABLON is particularly overcrowded, with 48 bronze figures representing the guilds and ten statues of national heroes, and there is a busty goddess at every turn in the PARC DE BRUXELLES.

The cemeteries of Brussels are full of wistful women cast in bronze, and there are three separate collections of sculpture at the MUSÉES ROYAUX DES BEAUX-ARTS. They are to be admired in the new **Galerie de Sculpture** at the MUSÉE D'ART ANCIEN (page 101), the **Jardin des Sculptures** off rue de la Régence (map **6F4**; see pages 83 and 107), and the MUSÉE CONSTANTIN MEUNIER (page 114). But the diminutive but inevitable star is the . . .

Manneken Pis

Rue de l'Étuve and corner of rue du Chêne. Map 3E3 ✿ *Tram 52, 55, 58, 81 to Bourse.*

Brussels is exceedingly proud of this fountain of a small boy relieving himself in public. Visitors are frequently surprised at its diminutive size and have been known to walk right past one of the city's most advertised sights, although the streets lined with full working models and cheeky corkscrews confirm its presence in the area.

At least six different traditions are attached to the Manneken Pis, which is considered Brussels' oldest citizen. Two go back to the times of the crusades, while another claims the town was saved when the little boy's action doused flames threatening to engulf the city. More recently, in 1450, a witch condemned a little boy to relieve himself for eternity after

he did so at her front door. The most plausible revolves round the gratitude of a wealthy citizen who erected a fountain to his son, lost during a local carnival and later found engaged in that activity.

There has been a fountain, called the Manneken Pis, on the site since 1452, but it was only in 1619 that a bronze version was installed. It has been kidnapped many times — by English and French soldiers, by students and in 1817 by an unfortunate ex-prisoner, Antoine Licas, who was later condemned to hard labor for life for his pains.

The statue has an extensive wardrobe, ranging from national and military uniforms to sporting and more casual outfits. According to tradition the first costume was donated in 1698 by Maximilian Emmanuel, governor of the Netherlands. He currently has over 520 costumes, some of which can be seen in the Museum of the City of Brussels in Grand'Place. Some are worn on specific dates, so on April 6th, the day the US army entered World War I, the statue is resplendent in the uniform of an American Military Police Master Sergeant.

VIEWPOINTS ◈

Brussels is built on a rolling landscape that offers various panoramic views. The most obvious viewpoints are located along the summit of the escarpment separating the Lower Town from the Upper Town. Stand at the top of the MONT DES ARTS for a romantic, if not entirely authentic, view of the Lower Town. The slender spire of the HÔTEL DE VILLE dates from the 15thC, but the Baroque gable houses in the foreground were built in the 20thC.

Visitors to the nearby MUSÉE INSTRUMENTAL can drink coffee on the Art Nouveau roof terrace overlooking the old town. For a more sweeping view, go to place Poelaert, which stands above the rooftops of the MAROLLES. On a clear day, you'll see the spheres of the Atomium glinting in the distance.

The ATOMIUM boasts a panoramic view from the top sphere, but it is a disappointment to discover that the main sights of the city are too far off to distinguish. Yet you might enjoy trying to spot the smoldering mass of a miniature Vesuvius at the MINI EUROPE theme park below.

Several parks in the city are on elevated sites with attractive views. The upper slopes of the PARC LEOPOLD offer a panoramic view of the buildings of the European Quarter, and a brisk climb in the PARC DUDEN gets you to a summit with a view of the city's western suburbs.

Some of the city's skyscraper hotels offer panoramic views from the bedrooms or restaurants. Book a window table at the **Plein Ciel** restaurant in the **Hilton Hotel** to enjoy the Upper Town from the 27th floor. Or stay at the **Sheraton Hotel** to splash in a rooftop pool overlooking the Lower Town business district. But the rooms with the best views in Brussels are at the AMIGO HOTEL. Ask for a 6th-floor room with a balcony facing the Hôtel de Ville.

Museums

Brussels has a wealth of museums devoted to subjects as diverse as Belgian beer and local sewers. Some of the greatest art in Europe is to be found in the art galleries of Brussels, which few tourists ever visit. The traveler in Brussels can often enjoy the rare pleasure of being utterly alone in a room filled with Flemish masterpieces, or wandering undisturbed amid Classical treasures.

Several of the major museums, the MUSÉE D'ART ANCIEN, the MUSÉE D'ART MODERNE, the MUSÉE INSTRUMENTAL and the MUSÉE BELLEVUE, are clustered around PLACE ROYALE (page 137) in the Upper Town. A further cluster of important collections is found in the PARC DU CINQUANTENAIRE; the elevation on page 97 pinpoints the MUSÉES ROYAUX D'ART ET D'HISTOIRE, MUSÉE DE L'ARMÉE and AUTOWORLD. There are a number of other museums dotted throughout the city.

The Royal Museums *(Musées Royaux)* are normally open free of charge unless a special exhibition is running. They are the MUSÉE D'ART ANCIEN, MUSÉE D'ART MODERNE, MUSÉE DE L'ARMÉE, MUSÉE D'ART ET D'HISTOIRE, MUSÉE BELLEVUE, MUSÉE CONSTANTIN MEUNIER, TOUR JAPONAISE, MUSÉE WIERTZ and KONINKLIJK MUSEUM VOOR MIDDENAFRIKA.

Entries are arranged alphabetically. All museums whose names begin with "Musée/s de" are listed alphabetically under **M** for Musée.

ATOMIUM
AUTOWORLD
CENTRE BELGE DE LA BANDE
  DESSINÉE
CINQUANTENAIRE MUSEUMS
FONDATION POUR L'ARCHITECTURE
HISTORIUM
KONINKLIJK MUSEUM VOOR
  MIDDENAFRIKA
MAISON ERASME
MINI EUROPE
MUSÉE DE L'ARMÉE ET DE L'HISTOIRE
  MILITAIRE
M. D'ART ANCIEN
M. D'ART MODERNE
M. BELLEVUE
M. DE LA BRASSERIE
M. VAN BUUREN
M. CHARLIER
M. DU CINÉMA

M. COMMUNAL
M. COMMUNAL D'IXELLES
M. DU COSTUME ET DE LA DENTELLE
M. DES ÉGOUTS
M. DES ENFANTS
M. DE LA GUEUZE
M. DE L'INSTITUT ROYAL DES
  SCIENCES NATURELLES
M. HORTA
M. INSTRUMENTAL
M. DU JOUET
M. CONSTANTIN MEUNIER
M. DES POSTES
  ET TÉLÉCOMMUNICATIONS
M. ROYAUX D'ART ET D'HISTOIRE
M. ROYAUX DES BEAUX-ARTS
M. DU TRANSPORT URBAIN
M. WIERTZ
PAVILLON CHINOIS
TOUR JAPONAISE

ATOMIUM

Boulevard du Centenaire
☎*(02)477.09.77. Map 1B3* 🔲
*Open daily 9.30am-6pm. Top floor
only remains open until 10pm
during summer months* 🚶 ⫷ 🅿
Metro to Heysel.

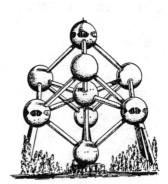

The nine steel spheres of the Atomium glint eerily in the sunlight
above the jumbled roofs of Jette.
The building was put up for the
1958 World Fair in Brussels. Representing the nine atoms of an
iron crystal magnified several billion times, the Atomium, 102m (335
feet) high, is one of the great surviving futuristic follies of the 1950s.

As the years went by, the Atomium became a rather aged and creaky
relic of the atomic age. The interior was recently purged of dusty clutter
and revamped as a museum of medicine called the **Biogenium**. Four of
the spheres are now occupied by ponderous exhibitions on diseases and
their treatment.

You may find the exhibition rather disappointing, but the structure
itself is still fun to explore, as you climb between the spheres on long
iron staircases, or peer out of the porthole windows to the road below.
The view from the top sphere takes in the miniature spires of MINI EUROPE
and the Heysel stadium, but the center of Brussels is too far away to make
out much.

At night, when the spheres are illuminated by tiny lights, the Atomium
takes on the air of a sci-fi spaceship from a Fifties comic. The view from
the top floor is best on summer nights when MINI EUROPE is spotlit.

AUTOWORLD

Esplanade du Cinquantenaire 11 ☎*(02)736.41.65. Map 1C3* 🔲 *Open
10am-5pm* 🚶 ⇌ *Metro to Mérode.*

One of the vast iron and glass halls of Leopold II's 1880 Palais du
Cinquantenaire is crammed with a private collection of 450 gleaming
vintage cars and trucks. Car enthusiasts can inspect the upholstery on a
Model-T Ford, or marvel at the chrome trim on a 1938 black Cadillac
that once carried President Roosevelt and his G-Men bodyguards. The
oldest model in the collection is Léon Bollée's 1896 *voiturette,* in which
chic couples once bounced along French roads.

Autoworld preserves a selection of rare, Belgian-made vehicles, in-
cluding two study Minerva cars that carried King Albert on state visits.
But perhaps the most evocative exhibit is the 1956 Cadillac in which John
F. Kennedy rode through Berlin in 1963 to deliver his famous *Ich bin ein
Berliner* speech.

See also CINQUANTENAIRE MUSEUMS, which includes a plan of the group
of museums.

CENTRAL AFRICA, MUSEUM OF
See KONINKLIJK MUSEUM VOOR MIDDENAFRIKA, page 98.

CENTRE BELGE DE LA BANDE DESSINÉE (Comic Strip Museum) ★ ▥
Rue des Sables 20 ☎*(02)219.19.80. Map 4D4* ▨ *Open 10am-6pm, closed Mon* ✹ ⇶ ▣ *Metro to de Brouckère. Reading Room and Library open Tues-Thurs 10am-5pm; Fri noon-6pm; Sat 10am-6pm* ✗ *if requested in writing.*

Tintin's gleaming red and white rocket, instantly recognizable to avid readers of "Operation Moon," greets visitors to the clean, cool interior of the national comic strip museum, a stone's throw from rue Neuve. Tintin's creator, Hergé, is still the best known of Belgium's designers of **bandes dessinées** or **BDs**.

The museum, opened in 1990, is a long-overdue tribute to more than 600 other Belgian designers who, over the past 60 years, gave readers of all ages characters from Lucky Luke to the Smurfs — or Stroumphs, as they are called in French — and made Belgium Europe's leading center for comic strip art. A series of special shows complement the permanent exhibition of more than 400 original plates and a collection of 25,000 sketches and drawings. There is a short section explaining the evolution of animation, but generally the displays are geared to adults and aficionados, and there are 20,000 albums available for consultation in the reading room.

Many people come just to admire the impressive restoration of the former Magasins Waucquez, a department store designed by Belgium's Art Nouveau supremo, Victor Horta, or to visit the Horta brasserie for a break during shopping. A museum shop carries thousands of new titles, cartoon memorabilia and souvenirs. It also provides a good place of contact for serious collectors needing a pointer to one of the specialist stores, which number more than 30 in Brussels.

CINQUANTENAIRE MUSEUMS
Parc du Cinquantenaire. Map 1C3. Metro to Mérode.

Three major museums occupy a vast complex in the PARC DU CINQUAN-TENAIRE, built for the 1880 Brussels Exhibition, which celebrated the 50th anniversary *(cinquantenaire)* of the Belgian revolution.

The complex is best approached from Mérode metro station. Climb the steps behind the fountain to reach an esplanade terminated by a triumphal arch. Built in 1905 by Charles Girault to commemorate the 75th anniversary of the Belgian revolution, the arch is surmounted by a bronze quadriga. The female figures at its base represent the provinces of Belgium: notice the plump figure of Antwerp holding aloft a ship.

A private collection of vintage cars known as AUTOWORLD occupies the large hall on the left side of the esplanade. The hall opposite contains the **Brussels Air Museum**, one of the departments of the military museum. Go through the door to the right of the arch to enter the MUSÉE DE L'ARMÉE. Or enter the MUSÉES ROYAUX D'ART ET D'HISTOIRE by the entrance to the left of the arch (see the illustration on page 34).

The museums are all free with the exception of Autoworld. Do not try to see everything at once. Even the most avid museum visitor will

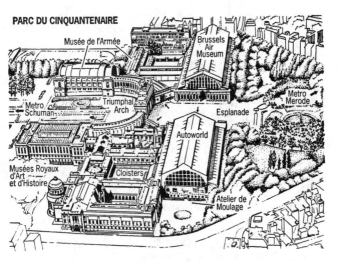

PARC DU CINQUANTENAIRE

Musée de l'Armée • Brussels Air Museum • Metro Merode • Metro Schuman • Triumphal Arch • Esplanade • Autoworld • Musées Royaux d'Art et d'Histoire • Cloisters • Atelier de Moulage

probably find a two-hour visit sufficient. Take a break in the park, or go to a café for a coffee or lunch in between visits. The café in the Musées Royaux d'Art et d'Histoire is rather gloomy, and it is better to head up the avenue de Tervuren to **La Terrasse** *(#11)*, an old Belgian café with plump leather sofas. As the name suggests, the café has a terrace where you can eat out on sunny days as the traffic roars past.

COMIC STRIP MUSEUM
In a fine Art Nouveau building, a tribute to the many Belgian artists and designers who, over 60 years, have made Belgium Europe's leading center for comic strip art. See CENTRE BELGE DE LA BANDE DESSINÉE, opposite.

FONDATION POUR L'ARCHITECTURE
Rue de l'Ermitage 55 ☎*(02)649.02.59. Map 1C3* ☎ *Open Tues-Fri 12.30-7pm; Sat, Sun 11am-7pm. Tram 93, 94 to Lesbroussart.*
A former 19thC brick pumping house off avenue Louise has been skillfully transformed into an exhibition space devoted to modern architecture. Expect stimulating displays featuring architects' plans, photographs, models and videos.

HISTORIUM
Anspach Centre (level 1), place de la Monnaie ☎*(02)217.60.23. Map 3D3* ☎ *but* ☎ *for children below 1.2m (47 inches)* ✱ *Open daily 10am-6pm. Tram 52, 55, 58, 81 to Bourse.*
The Historium is a stimulating waxworks museum modeled on Madame Tussaud's in London. Models of famous Belgians such as Charles V or Albert I are displayed in settings to conjure up the Burgundian

court or a medieval battlefield. The Historium is equipped with the latest headphone technology to provide pre-recorded commentary in four languages (French, Dutch, German and English). The historical background has been meticulously researched, and special effects such as a rat scuttling through a World War I trench are rather enjoyable.

JAPANESE PAGODA
See TOUR JAPONAISE, page 119.

KONINKLIJK MUSEUM VOOR MIDDENAFRIKA (Central Africa Museum) 🏛
Leuvensesteenweg 13, Tervuren ☎(02)767.54.01 ☒ ✗ (optional) ✽ Open mid-Mar to mid-Oct 9am-5.30pm; mid-Oct to mid-Mar 10am-4.30pm. Closed Mon.
Set in beautifully maintained French-style grounds, the museum was the brainchild of Leopold II. Indeed, it was almost solely through his efforts that Belgium became involved in the European race for empire. In 1885 he became the personal sovereign of the Independent Congo State, a country the size of Western Europe. For the next 75 years, many thousands of Belgians worked in the Congo. Supporters of their involvement stress the knowledge and economic and social infrastructure they provided. But critics point to the wealth, especially ivory and rubber, that was taken from the country at great cost. It was estimated that between 1885 and 1900, three million people died in the Congo. When Leopold II died in 1908, the Congo passed from his private hands into the hands of the Belgian state.

It was in 1897 that Leopold II organized an exhibition on the Congo and, flushed by its success, decided the following year to create a more permanent Congo museum. The work, entirely paid for from Leopold's private Congo income, was designed by the French architect Charles Girault to create a spectacular mock *château* modeled on the Petit Palais in Paris. It opened in 1910, the year after Leopold's death, on the occasion of yet another World Exposition. Today the museum plays an important role in the scientific knowledge of Africa.

In 1960, the year of the Congo's independence, the museum's scope was widened to include Central Africa and, latterly, to North and South America and the South Sea Islands. It now contains a wealth of exhibits, although only a small part of the collections are on display in the 20 exhibition areas. With 50,000 samples, the museum contains the second largest wood collection in the world. A large number of maps chart the progress of European knowledge of Africa through the centuries. Special attention is given to the Belgian presence in Africa, and separate collections of decorative items, masks, sculpture and other aspects of African civilization are on display.

The museum displays the extraordinary riches of the Belgian Congo, now Zaire, within its airy marble halls. The rotunda overlooking the formal gardens contains statues from the 1897 Exposition, including bronze figures depicting the benefits brought by Belgium to the Congo. Other figures show the indigenous people engaged in hunting or wood carving. The museum owns many examples of superb Congolese workmanship, the most impressive of which is a canoe (**room 11**) fashioned from a single tree trunk, measuring over 22m (70 feet). About one hundred people manned this craft, which was used both for river transport and war expeditions.

Room 13 gives some idea of the serious scientific work the museum carries out, with its cabinets of insects and butterflies carefully catalogued in neat handwriting. The collection of freshwater fish in **room 14** is but a tiny sample of the half-million different species owned by the museum.

Enormous murals of the dramatically varied Congo landscape decorate **room 14**, together with a frieze of 32 historical photographs of the swollen Congo river, showing fishermen laying nets, and remote settlements of huts. One remarkable photograph shows a boa constrictor in the act of swallowing its prey. Another provides a distant glimpse of a steam train laboring up a steep mountainside on the line built to link two ports on the Congo separated by the Stanley Falls.

The museum has many meticulously constructed dioramas of lions, zebras and other African animals in their natural habitat. The most impressive of these miniature landscapes, which were created for the 1958 World Fair in Brussels, illustrates the different zones of natural vegetation on the slopes of the Ruwenzori massif, an extinct volcano. The first diorama shows the base of the volcano covered by dense equatorial forest, with civet-cats skulking in the undergrowth, and green parrots peering out from a tangle of creepers. The next zone is mountain forest, home to the sleek-feathered, dark blue Lady Ross touraco. The vegetation turns to bamboo forest, followed by wooded heath, with beards of lichen hanging from the trees. This gives way finally to the alpine zone, the domain of the eerie white-collared crows.

The museum owns a spectacular collection of African art (**rooms 6-7**). The art of the Congo is organized according to tribes, and shows the range of styles that have evolved, from the menacing black angular masks of the Salampasu tribe (who lived in the southern region near the Angolan border), to the rounded female figures of the Luba (from the mountains close to Zambia).

Most of the sculpture and tools in the museum are made from the shiny dark brown and black woods of the Congo. Leopold's colony supplied much of the timber used to construct the sweeping staircases and sumptuous furnishings characteristic of Belgian Art Nouveau.

The museum possesses a fascinating collection of mementoes of Africa explorers, including a battered suitcase owned by Henry Morton Stanley, a journalist paid by Leopold II to explore the Congo. An old label attached by Stanley's wife is still legible. "This portmanteau belonged to H.M. Stanley," it declares. "It was carried across Africa. It must never be removed from my room and *never* on any account be used."

The museum now owns most of the private papers of Stanley, among them a letter to James Gordon Bennett, the *New York Herald* publisher who financed his expedition in search of Livingstone. "Animated only with the desire to do my duty to the *New York Herald*," Stanley wrote, "I halted at nothing, was ever pushing on until my men cried out from sheer fatigue, 'Have Mercy!' " Stanley eventually found the Scottish explorer, prompting the famous utterance, "Dr Livingstone, I presume."

MAISON ERASME

Rue Chapitre 31 ☎*(02)521.13.83. Map* **1C2** ☒ *Open 10am-noon, 2-5pm. Closed Tues; Fri. Metro to Saint-Guidon.*

Tucked away in a leafy garden in industrial Anderlecht, the Erasmus Museum is one of the secret delights of Brussels that few tourists ever track down. The museum occupies a 15thC brick house where the Dutch humanist Erasmus spent five months in the summer of 1521 recuperating from an illness.

Anderlecht was then just a small village in the rolling Pajottenland. Erasmus fled there from Leuven, where he taught theology, to stay with his friend Pieter Wychman, a canon at the nearby church of Saint-Pierre.

Local craftsmen skilled in medieval building techniques have expertly reconstructed the step-gabled house where Erasmus stayed. The walls have been rebuilt using authentic 16thC Spanish bricks, and the rooms are furnished with antique Gothic linenfold chests, pewter vases and religious statues. The Renaissance Hall on the ground floor is hung with sumptuous pale blue Cordoba leather stamped with gilt patterns.

On even the dullest days, the museum is suffused with the warmth of the Flemish Renaissance. The walls are crammed with reproductions of portraits of Erasmus by Holbein and Dürer. A woodcut by Dürer shows the genial scholar seated at his desk, wearing two coats and a hat to keep warm, and holding the ink bottle to prevent the contents from freezing.

In an evocative room known as Erasmus' Study, a wooden desk stands next to a stained glass window overlooking the replanted medieval garden. Dappled sunlight falls across the yellowed pages of an old book, and it is all too easy to imagine Erasmus sitting there penning one of the 40 or so letters he wrote from Anderlecht. The setting is entirely imaginary, however, and the chair is carved on the back 1548, by which date Erasmus had been dead for 12 years.

A room upstairs contains glass cases crammed with moldering volumes bound in old leather. The works include Erasmus's *In Praise of Folly*, written in 1509 at the age of 40. Despite preaching toleration, Erasmus was hounded for much of his life by fanatical theologians at Leuven University and elsewhere. At the end of his stay in Anderlecht, he left Brabant for good, settling in Basel. Yet he retained a fondness for this region of Europe, writing to a friend a few days before he died, "If only Brabant were closer!"

MINI EUROPE

Bruparck ☎*(02)478.05.50. Map* **1B3** ☒ *but* ☒ *for children below 1.2m (47 inches). Open Sept-Jun, daily 9am-6pm; Jul, Aug, Mon-Fri 9am-8pm, Sat, Sun 9am-9pm* ✳ ═ *Metro to Heysel.*

A landscaped park beneath the ATOMIUM has been laid out with miniature replicas of famous buildings from the member states of the European Community. Winding paths lead visitors past fastidiously-constructed scale models of the Sacré-Coeur in Paris or the Leaning Tower of Pisa.

The special effects include a harbor fire, an eruption of Vesuvius and the simulated launch of an Ariane rocket.

MUSÉE ROYAL DE L'ARMÉE ET D'HISTOIRE MILITAIRE (Royal Museum of the Army and Military History)

Parc du Cinquantenaire 3 ☎*(02)733.44.93. Map 1C3* 🖾 *Open Tues-Sun 9am-noon, 1-4.40pm. Metro to Mérode.*

The vast army museum provides a sobering reminder of the countless wars that have been fought on Belgian soil. Founded in 1910, the museum occupies an entire wing of the 1880 Cinquantenaire palace. Gleaming suits of 15thC armor and menacing pikes are displayed in the attractive **Salle des Provinces Réunies**, while some dusty relics collected from **Waterloo** (see EXCURSIONS on page 153) occupy glass cases in the entrance hall.

The museum owns a vast collection of 19thC military uniforms, which are displayed in rows of antiquated glass cases. You will find relics from long-forgotten 19thC wars, alongside curiosities such as Leopold II's tricycle.

A vast gloomy hall is crammed with equipment salvaged from World War I, including guns, vehicles and faded photographs. A nearby hall contains mementoes of World War II. American tanks that blasted through the Ardennes in 1944 are sometimes on show in an inner courtyard of the museum.

A chilly 19thC hall is devoted to the **Brussels Air Museum**, which has a sizeable collection of historic planes. On the first Saturday of every month, the **Marché du Vieux Papier** is held in the air museum. Dealers set up stalls next to the fighter aircraft to sell old books and postcards.

MUSÉE D'ART ANCIEN ★

Rue de la Régence 3 ☎*(02)513.96.30. Map 6F4* 🖾 *Open Tues-Sun 10am-noon, 1-5pm* 🚽 🖦 *Tram 92, 93, 94 to place Royale.*

The foremost collection of Belgian painting and sculpture, the Musée d'Art Ancien began rather unpromisingly as a collection of rejected paintings. The French revolutionary army had plundered churches and art collections throughout Flanders in the late 18thC, and carted off the most valuable works to Paris. The Paris Louvre eventually became so swamped with booty that a Napoleonic decree was enacted to set up provincial museums throughout the Empire.

One such museum was opened in Brussels, receiving two separate batches of paintings in 1802 and 1811. The returned works included several altarpieces by Rubens that had been ripped out of Flemish churches.

The Musée d'Art Ancien gradually built up a prime collection of Dutch and Flemish paintings. It is now displayed in a monumental Neoclassical building that positively bristles with national pride. Designed by Alphonse Balat in 1887-80, the building has an intimidating entrance flanked by colossal columns of Scots granite and oversized statues representing the Arts. It is perhaps too grand a backdrop for the intimate paintings of Early Flemish Masters, but it sets just the right tone for Rubens and 19thC Belgian art.

For a fuller account of Belgian art, see also FIVE CENTURIES OF BELGIAN PAINTING on page 38.

MUSÉE D'ART ANCIEN

SECOND FLOOR   BROWN ROUTE (17th-18thC)

52-54,	
57-60,62	Flemish Baroque
62	Rubens
50	Spanish Baroque
61	French Baroque
60	Dutch Baroque
50-51	Italian painting 14th-18thC
55-56	Della Faille Bequest

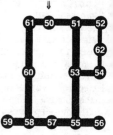

FIRST FLOOR   BLUE ROUTE (15th-16thC)

10-17	Flemish Primitives
21-34	16thC Flemish painting
31	Bruegel
17,24,25	Dutch painting
18-20	German painting
11,12,15,16	French painting
37-45	Delporte Bequest

GROUND FLOOR   YELLOW ROUTE (19thC)

69-70	Neoclassicism, Romanticism
72-80	Realism
79	Meunier
82-84	Drawings and watercolors
80-85	Symbolism
87	Luminism
88	Evenepoel
89	Ensor
90-91	Impressionism
91	Hess-Vandenbroek Bequest

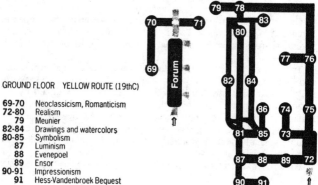

Orientation

The collection of paintings and sculpture in the Musée d'Art Ancien is vast, and even the most diligent visitor is likely to get lost in the maze of rooms, numbering 91 in all. The main departments are distinguished by signs in different colors, and the museum plan *(detailed copy sold at the main desk — simple version on opposite page)* is a helpful aid to the bewildered.

Once you have dropped off your coat and bag at the cloakroom *(garderobe)*, enter the airy main hall known as the Forum to get your bearings. The first door on the right leads to the Artshop, which sells postcards, art books, toys and T-shirts. The second door on the right leads to the adjoining Musée d'Art Moderne via an escalator (green route).

Go through the door at the far end of the Forum to get to the **15th-16thC collection** on the first floor (blue route), and the **17th-18thC collection** on the second floor (brown route). Back on the ground floor, go through the door to the right of the Neptune fountain to reach the **19thC collection** (yellow route). Descend to the basement by the stairs to the left of the fountain to find the **sculpture gallery** and the **museum café**.

Bear in mind that the Musée d'Art Ancien closes from noon-1pm. You can pass the time either in the modern art museum *(closed 1-2pm)* or by taking a break for lunch. The museum café *(open 11am-4.30pm)* serves plump, filled *baguettes*, and a dish of the day, but the surroundings are rather lugubrious. For excellent and inexpensive sandwiches, squeeze into the convivial **New York** *(rue de Namur 8)*.

The 15th-16thC collection

In **room 11**, you meet the Early Flemish painters Robert Campin (here labeled the Master of Flémalle) and his pupil Roger van der Weyden. You might find the medieval symbolism in the Master of Flémalle's *St Gregory's Mass* difficult to grasp, but concentrate on the details such as the tiled floor. His *Annunciation* is a more familiar subject, treated with enormous sensitivity. Admire the vase of lilies on the table or the open book with its curled pages. The next two generations of Flemish painters were mesmerized by Campin's realism.

The Brussels city artist Roger van der Weyden went in a different direction. He laid the foundations of Flemish portrait painting, in his studies of Burgundian nobles dressed in fashionable black gowns. Antoine, the Great Bastard of Burgundy, was not blessed with the most fetching of names, but he appears a handsome young man in Van der Weyden's portrait *Man with the Arrow*. The arrow may be symbolic, but most art critics now think not. The *Portrait of Laurent Froimont* is one panel of a diptych. The Virgin and Child which was once fixed to it is now in the Caen fine arts museum. Walk around the back of the painting to see a grisaille representation of St Lawrence. Froimont's coat-of-arms was also to be seen on the back until a zealous French revolutionary scratched it off.

The *Pietà* by Van der Weyden is set against a dramatic fiery sunset. Rubens would use a similar twilight sky in a *Crucifixion* in Antwerp. By contrast, the *Pietà* by Petrus Christus in the same room is a rather tame composition. None of the figures seems particularly perturbed by the dead Christ.

Room 13, to one side, contains two large paintings by Dirk Bouts and nothing else. They hang on special stone walls imitating the original location in the courtroom of Leuven town hall. The two paintings belong to a series of four works called *The Justice of Emperor Otto*, which were intended to warn judges of the penalties of corruption. Bouts died before the painting was finished, and his son added the final touches.

The man in the white gown in the painting to the left was falsely accused of a crime by the Emperor's wife, who is standing behind a wall with her husband. The woman in the red dress is the dead man's wife. In the second painting, she proves her husband's innocence by grasping a red-hot iron without feeling pain — a medieval lie detector test. The Emperor's wife is then burned at the stake.

After the epic scale of Bouts, it is all too easy to overlook the small paintings from Bruges (**rm 14**). There are no Van Eycks, alas, but the miniature panels by Memling are exquisite. The portraits of Willem Moreel and his wife Barbara van Vlaenderberch hang side by side, as Memling intended. Moreel was a wealthy spice merchant in Bruges, with sufficient funds to commission a further triptych by Memling, which now hangs in Bruges. Look out for the vivid scarlet of the Virgin's gown in Memling's *Virgin and Child*. Scarlet cloth was the most expensive, in the medieval world.

The contemporary of Memling who painted the *Triptych of Jan de Witte* is known only as the Master of 1473. He had little talent when it came to painting children or hands, but he was gifted with a keen eye for flowers and rich fabrics.

The next room (**rm 15**) shifts attention back to 15thC Brussels. You may notice that the women are dressed less fashionably than those of Bruges. A little painting of *The Miracle of the Virgin* by the Master of Sainte-Gudule is mainly of interest for the view of Brussels Cathedral and the astonishing pointed shoes worn by the man on the left.

The mood of Netherlandish art turned to apocalyptic gloom in the early 16thC (**rm 17**). The *Temptation of St Anthony* was a favorite theme of Renaissance artists. It resurfaced in the 20thC in a painting by Dalí in the adjoining Musée d'Art Moderne. An anonymous artist painted a tiny work showing the beleaguered St Anthony in the midst of a dark forest.

Hieronymus Bosch painted a large triptych on the same subject, filled with bizarre animals and blazing cities. The original is in Lisbon; the painting here is a 16thC copy. Bosch's *Calvary with Donor* is a tranquil painting compared with the Van der Weyden *Pietà*, and the donor looks strangely incongruous in his fashionable Burgundian clothes.

Now look at Gerard David's *Madonna with the Porridge Spoon* (**rm 21**). This shows the state of painting in late 15thC Bruges, when the Flemish city had become a backwater. The mood is tranquil and domestic, like a 17thC Vermeer interior. The portrait of the child is unusually tender for a medieval artist.

The paintings that follow (**rms 22-25**) come mainly from the Renaissance palaces of Antwerp. You should try to imagine them hanging on walls of gilded leather in 16thC merchants' homes. Do not miss the *Little Girl with Dead Bird* by an unknown 16thC painter (**rm 22**). A troubled blue-eyed girl in a bonnet is holding a dead bird. Art historians have tried, but failed, to identify the girl in this extraordinary image of childhood confusion. The artist likewise remains a mystery.

Flemish artists became increasingly skilled at painting children in the 16thC. Look for the child reading a book upside down in Quentin Metsys's *Altarpiece of the Brotherhood of St Anne,* painted in 1509 for a chapel in the Pieterskerk in Leuven. Or find the little boy in Metsys's *Virgin and Child.*

Now look at Jan Gossaert's *Venus and Cupid* (**rm 25**). The result of an Italian journey in 1508, the small work displays a new fascination with plump female nudes. The art of Rubens is not far off.

Go into **room 26** and stand in front of Bernard van Orley's triptych, *The Virtue of Patience.* Margaret of Austria commissioned this work on the trials of Job in 1521. Margaret's life was filled with tragedy; her first marriage was dissolved for political expediency, and two subsequent husbands died. Her resigned dignity is visible in Van Orley's portrait (here a copy).

Look in the same room for the *Portrait of Dr Joris van Zelle,* a physician in Brussels who lived on the place Saint-Géry. Van Orley, who had a house nearby, painted this affectionate portrait of his 28-year-old friend in 1519. The double hands on the tapestry probably symbolize the friendship between artist and sitter, though the cryptic letters remain a mystery.

Pause in **room 28** to look at Jan van Coninxloo's *St Benedict Altarpiece* of 1552. It may not be a great painting, but the scene involving the miracle of the broken cup (left panel) takes us inside a Flemish kitchen of the 16thC to show off gleaming brass pots and a caged bird.

The Bruegel room (**rm 32**) contains four paintings by Pieter Bruegel the Elder. Bosch's fantasies influenced Bruegel's early Antwerp works, such as the *Fall of the Rebel Angels,* painted in 1562, and the sadly faded *Adoration of the Magi* from 1557. After moving to Brussels in 1563, Bruegel discovered the Flemish villages of the Pajottenland, w of Brussels. *The Numbering at Bethlehem* shows the census, ordered by the Emperor Augustus, taking place in a snowbound Pajottenland hamlet in the winter of 1566. The *Fall of Icarus* illustrates Bruegel's melancholy world view. You have to look closely to see the tiny splash where Icarus has hit the water, while a ship sails past and a plowman continues working as if nothing had happened.

The next rooms contain several works by Pieter Bruegel the Elder's two sons, Pieter and Jan. Pieter Bruegel the Younger piously copied many of his father's paintings, such as the *Wedding Dance* (**rm 33**), which is a copy of a work by Bruegel the Elder in Vienna.

Be sure to visit the **Delporte Bequest** (**rms 37-45**), which forms a small museum in its own right. It displays works collected by Dr Franz Delporte, whose tastes ranged from Flemish Renaissance paintings to African art. Look out for the tiny painting by Pieter Bruegel the Elder of a *Winter Landscape with Skaters and a Bird Trap* (**rm 44**), set in a

Pajottenland village on a crisp winter's day. Bruegel hints at the transience of existence by showing children playing games on thin ice, and birds pecking crumbs near a makeshift trap.

Take the elevator down to the basement café, if you feel weary, before going up to the second floor to follow the brown route.

The 17th-18thC collection

Pieter Paul Rubens was the leading Flemish painter of the 17thC. Many of his greatest works are in Antwerp (where he lived), but Brussels has built up a sizeable collection. The largest canvases are the altarpieces painted for churches in Ghent, Tournai and elsewhere (**rm 62**). They were plundered by the French, but subsequently returned to Brussels, where they now hang frameless and rather forlorn. You have to imagine flickering candles and a whiff of incense.

Another room (**52**) has a series of 12 cartoons drawn by Rubens in 1636. One shows the *Fall of Icarus* at the moment the boy begins to plunge to earth. Bruegel, as we have seen, picked a less dramatic moment to paint. The cartoons were preliminary studies for paintings to decorate a hunting lodge outside Madrid. But perhaps his most astonishing work is the *Studies of a Negro's Head*.

French 18thC artists such as Watteau and Delacroix learnt much from Rubens paintings. You may notice an unfinished canvas by Rubens of *The Miracles of St Benedict*. Delacroix was so impressed by this painting that he made a copy, which now hangs nearby. English landscape painters such as Constable and Gainsborough were likewise inspired by such Rubens studies of nature as *Landscape with the Hunt of Atlanta*.

Now look at paintings by Rubens' pupils such as the animal painter Frans Snyders, and Anthony van Dyck (who spent much of his life in London). Van Dyck captured the spirit of Baroque Europe in portraits such as *A Genoese Lady with her Daughter*. Another Rubens pupil, Jacob Jordaens, developed a rather grotesque Baroque. In a curious collaboration, Jordaens painted the figures in *Allegory of Fecundity* (**rm 57**), while Snyders added the fruit.

The painting by Hieronymus Francken the Younger of *The Cabinet of Jan Snellinck* illustrates a 17thC Antwerp merchant's collection of paintings and curiosities. The walls are covered with floor-to-ceiling paintings as if they were a kind of wallpaper.

The museum has a small collection of Dutch Baroque, including Rembrandt's *Portrait of Nicolaes van Bambeeck*, painted when the artist was 35. Look closely to see the painted black frame on which the sitter rests his left hand. Then pause at the top of the stairs to look at the paintings of 17thC Brussels by various artists before leaving this floor.

The 19thC collection

Although frequently overlooked, the 19thC rooms contain some exceptional works by Belgian Romantics and Impressionists. Start with the three rooms of early 19thC painting off the Forum (**rms 68-70**). Join the admirers in front of Jacques-Louis David's *Death of Marat*, painted in 1793. David had fled to Brussels from Paris in 1816. He died in 1825 and was buried beneath an obelisk in the CIMETIÈRE DE BRUXELLES.

Now follow the yellow route to reach the 19thC wing. Linger in **room 81** to enjoy the exceptional vitality of Belgian art of the 1880s and '90s. The Brussels group known as Les XX showed experimental art at its exhibitions. Look out for Théodore van Rysselberghe's portrait of Octave Maus, founder of Les XX, who is shown in an artful room filled with Oriental lamps and fragile vases. Under the influence of Seurat, Van Rysselberghe later produced Pointillist paintings such as *The Walk* and *Portrait of Madame Maus.*

You see new ideas taking shape in Henri Evenpoel's Impressionist paintings of Belgian interiors of the 1890s, with their Japanese porcelain and fans (**rm 81**). Evenpoel painted several captivating portraits of children, such as *White Dress* and *Henriette Wearing a Large Hat.* He died prematurely in Paris in 1899, aged 27.

Emile Claus, who fled to Britain during World War I, painted a strange, Impressionist view of London on a day of watery sunshine in the spring of 1916 (**rm 87**). Be sure not to miss the intimate furnished room (**91**) filled with voluptuous French paintings of the 1880s and '90s, including a Monet landscape, a Sisley and several Renoirs. Another room (**88**) has a Gauguin painting from his Pont-Aven period, and a Bonnard nude.

James Ensor was the most innovative of the 19thC Belgians. Linger in the Ensor room (**89**) to compare his somber early paintings of Ostend interiors with the vibrant Expressionist style that began in about 1883.

Sculpture

The marble statues in the museum come mainly from the Parc de Bruxelles, where the originals have been replaced by copies. Baroque statues of Diana and Narcissus strike flamboyant poses at the foot of the main staircase. Carved by Gabriel Grupello, they once stood in the garden of the Tour et Tassis palace. Copies made in the 19thC stand near the round pond in the PARC DE BRUXELLES.

Grupelle designed the hefty fountain at the foot of the staircase as a wine-cooler for the Guild of Fishmongers. The furious-looking Neptune sits in the basin shaking his fist at a horse (which once spurted jets of water), while a demure Juno holds her nipple (from which water once trickled onto the wine bottles).

The vaulted brick cellars of the old museum have been tastefully restored for the new **Galerie de Sculpture** *(this part of the museum is subject to occasional closures: call ahead),* which contains works by Belgian sculptors from the 18thC and 19thC.

The **Jardin des Sculptures** *(rue de la Régence 🖾 open daily 10am-105pm)* was recently created on the slope next to the museum to display several works by Belgian sculptors.

MUSÉE D'ART MODERNE (Museum of Modern Art) ★

*Place Royale 1 ☎(02)513.96.30. Map **6F4** 🖾 Open Tues-Sun 10am-1pm, 2-5pm 🚉 🚊 Tram 92, 93, 94 to place Royale.*

The modern art museum is located in a controversial building sunk eight floors below the cobbled courtyard of the Palais de Charles de

Lorraine. Some of the rooms receive natural light from a sloping glass well in the middle of the square, but others are windowless. After a heated debate that ran for many years, the subterranean building was proposed as a way of preserving intact the 18thC palace.

For a fuller account of Belgian art, see also FIVE CENTURIES OF BELGIAN PAINTING on page 38.

Orientation
The visitor must first get to grips with the logic of the building's layout. You enter the museum either through a Neoclassical house on the corner of place Royale, or via an escalator off the main hall of the Musée d'Art Ancien. After dropping off your coat and bag at the cloakroom (garderobe) on level -2, you follow the signposted green route. This follows a downward spiral route to the deepest gallery at level -8. You can return to level -3 by a large elevator fitted with armchairs.

Level -3
Some of the most exciting modern works lurk in the shadowy recesses of level -3, officially devoted to recent acquisitions and temporary loans. Expect to find lingering Belgian Surrealism, quirky mechanical inventions, pulsating video screens and the inevitable old junk turned into art.

Brabantine Fauvists
The ragged groups of Belgian artists labeled the Brabantine Fauvists are hung in daylit rooms at **level -4**. The paintings by Rik Wouters especially capture the tranquil domesticity and languid torpor of Brussels on the eve of World War I. Interned in Amsterdam after war broke out, Wouters developed a more melancholy style as even the title of one painting reveals — Still Life, Somber Mood was painted in 1915. Wouters died of eye cancer in Amsterdam a few months later.

Look now at the Symbolist paintings of Léon Spilliaert. His paintings often show the beach and buildings of his native Ostend, yet they are far from the usual romantic sea images. In one somber painting, a solitary woman walks along a darkening beach. Another ominous work from 1910 depicts an airship in a hangar. His Self Portrait (1907) shows a face haunted by fears.

The cataclysm of World War I left its mark on Belgian art. Inspired by German Expressionism, the Flemish Expressionists turned their attention to peasant life and innocent images of childhood. Constant Permeke painted melancholy landscapes awash with earthy browns and black. Gustave de Smet was no less somber in his studies of poor Belgian families.

Belgian Surrealism
Like recurring dreams, the paintings of Paul Delvaux (**level -5**) feature disturbing images of erotic nudes, night trains and skeletons. Delvaux studied at the Brussels Académie Royale des Beaux-Arts, and his paintings are sometimes set in the Quartier Leopold or at the Boitsfort rail station.

The museum's Magritte collection (**level -6**) was boosted recently by a sizeable legacy of paintings donated by his wife Georgette, who died in 1987. Many of the paintings once hung in the Magrittes' rather stuffy bourgeois home in rue des Mimosas in Schaerbeek. The haunting nude portraits of Georgette in *La Magie Noire* (Black Magic) and *Le Galet* (The Boulder) were formerly displayed in a corner of Magritte's studio above a somewhat ugly green sofa. The paintings feature bizarre elements such as a night street scene with a clear blue sky. Don't expect much help from the titles, which were often proposed by friends in late-night gatherings.

The next room helps you locate Belgian Surrealism in a European context. Giorgio de Chirico's *The Melancholy of a Beautiful Day* (1913) is the type of enigmatic city scene that influenced Delvaux in the 1930s. Dalí's *Temptation of St Anthony* gives a Freudian twist to the Biblical story of moral temptation popularized by Flemish Renaissance painters.

Recent Belgian art

The *Jeune Peinture Belge* (Young Belgian Painting) movement that flourished briefly in the 1940s produced dark and pessimistic abstract paintings. The mood of anxiety finally vanished from Belgian art with Cobra, the postwar Northern European art group. Corneille's *A New Dawn Full of Birds* reflects postwar optimism in its very title. But gloomy gray tones return in the room devoted to the Zero group at **level -7**.

By contrast, the recent modern art at **level -8** is joyfully off-beat and bizarre. The museum admits to being at a loss to categorize these diverse works, and you can immediately see why, as your eye wanders from old wooden posts leaning against a wall to mock Classical ruins. The Surrealist tradition of bizarre titles remains strong, and even the names of some artists are a source of further confusion, such as the Belgian who signs his works "Denmark."

The quirky Belgian Marcel Broodthaers solemnly displays a red casserole overflowing with mussels, and creates a mock museum cabinet filled with bizarre objects including a blank canvas and a lump of coal wrapped like a precious jewel. Arman creates distinctive works by sticking squeezed paint tubes onto a canvas in *Homage to Jackson Pollock*, or by gluing two smashed violins onto the canvas in *Angry Violins*. Edward Kienholz constructs a grim Cross covered with fur, which he titles *We'll Catch the Boss and Put Him on a Cross*. The pleasure principle reaches a glorious climax in a bizarre mechanical construction by Jean Tingueley. Push the button to start the mechanism.

MUSÉE BELLEVUE

Place des Palais 7 ☎*(02)511.44.25. Map* **6**F4 ▣ *Open Sat-Thurs 10am-5pm. Tram 92, 93, 94 to place Royale.*

This elegant museum occupies a former 18thC hotel built by Barnabé Guimard as part of the PLACE ROYALE quarter. The miscellaneous collection of decorative arts includes porcelain, furniture, jewelry and fans. The collections are perhaps mainly of interest to experts, but it is interesting to wander in the 18thC period rooms furnished in Louis XIV, Empire and Napoleon III styles.

MUSÉE DE LA BRASSERIE (Museum of Brewing)

Maison des Brasseurs, Grand'Place 10 ☎*(02)511.49.87. Map* **3E3** ▨
Open Mon-Fri, 10am-noon, 2-5pm; Apr 1-Oct 31 only, open Sat 10am-noon ♨
Tram 52, 55, 58, 81 to Bourse; metro to Gare Centrale.

What better starting point for getting some advice on Belgian beers before putting that knowledge to the test in one of Brussels' many cafés. The hops climbing the outside pillars of this guild house, built on the GRAND'PLACE in the Classical style, confirm that you have the right place. Press the bell and go down a narrow staircase to the basement. Authentic equipment from an 18thC Hoegaarden brewery, various trappings and memorabilia from the brewing trade, and a multilingual cassette commentary explain the industry, while books on beer, posters and other items can be bought.

In an adjoining room is a beautifully decorated 19thC-style café where visitors are offered a glass of draft beer, whose price is included in the entry fee. The highly knowledgeable curator is happy to talk about all aspects of Belgian beer, but he will not reveal the name of the brew you are drinking. That is his secret and he rings the changes, selecting produce from 50 to 60 breweries.

MUSÉE DAVID ET ALICE VAN BUUREN

Av. Leo Errera 41 ☎*(02)343.48.51. Map* **1D3** ▨ *⚹ Open Mondays only*
2-4pm. Closed July. Tram 23, 90 to Cavell.

A handsome suburban villa in Uccle built in 1923 by David van Buuren, a Dutch banker, contains a remarkable collection of paintings. A version of Bruegel's *Fall of Icarus* hangs in the living room, but the collection is particularly interesting for works by Constant Permeke and other artists of the Second Latem Group (see page 42). The garden was planted by Alice van Buuren, with masses of rhododendrons and a maze modeled on one at Versailles.

MUSÉE CHARLIER

Av. des Arts 16 ☎*(02)220.26.90. Map* **4D6** ▨ *Open Mon-Thurs 1.30-5pm, Fri*
1.30-4.30pm. Scheduled to reopen in May 1993. Metro to Madou.

A subdued light fills the Hôtel Charlier, a 19thC mansion in Saint-Josse once owned by the sculptor Guillaume Charlier. Decorated in 1890 by Victor Horta (three years before his first Art Nouveau commission), it contains a private collection of paintings by Constantin Meunier, James Ensor and Emile Claus. The house suffered considerable damage during the construction of the metro in the 1970s. Go there once it has reopened, for the rare pleasure of seeing 19thC Belgian paintings in a *fin-de-siècle* setting. Look out for occasional concerts held here.

MUSÉE DU CINÉMA (Cinema Museum)

Rue Baron Horta 9 ☎*(02)507.83.70. Map* **4E4** ▨ *Children under 16 not*
admitted. Open daily from 6pm. Metro to Gare Centrale; tram 92, 93, 94 to
place Royale.

Cinema fans flock to the two-screen museum in the Palais des Beaux-Arts to watch classic films in the original language. The weekly program is displayed outside the museum, and is also listed in *The Bulletin*. Silent German and US classics are generally screened in one theater, while more recent movies are shown in the other. Tickets are inexpensive and seats sell out fast.

MUSÉE COMMUNAL (Brussels City Museum)

Grand'Place, Maison du Roi ☎(02)511.27.42. Map 3E3. Open Mon-Fri 10am-12.30pm, 1.30-5pm (Oct-Mar, closes at 4pm); Sat, Sun, hols 10am-1pm; sometimes closed weekends — call ahead. Tram 52, 55, 58, 81 to Bourse; metro to Gare Centrale.

The Brussels city museum occupies a handsome building facing the town hall. It is rather confusingly known as the **Maison du Roi**, though no king ever stayed there. Charles V ordered the construction of the Maison du Roi in 1514-25. The architects Antoon and Rombout Keldermans designed the building in a florid Late Gothic style. Counts Egmont and Hoorn were imprisoned here in 1568 on the night before their execution on Grand'Place. The building had fallen into ruin by the 19thC, but Victor Jamaer fastidiously rebuilt it in the 1870s using 17thC engravings as his guide.

The museum now occupies all three floors of the Maison du Roi. Wander through the ground-floor rooms to get an insight into the artistic brilliance of medieval Brussels. Inspect the remarkable carved details on the medieval retables and study the medieval stone sculpture rescued from the Hôtel de Ville and Notre-Dame du Sablon. Look out for the painting of *The Marriage Procession* by Pieter Bruegel the Elder, showing a country wedding in a Pajottenland village.

Go up the stairs to pore over the maps and plans of Brussels, which illustrate the city's grand plans and even grander disasters. Watercolors show the picturesque River Senne and some streets that have vanished forever. The top floor is reserved for a collection of more than 520 glittering and gaudy costumes worn by the MANNEKEN PIS from 1698 to the present day.

MUSÉE COMMUNAL D'IXELLES

Rue Jean van Volsem 71 ☎(02)511.90.84. Map 6l6 ▣ (except for special exhibitions). Open Tues-Fri 1-5.30pm; Sat, Sun 10am-5pm. Tram 81 to place Flagey.

A former 19thC abattoir in Ixelles boasts a distinguished collection of paintings and sculpture. Opened in 1892, the Ixelles museum has inherited various bequests from local art collectors to become one of Belgium's foremost museums of art.

Art enthusiasts who puff up the hill will find Dürer's captivating drawing *The Stork*, together with paintings by Boucher and Delacroix. The museum has amassed important works by some of the artists who lived in Ixelles in the 19thC. A sculpture by Rodin is a relic of the period he worked in an atelier in the nearby rue Sans Souci *(#111)* from 1871-77.

You will find works by 19thC Belgian Impressionists and 20thC Symbolists such as Spilliaert. Look out for the paintings donated by Octave Maus, the leader of the energetic group Les XX.

The museum has built up a sizeable collection of 19thC posters advertising patent cures or mineral waters. They include a virtually complete set of Toulouse-Lautrec posters in vivid red and black. There is an enigmatic Magritte *(The Contented Donor)*, and a Delvaux from 1944 showing nude women in a Classical landscape. Watch out for major exhibitions at the museum.

MUSÉE DU COSTUME ET DE LA DENTELLE (Museum of Costume and Lace)
Rue de la Violette 6 ☎*(02)512.77.09. Map* **3E3** *(just behind town hall). Open Mon-Fri 10am-12.30pm, 1.30-5pm; Sat, Sun, hols 2-4.30pm. Tram 52, 55, 58, 81 to Bourse.*

Traditional Belgian lace is famous the world over for its intricate patterns and painstaking needlework. The lace museum has built up a varied collection of lace collars, tablecloths and dresses. Several lace shops are located in the neighborhood, although much of the modern lace on sale is produced in the Far East. Another important lace collection can be studied at the MUSÉES ROYAUX D'ART ET D'HISTOIRE.

MUSÉE DES ÉGOUTS (Sewers Museum)
Porte d'Anderlecht. Map **3E1** ☎*(02)513.85.87* ✗ *(compulsory) Wed only at 9am, 11am, 1pm, 3pm. Tram 18 to Porte d'Anderlecht.*

The Sewers Museum occupies one of two 19thC Neoclassical gatehouses at the Porte d'Anderlecht. Visitors interested in venturing below the city streets are taken on a guided tour through the sewer tunnels. You are led along damp catwalks to look at an underground stretch of the polluted River Senne and an impressive weir. Sewer technology is explained in an elegant little museum painted in soothing pastel colors.

MUSÉE DES ENFANTS (Children's Museum)
A hands-on museum near Ixelles. See BRUSSELS FOR CHILDREN on page 206.

MUSÉE DE LA GUEUZE (Gueuze Museum)
Rue Gheude 56 ☎*(02)521.49.28 or 520.28.99. Off map* **5F1** ▨ ✗ *optional. Open Mon-Fri 9am-4.30pm; Sat 10am-6pm. Closed Sun; Jun 1-Sept 30.*

This last working artisanal gueuze brewery in Brussels gives visitors an opportunity to see the whole process for making *lambic*, the base for four beers: *gueuze, faro, kriek* and *framboise.* Special conditions and micro-organisms, to be found only in the Senne valley, are necessary to produce the somewhat acidic, flat lambic. Lambic can be drunk young, after 15 days, or after one, two or three years.

The brewery was founded by Paul Cantillon in 1900, although brewing did not start there until 1937. Among its many visitors was former US Secretary of State George Schultz in 1986.

Good times to visit are the first Saturdays of November and March, when the brewery has a full open day, complete with breakfast coffee and croissants. The brewery's produce can be tasted on the premises and bottles bought to take away. To taste authentic Cantillon gueuze, when the brewery is closed, try DE ULTIEME HALLUCINATIE (see CAFÉS, page 179).

MUSÉE HORTA ★ 🏛

Rue Américaine 25 ☎*(02)537.16.92. Map 1D3* 🚻 *Open Tues-Sun 2-5.30pm. Tram 81, 91, 92 to Janson.*

Built in 1898-90 as a family house and studio, the Musée Horta house is suffused with the alluring sensuality of Art Nouveau. Every element in the building combines into an organic whole, with the curvaceous staircase ascending through the building like a tendril of ivy. Each room has a different quality of light, from the bright tiled dining room on the ground floor to the mellow golden attic.

The former studio contains architectural drawings and models to illustrate Horta's extraordinary talents. Temporary architectural exhibitions are occasionally held here.

MUSÉE DE L'INSTITUT ROYAL DES SCIENCES NATURELLES (Natural Science Museum)

Rue Vautier 29 ☎*(02)627.42.11. Map 1C3* 🚻 *Open Tues-Sun 9.30am-4.45pm* ⚦ 💺 *Metro to Maelbeek.*

Sited on a hill in the romantic PARC LEOPOLD, the Belgian Natural Science Museum was opened by King Leopold II in 1891. The original collection of fossil finds and stuffed animals was grandly displayed in a vast hall with iron columns and balconies. An unlovely modern wing was added at the back to contain the ever-growing collection of minerals, insects and skeletons.

The science museum was urgently needed in 1891 to accommodate a collection of nine giant **iguanodon skeletons** that had been discovered in a coal mine in Wallonia. The skeletons were originally reassembled in the CHAPELLE DE NASSAU before being moved to specially-built cabinets in the **Prehistoric Hall** of the museum. The total find amounted to nine near-perfect dinosaur skeletons and 20 incomplete ones. The Belgian paleontologist Louis Dollo labored for several years to fit the pieces together, and eventually decided that the 29 dinosaurs had perished simultaneously in a bog during the Jurassic Age. The cause of the disaster remains a mystery.

The prehistoric collection includes a perfectly-preserved skeleton of a Neanderthal man, found near the Wallonian village of Spy. The **Man of Spy** is displayed in a reconstructed 19thC archeologist's study, furnished with chests crammed with neatly-labeled bones.

Be sure to delve into the mock cave labeled **Paleolithic Bestiarium**, just off the prehistoric hall. The fiberglass walls are daubed with replicas of cave paintings from Lascaux and other grottos in Europe.

Other rooms in the museum have been recently revamped after years of neglect. A collection of some 5,000 butterflies and beetles occupies the renovated insect hall. Another modern room contains exotic shells artfully lit by pinpoint lamps.

Children particularly enjoy the **Whale Hall** on the upper floor. Several immense rib cages are eerily lit by blue spotlamps to evoke the underwater world of the whales. You can go into a replica bathyscaphe which simulates a deep-sea dive, or stand on a mock ship's bridge to gaze down on the whales.

MUSÉE INSTRUMENTAL (Museum of Musical Instruments) 🏛
Rue Montagne de la Cour. Map 6F4. Contact tourist office (page 59) to confirm that the museum is open ⇐ *Tram 92, 93, 94 to place Royale.*
One of the world's foremost collections of old musical instruments was established in Brussels in the 19thC. The collection languished for many years in an old building on the Sablon, until the city finally resolved to create a spectacular new museum in an abandoned Art Nouveau department store located off place Royale. The new museum is scheduled to open in 1993.

The collection of some 6,000 instruments includes violins, pianos and bagpipes. The majority of the exhibits are European, but some were brought from the former Belgian Congo (now Zaire), while a set of 97 Hindu instruments was presented to King Leopold II by an Indian prince.

The new museum occupies the Old England department store built in 1899 by Paul Saintenoy, and an adjoining 18thC town house on place Royale, designed by Guimard. The flamboyant wrought-iron decoration of the department store has been fastidiously restored, and the roof terrace overlooking the Lower Town has been reopened.

Look out for posters advertising concerts in the museum and children's workshops in the *atelier pour enfants*.

MUSÉE DU JOUET (Toy Museum)
Every conceivable kind of old toy. See BRUSSELS FOR CHILDREN, page 206.

MUSÉE CONSTANTIN MEUNIER
Rue de l'Abbaye 59 ☎*(02)513.96.30. Map 1C3* 📷 *Open Tues-Sun 10am-noon, 1-5pm. Ring bell. Tram 93, 94 to Abbaye.*
The Constantin Meunier Museum occupies the solid bourgeois home of Belgium's greatest 19thC sculptor. Originally a painter, Meunier later turned to producing sculpture in a grimly realistic style. His monumental bronze figures of reapers and stevedores stand somewhat menacingly in the large former studio at the back of the house. Other rooms contain sketches of London railway bridges and tobacco workers in Seville.

MUSÉE DES POSTES ET TÉLÉCOMMUNICATIONS
Place du Grand Sablon 40 ☎*(02)511.77.40. Map 5F3* 📷 *Open Tues-Sat 10am-4pm, Sun 10am-12.30pm. Tram 92, 93, 94 to Petit Sablon.*
The museum of post and telecommunications occupies the upper floors of a handsome old building on the Sablon. Visitors are few, apart from the occasional philatelist poring over the enormous collection of rare postage stamps.

Other rooms have old mailboxes and Belgian postmen's uniforms, while the top floor has an interesting collection of hand-cranked phones and telex machines.

Turn right on leaving the museum and walk up the hill to see, on the far side of the rue de la Régence, a bronze plaque marking the site of the Palais of the Tour et Tassis family, which organized Europe's first postal service in the 16thC.

MUSÉES ROYAUX D'ART ET D'HISTOIRE (Royal Museums of Art and History) ★

Av. J.F. Kennedy, Parc du Cinquantenaire ☎*(02)741.72.11* ☷ *Open Tues-Fri 9.30am-4.50pm; Sat, Sun 10am-4.50pm* 🚗 💂 *Metro to Mérode.*

The vast museum of art and history in the Parc du Cinquantenaire is packed with a diverse collection of archeological finds, mosaics, sculpture, tapestry, glass and porcelain. The collection is largely composed of Belgian antiquities, but there are sizeable sections devoted to Egypt, the Classical world, the Middle East, the Orient and the Americas.

The works were originally displayed in a vast iron-and-glass hall built in 1880. Gutted by fire in 1946, the museum was rebuilt in a sober Art Deco style. Formerly an echoing and forbidding institution that most Belgians avoided, the museum has been given a radical face-lift, making it more visitor-friendly. The rooms are now teeming with Belgian schoolchildren during the week, although the atmosphere remains studious on weekends. You may find that certain departments have moved, but the attendants will put you on the right track.

The museum runs a lively program of lectures and guided tours in French, Dutch or English. Details are listed in the museum's newsletter *Per Musea,* which is available at the information desk.

Orientation

A museum on this scale must be taken in easy stages. Concentrate on a single department if you have only a little time to spare, and be sure not to miss the collection of decorative arts in the cloisters.

The museum bookstore sells an enticing glossy catalogue in English. For an unusual souvenir, investigate the **Atelier de Moulage** *(open Mon-Fri 9am-noon, 1.30pm-4pm* ☷*)*. Situated behind AUTOWORLD (see plan on page 97), the plaster cast workshop sells models of Roman busts and Egyptian deities.

The museum restaurant looks basic, but you may be tempted by the dish of the day chalked up at the entrance. There are plenty of restaurants nearby on avenue de Tervuren. For a plain Belgian lunch in a handsome old interior, try **La Terrasse** *(av. de Tervuren 11).*

Egypt

Begin a tour in the Egyptian Rooms on the second floor. Look out for a relief depicting Queen Tiy in the New Kingdom room (**rm 4**). Several ship models date from the Middle Kingdom, but the most remarkable relic is the reconstructed **Mastaba of Neferirtenef**, a tomb from Sakkara presented to Belgium in 1905. Go inside to see reliefs depicting scenes of everyday life in about 2400BC. A rather somber room (**rm 5**) contains a remarkable collection of funeral relics, including the **Sarcophagus of Chonsoetefnacht** from the 4thC BC. Go into the adjoining room to peer into a curious reconstruction of the **Tomb of Nakht**, built for a gardener at the Temple of Amon in the 18th Dynasty. The replica hieroglyphics were painted on linen in 1928.

Don't miss the room near the main staircase which has old wooden cabinets filled with samples of marble quarried during the Roman Empire.

Before going down the stairs to the first floor, look over the balcony for a close-up view of the masks on the architrave of the Portico of Apamea.

Rome and Greece

The first floor is divided into Greek and Roman antiquities. Go first into the **Classical Greek** rooms (**rm 9-13**) to look at the black-figure and red-figure vases. Pause in the room of Greek sculpture (**rm 11**) to admire the idealized human figures, now missing legs, heads and arms. A curious collection of bronze mirrors decorated with mythological scenes is found in the **Etruscan room** (**rm 13**). A small room nearby with Greek satyrs and other figures is dedicated to Jean de Mot, a conservator at the museum killed at Passchendaele a few weeks before the end of World War I.

The giant Corinthian columns of the **Great Colonnade of Apamea** on one side of the hall (**rm 12**) once stood on the principal street of Apamea, the capital of Roman Syria. Wander through the gallery behind the columns to see fragments of **mosaics from the Great Colonnade**. They are decorated with various animals, including a lion attacking a wild boar. Also from Apamea, the abstract mosaics on the wall opposite the colonnade were found in the Synagogue.

Now look over the balcony to see the impressive **Hunting Mosaic of Apamea** on the first floor. The mosaic, depicting a hunt with lions and Romans on horseback, was unearthed by Belgian archeologists in the 1930s. Created in the 5thC, it once decorated the governor's residence in Apamea.

Wander amid the Roman heads, some broken, some intact, that stand on pedestals in the adjoining room (**rm 15**). Look out for the **fresco** from Boscoreale, near Pompeii, which is skillfully painted to suggest real marble and three-dimensional architecture.

Go down one flight of stairs to look more closely at the hunting scene. Examine the medical equipment and glass in the display cabinets, then enter the darkened room nearby to peer over the balcony. You will see a detailed **scale model of Rome** in the room below. The work of a Belgian architect, it shows the heart of the 4thC BC city. The best time to be there is when the taped commentary is being run, and buildings such as the Colosseum and Trajan's column are picked out by spotlights.

Islam and Byzantium

Go through to the **Islamic Room**, which is filled with dark carpets and ornate porcelain. Enter the round hall beyond to look at glinting Byzantine icons and Armenian ceramics. Admire the glazed dome, then go up to the first floor to find a curious collection of antique movie cameras.

European Decorative Arts

The rooms that remain to explore are mainly devoted to Belgian decorative arts. From the Byzantine room, go down the corridor, glancing into the side rooms containing Belgian silverware. You enter a mock **Renaissance hall** containing medieval brass memorials and old iron signs. Locate the **Salle Mosane** in the corner of the hall. This secure little room contains treasures of medieval Mosan art, such as the reliquary of Pope Alexander and the tiny portable altar of Stavelot. The exquisite craftsmanship from the Meuse valley prefigured medieval Flemish art.

The adjoining room displays precision instruments including two huge 17thC wooden globes by Vincentius Coronelli representing the earth and sky.

Now cross the hall and enter the vaulted **Cloisters** opposite. This mock Late Gothic building contains exceptional works of **European decorative art** in four separate wings.

The vaulted w cloister (parallel to the large hall known as the Great Narthex) contains medieval tombs, fonts and fragments of stained glass from Brussels Cathedral.

Back in the great hall, a left turn gets you to the s cloister. Glance in the **Ypres Room (rm 17)**, furnished in 15thC style, like a Master of Flémalle interior, with a large fireplace, old chests and a 15thC Tournai tapestry depicting sheep-shearing.

Elaborate **retables** were carved in Brussels, Antwerp and Mechelen to stand in local churches behind the altar. Too unwieldy to be shipped abroad, they have mostly remained in Belgium. The Art and History Museum has an unrivaled collection of these works, which combined the medieval skills of woodcarving, gilding and painting. The **Passion Retable of Claudio Villa and Gentina Solaro** was assembled in Brussels in about 1470. The carved figures represent episodes from the New Testament. Picture the flickering candlelight that once glinted on the gilt decoration (most of which has flaked off). The two kneeling figures in the foreground — the man clad in armor and the woman in a red brocade dress — represent the donors.

Seven grisly martyrdom scenes decorate the **St George's Retable**, constructed in Brussels in 1493 by the sculptor Jan Borreman. The long wooden structure originally stood behind the altar in a Leuven church. Retable design became increasingly elaborate in 16thC Antwerp. For proof, look at the **Maria Retable of Pailhe** carved in about 1510-25. Exotic costumes and foreign faces reflect the cosmopolitan spirit of Renaissance Antwerp.

For dazzling craftsmanship, marvel at the **Passion Retable of Oplinter**, carved in Antwerp in about 1530. Though the figures are dressed in Renaissance fashions, the work is steeped in medievalism. The frame is like a Gothic cathedral in miniature, and all the poses are inherited from the Flemish Primitives. The full force of the Renaissance can be seen in the **Judgment of Solomon Retable**, carved in Mechelen in the late 16thC.

The secrets of the Flemish retable workshops are revealed in a side room (**rm 33**). A replica workshop shows three waxwork figures working on different tasks. The construction of a large retable required the carving and gilding of hundreds of human figures and architectural details. You can perhaps best appreciate the enormous labor involved by studying the fragments of dismantled retables in the collection.

Turning into the E cloister, you enter a room hung with three huge Brussels tapestries. In the 16thC, European nobles were prepared to pay enormous sums for tapestries marked with the letters "BB," symbolizing Brussels, Brabant. One such order was placed by Ferrante Gonzaga, Duke of Guastalla, for a series of eight tapestries. The tapestries were woven in Jean Baudouyn's workshop in 1546-7. As Charles V's supreme military leader, Gonzaga chose the bellicose theme of *The Fruits of War*, based on paintings by an Italian Renaissance artist. All but one of the works have been lost or damaged. You see here the sole survivor, depicting *The Triumphal Procession of the General*. The art of tapestry weaving is explained in a side room containing an old loom (**rm 31**).

The romantically-inclined refer to the wooden cradle in the E cloister as **Charles V's cradle**. It is decorated with the coats-of-arms of Charles's parents, the Emperor Maximilian and Mary of Burgundy. By the time it rocked Charles V to sleep, the cradle had probably already been used for his elder siblings Philip and Margaret.

A Renaissance door leads into a room with a miscellany of furnishings, including a grand wooden staircase rescued from a demolished house in Brussels, and a majolica-tiled floor from an Italian family chapel.

Before leaving the museum, search for the **Carriage Museum**, which contains elegant 18thC and 19thC coaches and harnesses.

MUSÉES ROYAUX DES BEAUX-ARTS (Royal Fine Arts Museums) ★
Rue de la Régence 3. Map 6F4 ⬛ *Tram 92, 93, 94 to place Royale.*
One of the great picture galleries of the world, the Musées Royaux des Beaux-Arts combines the MUSÉE D'ART ANCIEN and the MUSÉE D'ART MODERNE. The two buildings are linked by an escalator. The museum organizes a busy program of lectures, poetry readings, lunchtime concerts and workshops. The dates are listed in a quarterly bulletin.

MUSÉE DU TRANSPORT URBAIN BRUXELLOIS (Brussels Public Transport Museum)
Av. de Tervuren 364b ☎*(02)515.31.08. Map 2C4* ⬛ *Open first Sat in Apr to first Sun in Oct, Sat, Sun, hols only 1.30-7pm* ⬛ ⬛ *Tram 39, 44 to Woluwé Dépôt.*
A disused 19thC depot houses a collection of antiquated Brussels trams and buses. One of the old trams rumbles out to Tervuren on summer weekends.

MUSÉE WIERTZ
Rue Vautier 62 ☎*(02)648.17.18. Map 1C3* ⬛ *Open Tues-Sun 10am-noon, 1-5pm. Sometimes closed on weekends; call ahead. Metro to Maelbeek.*
A secret museum near the Parc Leopold contains an extraordinary collection of 19thC paintings. Tucked away behind an old iron gate, the Musée Wiertz attracts just a trickle of offbeat tourists and art-lovers, but it is well worth a glance as an eccentric relic.

The museum occupies the home and studio of the Belgian Romantic painter Antoine Wiertz (1806-65). His early works, which hang in three small rooms, include glowing Italian landscapes and curious erotic portraits. But Wiertz was no ordinary northern Romantic; he saw himself as a worthy successor to Rubens or Michelangelo and, to prove the point, he toiled away in an abandoned factory on colossal canvases depicting violent mythological scenes. The Belgian government of the day was so impressed that it agreed in 1850 to build Wiertz an enormous atelier. In return, the artist bequeathed all his paintings to the state, on the condition that they remained attached to the walls for ever.

The state has kept its side of the bargain and the paintings have been gathering dust for more than a century. You will see scenes as gruesome as any horror movie, such as *Polyphemus Devouring the Companions of Ulysses,* and *The Suicide,* in which a man blows out his brains. A painting called *Buried Alive* shows the sheer terror of a man trapped in a coffin, while another work depicts a hungry mother driven to eating her child. The flesh and violence is rather overloaded, but it is enjoyable to wander in the restored atelier with its elegant 19thC brass railings.

PAVILLON CHINOIS

Av. Van Praet 44 ☎*(02)268.16.08* ☷ *Open Tues-Sun 9.30-noon, 1.30-4.50pm. Scheduled to reopen in 1993. Tram 92 to Araucaria.*

An exquisite Chinese pavilion stands in the park opposite the TOUR JAPONAISE. Bought by Leopold II at the 1900 Paris Exhibition, the pavilion is furnished in a glittering Rococo style. Over the years the building became dilapidated, and was eventually closed for restoration. Once the pavilion reopens (scheduled for 1993), its collection of Chinese porcelain can be enjoyed in the most sumptuous of settings.

On leaving the pavilion, turn right to look at a **replica of the Neptune Fountain** in Bologna, commissioned by Leopold II as part of a unfinished plan to create an avenue lined with great world architecture.

PORTE DE HAL

The 14thC city gate with its 19thC turrets and round tower has now been restored as a museum of Belgian folklore. See LANDMARK BUILDINGS on page 125.

SEWERS MUSEUM

See MUSÉE DES ÉGOUTS.

TOUR JAPONAISE (Japanese Pagoda)

Av. Van Praet ☎*(02)268.16.08. Map 1B3* ☷ *Open Tues-Sun 10am-4.45pm. Tram 92 to Araucaria.*

The Japanese Pagoda is perhaps the most eccentric of Leopold II's gifts to Brussels. The idea of building a replica pagoda next to the royal palace in Laeken came to the elderly Belgian monarch on a visit in 1900 to the Paris Universal Exhibition. Leopold had been particularly impressed in Paris by an exhibition incorporating a jumble of exotic buildings from every continent. The architect king began to plan the creation of an avenue lined with faithful copies of exotic buildings. Funds ran out when the folly was far from complete, and three isolated buildings in a maul of traffic are all that survive.

Perched on a rocky summit, the five-floor Japanese Pagoda is roughly modeled on traditional Buddhist architecture. The tower was built specially for Leopold, but the entrance pavilion was shipped back from Paris after the exhibition.

Leopold gifted the pagoda to the nation, but it was a difficult building to run, and the museum in charge kept it closed for almost half a century. The pagoda was recently renovated to house a collection of Japanese porcelain. A new entrance lodge in Japanese style was built in a leafy hollow in the park opposite. This leads to a tunnel under the main road, which emerges in a tiny Japanese garden with trickling fountains and fish ponds.

The shadowy interior is richly decorated with carved wood, red lacquer and gilded details. Wooden cabinets contain a few spotlit examples of wafer-thin Imari porcelain.

A broad ceremonial staircase lit by clusters of iron lamps leads to the base of the tower. Notice the stained glass windows decorated by Jacques Galland with scenes inspired by Japanese legends. Visitors may be frustrated to arrive at the top of the stairs and find the doors to the tower locked, yet the building is still worth a visit.

Landmark buildings

Isolated buildings in Brussels are often strikingly original, although the overall urban planning leaves much to be desired. The Baroque architecture of GRAND'PLACE (page 131) is gloriously excessive, whereas the 18thC squares such as PLACE DES MARTYRS (page 136) attain a quiet dignity.

The grand projects of Leopold II created several monstrous edifices that sometimes sit awkwardly amid the older buildings. The PALAIS DE JUSTICE looms menacingly over the MAROLLES quarter, while the sprawling museum complex in the PARC DU CINQUANTENAIRE provides a rather intimidating setting for medieval works of art.

Brussels is famous above all for its outstanding Art Nouveau architecture. The city is dotted with enticing buildings by Victor Horta and his contemporaries. Some are private dwellings, but you can get inside the MUSÉE HORTA, the CENTRE BELGE DE LA BANDE DESSINÉE and the ESPACE PHOTOGRAPHIQUE CONTRETYPE. Follow WALK 3 (page 84) to discover the Art Nouveau architecture of Ixelles.

More recent architecture in Brussels is rarely inspiring, but it is instructive to stroll amid the curious buildings designed in the 1970s by Lucien Krol at the Brussels campus of the Université Catholique du Louvain-la-Neuve *(metro to Alma)*.

Take an **Arau** tour (see USEFUL ADDRESSES on page 60) for the chance to see the city's architecture as its inhabitants do. You should look out also for stimulating exhibitions at the FONDATION POUR L'ARCHITECTURE (page 97).

Apart from the many historic buildings ranging from museums to shops and restaurants that are open to the public, there is also one prime opportunity to look inside private castles, artists' studios, Art Nouveau homes, theaters and even barracks. For on Heritage Day, in mid-September, historic buildings throughout Belgium open their doors to the public for just one day each year. Look out for the flag decorated with the EC ring of stars, which identifies the buildings that are open free of charge.

This section covers the following buildings:

BIBLIOTHÈQUE ROYALE	HÔTEL DE VILLE
BOURSE	PALAIS DE JUSTICE
GALERIE BORTIER	PALAIS DU ROI
GALERIES SAINT-HUBERT	PORTE DE HAL

BIBLIOTHÈQUE ROYALE (Royal Library)

Dating back to the 15thC, this is now part of the MONT DES ARTS complex. It contains the 16thC Brabant Gothic CHAPELLE DE NASSAU, the **Musée de l'Imprimerie** and the **Archives Générales du Royaume.** See OFF THE BEATEN TRACK, page 139.

BOURSE (Stock Exchange) 🏛

Boulevard Anspach. Map 3D3. Not open to the public. Tram 52, 55, 58, 81 to Bourse.

The Brussels **stock exchange**, designed by Léon-Pierre Suys in a heavy Neo-Renaissance style.

The Brussels stock exchange was erected in 1871-73 in an ornate Classical style. The exterior is laden with symbolic sculpture representing subjects dear to a stockbroker's heart, such as commerce, industry and work. The frieze running along the south facade *(facing rue Henri Maus)* includes figures carved by the young Rodin during his stay in Brussels.

The Bourse is overlooked by teeming cafés, such as LE FALSTAFF and LE CIRIO (see CAFÉS, page 177).

GALERIE BORTIER

Entrances on rue St-Jean and rue de la Madeleine. Map 4E4 🚇 *Metro to Gare Centrale.*

A seductive arcade lined with wood-paneled shops curves around the back of a former market near Grand'Place. Built by Cluysenaar soon after his GALERIES SAINT-HUBERT, the Galerie Bortier was a far less successful venture. Its cramped shops are now occupied by antiquarian booksellers and dealers in prints, and these lend the place the musty atmosphere of a private club. You go there to admire the glass roof, or to browse in the racks of mainly French fiction. Sadly, there is no café where you can bask in Bortier's somehow sad brownish light.

GALERIES SAINT-HUBERT ★ 🏛

Entrances on rue du Marché aux Herbes, rue de la Montagne aux Herbes Potagères and rue des Dominicains. Map **4**E4-D4 *Open at all times. Metro to Gare Centrale.*

Elegant female statues and polished marble pilasters lend an air of *outré* elegance to the Galeries Saint-Hubert. Situated off Grand'Place, the three connected galleries were built by Jean-Pierre Cluysenaar in 1847. They were the first grand galleries to be built in Europe, rising through three floors to a roof of iron and glass. The sensational style was later copied in Milan by the architect of the Galleria Vittorio Emanuele II.

A Classical entrance on rue du Marché aux Herbes is inscribed *Omnibus omnia* (everything for everyone). The long **Galerie de la Reine** runs N to rue des Bouchers. The **Galerie du Roi** continues at a slight angle from rue des Bouchers to rue de la Montagne aux Herbes Potagères. The more modest **Galerie des Princes** runs at a right angle from the Galerie du Roi to rue des Dominicains.

The architectural details have been impeccably preserved. Glance at the iron lamps and the illuminated clocks, or peer into the shop interiors to see the old wooden fittings and antique paintings. You can buy Italian gloves, Belgian chocolates or English shoes in the elegant shops. The prices are sometimes high, but you can purchase a print of Old Brussels for a few hundred francs at **Galerie Apollo** *(Galerie du Roi 25).*

A plaque on the wall *(Galerie du Roi 7)* commemorates Belgium's first movie screening in 1896. For Belgian gourmets, however, a more important event was the invention of the world's first praline chocolate at the **Neuhaus** shop *(Galerie de la Reine 25).*

Part of the success of the Galerie can be attributed to the diversity of activities under one roof. The arcades contain apartments, three restaurants, two cafés, a newsdealer's shop, two bookstores, a theater and an excellent cinema.

It is quite possible to spend an entire rainy day within the arcades. Visit **Tropismes** bookstore *(Galerie des Princes 11)* to admire the sumptuous interior. The stock is mainly French fiction and art, but a small selection of English novels occupies a corner. **Mokafé** *(Galerie du Roi 9)* is a solid café offering excellent espresso coffee and tempting cakes. Serious new films are screened in the Art Deco **Arenberg** cinemas, and you can eat Belgian brasserie food at the Taverne du Passage *(Galerie de la Reine 30).*

The atmosphere is especially strange after dark, when the lamps are lit and the roof becomes virtually invisible. Stroll through at night to listen to a quartet busking, or squeeze into Mokafé for a *digestif.*

HÔTEL DE VILLE (Town Hall) ★ 🏛

Grand'Place ☎*(02)512.75.54. Map 3E3* 📧 ✗ *compulsory (in French, Dutch, English or German): depart from the desk at the visitors' entrance, reached through the courtyard. The 30min tours begin at unpredictable times, Tues-Fri 9.30am-12.15pm, 1.45-4pm; Sun, hols 10am-noon, 2-4pm. Go to the information desk at the visitors' entrance to find out the approximate departure times for tours in different languages. Tram 52, 55, 58, 81 to Bourse.*

The Brussels town hall is an exquisite memento of the florid Flemish Gothic style of the 15thC, laden with tiers of statues ranging from bearded knights in chain mail to drunken customers in bawdy taverns. Begun in 1402, the building was gutted by fire during the bombardment in 1695. The wing on Grand'Place was faithfully reconstructed in Gothic style, while the rear wing was rebuilt in Louis XIV style. Now one of 19 town halls in Brussels, the Gothic building provides a spectacular setting for local council meetings and marriages of couples fortunate enough to live in postal district 1000.

The traveler with time to spare should look closely at the sculptures, which cover virtually every available surface. Most are 19thC works representing local rulers, artists and Biblical figures, but a few are quirky scenes cut by medieval masons to illustrate a local joke.

The oldest part of the building is the **left wing**. An early example of Brabant Gothic, it was designed, the experts believe, by Jacob Van Thienen and Jan Bornoy. The vaulted rooms off the arcade known as the **Salle Ogivale** *(open Mon-Sat 11am-6pm, Sun 10am-1pm)* are used for occasional exhibitions of paintings and crafts.

The old wing was largely copied by the unknown architect who added the **right wing** in the 1440s. A local police station and a cramped tourist office now occupy part of the wing. Ignore the traffic policemen in windproof leather jackets, and look in the arcade for the bizarre capital showing a scene with men shoveling chairs. The reason for this puzzling motif is that there was once a building here called *De Scupstoel*—literally the "shovel chair."

When not wrapped in scaffolding, the slender white **spire** of the town hall makes a deep impression, especially when you glimpse it down rue Chair et Pain, a narrow medieval lane. Victor Hugo, who rented a hotel room opposite the town hall in 1837, praised it as "a jewel comparable to the spire of Chartres." The spire was built by Jan Van Ruysbroeck in 1449-54, and is topped by a copper weather vane by Martin Van Rode showing St Michael slaying the dragon. It was once possible to climb to the top, but the tower has been closed for many years.

Go through the arch under the tower to reach the **courtyard**. When not jammed with official cars, this is a seductive spot at the heart of the city, with splashing fountains and the scent of spring blossom. The two 18thC fountains on the rear wing are decorated with muscular gods representing the Scheldt and the Meuse, the two great rivers of Belgium.

✗ You will have to join a guided tour to get inside the building. While you wait, read the faded notices from 1914, in which Burgomaster Adolphe Max urged the citizens of Brussels to resist the German army. Official guides rush tourists rather brusquely through the building, leaving you with little time to enjoy the grand Baroque ceilings and faded Brussels tapestries. The **Salle du Conseil Communal** is the glittering 17thC setting for bilingual meetings of the local council. The **Salle d'Attente** is hung with nostalgic paintings of the river Senne before it was put underground, while the **Salle des Marriages** is decorated with mock Gothic wood paneling to provide a suitable background for a Belgian wedding.

PALAIS DE JUSTICE (Law Courts) 🏛

Place Poelaert. Map 5G3 📷 *Open Mon-Fri 9am-6pm. Metro or tram 91, 92, 93, 94 to Louise.*

The Brussels court of justice was designed by Joseph Poelaert in an overblown Neoclassical style. Sited on a summit where the gallows once stood, the Palais de Justice was intended to intimidate the unruly inhabitants of the Marolles district below.

Seventeen years in the making, the monstrous building was the greatest 19thC construction project on mainland Europe. The awesome Palais de Justice is larger than St Peter's in Rome, with a warren of 245 dingy offices and 27 court rooms. Poelaert died before the building was completed, apparently a broken man. On weekdays, you can wander into the vast *Salle des pas perdus,* the waiting hall where lawyers huddle in conversation with their clients, to experience the sheer despotic terror of the architecture.

PALAIS DU ROI

Place des Palais. Map 6F5 📷 *Tram 92, 93, 94 to place Royale.*

Facing the PARC DE BRUXELLES, the royal palace was built by Leopold II in 1905. The architect Henri Maquet created a building in ponderous Louis XIV Baroque style, entirely ignoring the audacious Art Nouveau movement that was then flourishing in Brussels.

The palace is briefly open for a few weeks every year, when long lines of people wait to file through the stately rooms. The most spectacular rooms are the **Throne Room** built by Alphonse Balat, with glittering mirrors and columns decorated with gold-leaf, and the **Hall of Mirrors** by Maquet, inspired by Versailles. Sadly, the palace contains few personal mementoes of the royal family — you must go to the MUSÉE DE LA DYNASTIE for photographs and other relics.

PALAIS STOCLET

Avenue de Tervuren 281. Map 2C4. Not open to the public. Tram 33 or 44 to Père Damien.

One of the pioneering buildings of the Modern Movement, the Palais Stoclet was designed in 1905 by the Viennese architect Josef Hoffman (1870-1956) for the Belgian industrialist Mons Stoclet. The sober geometric style of the Palais Stoclet stands in stark contrast to the curled ironwork of Belgian Art Nouveau houses erected at the same time.

The Palais Stoclet is modeled on the strict principles of the Wiener Werkstätte, a movement founded in 1903 by Josef Hoffman and Koloman

Moser. The interior is furnished with murals by Gustav Klimt, but no one, except for the occasional art historian, is ever admitted to the house. Most people must be content with a glimpse of the marble exterior, the heroic male statue on the roof and the clipped trees.

PORTE DE HAL

Boulevard du Midi
☎ *(02)534.25.52. Map* **5***H2*
▨ *Open Tues-Sun 10am-5pm.*
Metro or tram 18 to Porte de Hal.

The only relic to have survived from the second city wall is the Porte de Hal. The 14thC brick hulk was saved when the city wall was knocked down in the 18thC simply because it was in use as a prison. The grim city gate was transformed into a fanciful turreted castle by a 19thC architect. For a true impression of the building, you must ignore the half-round tower, the battlements and the pointed turrets with their wrought iron flourishes. The city gate was recently restored as a museum of Belgian folklore.

Ecclesiastical buildings

The old Catholic churches of Brussels often feature dark and mysterious interiors, filled with faded Baroque paintings and flickering red candles. Many are flamboyant Brabant Gothic churches built of a soft white sandstone, such as the CATHÉDRALE SAINT-MICHEL and ÉGLISE NOTRE-DAME DU SABLON. The suburbs are dotted with ancient abbeys that once stood in the countryside, including the ABBAYE DE LA CAMBRE and the ABBAYE DU ROUGE-CLOÎTRE. Several ancient churches survive in the suburbs, including the **Chapelle de Marie la Misérable** in Woluwé Saint-Pierre, named after a local girl who refused to be seduced by a nobleman, and was buried alive after he falsely accused her of theft.

Many churches of Brussels have been spared from demolition by ingenious schemes. The CHAPELLE DE NASSAU is now part of a library, while the **Chapelle de la Madeleine** (see CURIOSITIES, page 91) was carefully rebuilt in a new location during the construction of Gare Centrale. A synagogue stands on rue de la Régence, but perhaps the most curious church is the **Église Orthodox Russe** *(av. De Fré),* which was modeled on a church near Moscow.

The following ecclesiastical buildings are described in alphabetical order in this section:

ABBAYE DE LA CAMBRE
ABBAYE DU ROUGE-CLOÎTRE
BASILIQUE DU SACRÉ-COEUR
CATHÉDRALE SAINT-MICHEL
CHAPELLE DE NASSAU
ÉGLISE NOTRE-DAME DE FINISTÈRE

ÉGLISE NOTRE-DAME DE LA
  CHAPELLE
ÉGLISE NOTRE-DAME DU
  SABLON
ÉGLISE SAINT-DENIS
ÉGLISE SAINT-NICOLAS

ABBAYE DE LA CAMBRE

Entrances at square de la Croix-Rouge, av. Emile De Mot and av. Duray. Off map **6**I5. *Abbey church open Mon-Fri 9am-noon, 3-6pm, Sat 3-6pm, Sun 9am-12.30pm; abbey gardens open at all times* ▣ *Tram 23, 90, 93, 94 to Étoile, then walk down av. de la Folle Chanson.*

Tucked away in a wooded hollow near the Bois, the Abbaye de la Cambre is an unexpected relic of the Middle Ages. Hemmed in by heavy traffic and glass skyscrapers, the abbey grounds have lost their original tranquility, although they remain a pleasant spot in which to stroll or sit.

The abbey was founded in 1201 in the wooded Maelbeek valley. The buildings were badly damaged in the 16thC, and later rebuilt in Baroque style. Dissolved in 1796 by the French Revolutionaries, the abbey fell into ruins. The Late Gothic church has been restored and the 14thC cloister remains intact. Some of the former abbey buildings are now occupied by the Belgian cartographic institute.

The formal gardens rising to the s of the abbey were laid out in the 1720s. The three terraces linked by monumental Baroque stairways were fastidiously restored by Jules Buyssens in the 1930s, using old engravings of the site. Now planted with yew topiary and boxwood, they provide a retreat from the din of traffic on avenue Louise.

ABBAYE DU ROUGE-CLOÎTRE

Rue du Rouge-Cloître 4 ☎*(02)660.55.97. Map* **2**D4 ▰ ▰ *Metro to Herrmann-Debroux, then walk along av. Herrmann-Debroux, cross chaussée de Wavre, and turn left and first right down drève du Rouge-Cloître; or tram 44 to Auderghem Forêt, then a 10min walk through the woods down the sentier des Ronces.*

A cobbled lane on the w edge of the city leads to a secluded abbey built by Augustinian monks in the 14thC. It was named the Red Monastery because the walls were once decorated with a reddish tint.

Afflicted by a nervous breakdown, the Flemish painter Hugo van der Goes lived out the last years of his life as a lay brother at Rouge-Cloître. Famous for his religious paintings, he was visited at the abbey by the Emperor Maximilian of Austria. Tormented by a sense of failure, Van der Goes attempted suicide in 1480 and died the following year.

In the 16thC, the abbey was a favorite pilgrimage spot of Charles V and his son Philip II. Like most Belgian abbeys, it was closed down by the French Revolutionaries. Many of the old buildings were torn down, and all that now remains are the priory, chapter house, guest quarters, farm and mill.

The farm buildings are now used by local art groups for painting and craft classes. The guest house has been turned into a smart restaurant, and in the summer, metal tables are spread out on the lawn, where you can order a sandwich and a beer, or tuck into a slice of fruit tart.

The abbey makes a good starting point for rambles in the FORÊT DE SOIGNES (see pages 87-8 and 145). Simply follow the Chemin des Étangs along the edge of the fish ponds. Formerly a source of fish for the abbey, the ponds are still teeming with overfed carp.

BASILIQUE DU SACRÉ-COEUR

Place de la Basilique. Map 1B2. Open Easter-Oct 8am-7pm; Nov-Easter 8am-5pm. Tram 19 to Bossaert.

The Basilique began as one of Leopold II's pet projects to celebrate the 50th anniversary of Belgian independence. The project was shelved due to lack of funds, but Leopold raised the idea again for the 75th anniversary celebrations in 1905. Work began on a Neo-Gothic church, but it was halted by the outbreak of war. The basilica was finally completed in 1930 as a memorial to the dead of World War I. The vast interior is built in a rather chilling Art Deco style.

CATHÉDRALE SAINT-MICHEL ★ 🏛

Parvis Sainte-Gudule ☎*(02)217.83.45. Map 4D4* 📷 *Open 7am-6pm. Tram 92, 93, 94 or metro to Parc.*

With its splendid twin towers and soaring interior, Brussels Cathedral is one of the triumphs of Brabant Gothic architecture. It stands rather awkwardly on the slopes above the Lower Town, surrounded nowadays by 19thC and 20thC office buildings. The best view is from the top of rue d'Arenberg.

Modeled on the Gothic cathedrals of northern France, the cathedral was begun in 1226 under Duke Henry I of Brabant. The intricate Late Gothic craftsmanship dates from the 15thC, when architects such as Jacob van Thienen and Jan van Ruysbroeck were in charge of the project. The N tower was completed in 1451 and its counterpart to the S in 1475-80. The 15thC church became a favorite subject for Flemish painters, including the anonymous artist known as the Master of Sainte-Gudule, whose works can be seen in the MUSÉE D'ART ANCIEN.

The Gothic building replaced an older 11thC Romanesque church, whose foundations were recently excavated. Masonry and even human bones can be seen partly exposed through glass panels set in the floor of the church. The crypt, which is rarely open, contains extensive Romanesque foundations.

Originally named after St-Michel, the patron saint of Brussels, the church later became the Église St-Michel et Ste-Gudule after the relics of a local saint were moved there. Gudule, a local girl, was witness to a modest miracle one night when her candle blew out, but miraculously relit in answer to her prayers. The name Gudule was dropped when the church became a cathedral in 1961, but she still lends her name to streets and squares nearby, such as the parvis Ste-Gudule in front of the cathedral.

The Dukes of Brabant and the painter Roger van der Weyden are among the famous figures buried in the church.

CHAPELLE DE NASSAU

*Bibliothèque Royale Albert I, Mont des Arts. Map **4**E4-F4. Enter the library, go up the stairs and turn left to reach the chapel. Open during temporary exhibitions only, Mon-Sat noon-4.50pm* ▣ *Tram 92, 93, 94 to place Royale; metro to Gare Centrale.*

Incorporated into the National Library in the 1950s, the Nassau Chapel is a little-known relic of 15thC Burgundian Brussels. The exterior wall of honey-colored sandstone can be seen in the arcade in front of the library. A modern relief nearby shows the original Nassau palace, built for Engelbert II of Nassau, the powerful governor-general of the Low Countries under Philip the Fair. William of Orange occupied the palace in the 16thC, but fled to Holland to escape the fate of the counts of Egmont and Hoorn, who were executed on Grand'Place for their opposition to Philip II.

The Austrians were to blame for the destruction of the palace in the 18thC. Charles of Lorraine bought the building in 1756 and promptly tore down everything, save the chapel. He built a grand, if rather dull, Neoclassical palace in its place.

The little chapel was used for a time as a beer warehouse, before the science museum took it over as a laboratory in the 19thC. The remarkable dinosaur skeletons found at Bernissart (see MUSÉE DE L'INSTITUT ROYAL DES SCIENCES NATURELLES, page 113) were put together in the chapel. Now part of the national library, the chapel is a graceful structure of slender stone columns and Late Gothic vaulting. The chapel forms the perfect setting for exhibitions of 15thC illuminated manuscripts.

ÉGLISE NOTRE-DAME DE FINISTÈRE

Rue Neuve ☎*(02)217.52.52. Map **4**C4* ▣ *Metro to de Brouckère.*

This 18thC Baroque church stands on a street that was *neuve* (new) back in 1617. Rue Neuve is now lined with boutiques blasting out the latest pop songs, but the church has kept its dignity. Go inside to savor the scent of candle wax and the dull gleam of the polished wood confessionals. Look for the medieval statue of Notre-Dame du Bon Succès, which was brought on a Scots ship from Aberdeen in 1625, and don't miss the remarkable Baroque altar featuring plump little cherubs struggling with ropes to hold aloft a wooden canopy.

ÉGLISE NOTRE-DAME DE LA CHAPELLE

Place de la Chapelle ☎*(02)512.03.70. Map **5**F3* ▣ *Tram 92, 93, 94 to Petit Sablon.*

The church at the bottom of the Sablon is a curious mixture of styles. Founded in 1134 on a site outside the city walls, the Église de la Chapelle has a squat, Early Gothic choir, and a noticeably taller Late Gothic nave. The w tower was destroyed in the 1695 bombardment and rebuilt in a curious Baroque style by Anthonis Pastorana, the architect of the guild house of the boatmen at Grand'Place 6.

Look out inside for the memorial to Pieter Bruegel the Elder. Bruegel married Maria Coecke, the daughter of a Flemish artist, in the Église de la Chapelle in 1563. He died only six years later, and was buried here in the church.

ÉGLISE NOTRE-DAME DU SABLON ★ 🏛

Rue de la Régence. Map 6F4 👁 *Open 9am-6pm. Tram 92, 93, 94 to Petit Sablon.*

The church on the Sablon was built in the 15th and 16thC in a harmonious Brabant Gothic style. Originally the church of the archers' guild, it was built to contain a miraculous statue of the Virgin brought by ship from Antwerp. The statue has formed the centerpiece of the annual *Ommegang* procession since the Middle Ages.

The fragile white stone of the exterior is now black with pollution and sadly dilapidated, but the interior remains spectacular, with its harmonious Gothic lines and ancient stained glass windows. A Baroque chapel was built at the E end in the 17thC by Lucas Fayd'herbe for the Tour et Tassis family, who lived nearby in a palace on the Sablon. The first international postal system was established in Brussels by François de Tassis in 1516.

ÉGLISE SAINT-DENIS

Chaussée de Bruxelles. Map 1D2 👁 *Unpredictable opening hours. Tram 18, 52 to Saint-Denis.*

This crumbling stone church stands near a huge automobile factory in Forest commune. The charm of Saint-Denis lies in its curious jumble of styles, with 12thC Romanesque combined with 13thC Brabant Gothic. If by any chance the door is unlocked, go inside to admire the bare stone walls, and the 11thC tomb of Saint-Alène located in a Romanesque chapel.

The remains of the **Abbaye de Forest** stand next to the church. The abbey was founded in the 13thC by Benedictine monks, but rebuilt in Baroque style in the 18thC.

The restored cloister buildings are now occupied by a restaurant and art gallery.

ÉGLISE SAINT-NICOLAS

Rue au Beurre 1 ☎*(02)512.29.18. Map 3D3. Open Mon-Fri 7.30am-6.30pm, Sat 9am-5.30pm, Sun 7.30am-7.30pm* 👁 *Tram 52, 55, 58, 81 to Bourse.*

Flickering red candles illuminate the shadowy interior of Saint-Nicolas, picking out the low Gothic arches and murky Baroque canvases. Situated off Grand'Place, Saint-Nicolas is one of Brussels' oldest churches. It was once the merchants' church, and is dedicated to their patron saint, Bishop Nicholas of Myra.

Saint-Nicolas was originally built in Romanesque style in the 12thC (or perhaps even the 11thC), but little remains of the old building apart from a rough fragment of wall in the porch (next to the right-hand door). The nave is 13thC, and the choir — which has a pronounced tilt to the left — was built in 1381.

Saint-Nicolas was damaged by Iconoclasts in 1579 and again by the French bombardment in 1695. It was quickly rebuilt and embellished with a lofty Baroque belfry, which toppled down in 1714. The squat building is now virtually hidden by tiny shops built up against the walls, where you can buy vegetables, Alessi coffee pots, rye bread or hot waffles.

The rather cramped interior of Saint-Nicolas is filled with a confusing clutter of old paintings and sculptures. Among the engaging curiosities, look out for the Martyrs of Gorcum reliquary, an ornate Neo-Gothic work of 1868.

Streetscapes and neighborhoods

Despite the massive upheavals of the past 30 years in Brussels, the old town retains several impressive Baroque and Neoclassical squares, including GRAND'PLACE, PLACE DES MARTYRS and PLACE ROYALE. Leopold II left his mark on the city by creating broad boulevards along which traffic now thunders, such as the ravaged AVENUE LOUISE and avenue de Tervuren (see TRAM RIDES, page 89). The traveler can still find the atmosphere of old Brussels in districts such as the MAROLLES and PLACE SAINTE-CATHERINE.

In the following pages we explore:

AVENUE LOUISE	PLACE DU GRAND
GRAND'PLACE	SABLON
ÎLOT SACRÉ	PLACE ROYALE
MAROLLES	PLACE SAINTE-CATHERINE
MONT DES ARTS	PLACE ST-GÉRY
PLACE DES MARTYRS	SQUARE MARIE-LOUISE

AVENUE LOUISE

Upper Town. Map 6G4-I5. Trams 93, 94 go down the entire length of av. Louise; trams 91, 92, 93, 94 to place Louise (for the N end of av. Louise); tram 81 to Lesbroussart (at #191); tram 23, 90 to Legrand (for the Bois de la Cambre).
Named after Leopold II's oldest daughter, avenue Louise was created in 1864 to link place Louise with the Bois de la Cambre. Planted with four rows of chestnut trees, the broad avenue became a fashionable artery to parade down in the late 19thC. Elegant Classical and Art Nouveau town houses were built, and smart cafés opened on strategic sites.

Most of the allure was lost in the 1950s, when a highway was built down the avenue to provide a fast route to the 1958 Brussels Exhibition. The construction of overscaled apartment blocks and skyscrapers has added further injury to the avenue. The best-preserved stretch of avenue Louise is now the *goulet* (bottleneck) from place Louise to place Sté-phanie. It is worth exploring the pedestrianized rue Jean Staes, off avenue Louise, recently rebuilt in 19thC style. The twin buildings on place

Stéphanie (named after another of Leopold II's daughters) are pleasing attempts at modernity, while the reconstruction of the 19thC Wiltcher's Hotel *(#71-83)* may restore some of the old grandeur to avenue Louise.

Fashion boutiques and art galleries occupy some of the surviving town houses. **Nihoul** continues to sell chocolates and cakes on the avenue *(#300),* while the **Galerie Isy Brachot** *(#62)* exhibits fashionably minimal modern sculpture.

You can walk down the length of the avenue in about 30 minutes, but the isolated mementoes of the old artery are perhaps best viewed from the window of a tram as it gently rumbles down the tree-lined tracks (see TRAM RIDES on page 88).

GRAND'PLACE ★ 🏛

Lower Town. Map 3E3. Tram 52, 55, 58, 81 to Bourse; metro to Gare Centrale.

The intimate Grand'Place is one of the most scintillating urban squares in the world. It lies slightly off the beaten track, enclosed and compact, providing an unexpected interlude in the city center. You go there to gaze at the HÔTEL DE VILLE or to visit the MUSÉE COMMUNAL. But you are also drawn to Grand'Place simply to admire the extraordinary Baroque sculpture of the guild houses, with their gilt details glinting in the sunlight as in a painting by Rembrandt.

The buildings on Grand'Place were mainly built in 1697-99, after the bombardment of the old town in 1695 by Marshal De Villeroy. The French attack reduced most of Brussels to rubble, with some 4,000 houses and 16 churches destroyed. A series of prints in the MUSÉE COMMUNAL shows the ruins of the old town in 1695.

The 17thC houses were mainly built in a rich Italian Baroque style introduced to Flanders by Pieter Paul Rubens. The palatial Roman and Genoese style had to be trimmed to fit the narrow plots on the market square, leading to an elongated style that recalls the Gothic age. Most of the buildings were the creation of the guilds, such as the brewers, bakers and butchers. Each guild aimed to outshine the others with a facade weighed down with Baroque statues representing gods, kings, slaves and cherubs.

Grand'Place is forever bustling, with children chasing pigeons across the cobblestones, and groups of dazed tourists hurrying to keep up with their guide. Flower sellers set up striped awnings on most mornings to sell geraniums or azaleas, but the most spectacular sight is the Sunday bird market, where dealers sell racing pigeons, songbirds and the occasional swan.

Even on rainswept winter days, Grand'Place has a glowing, convivial atmosphere, like the grand lobby of an old theater. The ideal place to admire this Baroque spectacle is at a window table in one of the cafés on the square, preferably in the morning when most are quiet. With their old wooden tables, blazing fires, and dusty aspidistras in gleaming brass pots, the cafés on Grand'Place reflect the comfortable, bourgeois spirit of Brussels. Go to **La Brouette** *(#3)* or **La Chaloupe d'Or** *(#24-25)* for the best coffee. Or take a window table on the mezzanine of the **Roi d'Espagne** *(#1-2)* for a captivating view of the square through small barred windows. In summer, you can join the crowds on one of the terraces.

Grand'Place has long been the setting for magnificent parades and festivities. Even today, you may come across a jazz concert or a medieval pageant. The annual *Ommegang* parade held on Grand'Place in late June-early July (see THE BRUSSELS CALENDAR, page 69) is the most spectacular of the events, featuring giants, stilt-walkers and genuine Belgian aristocrats representing their forefathers.

Almost every year, in mid-August, a huge carpet of more than half a million begonias is created in the middle of the square. The flowers from nurseries near Ghent are laid out in colorful patterns copied from old tapestries. The carpet lasts only two days, after which the blossoms fade.

Orientation

Each of the six cobbled lanes leading into Grand'Place provides a different view, but the most spectacular approach is down the quiet rue Chair et Pain. Taking this route, you will see the spire of the HÔTEL DE VILLE framed by the narrow street.

Turn left on Grand'Place to sit on the worn stone bench outside the MUSÉE COMMUNAL (see page 111). You can see most of the important buildings from here. The row of guild houses on the right *(#1-6)* are

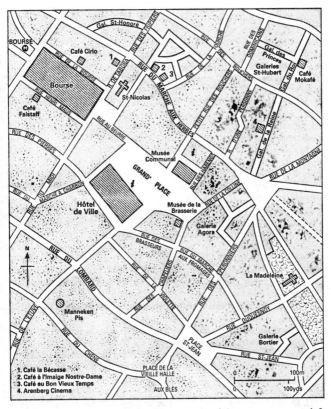

1. Café la Bécasse
2. Café à l'Imaige Nostre-Dame
3. Café au Bon Vieux Temps
4. Arenberg Cinema

architecturally the most interesting. The side of the square to your left (#13-19) appears to be occupied by a single palace, but the facade conceals six houses. The row of houses opposite, to the left of the Hôtel de Ville, includes the MUSÉE DE LA BRASSERIE (see page 110)

The guild houses
The guilds vied with one another to create the most opulent buildings, each adorned with symbolic sculpture appropriate to the trade practised. Many have names, such as "The Fox" or "The Wheelbarrow," which are usually inscribed in Dutch as this was the common language of the guilds in the 17thC. Today the guild houses are put to a variety of uses, as banks, shops, cafés and restaurants.

    Maison du Roi d'Espagne *(The King of Spain #1):* The palatial Maison du Roi d'Espagne was built by Jean Cosyns for the bakers' guild in 1697. Notice the statues on the balustrade symbolizing the six elements required to make bread — Energy, Grain, Wind, Fire, Water and

Prudence. A trumpet-blowing figure of Fame perched on top of the green dome adds further splendor to the building. Yet the most lavish decoration is the bust of King Charles II of Spain — a rather unflattering portrait — surrounded by flags, cannon and chained prisoners.

La Brouette *(The Wheelbarrow #3):* Jean Cosyns probably built the adjoining house known as La Brouette for the guild of candlemakers. The figure at the top of the gable is St Giles, patron saint of candlemakers.

Maison du Sac *(The Sack #4):* The Maison du Sac belonged to the guild of joiners. It was designed by a cabinet-maker called Antoon Pastorana, who hit on the curious idea of creating an elaborate Baroque pediment in the form of a 17thC wooden cupboard.

Maison du Louve *(The She-Wolf #5):* The Maison du Louve, which originally belonged to the guild of archers, was twice rebuilt following fires. The present building was designed in 1691 by Pieter Herbosch. The pediment is surmounted by a phoenix rising from the ashes to symbolize the reconstruction. The She-Wolf was one of the few guild houses to survive the bombardment in 1695. Look out for the relief above the door, showing Romulus and Remus being suckled by a she-wolf, and the four Baroque caryatides on the second floor representing Truth, Falsehood, Peace and Disorder.

Maison du Cornet *(The Horn #6):* The curious Maison du Cornet was designed by the cabinet-maker Anthonis Pastorana in 1697. Perhaps the most bizarre guild house on Grand'Place, it was built for the guild of boatmen, and features a pediment resembling the stern of a Spanish galleon. Notice the medallion on the stern, which features the plump Hapsburg profile of King Charles II.

Maison du Renard *(The Fox #7):* The Maison du Renard belonged to the peddlers and haberdashers. They advertised their far-flung travels with four statues of plump women, representing the continents that were known at that time. America is symbolized by a woman clutching gold ingots, recalling the vast riches shipped to Antwerp from the New World by the Spanish.

L'Étoile *(The Star #8):* The house to the left of the Hôtel de Ville is called L'Étoile. The entire building was demolished in the 19thC to widen the crowded street leading to the MANNEKEN PIS, but Burgomaster Charles Buls insisted that it had to be rebuilt. The open arcade, which replaces the original ground floor of the house, was a neat solution to the problem of crowds. An Art Nouveau plaque was placed in the arcade in 1899, in commemoration of Buls.

Maison du Cygne *(The Swan #9):* The Maison du Cygne was originally a private house, but the butchers' guild bought it in 1720 and added a bulbous Baroque roof. The building later contained a café frequented by Karl Marx during his exile in Brussels. The Belgian Workers' Party was founded here in 1885, but the Maison du Cygne has now abandoned its working-class roots to become one of the city's most luxurious restaurants (see RESTAURANTS A TO Z).

Maison des Brasseurs *(Brewers' House #10):* The handsome Maison des Brasseurs was built in Classical style by G. De Bruyn. The building once had a magnificent equestrian statue of Maximilian Emmanuel of

Bavaria, governor of the Spanish Netherlands, but the brewers prudently replaced it in 1752 with a statue of Charles of Lorraine, when the Netherlands passed into the hands of the Austrian Hapsburgs. The building now houses the MUSÉE DE LA BRASSERIE.

Maison des Ducs de Brabant *(The Dukes of Brabant #13-19):* The glittering Classical front of the Maison des Ducs de Brabant occupies the entire s side of the square. The name is a recent and rather confusing invention, derived from the busts of the Dukes of Brabant decorating the bases of the pilasters. The facade in reality conceals six houses with individual names. G. de Bruyn designed the building in a similar style to his Maison des Brasseurs.

Chaloupe d'Or *(The Golden Caravel #24-25):* The Chaloupe d'Or was also built by G. De Bruyn for the guild of tailors. The figure perched on the gable top is St Boniface, patron saint of tailors, holding aloft a pair of scissors.

ÎLOT SACRÉ
Rue des Bouchers and neighboring streets. Map 3D3-4E4. Tram 52, 55, 58, 81 to Bourse.

This picturesque tangle of medieval lanes near Grand'Place is crammed with restaurants. It is great fun to stroll through the neighborhood, glancing at the flamboyant displays of dripping seafood, and the flickering fires inside the old restaurants. The cooking tends to be plain and unpretentious, though you can generally count on being served a serious Belgian meal at **Aux Armes de Bruxelles** *(rue des Bouchers 13),* **Chez Vincent** *(rue des Dominicains 8)* or, for mussels and fries, **Chez Léon** *(rue des Bouchers 18).*

MAROLLES
Lower Town. Map 5G2-3. Metro to Porte de Hal.

The Marolles is an old and poor quarter of Brussels, where the locals still chat in a unique dialect that few outsiders can fathom. Pieter Bruegel the Elder lived in a brick-gable house that is still standing *(rue Haute 132),* although there is little now to see except for a plaque. Bruegel and his wife were buried in the local church, the ÉGLISE DE LA CHAPELLE.

A few fashionable restaurants have opened in the quarter recently, but the stubborn Marolles quarter has proved difficult to gentrify. You can savor the spirit of the neighborhood by wandering along rue Haute, with its old-fashioned hatter *(#158)* and crowded cafés, or by poking around the dusty junk shops along rue Blaes.

A rambling flea market is held every day on place du Jeu de Balle *(7am-2pm).* You might find a dusty Art Deco lamp, a damp copy of *War and Peace* minus the first 10 pages, a fork with one prong, or a tattered copy of the 1963 Bruges telephone directory. Locals sift through the accumulated debris in the hope of finding a lost Rubens, but only early risers have any prospect of finding a genuine bargain. Go to the café **De Skieven Architek** *(place du Jeu de Balle 50)* for a simple lunch in a bustling café decorated with *trompe l'oeil* murals.

MONT DES ARTS

N of place Royale. Map 6F4. Metro to Gare Centrale, or tram 92, 93, 94 to place Royale.

The Mont des Arts (or Albertine) was designed in 1934 as a memorial to King Albert, who died that year in a climbing accident. Plans to develop the slope between the Lower and Upper Towns had been drawn up in the 19thC, but the various projects had to be abandoned. The 1930s project was halted because of World War II, and the Mont des Arts was not finally built until 1954-65.

The focal point of the Mont des Arts is a formal garden cut into the slopes of the Coudenberg. Stand at the bottom of the hill beside the statue of King Albert to view the complex. The flight of steps on the right marks the course of the old rue Montagne de la Cour, where the 15thC painter Roger van der Weyden lived.

The steps ascend to the ultimate in intimidating libraries, the BIBLIOTHÈQUE ROYALE ALBERT I. The gray edifice incorporates the diminutive CHAPELLE DE NASSAU, a relic of the 15thC palace of the Nassau family.

The **Palais des Congrès**, a large congress center, occupies the building to the left. It incorporates several subterranean halls built under the MONT DES ARTS. If an opportunity arises, go inside to look at the mural by Magritte titled *Les Barricades Mystérieuses*.

Look out for the inconspicuous **carillon** mounted on the bridge spanning the road to the left. Twelve mechanical figures represent national heroes such as Philip the Good and Rubens. Politically correct in every detail, the carillon is programmed to play alternately a Flemish folk song and a melody by the Walloon composer Grétry.

PLACE DES MARTYRS ▥

Off rue Neuve. Map 4C4-D4. Metro to de Brouckère.

The pleasing symmetry of place des Martyrs was created in 1775 by Claude Fisco. The Neoclassical square was named "Martyrs Square" in memory of the soldiers killed during the Belgian Revolution. A memorial designed by Guillaume Geefs features a female figure representing Patriotism and four *bas-reliefs* illustrating episodes during the four days of street fighting in September 1830. The square was until recently woefully derelict, but work began in 1992 to restore it to its 19thC state.

PLACE DU GRAND SABLON

Upper Town. Map 5F3-6F4. Tram 92, 93, 94 to Petit Sablon.

The sloping square of the Sablon has in recent years become one of the most elegant quarters of Brussels. Restored 17thC brick-gable houses are occupied by antique stores and fashionable cafés.

The main sights on the Sablon are the ÉGLISE NOTRE-DAME DU SABLON, the PLACE DU PETIT SABLON, and the MUSÉE DES POSTES, but it is pleasant just to stroll aimlessly around the neighborhood. Start the day with a coffee and croissant at one of the cafés on the Sablon, or go for a lunchtime sandwich to the café **Comte d'Egmont** *(rue Sainte-Anne 18)*. Chocophiles buy irresistible Belgian pralines and cakes at **Wittamer's** *(#12)*. The restaurants on the Sablon tend to be pricey, but you can sometimes find inexpensive bistros off the square, in rue Sainte-Anne, rue des Minimes and rue de Rollebeek.

Delve down the cobbled lanes off the Sablon to find intriguing boutiques specializing in the offbeat. Admire the sensual African sculpture at Impasse Saint-Jacques 8, and wander into the courtyard of the Antique Fair Centre *(place du Grand Sablon 37)* to look at the giant pots and curious Belgian sculpture on sale.

The Sablon looks its best on Saturday and Sunday, when antique dealers dressed in green padded jackets organize an outdoor market beside the church. The atmosphere is romantic, especially in winter, with lights strung between the striped awnings. The stalls stock Belgian family silver, prints of Brussels, old lace and leather-bound books, but the prices are high. Look out for the Christmas market on the Sablon (see THE BRUSSELS CALENDAR on page 71), when rustic stalls sell Finnish wooden decorations and German mulled wine.

PLACE ROYALE 🏛

Summit of the Mont des Arts. Map 6F4. Tram 92, 93, 94 to place Royale.

Dominating the high ground above the old town, place Royale is the most elegant of the city's Neoclassical squares. It stands on the site of the medieval Ducal Palace, which burned down in 1731. A plaque on the wall of the MUSÉE BELLEVUE indicates the location of the 15thC great hall and royal chapel.

The site of the palace was leveled to create an elegant Neoclassical square designed by Barnabé Guimard. The church of **St-Jacques sur Coudenberg** forms the centerpiece of the plan, with eight identical white town houses enclosing the cobbled square. The MUSÉE D'ART MODERNE now occupies one of the buildings *(#2)*, while the MUSÉE BELLEVUE is situated in another. A third has been restored to house part of the cherished collection of the MUSÉE INSTRUMENTAL.

Below the cobblestones, an old street survives from the Middle Ages. The cellars of the medieval royal chapel have been uncovered nearby, and the city has ambitious plans to create a new museum in the subterranean passages *(entrance at # 10),* although an opening date remains unfixed.

PLACE SAINTE-CATHERINE

N of place de Brouckère. Map 3D2-3. Metro to de Brouckère.

A lively old market square overlooked by a crumbling 19thC church. The only surviving food market in the old town takes place here every day except Sunday *(7am-5pm).* It is a good place to buy Flemish potatoes, Belgian fries and Breton oysters to eat on the spot. There are several good fish restaurants in the neighborhood, including the outstanding **La Belle Maraîchère** *(place Sainte-Catherine 11).*

PLACE SAINT-GÉRY

N of the Bourse. Map 3D2. Tram 52, 55, 58, 81 to Bourse.

Lost in the tangle of streets N of Grand'Place, place Saint-Géry is a sadly neglected quarter of the old town. The square marks the site of an island, the Grande Île, where St-Géry, Bishop of Cambrai, founded a church in the 7thC. The Dukes of Lorraine built a castle on the island in the 10thC.

The decline of the Saint-Géry quarter began when the Dukes of Brabant moved their residence to the heights above the old town. The urban decay accelerated during the French Period, when the revolutionary government ordered the demolition of Église Saint-Géry. But the biggest blow to the quarter came in the 19thC when the picturesque but putrid River Senne was put underground.

A handsome covered market was built in the middle of the square in 1881, incorporating a curious obelisk-shaped fountain from Grimbergen abbey. The iron-roofed market hall closed down in the 1970s, and looked as if it was doomed to be demolished. It was briefly revitalized as a shopping center, but the project failed, leaving the empty market again facing an uncertain future.

Other projects have helped somewhat to improve the neighborhood. Several old houses have been carefully restored as apartments, and a stretch of the River Senne has been exposed in a hidden courtyard *(#23)*.

SQUARE MARIE-LOUISE

N of the European Quarter. Map 1C3. Metro to Schuman, then a 5min walk down rue Archimède.

A series of tiered gardens rising up from square Marie-Louise to square Ambiorix were created by Gédéon Bordiau in 1890. A picturesque pond on square Marie-Louise is surrounded by artificial grottos, while square Ambiorix is landscaped with formal gardens. Elegant mansions in various styles overlook the gardens, including an Art Nouveau mansion built by Victor Horta for Baron Van Eetevelde, an administrator in the Congo *(av. Palmerston 4)*.

The **Maison de Saint-Cyr** *(square Ambiorix 11)*, built by Gustave Strauven in 1896, shows a more flamboyant version of Art Nouveau, with its scintillating display of ironwork on the balconies and roof. See illustration on page 35.

Off the beaten track

Travelers who want to go deeper into the history or culture of Brussels should spend some time exploring the sights off the beaten track. Few visitors are aware of the existence of the MEDIEVAL WALL or the ENCLOS DES FUSILLÉS, and the hidden MAISON DE LA BELLONE is a surprise even to people who have lived in Brussels for years. Brussels cemeteries are rich in architectural and sculptural details, while the METRO STATIONS are sometimes decorated with spectacular modern art.

Read the section on VIEWPOINTS for recommended places to go for a panoramic view of the city (◀€). Brussels is dotted with unexpected and bizarre sights, which can be found under CURIOSITIES. And when it all gets too much, head for one of the resting places listed under INTERLUDES.

This section lists the following sights.

BIBLIOTHECA WITTOCKIANA
BIBLIOTHÈQUE ROYALE
BRASSERIE WIELEMANS
CENTRE CULTUREL LE
  BOTANIQUE
CIMETIÈRE DE BRUXELLES
CIMETIÈRE DE LAEKEN

L'ENCLOS DES FUSILLÉS
ESPACE PHOTOGRAPHIQUE
  CONTRETYPE
MAISON DE LA BELLONE
MEDIEVAL WALL
METRO STATIONS
THÉÂTRE TOONE

BIBLIOTHECA WITTOCKIANA

Rue du Bemel 21-23 ☎*(02)770.53.33. Map* **2C4** 🚽 *Open Tues-Sat 10am-5pm. Tram 39, 44 to Jules César.*

A massive stone slab resembling an old book stands at the entrance to the Bibliotheca Wittockiana. This specialized private collection of rare, bound books is housed in a striking concrete building near the Parc de Woluwé. The institute organizes temporary exhibitions of illustrated books and rare bindings. A small back room contains a bizarre private collection of several hundred terracotta and antique silver teething rings, including one incorporating a tiny bird cage and another decorated with 20 bells.

BIBLIOTHÈQUE ROYALE

Mont des Arts ☎*(02)519.53.11. Map* **4E4-F4** 🔲 *(exhibitions only). Open Mon-Fri 9am-7.50pm; Sat 9am-4.50pm. Metro to Gare Centrale or tram 92, 93, 94 to place Royale.*

The Bibliothèque Royale dates back to the 15thC, when the Dukes of Burgundy assembled a distinguished collection of illuminated manuscripts in the Coudenberg palace. The current library was planned in 1935 as a memorial to King Albert I, who died in a climbing accident. Halted by the outbreak of World War II, the library, now part of the MONT DES ARTS complex, was not finally completed until 1969.

The Royal Library stands on the site of the Hôtel de Nassau, of which all that remains is the 16thC Brabant Gothic CHAPELLE DE NASSAU (level 0). Rare 15thC manuscripts are occasionally displayed in the elegant chapel. The **Musée de l'Imprimerie** (corridors of level 2) exhibits several hundred printing presses and typefaces from the 19th and 20thC.

Other exhibitions likely to be of interest to bibliophiles are occasionally held in the **Archives Générales du Royaume** *(rue de Ruysbroeck 2* ☎ *(02)513.76.80, map* **6F4** 🔲 *open Tues-Sat 9.30am-4pm).*

BRASSERIE WIELEMANS

Av. W. Ceuppens. Map **1D2**. *Tram 18 to Wielemans.*

An abandoned 19thC Brussels brewery has been saved from demolition by the energetic local history group La Fonderie. They plan eventually to restore the great hall of the Wielemans brewery, which was built in 1931. With its huge glass windows and shiny copper vats, the brewing hall was once one of the largest of its kind in Europe. When the plan is completed, the former brewery will be used as a cultural center and café.

CENTRE CULTUREL LE BOTANIQUE 血

Rue Royale 236 ☎*(02)217.63.86. Map* **4**C5 ▣ ═ *Open Tues-Sun 11am-6pm. Metro or tram 92, 93, 94 to Botanique.*

A grand 19thC greenhouse in the old JARDIN BOTANIQUE (see PARKS, page 146) has been converted into a lively center for French language culture, where you can expect innovative theater, international films and contemporary music. Temporary exhibitions are staged in a large hall, while novels by Walloon authors, and artful Belgian postcards are sold in a little bookstore. Bask in the winter sun on one of the benches in the central rotunda or go to the brasserie to eat an inexpensive meal amid the potted plants. It's wise to dress lightly in summer, as it tends to get sweltering under the glass.

CIMETIÈRE DE BRUXELLES

Av. du Cimetière de Bruxelles. Map **2**B4. *Open dawn-dusk* 🚌 *Bus 66 or 67 to Cimetière de Bruxelles.*

A leafy 19thC cemetery near the Nato headquarters, filled with tombs commemorating Congo explorers, military leaders and 19thC musicians. A large monument in a shady corner was erected to the British soldiers killed at Waterloo. Other monuments recall the French and German soldiers who died in Belgian hospitals during the 1870 Franco-Prussian War.

The cemetery is laid out rather like a city, with the most prominent citizens occupying the rond-point des Bourgmestres. Several 19thC Brussels burgomasters are buried here, including Jules Anspach (who created the *grands boulevards*), Charles Buls (responsible for saving the historic heart of Brussels) and Adolphe Max (deported for resisting the Germans during World War I). An obelisk nearby commemorates the French painter Jacques-Louis David, who died in exile in Brussels in 1825.

CIMETIÈRE DE LAEKEN

Parvis Notre-Dame. Map **1**B3. *Open 8.30am-4.30pm. Tram 94 to Royauté, then a 5min walk down rue du Champ de l'Église.*

Many of the foremost 19thC Belgians are buried in Laeken cemetery in grandiose tombs adorned with Neo-Gothic pinnacles or wistful nymphs. A weeping willow shades the colossal tomb of Maria Félicita Garcia, the famous Spanish singer who first performed in Naples at the age of five. Look through the double bronze doors to see a marble statue by Guillaume Geefs showing La Malibran (as she was affectionately known) playing the role of Norma in Bellini's opera.

Wandering along the avenues at random, you will find dilapidated chapels, miniature mosques and even a mock menhir. Look out for the Neoclassical tomb of Joseph Poelaert, who died in 1879 while working on the Palais de Justice, and descend (if you dare) into the dim and dusty network of 19thC catacombs at the far end of the cemetery.

Many of the tombstones in the cemetery bear the signature *Salu*. They were carved by Ernest Salu, or his son, in the romantic 19thC Ateliers Salu at the cemetery gate. The workshop may soon be opened as a **Musée de l'Art Funéraire**. Statues and gravestones will be displayed in the 19thC workshops where the Salu family toiled until 1984. The craggy bust of *père Salu* stands on a pedestal near the main gate, decorated with tendrils of fake greenery and a lithe young girl to evoke eternal youth.

L'ENCLOS DES FUSILLÉS
Rue Colonel Bourg. Map 2C3 ▣ *Tram 23, 90 to Diamant, then a 10min walk.*
A cobbled lane near the Belgian broadcasting tower leads to the hidden firing range where the German army executed many Belgian resistance workers. Some 342 concrete crosses mark the graves of people shot in 1914-18 and 1940-45. The British nurse Edith Cavell *(grave #4)* was executed here on October 12, 1915. After aiding Allied soldiers to escape to neutral Holland, she was arrested as a spy and sentenced to death at the Palais de la Nation. Her last words were, "Patriotism is not enough, I must have no hatred in my heart."

A nearby cross *(#11)* marks the grave of Gabrielle Petit, a Belgian woman shot in 1916 for belonging to the resistance. A statue on place Saint-Jean *(map 3E3)* commemorates this exceptional woman, who once entered a German barracks disguised as a soldier.

ESPACE PHOTOGRAPHIQUE CONTRETYPE ᛗ
Av. de la Jonction 1 ☎*(02)538.42.20. Map 1C3* ▣ *Open Tues-Sun 1-6pm. Tram 91, 92 to Ma Campagne.*
A photographic gallery occupies the spectacular Art Nouveau mansion built by Jules Brunfaut in 1902. The house was originally owned by Edouard Hannon, an engineer and keen amateur photographer. Go inside to look at the flamboyant staircase decorated with murals by Paul Beaudouin.

MAISON DE LA BELLONE
Rue de Flandre 46 ☎*(02)513.33.33. Map 3D2* ▣ *Open Tues-Sat 1-6pm. Metro to Sainte-Catherine.*
A hidden Baroque town house reconstructed in Italo-Flemish style after the 1695 bombardment. Festooned with military trophies, the house was designed in 1697 by Jan Cosyns, the architect of the Roi d'Espagne on GRAND'PLACE (page 133). Named after Bellona, the Roman goddess of war, the Maison de la Bellone was bought by the city in the 19thC. It now provides an opulent setting for unusual exhibitions on French theater in Brussels.

MEDIEVAL WALL
Lower Town. Maps 3 and 4.
Fragments of the first city wall crop up unexpectedly in the Lower Town. The wall was begun at the end of the 12thC by Duke Henri I of Brabant, and replaced in the 14thC by the second city wall, of which all that survives is the turreted castle of the PORTE DE HAL.

The most impressive relic of the first Brussels wall is the **Tour Noire** on place Sainte-Catherine *(map 3D2-3)*. This 13thC stone tower was saved from demolition in the 19thC by Charles Buls, but its survival is now threatened by a new property development. With luck, the tower will be incorporated into a new hotel planned for the site, as happened to a stretch of wall to the N, which was reconstructed in the atrium of the SAS Royal Hotel.

Another solitary tower, the **Tour d'Anneessens**, stands incongruously next to a garage at the end of rue de Rollebeek *(map 5 F3)*. The tower is named after François Anneessens, who led an unsuccessful revolt against Austrian rule in the 18thC. The rebel leader was probably imprisoned in this tower before his execution.

A long stretch of the 13thC wall runs to the s along rue de Villers *(map 3 E3-F3)*. Battlements and a turret appear amid an urban wasteland.

METRO STATIONS

Many metro stations in Brussels are enlivened by paintings or sculptures specially commissioned by the public transport authority. Certain works of art are worth making a special trip to see. The metro system is explained on page 50, and the stations can be pinpointed on the tram and metro systems map at the back of the book.

Look out for the large mural by Paul Delvaux as you descend to the platform at **Bourse** station. Titled *Our Old Brussels Trams,* the work depicts several historic Brussels trams outside the Woluwé depot (now the MUSÉE DU TRANSPORT URBAIN BRUXELLOIS).

Commuters descending to **Parc** station are confronted with a whimsical sculpture by Marc Mendelson called *Happy Metro to You,* featuring colorful wooden figures representing office workers. Hankar station features a giant mural titled *Our Times,* painted by Roger Somville in 1976.

Wander through the station at **Comte de Flandre** to see eerie bronze figures by Paul van Hoeydonck suspended above the tracks. Or take line 1B out to **Stockel** station to look at the spectacular mural representing famous characters from Hergé cartoons. En route back to the city center, alight with the university students at **Alma** to look at the curious organic architecture featuring undulating walls and mushroom-like columns.

Continue to **Vandervelde** station, where Paul de Gobert has decorated the walls with a vast panorama painting on the metro platform, which shows the view from the Groenenberg, looking N up the Woluwé valley. The station tunnel was specially built with a round arch to complete the illusion.

Take line 1A in the direction of Heysel to look at **Stuyvenbergh** station, where a row of eerily spotlit ceramic statues stand along one wall. They were created by Yves Bosquet in memory of Queen Elisabeth, who lived nearby in the Château du Stuyvenbergh.

Take line 1B out to **Bizet** station to see the newest work of art, which celebrates the French composer Georges Bizet. On the return trip, get off at **Aumale** to see enlarged photographs by Jean-Paul Laenen showing the neighborhood of the station during the construction of the metro.

THÉÂTRE TOONE

Impasse Schuddevelde, Petite rue des Bouchers 21 ☎*(02)511.71.37. Map 3D3* ▨ *Performances Mon-Sat at 8.30pm. Metro to de Brouckère.*

A narrow cobbled lane in the ÎLOT SACRÉ leads down to an old tavern where the famous Toone puppet theater gives performances. Toone and its cast of marionettes are as unique to Brussels as the Mannekin Pis, putting on a raucous and irreverent show that harks back to the Middle Ages and evokes the images captured in Bruegel's masterly scenes of peasant life.

The company takes the classics, from Greek tragedy to Shakespeare, and portrays them with inimitable *Bruxellois* style and a Belgian-French accent so thick you could cut it with a knife. The company's verve and humor gives the shows a wide appeal.

Parks and open spaces

With their exotic scents, cool shade and vivid colors, the many parks of Brussels provide attractive interludes for the traveler. The green spaces vary enormously, from tiny rambling gardens concealed behind old houses to the vast tracts of beech forest just beyond the city limits.

There is no single landscaping style in Brussels. Some spaces are laid out like French parks, with gravel paths, pleached fruit trees and chaste statues; others are inspired by English gardens, with meandering walks and ponds lined with wistful willows. Each neighborhood has its own parks where the locals go to chat or push a baby carriage, and everyone has their favorite spots. But no visitor should leave Brussels without at least strolling through the PARC DE BRUXELLES and the BOIS DE LA CAMBRE.

This section describes the following parks, gardens and forests:

BOIS DE LA CAMBRE	PARC LEOPOLD
BRUPARCK	PARC TENBOSCH
FORÊT DE SOIGNES	PARC TOURNAY-SOLVAY
JARDIN BOTANIQUE	PARC DE WOLUWÉ
PARC DE BRUXELLES	PARC DE WOLVENDAEL
PARC D'EGMONT	PARK VAN TERVUREN
PARC DU CINQUANTENAIRE	SENTIER DU CHEMIN DE
PARC DUDEN	FER
PARC JOSAPHAT	SQUARE DU PETIT SABLON

BOIS DE LA CAMBRE ★

At the s end of av. Louise. Entrances off av. Franklin Roosevelt and chaussée de Waterloo. Map 1C3-D3 🖸 *Open at all times* ♣ ☱ ⬛ *Tram 93, 94 to Legrand (for N end of park) or Marie-José (for Chalet Robinson).*

The wooded hills and deep valleys of the Bois de la Cambre provide a seductive retreat on the southern edge of the city. Once part of the Forêt de Soignes, the Bois was bought by the city in 1862 and turned into a park by the German engineer Edmond Keilig. The main entrance at the s end of avenue Louise is marked by two abandoned Neoclassical pavilions that once stood at the Porte de Namur. Some areas such as the Chemin de l'Aube to the E of the Bois have been left wild, while other spots like the Pelouse des Anglais feature sweeping lawns for sunbathing and picnics.

Paths for walkers and horseback-riders meander through the woods, although the idyllic peace is sometimes shattered by fast road traffic. Note that the main roads through the forest are sometimes closed to traffic during the summer months.

An artificial lake with an island in the middle forms the centerpiece of the Bois. An antiquated mechanical ferry takes people across to the island. Until recently, there was a rustic restaurant known as the **Chalet Robinson**. The restaurant has burned down, although there are plans to rebuild it.

You can still cross to the island to rent a boat and row around the island, or take your children to the adventure playground. Look out for the conversation benches opposite the island, where notices in several languages invite people to talk.

The main action for children is at the N end of the Bois, where they can join the cosmopolitan crush at the adventure playground next to the **Jardin du Bois** café, or roller skate at the outdoor rink near the **Théâtre du Poche** (see BRUSSELS FOR CHILDREN, page 207).

Adults, too, might look out for posters announcing concerts in the summer on the **Pelouse des Anglais** *(Sun at 11am)*.

BRUPARCK

Boulevard du Centenaire 20 ☎*(02)477.03.77. Map* **1**B3 ✽ *Opening hours vary for different attractions. Metro to Heysel.*

Bruparck is the catchy name for a cluster of attractions on the N edge of the city. Situated beside the huge Brussels Exhibition Centre, the park features buildings in various styles ranging from the futuristic to the nostalgic. You buy a separate entrance ticket for each of the seven or so main attractions.

Visit the futuristic ATOMIUM (see MUSEUMS, page 95) for a panoramic view of the Bruparck, then wander into MINI EUROPE (see MUSEUMS, page 100) to admire the detailed scale models of historic European buildings. If it rains, you can go to the **Planetarium** *(☎(02)478.91.06)* to view the night sky projected onto a dome, or choose a film from the 24 on offer at the giant KINEPOLIS cinema complex (page 186). Take your children to splash around in the sophisticated OCÉADIUM pool (page 212) or treat them to a giddying wrap-around film at the **Imax** cinema.

Restaurants and cafés occupy a cluster of mock Flemish gable houses called **the Village** (⌧). You can eat a standard hamburger, a pot of mussels at a branch of Chez Léon, or a sophisticated lunch in an old railway dining car. The Village has an adventure playground for children and a gaudy carousel with wooden horses to ride.

CIMETIÈRE DE BRUXELLES

A 19thC cemetery near the Nato headquarters. See OFF THE BEATEN TRACK on page 140.

CIMETIÈRE DE LAEKEN

Burial place of many leading 19thC Belgians. See OFF THE BEATEN TRACK on page 140.

FORÊT DE SOIGNES

s and ε of Brussels. Map 2E4-D6, and walk map on page 87 ♣ Tram 94 to Coccinelles (s area of forest) or tram 44 to Quatre Bras (ε area of forest).

Keen ramblers visiting Brussels should be sure to pack a pair of tough boots for hiking in the vast forest beyond the city boundary. The Forêt de Soignes (Zonienwoud in Dutch) is not as well known as the Bois de Boulogne in Paris, yet it offers endless itineraries for country walks within easy reach of the city.

The 4,350-hectare (10,750-acre) Forêt de Soignes is all that remains of an ancient forest that once extended from Picardy to the Ardennes. The forest has been settled since prehistory, and mysterious burial mounds can still be seen near the path known as the Sentier des Tumuli. During the Middle Ages, monks in search of solitude built several monasteries deep in the woods. An abbey at Groenendaal sheltered the medieval Christian mystic Jan van Ruysbroeck, while the painter Hugo van der Goes retreated to the Abbaye du Rouge-Cloître. Many of the religious buildings have vanished, but a few are still intact, including the ABBAYE DE LA CAMBRE, which originally stood in a wooded valley s of the city walls, and the ABBAYE DU ROUGE-CLOÎTRE, which stands in a wooded hollow to the ε of the city.

A Flemish tapestry in the Musée Communal shows that the original Forêt de Soignes was a tangle of gnarled oak trees, but the ecology changed dramatically when the Austrians replanted the forest with lofty beech trees.

The rambler has a bewildering choice of paths to follow in the woods. The first step is to buy a good map such as the IGN 1:25,000 map of the Forêt de Soignes, which marks footpaths, cycle tracks and bridle paths for horses. In planning a ramble, use public transport on the outward journey and walk back into the city, or plot a circular walk. Paths through the forest are of two types: long straight avenues known as *drèves* created by the Austrians, and ancient meandering paths marked *sentiers* or *chemins*. The meandering paths are often the more interesting to follow for long distances.

An easy initiation into the forest is to take tram 94 to the Coccinelles halt, cross the road and head down the drève du Comte (see WALK 4, page 87). Or take tram 44 out to Tervuren, getting off at the Quatre Bras stop.

Whatever the walk you choose, be sure to take your own food and refreshments, as there are no restaurants or cafés in the forest. You will find a cluster of popular Flemish restaurants on the ε edge of the forest at Jezus-Eik, and a few local restaurants clustered around place Wiener in Boitsfort.

GEOGRAFISCH ARBORETUM TE TERVUREN (Tervuren Geographical Arboretum)

Sint-Janskruispunt, Tervuren ☎(02)767.92.42. Map 2D5 ▣ Open at all times ♣ Tram 44 to Quatre Bras, then follow the Koninklijke Wandeling for about 20mins to reach the main entrance.

A magnificent arboretum was planted in 1902 in the Forêt de Soignes by the botanist Charles Bommer. Originally Leopold II's private estate, it was opened to the public in 1903. Exotic trees from almost 20 temperate countries are clustered according to their place of origin. Some 40 numbered plantations cover areas as diverse as Manchuria and the Mississippi. The map of the Forêt de Soignes published by IGN includes a detailed plan of the arboretum.

JARDIN BOTANIQUE (Botanical Garden)
Entrances at rue Royale 236 and rue Gineste (facing the Palace Hotel). Map 4C5. Open 7.30am-5.30pm ▣ ⇥ *Metro to Rogier; metro or tram 92, 93, 94 to Botanique.*

The former Jardin Botanique was landscaped in formal terraces in 1826. Much of the greenery was destroyed to build a major highway, but there is still a romantic pond and a few benches overlooking clipped box hedges. The park is dotted with 19thC bronze statues representing the seasons, including works by Constantin Meunier. Go for a coffee to the brasserie of the CENTRE CULTUREL LE BOTANIQUE (page 140), in what was formerly the vast Neoclassical greenhouses, or take your children to the playground. The city's botanical gardens now flourish on an old country estate at Meise, N of Brussels.

PARC DE BRUXELLES ★
Entrances on rue Royale, place des Palais, rue Ducale and rue de la Loi. Map 6E5-F5 ▣ *Open 6am-9pm* ❀ ▣ *(summer only). Metro or tram 92, 93, 94 to Parc.*

Situated between the palace and the parliament, the Parc de Bruxelles is the city's most elegant park, dotted with old iron lampposts and seductive Baroque statues. The long avenues lined with pleached lime trees were laid out in 1774-87 by the French architect Barnabé Guimard, who designed PLACE ROYALE at the same time.

Created on the site of the famous Renaissance gardens of the Dukes of Burgundy, the rectangular park epitomizes the stiff formality of the 18thC. The avenues were laid out in a *patte d'oie* (goose foot) pattern popular with French landscape gardeners. Two large basins provide focal points in the design. The paths are lined with elegant Baroque statues representing Greek gods or Classical virtues. Some statues formerly graced the labyrinth in the ducal park, while others were rescued from the royal castle at Tervuren after fire gutted the building. The garden of the Tour et Tassis mansion on the Sablon provided other statues. Most of the works in the park are copies; the originals are now kept in the MUSÉE D'ART ANCIEN.

The Parc de Bruxelles is dotted with elegant buildings such as the 18thC **Théâtre Royal du Parc** and the **Waux Hall**, which was modeled on the Vauxhall Theatre in London. Belgian aristocrats and international businessmen continue to wallow in the mock-English ambience of the **Cercle Gaulois**, a private club behind the theater.

The park is particularly beguiling in the summer. Office workers can pick up a sandwich at **New York** *(rue de Namur 8)* to eat in the park, or drink a beer at a kiosk under the trees. Concerts and puppet shows are staged in the summer at a 19thC iron bandstand, and children can play in a little park with climbing frames and an iron boat. But perhaps the ideal summer pursuit is to sit on a bench overlooking the round pond to read Charlotte Brontë's *The Professor*, which is mainly set in the neighborhood of the park.

PARC D'EGMONT

Entrances on boulevard de Waterloo and rue du Grand Cerf. Map 6G4 🔄 *Open 8am-dusk* ✿ *Metro or tram 91, 92, 93, 94 to Louise.*

A secret little park not far from the shopping arcades of the Upper Town. Originally the property of the Egmont family, the park adjoins the closely-guarded 18thC Palais d'Egmont where EC conferences are sometimes held. Tucked away in a corner is a 15thC stone well that stood on the site of Galerie Ravenstein. Children appreciate the bronze statue of Peter Pan surrounded by scuttling rabbits and mice.

PARC DU CINQUANTENAIRE

Entrances at av. de la Joyeuse Entrée and Porte de Tervuren. Map 1C3 🔄
Open at all times. Metro to Schuman or Mérode.

Jogging Eurocrats keep themselves trim by pounding down the dusty alleys of the Parc du Cinquantenaire. This formal park was created by Leopold II for the 1880 Brussels Exhibition, a lavish event staged to celebrate the fiftieth anniversary (*cinquantenaire* in French) of Belgian independence. A triumphal arch straddles the park, linked by double colonnades to the former exhibition halls, now three vast, major museums (see plan and entry under CINQUANTENAIRE MUSEUMS on pages 96-7).

The architect king would perhaps weep if he saw the damage done to the park by a road tunnel that surfaces briefly in the middle of his flower beds. Away from the traffic, some interesting 19thC statues and monuments survive. Tucked away in a corner next to the avenue de Cortenberg is a mock **mosque**. Visitors in 1880 could admire a vast panoramic painting of Cairo in the circular interior. The building was later transformed into a genuine mosque for Brussels' Muslims.

The most intriguing edifice in the park is the **Pavillon des Passions Humaines** *(near the av. de la Joyeuse Entrée)*. This Neoclassical temple (an early Horta building) contains an erotic sculptural frieze by Jef Lambeaux depicting *Les Passions Humaines* (the human passions). The writhing nudes caused such a furor when they were unveiled in 1889 that the temple was promptly closed. It has remained locked ever since, although the Musées Royaux d'Art et d'Histoire occasionally organize guided visits for the curious, as does **Arcadia** (for details see BUS TOUR OPERATORS on page 60).

It was briefly fashionable to live near the Parc du Cinquantenaire, and the painter Paul Gauchier designed himself a flamboyant Art Nouveau house at rue des Francs 5.

PARC DUDEN

Entrances at square Laine, av. Victor Rousseau and av. Gabriel Fauré. Map 1D3 🔄 *Open 8am-dusk* ◁ *Tram 18 to Rochefort, or bus 48 to Laine.*

Willem Duden, a lace merchant from Germany, owned a vast private estate in Forest which was turned into a public park in 1911. The steep paths, deep ravines and curious 19thC Italianate villa make this one of the city's most romantic parks. Climb the steps s of square Laine for a view of the Palais de Justice, or wander to the summit to the E to watch the sun setting.

PARC JOSAPHAT

Boulevard Josaphat. Map 1B3. Open 8am-dusk 🚊 *Tram 23 to Chazal or Héliotropes.*

A romantic 19thC park tucked away in a deep valley, with winding paths, rocky outcrops and shady ponds. The park is thickly planted with exotic trees and dotted with 19thC statues. Look out for the bizarre tables and benches made from concrete molded to resemble wood. The **Laiterie du Parc** has a vast terrace where you can drink a Belgian beer. Concerts are staged in the summer at a nearby 19thC bandstand.

PARC LEOPOLD

Rue Belliard. Map 1C3 🚊 *Open 8am-dusk* ♿ *Metro to Schuman.*

A romantic park originally created as a zoo in 1851 on the slopes overlooking an old pond. The park is dotted with ponderous 19thC scientific institutes, including the MUSÉE DE L'INSTITUT ROYAL DES SCIENCES NATURELLES (see page 113). The park is well placed for a brief stroll between meetings at the Brussels seat of the European Parliament.

PARC TENBOSCH

Entrances on chaussée de Vleurgat and square Henri Michaux. Map 1C3. Open mid-Oct to mid-Mar 8am-6pm, mid-Mar to mid-Oct 8am-9pm ♣ *Tram 93, 94 to Vleurgat, or bus 38 to Van Eyck.*

Another romantic park, this one is in Ixelles, with winding paths, ponds and shady benches where the locals gather to chat. It is best in spring when the blossom adds splashes of pink and yellow, but it remains interesting all year round thanks to careful planting. There are swings and a sandpit for children, and a curious flock of stray parrots squawking in the trees.

PARC TOURNAY-SOLVAY

Chaussée de la Hulpe. Map 2D4 🚊 *Open 8am-dusk* ♣ *Tram 94 to Boitsfort.*

A secret park on the fringe of the Forêt de Soignes near the rustic Boitsfort rail station. The winding paths and dusky rhododendron glades were created in 1890 in the romantic spirit of British landscape gardening. One path plunges down to a pond; another crosses a bridge spanning an ancient sunken road through the forest.

The park was created for the Solvay family, one of the powerful industrial dynasties of Belgium. A flamboyant Neo-Gothic castle overlooking the park was recently gutted by fire, leaving a wistful ruin with pigeons nesting in the blackened rafters, and weeds sprouting from the marble mantlepieces. Various plans to rebuild the castle have failed for want of funds, but it may one day be restored to its former splendor.

Only a few people ever discover the formal walled garden surrounding a pond. The paving stones there are made from 17thC tombstones. The aristocratic coats-of-arms were hacked off after the French revolution, but a few words and wistful cherubs are still visible.

On leaving the park, turn left down a cobbled lane known as the Chemin des Deux Montagnes. After plunging through a tunnel under the Solvay estate, you come to the *laiterie,* once a fashionable café and now a private house. Continue up the hill and under the railway line to reach the forest, or turn left along the lakeside road, the Chemin des Silex, to reach the old center of **Boitsfort**. Take tram 94 from place Wiener to get back to the city center.

PARC DE WOLUWÉ

Av. de Woluwé. Map 2C4 ☒ *Open at all times* ♣ *Tram 39, 44 to Chien Vert or Woluwé.*

A rolling park landscaped in English style, with spacious lawns and handsome trees. A good spot to jog or read a novel on a summer day, although the roar of traffic is hard to escape. Rowboats and pedalos are rented out in summer.

PARC DE WOLVENDAEL

Entrances at square des Héros and av. Wolvendael. Map 1D3 ☒ *Open 8am-dusk* ♣ ☰ 🅿 *Tram 92 to Héros, Wolvendael or Dieweg.*

A wild and rambling park in Uccle, with wooded slopes and deep ravines. Boots are a must in wet weather. The park's curiosities include a pavilion from an Amsterdam mansion designed in a florid Louis XV style (now a restaurant). The park has a children's playground and a mini-golf course (open in summer only).

PARK VAN TERVUREN

To the SE *of Brussels;* E *of Tervuren village. Map 2C6* ☒ *Open at all times* ♣ *Tram 44 to Tervuren.*

Charles of Lorraine planted extensive 18thC formal gardens to the E of the royal castle at Tervuren. The main feature in the park is De Zevenster, a star-formation of avenues radiating from a circle in the forest.

The medieval royal castle formerly stood on a promontory overlooking a narrow lake. Leopold II gave the castle to his bereaved sister Charlotte in 1853. Less than a year after she returned to Belgium, her husband Maximilian was executed in Mexico in 1867 (a famous painting by Manet in the Mannheim art gallery shows the execution), but her troubles were far from over. The Château de Tervuren burned down in 1879, and the unlucky princess had to move to another castle at Meise. All that remains of the royal castle at Tervuren is the Renaissance chapel of St-Hubert, which stands in a clump of trees on the waterfront.

The grounds between the lake and the KONINKLIJK MUSEUM VOOR MIDDENAFRIKA (see MUSEUMS, page 98) were landscaped in the 19thC by the Frenchman Lainé. Straight avenues are flanked by topiary, flower beds and statues. In the summer, rent a rowboat at the W end of the lake.

Leave the park by the Kapucijnenpoort to the s and follow the Isabelladreef to get to the arboretum (see GEOGRAFISCH ARBORETUM TE TERVUREN on page 145).

PLACE DU PETIT SABLON ★

Rue de la Régence. Map **6***F4* 🖭 *Open 8am-dusk. Tram 92, 93, 94 to Petit Sablon.*

A miniature park created in 1890 on the sloping ground to the N of the pl. du Grand Sablon. The park is positively mobbed with 19thC statues representing famous figures in the history of the Low Countries. The Protestant martyrs, Counts Egmont and Hoorn, look down upon gaudy flower beds planted with geraniums and marigolds, while a neat hedge encloses a semicircle of ten statues representing such great men as William of Orange and Mercator.

The park is encircled by an ornate iron railing with 48 Neo-Gothic pedestals surmounted by figures representing the medieval guilds of Brussels.

Romantic although it seems, this is not a popular park with courting couples. The park-keeper is inclined to tick off anyone caught kissing, or breaking any other regulation. Parents and lovers might prefer the more relaxed Parc de Bruxelles.

SENTIER DU CHEMIN DE FER

Access from av. Dehoux or av. de Tervuren at blvd. du Souverain. Map **2***C4* 🖭 *Metro to Démey; tram 39, 44 to Woluwé Dépôt.*

A stretch of abandoned railway line in Woluwé has been turned into a public footpath. The paved path runs through leafy suburbs for some 2.5 kilometers (1½ miles), with rustic benches along the way. Maps are posted at strategic points, but finding the start of the path can be difficult. It can be found up an unmarked path at the intersection of avenue Dehoux and chaussée de Watermael, near Demay metro station. Another access point is beside the PARC DE WOLUWÉ at the intersection of avenue de Tervuren and boulevard du Souverain.

Excursions

The attraction of Brussels as a tourist or business destination is greatly enhanced by the many historic cities within easy reach. The great Flemish cities to the north — **Bruges**, **Antwerp** and **Ghent** — are captivating to explore for a day or longer. Although less well publicized, the Walloon cities of **Liège** and **Namur** to the south are also worth exploring.

Several regions of attractive landscape lie close to Brussels. The windswept dunes of the North Sea coast make an invigorating day trip. You can take the train to **Knokke** and wander along the shore to the bird reserve of **Het Zwin**. Or go south to **Spa** or **Dinant** to hike in the wooded Ardennes.

The following excursions are described below:

BRUSSELS ENVIRONS
KASTEEL VAN BEERSEL
GRIMBERGEN

PAJOTTENLAND
TERVUREN
WATERLOO BATTLEFIELD

BRUSSELS ENVIRONS

The rolling Flemish landscape begins almost as soon as you leave Brussels, and there are many places nearby that are worth visiting. The giant beech trees of the **Forêt de Soignes** spread to the s and E, while Bruegel's **Pajottenland** undulates to the w. Even in the industrialized belt N of Brussels, patches of Flemish countryside survive around **Grimbergen**. Rent a car for the day, or take a local bus out of town to sniff the country air of **Brabant**.

For information on local bus services, call either the Flemish bus authority **De Lijn** (☎ *078.11.37.73, toll-free*) or the Walloon authority **TEC** (☎ *(02)287.29.11*).

KASTEEL VAN BEERSEL

Lotstraat, Beersel, Flemish Brabant, 8km (5 miles) s of Brussels
☎ *(02)331.00.24. Map 1E2* ▨ *Open Mar to mid-Nov: Tues-Sun 10am-noon, 2-6pm; mid-Nov to Dec, Feb: Sat, Sun 10.30am-5pm. Closed Jan. By train: to Beersel (Mon-Fri only). By tram: tram 55 to Uccle Calevoet station, then bus UB to Beersel. By car: on the A7 to exit 14.*
Tucked away in a wooded valley of the River Zenne (the Dutch name for the Senne), Beersel is a spectacular moated castle from the Middle Ages. The lofty triple towers linked by curtain walls have fended off every hostile army but one — a force from Brussels that breached the defenses in 1489.

The castle has been restored, but it retains a wild aspect. The wind whistles through the open windows, and visitors not prone to vertigo are free to scramble up wooden ladders into the loft, or down narrow passages into the dank dungeons. The eerie atmosphere is aided by the nesting pigeons, which are liable to fly off in a cloud of feathers as you poke your head into a dark alcove.

High above the castle, Beersel village is a typical Brabant *dorp*. The place for lunch is **De Drie Fonteinen**, opposite the church, where they brew their own Gueuze beer using rare yeasts that thrive in the Zenne valley. Try a typical Flemish dish such as *paling in 't groen* (eel with spinach) or *waterzooi* (chicken stew), or go on Thursday or Friday to join the locals as they tuck into steaming pots of Dutch mussels.

GRIMBERGEN

Flemish Brabant, 11km (7 miles) N of Brussels. Map 1A3. By bus: bus G from Gare du Nord. By car: take the Brussels Ring (beltway) to exit 18.
Grimbergen is an attractive Flemish village still blessed with narrow cobbled lanes and old iron signs hanging outside the local shops. The village is dominated by the unfinished Baroque abbey **church of St Servatius** (*open 10am-5pm*). Stroll into the nearby Prinsenbos park to

admire the romantic crumbling ruins of **Grimbergen castle**, or visit the **Museum of Country Crafts**, which is located in former Renaissance stables nearby.

The village is surrounded by placid meadows with pollarded willows and wayside shrines containing statues of the Madonna. Follow the footpath signposted *Maalbeek Wandeling* along the banks of the Maalbeek stream to reach two picturesque watermills. On summer days, you can sit on terraces beside the stream to sample a glass of dark Grimbergen beer.

PAJOTTENLAND

Flemish Brabant, to the w of Brussels. Map 1C1. By car: take exit 13 on the Brussels Ring (beltway) **i** *Oude Pastorie, Gaasbeek* ☎*(02)532.57.58.*

The Pajottenland is a tranquil area of gently rolling fields lying just a few kilometers beyond the western edge of Brussels. The inquisitive traveler can track down the villages in the rolling Pajottenland where Pieter Bruegel the Elder painted 16thC peasant weddings and boisterous country fairs. Head for **Sint-Anna-Pede** to find the church that appears in the background of the *Parable of the Blind,* or visit **Itterbeek** to look at the church that features in Bruegel's *Wedding Feast,* the original of which is to be seen in the New York Metropolitan Museum of Art.

The region is dotted with brick breweries producing traditional Belgian ales, including Gueuze, a local speciality. Beer-lovers can follow the 50-km (32-mile) Gueuze Route, which takes in some of the main breweries in the Pajottenland.

TERVUREN

Flemish Brabant, 13km e of Brussels. Map 2C **i** *Markt 7, Tervuren* ☎*(02)769.20.80. Tram 44 to Tervuren.*

The old Flemish town of Tervuren is attractively situated in the depths of the Forêt de Soignes (Zonienwoud in Dutch). Once the site of a royal château (destroyed by fire in 1879), Tervuren later became the setting for one of Leopold II grandest projects, the KONINKLIJK MUSEUM VOOR MIDDENAFRIKA (see page 98).

The PARK VAN TERVUREN (see page 149) still has a few relics from the 17thC, including the **Sint-Hubertus Kapel** at the w end of the park, once part of the royal palace, and the **Spaanse Huis**, at the e end of the park, once a watermill.

A sad reminder of Leopold II's colonial ambitions is to be found in the cemetery of **Tervuren church**, where a row of identical tombs commemorates seven unfortunate Congolese brought to Belgium for the 1897 Exposition, all of whom died from disease.

The peaceful GEOGRAFISCH ARBORETUM TE TERVUREN (see page 145) lies to the e of the town. Tervuren does not boast many restaurants; those with a car or strong legs should head through the forest to Jezus-Eik, where locals like to flock for solid Belgian Sunday lunch.

A rustic café near the Sint-Hubertus Kapel has a lakeside terrace, and boats for rent.

WATERLOO BATTLEFIELD

French Brabant, 17km (10 miles) s of Brussels. Map 2F4 i Waterloo tourist office, chaussée de Bruxelles 149 ☎(02)354.99.10. By bus: line W from place Rouppe. By car: take the chaussée de Waterloo from Brussels.

Waterloo battlefield is one of the great tourist sights in Belgium, with about 500,000 visitors each year tramping across the site. The rolling beet fields where Napoleon was finally defeated in 1815 are dotted with memorials to the soldiers killed in the one-day battle. Some 191,000 men fought at the Battle of Waterloo, of which 72,000 were commanded by Napoleon, 67,000 by Wellington and 52,000 by Blücher. When the battle started at about 11.30am, the French had 246 canons in the field against Wellington's 160. By the end of the fighting, the dead numbered some 13,000, of which about half were French. The wounded totaled about 35,000, almost two-thirds of whom were French.

The main feature on the battlefield is the **Lion de Waterloo**, a colossal earth mound erected by the Dutch on the spot where the Prince of Orange was wounded. You can toil to the summit to pinpoint the roads and farmhouses that played a crucial role in the battle.

A cluster of museums next to the Lion Mound offer a variety of interpretations of the battle. There is a dusty 19thC waxworks museum and a faded panoramic painting of the battle. A new **Visitors' Center** offers instead a diorama of the battle and a brief film. The battle is re-enacted every five years, with the next due in 1995.

But perhaps the best way to appreciate the significance of Waterloo is to get away from the cafés and tourists' paraphernalia, and tramp over the battlefield. Go to the crossroads where Lord Picton died, still wearing his top hat and tails, and wander out to Hougoumont farm where the walls are still pock-marked with bullet holes.

✎ **Le 1815**, a small but elegant, battle-themed hotel, has opened near to the Visitors' Center. See HOTELS A TO Z on page 158 for full details.

Where to stay

Making your choice

The choice of hotels in Brussels runs from grand 19thC palaces to modest town houses in leafy suburbs. It pays to be careful in choosing a hotel; some of the most expensive establishments offer little in the way of service or character, whereas an inexpensive family-run hotel sometimes retains old-fashioned Belgian charm.

Most of the hotels built by developers in the 1960s may be avoided by the discerning traveler, although some built in recent years are less impersonal. The **SAS Royal** must be singled out for its architecture and excellent location, while the **Stanhope** offers impeccable service in a country-house setting. We must wait to see whether the newly opened **Conrad Hotel**, located in the shell of a 19thC Art Nouveau hotel at place Stéphanie, will win the affection of travelers.

Most international hotel chains are represented in Brussels, including the following:

* The **Hilton** in the Upper Town *(boulevard de Waterloo 38, B-1000 Bruxelles, map* 6G4 ☎ *(02)504.11.11* Fx *(02)504.21.11)*
* The **Sheraton** in the Lower Town *(place Rogier 3, B-1210 Bruxelles, map* 4C4 ☎ *(02)224.31.11* Fx *(02)224.34.56)*
* The **Scandic Crown** in the Upper Town *(rue Royale 250, B-1210 Bruxelles, map* 4C5 ☎ *(02)220.66.11* Fx *(02)217.84.44)*
* The **Ibis** near Grand'Place *(rue du Marché-aux-Herbes 120, B-1000 Bruxelles, map* 4E4 ☎ *(02)514.40.40* Fx *(02)514.50.67)*

These hotels guarantee travelers a high standard of service, and for many, that will suffice. But by their very nature they scarcely reflect any local character. For a room with a four-poster bed, or a Japanese breakfast, or a view of the town hall, or an original work by a Belgian artist, you might do better to select one of the hotels described in this chapter

LOCATION

The key factor in selecting a hotel in Brussels is to choose the right· location. Those traveling on business may feel that they have to stay near to the European Commission, Nato or the Brussels Exhibition Centre. Yet Brussels is a relatively compact city, and you can easily base yourself in the heart of the old town, while traveling to meetings by metro or taxi. The metro gets you from place de Brouckère to Schuman (for the European Quarter) in about five minutes, or to Heysel (for the Brussels Exhibition Centre) in about 20 minutes. A taxi will get you to Nato from the city center in 15 minutes.

The most desirable location for most people is **off Grand'Place**. The traffic is quieter than elsewhere, and the quarter is thick with desirable restaurants and cafés frequented by tourists and locals alike.

Many of the grand old hotels in Brussels have vanished, but a few historic hotels survive almost intact. Most are located in the **Lower Town**, including the gently aging MÉTROPOLE, whose fusty charm contrasts with the gleaming modernity of the nearby SAS ROYAL. The Lower Town neighborhood is within walking distance of Grand'Place, and offers elegant shopping arcades, serious cinemas and a plentiful supply of restaurants. Several hotels are clustered around place Rogier, near the Gare du Nord. They include the ALBERT PREMIER, NEW SIRU and PALACE. This can be a noisy and occasionally seedy neighborhood, but, after years of neglect, it is slowly recovering its former allure. Its main advantage is the excellent location for getting around town by public transport.

The advantages of the **Upper Town** are the spacious streets, elegant parks and major museums. The main restaurants and cafés are clustered around the elegant Sablon square. The only really noteworthy hotel in this quarter is the PULLMAN ASTORIA.

Avenue Louise and the surrounding streets boast a number of modern hotels, both large and small. This mainly 19thC neighborhood has elegant shops, cinemas and restaurants, but the main attractions are the many parks and the diversity of Art Nouveau architecture in the vicinity.

Those visiting the EC institutions tend to opt for one of the modern hotels in the **European Quarter**. This area has a few Irish cafés and Italian restaurants, but it tends to be rather quiet at night. You may well find yourself taking the metro to place de Brouckère in search of nightlife.

A few hotels are to be found in the 19thC **suburbs**. They are sometimes — but not inevitably — in quiet locations, and may offer an opportunity to savor the charms of Belgian suburban life.

FACILITIES

Most hotels in Brussels are run with the business traveler in mind. Prices tend to be high, and the service is smooth rather than friendly. Modern hotels usually have underground garage parking for which a charge is made. Reserve ahead to secure a parking place. Rooms tend to have direct dial telephones and minibars, usually stocked with a thoroughly predictable range of drinks (Stella Artois rather than Hoegaarden Grand Cru).

Television in rooms is a constant even in inexpensive hotels. Televisions are normally linked to the local cable network, which transmits at least 25 channels in six languages, including the British BBC1, BBC2 and the American CNN. You can improve your rusty Italian by watching Rai Uno, or catch an occasional film in English on Flemish or Dutch TV. Some hotels supply a free program guide, but otherwise you will find a comprehensive weekly TV listing in English in *The Bulletin*.

Few hotels in Brussels are equipped with swimming pools or fitness rooms. The **Sheraton**'s rooftop pool and fitness center are superior to anything else that Brussels has to offer. The **Scandic Crown** has a health club and the **Copthorne Stephanie** has a modest pool. For ways to keep in trim while you are in Brussels, see SPORTS on page 210.

FOOD

Large hotels tend to serve a wholesome and generous buffet breakfast featuring muesli, rolls, croissants and possibly bacon and eggs. Inexpensive hotels are more likely to produce a "Continental breakfast" comprising crisp *baguette,* fresh *croissant* and coffee. The Continental breakfast is preferred by Belgians, but travelers used to a high-calorie breakfast may need a supplement by mid-morning.

The cost of breakfast is normally included in the price of the hotel room, except at some large hotels where the American custom of charging breakfast separately has been adopted. The price categories for hotel rooms given opposite include breakfast in all cases.

Several large hotels in Brussels have restaurants which offer sophisticated cuisine in an elegant setting. The **Sea Grill** at the SAS ROYAL offers outstanding seafood dishes in an intimate dining room. The **Alban Chambon** at the MÉTROPOLE serves sophisticated French cuisine in a glittering 19thC room. The **Brasserie** at the NEW SIRU prepares simple and inexpensive French meals. Most other hotel restaurants can be counted on to provide good cooking, though it may be more adventurous to venture out of the hotel to sample a neighborhood restaurant.

BARGAINS

The big Brussels business hotels find it hard to fill their rooms on weekends, and many offer substantial discounts on Friday, Saturday and possibly Sunday nights. The general rule is that the more expensive chain hotels offer the better deals. You can sometimes end up paying less at a luxury hotel offering a discount, than at a simple hotel offering no reduction. But the small hotel will often provide a more friendly atmosphere.

Call the Brussels tourist office to find out about the special deals available, or contact the hotels directly to ask if they have any special deals on offer. The **Stephanie** cuts more than 50 percent off its rates on Friday and Saturday. The **SAS Royal** offers a "senior citizen" rate from Friday to Sunday; the room price for those over 65 is cut by a percentage corresponding to the guest's age. The **Stanhope** is one of the few luxury hotels that resists the temptation of cutting weekend rates, seeking to maintain a dignified atmosphere.

RESERVATIONS

Rooms can usually be found on short notice if you can afford to pay top rates. Those on a tighter budget must generally reserve ahead, due to the more limited supply of inexpensive hotels.

The busy periods for tourists tend to coincide with public holidays in Germany, the Netherlands or the UK. The main dates to avoid are Easter, Ascension and All Saints' Day. The few inexpensive hotels in Brussels may well be fully booked on those dates, although the large hotels aimed at business travelers often have to work very hard for business.

It can also occasionally happen that all the main hotels in Brussels are swamped by an international conference or EC summit. Predicting this ahead is no easier here than anywhere else.

If you have problems finding a room, you should call **Belgique Tourisme Réservations** *(boulevard Anspach 111, B-1000 Bruxelles, map 3 D3* ☎ *(02)513.74.84* ☒ *(02)513.92.77, Mon-Fri 9am-6pm, Sat 9am-12.30pm),* a free nationwide reservation service that will attempt to locate a room to fit your needs. If all else fails, remember that the medieval city of Bruges, which has many attractive small hotels, is just one hour by train from Brussels.

TIPPING
Service charges are included in the hotel bill, although if you have stayed for a few days, it may be appropriate to leave a tip for the chambermaid.

CHILDREN
For those with young children, staying at a grand old hotel can be a catalog of disasters, ranging from damaged antiques to irritated fellow-guests. It is often more restful to take a room at one of the modern international hotels such as the **SAS Royal**, **Hilton**, **Scandic Crown** or **Ibis**, where they seem better able to plan for children's needs. Children get to share their parents' room at the SAS Royal at no extra charge except for breakfast.

APARTMENT HOTELS (see page 163) offer another solution to traveling with children.

ABOUT THIS CHAPTER
The following selection of hotels has been made with the aim not only of covering all the main areas and a wide range of prices, but with other factors in mind: for example a congenial atmosphere, or suitability for business travelers. There is also a brief section on apartment hotels, which are particularly useful for longer stays or when you need to have your own catering facilities.

Full details of all our recommended hotels are given, and symbols show those that are particularly luxurious (🏨) or simple (🏠) in style. Other symbols show price categories, and give a résumé of available facilities. See the KEY TO SYMBOLS on page 7 for the full list of symbols.

The prices corresponding to our price symbols (see below) are based on average charges for two people staying in a double room with bathroom/shower, inclusive of breakfast and Value-Added Tax (shortened to **TVA** in French or **BTW** in Dutch. In practice, charges for one person are not much cheaper.

Although actual prices will inevitably increase, our relative price categories are likely to remain the same.

Symbol	Category	Current price
▥	very expensive	more than 8,000 BF
▥	expensive	6,000-8,000 BF
▥	moderate	4,000-6,000 BF
▱	inexpensive	2,000-4,000 BF
▱	cheap	under 2,000 BF

157

FEATURED HOTELS CLASSIFIED BY AREA

LOWER TOWN
Albert Premier ▥
Métropole ▥▥ ⬙
New Siru ▥
Orion ▥
Palace ▥
SAS Royal ▥▥ ⬙
UPPER TOWN
Pullman Astoria ▥ ⬙
SUBURBS
Le 1815 ▥ to ▥
Lloyd George ▢ to ▢ ◖
Sodehotel ▥
Les Tourelles ▢ ◖

OFF GRAND'PLACE
Amigo ▥ to ▥ ⬙
Arlequin ▥
La Madeleine ▢ to ▢ ◖
AVENUE LOUISE
Copthorne Stephanie ▥
Manos Stephanie ▥
Mayfair ▥ ⬙
Mövenpick Cadett ▥ to ▥
Rembrandt ▢ to ▢ ◖
EUROPEAN QUARTER
Archimède ▥ to ▥
City Garden ▥
Stanhope ▥ ⬙

Brussels' hotels A to Z

LE 1815
Route du Lion 367-369, B-1410 Waterloo
☎(02)387.00.60 ☒(02)387.12.92 ▥ to
▥ 15 rms ⬅ ⬛ AE ⊙ ⊙ VISA ⌨ ▢
▣ ⬛ ⬛ ⬛ ⬛ ⬛ ⬛ ↻ ✓ Train to
Braine l'Alleud, then a 5min taxi ride.
Location: On the plain of Waterloo, 200m (220 yards) from the new visitors' center and 17km (11 miles) from the heart of Brussels. Uniquely placed on the site of one of Europe's most famous battles, Le 1815 is an ideal location for those wishing to combine business with pleasure. The hotel has been completely modernized, offering a conference room and heliport. Yet it also makes imaginative use of its central theme — the battle of Waterloo and its leading personalities. Visitors can stay in individually decorated roms dedicated to the Duke of Wellington, the Emperor Napoleon, and all the other generals involved in that historic encounter. A miniature 18-hole golf course in the hotel gardens highlights key events from the battle.

ALBERT PREMIER
Place Rogier 20, B-1210 Bruxelles
☎(02)217.21.25 ☒(02)217.93.31. Map
4C4 ▥ 285 rms AE ⊙ ⊙ VISA ✱ ▢ ▣
⬛ Y ▣ Metro to Rogier.

Location: Lower Town, 10 minutes' walk from Grand'Place. This Art Deco hotel was recently renovated in a tasteful Post-Modern style. The rooms are bright and airy, with a stylish decor. The room rates are kept low by dispensing with needless luxuries, though some might wish that there was a parking lot and restaurant attached. The square outside can be noisy, but the nearby JARDIN BOTANIQUE provides a patch of relative tranquility.

AMIGO ⬙
Rue de l'Amigo 1, B-1000 Bruxelles
☎(02)511.59.10 ☒(02)513.52.77. Map
3E3 ▥ to ▥ 183 rms ▤ ⌨ ⬅ AE
⊙ ⊙ VISA ✱ ▢ ▣ ⬛ Y ▣ ⬛ Tram 52, 55, 58, 81 to Bourse.
Location: In the Lower Town, just off Grand'Place. The aristocratic ambience and attentive staff make the Amigo one of the truly great hotels of Europe. It is frequented by a steady stream of statesmen, conductors, writers and film stars. The hotel was constructed in the 1950s, on the site of an old prison, known as the Amigo by the Spanish governors. Built using old red bricks and gray paving stones, the hotel blends in well with the older buildings in the neighborhood. The

bedrooms are spacious and comfortable, with handsome antiques and 19thC Belgian paintings. Each room has a different decor, and regulars often develop a fondness for one room. Ask for a 6th-floor room at the front of the hotel, for a balcony with a view of the Gothic HOTEL DE VILLE opposite.

ARCHIMÈDE
Rue Archimède 22, B-1040 Bruxelles
☎*(02)231.09.09* 🖷*(02)230.33.71. Map*
1C3 ▥ *to* ▥ *56 rms* � AE ⊙ ⊙ ▨
✱ ☐ ⌂ ▤ *Metro to Schuman.*
Location: In the European Quarter. The Archimède makes the curious claim of being the only hotel in Brussels with a sea view. This small hotel near the European institutions has won many friends by its combination of attentive service and quirky humor. Two mock butlers pose in the lobby, while the corridors are decorated with rare kimonos from the owner's private collection. The bedrooms are each slightly different, with zany Post-Modern desks and original Belgian prints. But the most appealing feature is the breakfast room, which is decorated with brass portholes and canvas chairs to create the atmosphere of a luxury yacht. The illusion is successfully completed by a vast mock sea view painted on the back garden wall.

ARLEQUIN
Entrances at Petite rue des Bouchers 16, rue de la Fourche 17-19, B-1000 Bruxelles
☎*(02)514.16.15* 🖷*(02)514.22.02. Map*
3D3 ▥ AE ⊙ ⊙ ▨ ✱ ☐ ⌂ *Tram 52, 55, 58, 81 to Bourse; metro to Gare Centrale.*
Location: Just 5 minutes' walk from Grand'Place. A plain, but perfectly adequate hotel in the heart of the old town. Hemmed in by 17thC buildings, the hotel is reached down a modern arcade. Say no to a room on the second floor, and ask for one facing the Hôtel de Ville, if possible. The hotel is next to the highbrow Actors' Studio cinema, in a quarter crammed with restaurants. The only drawback is that you must squeeze past trucks unloading crates of beer and

bags of mussels if you venture out in the early morning.

COPTHORNE STEPHANIE
Av. Louise 91, B-1050 Bruxelles
☎*(02)539.02.40* 🖷*(02)538.03.07. Map*
6H4 ▥ *142 rms* ▦ ▨ ⌂ ➥ AE ⊙ ⊙
▨ ✱ ☐ ⌂ ▦ ⌖ ✠ ⚥ ▤ *Tram 91, 92, 93, 94 to Stéphanie.*
Location: In the Upper Town near Galerie Louise. Owned by a British hotel group, the Stephanie possesses something of the relaxed ambience of a country house hotel. It is small enough to be friendly, yet more than efficient enough to serve the continent-hopping businessman. The rooms are generously proportioned, and all have been recently renovated with classic British furnishings. You get tea-making equipment in the room and a trouser press in the closet. The hotel sets you up for the day with an excellent British breakfast cooked to order, featuring bacon, sausage, scrambled eggs and mushrooms.

LLOYD GEORGE ▦
Av. Lloyd George 12, B-1050 Bruxelles
☎*(02)648.30.72* 🖷*(02)646.53.61. Map*
1C3 ☐ *to* ▥ *15 rms* AE ⊙ ⊙ ▨ ✱
⌂ *Tram 23, 90, 93, 94 to Étoile.*
Location: In Ixelles, facing the Bois de la Cambre. A friendly hotel situated in a Neo-Baroque town house built in 1925. The furniture is rather old-fashioned and the bathrooms need renovating, but the location is ideal for rambles in the BOIS DE LA CAMBRE, or in the gardens of the ABBAYE DE LA CAMBRE. The bohemian atmosphere makes the Lloyd George a favorite with impoverished academics visiting the nearby Université Libre de Bruxelles. Some rooms are cramped, but those for four people are spacious. Choose a room at the front for a view of the forest, or ask for one at the back to sleep soundly. Count on 20 minutes to get to the city center by tram.

MAYFAIR ▦
Av. Louise 381, B-1050 Bruxelles
☎*(02)649.98.00* 🖷*(02)640.17.64. Map*
1C3 ▥ *99 rms* ▦ ▨ ⌂ ➥ AE ⊙ ⊙ ▨

✢ ☐ ☒ ❄ ⛢ ☒ ▤ ⌷ Tram 93, 94 to Van Eyck.

Location: In a residential quarter of Ixelles, 5 minutes' walk from the Bois. A modern hotel furnished in impeccable taste with Baroque antiques and Japanese porcelain. The bedrooms are bright, if rather bland, with every comfort you might need to help you recover from a long day. Ask for one of the rooms with a balcony for a panoramic view of avenue Louise. Breakfast is served in the luxurious setting of the hotel's Louis XVI restaurant, and a small garden with a fountain provides a quiet spot for a drink. The hotel was bought recently by a Japanese company, and now boasts a serious restaurant with *sushi* bar and *teppan-yaki* tables.

LA MADELEINE 🏠

Rue de la Montagne 20-22, B-1000 Bruxelles ☒(02)502.13.50. Map 4E4 ▥ to ▥ 55 rms ▨ ◉ ▥ ✢ ☐ ☒ Metro to Gare Centrale.

Location: Off Grand'Place, 5 minutes' walk from Gare Centrale. A friendly hotel occupying two Neo-Baroque gable houses in the Lower Town. The smallish rooms are furnished in an unfussy, modern style, and those at the front have good views onto a quiet square. For budget travelers, the location opposite Central Station is ideal, and inexpensive rooms are available for single travelers or threesomes. Those with a car should park in the nearby Agora multistory garage, but be sure to remember the floor number to avoid a harrowing hunt.

MANOS STEPHANIE

Chaussée de Charleroi 28, B-1060 Bruxelles ☎(02)539.02.50 ▦(02)537.57.29. Map 6H4 ▥ 48 rms ▨ ➡ ▨ ◉ ▣ ▥ ✢ ☐ ☒ ⛢ ☒ Tram 91, 92, 93, 94 to Stéphanie.

Location: Off avenue Louise, 5 minutes' walk from place Louise. An intimate, family-run hotel gracefully furnished with antiques and paintings. The rooms are comfortable and stylish, with handsome Rococo desks and Italianate fabrics. Pleasing touches are everywhere, such as the gilt frame around the key rack and the vast bowls of flowers. The Suite Palace (#109 ▥) is rather special, with a mezzanine bedroom reached by a spiral staircase. The same family runs the nearby Hotel Manos.

MÉTROPOLE 🏠

Place de Brouckère 31, B-1000 Bruxelles ☎(02)217.23.00 ▦(02)218.02.20. Map 3D3 ▥ 400 rms ▨ ➡ ▨ ◉ ▣ ▥ ✢ ☐ ☒ ⛢ ☞ ☒ ☒ Metro to Brouckère.

Location: On a grand 19thC boulevard in the Lower Town. Celebrities have been staying at the Métropole since it opened in 1895. Built by theater architect Alban Chambon, it is a gloriously rich Neo-Renaissance monument, laden with heavy columns and statues. The restaurant, bar and café (see CAFÉS on page 178) have scarcely changed since the days when Sarah Bernhardt and Albert Einstein stayed here. An ancient elevator with an ornate iron grille still carries guests to the upper floors. The bedrooms have rather dated and dented furniture, and often antiquated bathrooms, but the owner is in no hurry to change. Some may prefer their accommodation to be more modern, but for many writers and artists the Métropole is the perfect Brussels hotel.

LE 1815 See page 158.

MÖVENPICK CADETT

Rue Paul Spaak 15, B-1050 Bruxelles ☎(02)645.61.11 ▦(02)646.63.44. Map 1C3 ▥ 128 rms ▨ ▨ ➡ ▨ ◉ ▣ ▥ ✢ ☐ ☒ ❄ ⛢ ☞ ☒ ☒ Tram 93, 94 to Lesbroussart.

Location: In a quiet street off avenue Louise. Mövenpick Cadett hotels have been carefully thought out to meet the needs of the traveling businessman. They have pared down their bedrooms to the absolute essentials. You get a big bed with a good mattress, a desk designed for the serious workaholic, and a single hi-tech armchair to collapse into at the end of a long flight. Breakfast consists of an ample selection of cereals, bread, rolls, eggs and sausages.

The hotel has a specialized wine bar and restaurant, but for some the most tempting feature is the round-the-clock availability of Mövenpick ice cream at the reception desk.

NEW SIRU

Place Rogier 1, B-1210 Bruxelles
☎(02)217.75.80 ☒(02)218.33.03. Map
4B4 ▥ 101 rms ▦ ━ ➟ AE ◉ ⬤
▥ ✦ ☐ ◪ ▰ ♈ Metro to Rogier.
Location: Lower Town, 10 minutes' walk from Grand'Place. An engagingly eccentric hotel where each bedroom contains a original work by a contemporary Belgian artist. This Art Deco building from the 1930s was converted into the world's first art hotel in 1989. You can choose a room with four granite rocks suspended above the bed (#211) or one with two arrows embedded in the ceiling (#513). The romantic traveler should ask for one of the octagonal rooms in the tower (ending in the digits 08), such as #408 with its voluptuous nude woman by Roger Somville (who painted the mural at Hankar metro station), or #208, which features a fresco on the ceiling above the bed. The rooms are cramped and sometimes noisy, but the Post-Modern interior is designed with such flair that the shortcomings are soon forgotten. The art theme continues in the corridors, where Belgian cartoonists have created works to illustrate themes such as "Memories of Travel" and "Unexpected Encounters." The hotel bakes its own bread for breakfast and runs a good brasserie. There is even a tiny theater in the basement, where experimental plays are staged.

PALACE

Rue Gineste 3, B-1210 Bruxelles
☎(02)217.62.00 ☒(02)218.76.51. Map
4C5 ▥ 360 rms ➟ AE ◉ ⬤ ▥ ✦ ☐
◪ ▰ ♈ ▤ Metro to Rogier.
Location: Lower Town, 10 minutes' walk from Grand'Place. Opened in 1908, the Palace in its heyday was one of the great European hotels, visited by the likes of Orson Welles and Rita Hayworth. It fell on hard times in the 1970s,

and came within a whisker of being demolished, but it has now been saved and carefully renovated by a Brussels hotel group. The corridors and rooms retain a certain grandeur, and some still have original furniture. The hotel is now mainly used for conferences, but romantic couples might still be tempted to book into the Grace Kelly suite (#150), which has kept the flashy 1950s decor installed for Princess Grace, including perhaps the most romantic bed in town.

PULLMAN ASTORIA 🏛

Rue Royale 103, B-1000 Bruxelles
☎(02)217.62.90 ☒(02)217.11.50. Map
4D5 ▥ 125 rms ▦ ➟ AE ◉ ⬤ ▥ ✦
☐ ◪ ▰ ♈ ▤ Metro or tram 92, 93, 94 to Botanique.
Location: In the Upper Town, 5 minutes' walk from the Jardin Botanique. One of the grand old hotels of Brussels, the Astoria was built in 1909 in a palatial style modeled on the Hotel Adlon in Berlin. The Astoria has the most glittering entrance hall in Brussels, with gilded mirrors and plump cherubs. It has seen many famous guests, including the Emperor Hirohito, Churchill and Eisenhower, and yet the staff nowadays seem sometimes rather nonchalant. The bedrooms are comfortable, if without special charm, and it may strike the traveler that this hotel has mislaid the touch that gave it its former sparkle.

REMBRANDT 🏚

Rue de la Concorde 42, B-1050 Bruxelles
☎(02)512.71.39 ☒(02)511.71.36. Map
1C3 ☐ to ▥ 15 rms ◉ ⬤ ▥ ✦ ◪
Tram 91, 92, 93, 94 to Stéphanie.
Location: In a quiet Ixelles street, 10 minutes on foot from place Louise. One of the most attractive little hotels in Brussels, located in a bright pink, 19thC corner house on a street off avenue Louise. The hotel is furnished with a tasteful collection of antiques, and its elevator must be one of the smallest ever made. The breakfast room is an intimate place in which to strike up a conversation with fellow travelers. The bedrooms are small, but bright and airy, with paintings and vases of fresh

flowers. Reserve your room several weeks ahead. The corner room (#6) is particularly bright and spacious.

SAS ROYAL 🏨

Rue du Fossé-aux-Loups 47, B-1000 Bruxelles ☎(02)219.28.28 🖷(02)219.62.62. Map 4D4 ▦ 281 rms ▤ ▣ ⇌ AE ◉ ▩ ‡ ☐ ▱ ▦ ⚍ ⚐ ⇌ ☿ ▤ Metro to Brouckère.

Location: In the Lower Town, a 10-minute walk from Grand'Place. This new hotel designed by a Belgian architect in a jazzy Art Deco style has rapidly established itself as one of the best business hotels in the city. The eight-floor atrium exudes pure American glitz, with its tiers of rampant greenery and nippy glass elevators. The bar tables are dotted around below, amid gurgling water and a restored fragment of 12thC city wall. Guests at SAS hotels get pampered almost to excess. They can pick a room decorated in Italian style (with quirky furniture), Scandinavian (with bare wooden floors), or opt for a warm-toned Oriental interior furnished with Colonial cane chairs. You can leave a recorded message on the room phone or check out using the TV screen.

The SAS staff cater to one's every whim with a quiet professionalism. They'll launder a shirt in three hours flat and pick up your favorite daily newspaper if it's in the shops. The staff rush to correct any defect in the room and let you stay put long after other hotels have hustled their guests out.

The business center on the ground floor has clued-up staff to fax, photocopy or find you a Tagalog translator. The hotel can handle a 300-person conference, or set up the hideaway **Rotonde** conference room at the top of the building for an intimate meeting. You can eat a tasty Scandinavian smørrebrød in the atrium or sample moist Norwegian salmon in the **Sea Grill** restaurant. Guests dashing for an early morning appointment can grab an express breakfast rather than the buffet spread, and anyone flying full-fare SAS or Swissair can check in their suitcases in the hotel lobby.

SODEHOTEL LA WOLUWÉ

Av. E. Mounier 5, B-1200 Bruxelles ☎(02)775.21.11 🖷(02)770.47.80. Map 2C4 ▦ 112 rms ▤ ▬ ▣ ⇌ AE ◉ ◉ ▩ ▣ ‡ ☐ ▱ ☿ ⚐ ☿ ▤ Metro to Alma, then a 5min walk across university campus (follow signs to Hôpital Saint-Luc).

Location: In Woluwé-St-Lambert, 10 minutes from the airport by shuttle bus. This is an attractive new hotel in a quiet semi-rural location facing an old wooden windmill (see CURIOSITIES on page 91). The bedrooms are comfortable and well equipped, with trouser press, safe and plugs for computer and fax. Ask for a room with a balcony, or think about paying the extra for a capacious suite with two rooms and two bathrooms.

The hotel has a good restaurant with a terrace, but its outstanding feature is a sophisticated auditorium seating 200, equipped with simultaneous-interpretation booths and a large screen. Owned by Sabena airlines, the Sodehotel runs a free shuttle service to the airport every 30 minutes. The nearby metro gets you directly to Schuman in 5 minutes (for the European Quarter) and Bourse (for the Lower Town) in 15 minutes. It is worth wandering to the nearby university campus to look at the unusual modern architecture (see METRO STATIONS on page 142).

STANHOPE 🏨

Rue du Commerce 9, B-1040 Bruxelles ☎(02)506.91.11 🖷(02)512.17.08. Map 6F6 ▦ 50 rms ▤ ▣ ⇌ AE ◉ ▩ ▱ ‡ ☐ ▱ ⚘ ⚐ ⚍ ☿ ▤ ▤ Metro to Luxembourg.

Location: Upper Town, in the heart of the business district. A comforting small hotel, angled at business travelers, tastefully decorated in the style of a British country house, with plump sofas, 18thC paintings and antique desks. Rooms are individually decorated like a private home, with TV sets tucked away in antique cabinets, and even the occasional 4-poster bed. Even the complimentary fruit and flowers vary from one room to another. The hotel has *trompe l'oeil* bookshelves in the bar and also the elevator, and a breakfast room decorated with pastel murals inspired by the Royal Pavilion at Brighton. You can watch stock market reports on the television, or ask for a fax machine in your bedroom.

LES TOURELLES 🏨

Av. Winston Churchill 135, B-1180 Bruxelles ☎*(02)344.02.84* 🖷*(02)346.42.70. Map* *1D3* ▢ *21 rms* ➡ *No cards* ▢ ▨ *Tram 23, 90 to Cavell.*
Location: On a leafy boulevard in Uccle. A rambling hotel occupies an quaint Normandy-style building with

half timbering and turrets. Once a girls' boarding school, the hotel seems old-fashioned and rather French, with creaking wooden staircases (there is no elevator) and an assortment of antique furniture. Les Tourelles has a wide variety of rooms on offer. The best room is the suite (#7 ▨), which comprises two rooms facing the garden and is tastefully furnished with antiques. Stay at Les Tourelles if you want to experience traditional Belgian courtesy, but give it a miss if you insist on double glazing and a garage. Count on 30 minutes to get into the town center by tram.

Apartment hotels

Apartment hotels offer a room with a kitchen and ample storage space for luggage. They are ideal for extended stays in the city, or for parents with small children, who don't wish to face the frazzle of restaurant meals.

The **Copthorne Stephanie** and the **Stanhope** (see entries in HOTELS A TO Z) have some apartment rooms to let for extended stays.

CITY GARDEN

Rue Joseph II 59, B-1040 Bruxelles ☎*(02)230.09.45* 🖷*(02)230.64.37. Map* *1C3* ▨ *95 rms* 🄰🄴 ◈ ◑ 🆅🅸🆂🅰 ✳ ▢ ▨ 🚇 *Metro to Arts-Loi.*
Location: In the heart of the European Quarter. This modern hotel offers bright bedrooms furnished in a sober modern style. The spacious rooms are ideal for prolonged business stays in Brussels; some have separate kitchens, while others are fitted with folding beds to allow the room to be used as an office. There are connections for fax and modem, and the beds are extra long. The reception and breakfast room are perhaps too functional for ordinary tourists, and the neighborhood is rather uninteresting after dark.

ORION

Quai au Bois à Brûler 51, B-1000 Bruxelles ☎*(02)221.14.11* 🖷*(02)221.15.99. Map* *3C3* ▨ *169 rms* ▢ 🄰🄴 ◈ ◑ 🆅🅸🆂🅰 ✳ ▢ ▨ *Metro to Sainte-Catherine.*
Location: In the Lower Town facing the old fish market. The French Orion group has designed an apartment hotel that concentrates on the basics. The rooms are modern and practical, if not palatial, and there is ample space to store suitcases. Orion have put a lot of thought into the eating arrangements in their apartments. Each double room has a modern kitchen with cooker, oven, refrigerator and enough dishes to serve six. Single rooms, though small, have a table to seat four at a pinch. The cupboards are packed with cooking utensils, including a coffee pot, colander, lettuce spinner and ample pots (including one that would do perfectly for mussels). The hotel's location off place Sainte-Catherine is ideal for laying-in essential supplies. There is a daily market on place Sainte-Catherine, and specialist shops in the neighborhood stock Dutch mussels, Ostend sole, Ardennes pheasant (in season), Belgian cheeses and good wines.

Eating and drinking

Dining out in Brussels

Whether they are Flemish or Walloon, whether they like substantial country dishes or the comforting delights of *cuisine ménagère*, whether or not they have the discriminating palate of an epicure, all Belgians love to eat. Together with the quality of the cooking, something that never fails to strike visitors to Belgium is the quantity of food absorbed, and the size of portions in restaurants. This is not new. When Victor Hugo was a political exile in Brussels, a man sitting at the next table in a restaurant said to him, "You must surely be French to eat so much bread." Hugo replied in his usual gruff manner, "And you must surely be Belgian to eat so much."

The Belgians are and have always been the *bons vivants* of Europe — just look at the Rabelaisian scenes that run through Flemish painting, from Bruegel to Jordaens. But their love of food, drink and revelry is a social phenomenon and goes hand in hand with religious, social and family rituals, some of which go back to early Christian times. Belgian folklore is still very much alive and almost any pretext is good enough for a party, a fête, a procession or a carnival. Such rituals are highly organized and are the responsibility of the guilds.

These guilds, which are so very much part of Belgian tradition today, are a remnant of the Middle Ages. Then, every aspect of life was regulated by them, not least the wine and food trade (the beer trade was mostly controlled by the monasteries). An evocative reminder of this, which also reflects the important role played by food in Belgian life, is the wealth of street names that relate to the acts of eating and drinking. Brussels alone has more than 120 streets named after some kind of foodstuff, from rue du Marché aux Fromages to impasse aux Huîtres, from Vieille Halle aux Blés to Petite rue au Beurre.

Belgium has an astonishing number of good restaurants, and those mentioned in this chapter are but the tip of the culinary iceberg.

CHOOSING WHERE TO EAT

Eating out in Brussels is easy; choosing where to eat could pose a problem. There are over 2,000 restaurants, from the world-famous ones like COMME CHEZ SOI to the local corner *estaminet* (café), where you can find anything from the ubiquitous *steak/frites* (steak and fries) to wonderful homemade soups and beef *carbonnades*.

Many restaurants close for part of July, while those in the EC area are frequently shut during August instead. It is advisable to telephone beforehand, and reservations are recommended all year round.

Symbols show those restaurants that are particularly luxurious (⌂) or simple (☻) in style. See the KEY TO SYMBOLS on page 7 for an explanation of the full list.

The prices corresponding to our symbols are based on the average price of a meal for one person, with house wine and Value-Added Tax (**TVA** or **BTW**) included. Although actual prices will inevitably increase after publication, our relative price categories are likely to remain the same.

Symbol	Category	Current price
▨	very expensive	over 3,000 BF
▨	expensive	2,000-3,000 BF
▨	moderate	1,500-2,000 BF
▨	inexpensive	1,200-1,500 BF
▢	cheap	800-1,200 BF

A GUIDE TO THE MENU

The international status of Brussels is reflected in the variety of cuisines from all over the world that are there for the tasting. Belgian cuisine is not a mere copy of neighboring France, and many items on the menu are uniquely Belgian. Like most countries dedicated to good food, Belgium offers a wide variety of cooking from the simplest country fare to the most sophisticated dishes. It is, however, rarely complicated, for elaboration only came with the inventive cuisine of gastronomes.

Waterzooi heads the list of the most talked-about dishes. There are even arguments as to whether it originated with fish or chicken. But does it matter? You will now find chicken, rabbit and shellfish versions quite easily. It is a mixture of lightly poached ingredients, enriched with cream and egg yolks. *Waterzooi* aficionados will always ask if a parsley root has been used in the flavorings — if not, it is not the real thing.

Croquettes de fromages (cheese croquettes) cause further concern. Some say that the Parmesan croquette is an upstart, while others claim it is equally good, and yet others reckon the *croquettes aux crevettes* (with shrimps) are even better. If visiting in the game season, try *faisan à la brabançonne* (pheasant with braised endives), or, in the month of May, *asperges à la flamande* (asparagus with melted butter and finely chopped hard-boiled egg). In spring you will find *jets de houblon* (hop shoots) which are delicious with scrambled eggs. *Anguilles au vert* (eels in a green herb sauce) is a very popular dish. *Boudin blanc* (white sausage) and *noir* (blood) are usually served with stewed apple and make a good snack for adults and children alike.

You will find *carbonnade* (casserole of beef) on menus, followed by the names of different regions — always basically the same recipe, with small local variations. Something *à la Liègeoise* usually includes juniper berries, although a *Salade Liègeoise* is a warm mixture of green beans, potatoes and bacon with a dressing of vinegar that has been poured into the pan in which the bacon was cooked and reduced by a third. *L'oie à l'instar de Visé*, one of Belgium's most elaborate dishes, is made from goose that has first been poached with a whole head of garlic, then sautéed. The cooked garlic is then puréed, added to some of the broth, and enriched with cream and egg yolks to make a wonderful garlic sauce.

There are also a number of Belgian cheeses. Almost every province has one or several representative cheeses; Brabant has *bettekees, stinkkees* (which, as its name implies, is strong smelling), *schopkees* and *pottekees;* Liège has numerous and well-known *herves* and *maquêyes;* Flanders the *Westfleteren* and *Watou* cheeses; Limburg the *wittekaas, boerenplatte-kaas* and *Limburger;* Hainaut the *Chimay* and the *boulettes de Beau-mont;* Namur its famous *cassettes* and *boulettes;* and the Maredsous the *Romedenne, Couvin, Coldes-Sarts, Surice* and *Floreffe.*

FEATURED RESTAURANTS AND CAFÉS CLASSIFIED BY AREA

The restaurants and cafés listed by area below can be found in alphabetical order on pages 167-172 and 177-9, except for those in the European Quarter, which are grouped together on pages 172-4.

GRAND'PLACE

≈ Brasserie de la Roue d'Or *Belgian* ▥

≈ Chez Jean *Belgian* ▥ ☖

≈ La Maison du Cygne *French* ▦ ⬠

▣ La Brouette

▣ La Chaloupe d'Or

▣ Le Roi d'Espagne

LOWER TOWN

≈ Les Années Folles *French* ▥

≈ Le Café de Paris *French/seafood* ▦

≈ Comme Chez Soi *French* ▦ ⬠

≈ L'Idiot du Village *French* ▥

≈ Jacques *Seafood* ▥ ☖

≈ La Manufacture *French* ▥

≈ Au Stekerlapatte *Belgian* ▥

≈ Les Trois Chicons *Belgian* ▥ ☖

▣ La Bécasse

▣ Le Cirio

▣ Le Falstaff

▣ La Fleur en Papier Dore

▣ Le Goupil le Fol

▣ L'Imaige Nostre-dame

▣ La Lunette

▣ Le Métropole

▣ La Mort Subite

UPPER TOWN

≈ L'Écailler du Palais Royal *Seafood* ▦ ⬠

≈ En Provence Chez Marius *Seafood* ▦

▣ De Ultieme Hallucinatie

AVENUE LOUISE

≈ La Porte des Indes *Indian* ▦ ⬠

EUROPEAN QUARTER

≈ L'Acte Unique *French* ▥

≈ Barbanera *Italian* ▦

≈ Momotaro *Japanese* ▥

≈ Mykonos *Greek* ▥

≈ Nordica *Danish* ▥

≈ Pom Noisette *French* ▥

≈ Al Pomo d'Oro *Italian* ▥

≈ Le Rocher Fleuri *Vietnamese* ▥ ☖

≈ Rosticceria Fiorentina *Italian* ▥ ☖

≈ Sole di Capri *Italian* ▦

≈ Le Stévin *French* ▥

≈ Takesushi *Japanese* ▥ ☖

≈ Villa de Bruselas *Spanish* ▦

▣ The Drum

▣ Kitty O'Shea's

SUBURBS

≈ Les Brasseries Georges *French* ▦

≈ Due Signori *Italian* ▥

≈ Le Fruit de ma Passion *French* ▦

≈ Monochrome *French* ▥

≈ L'Océan *Belgian* ▥

≈ La Quincaillerie *French* ▦

≈ Restaurant Saint-Boniface *French* ▥ ☖

La Tour d'Argent
Vietnamese ▯

Au Vieux Bruxelles
Belgian ▯ ☕

La Villa Lorraine
French ▥ ⌂

Bierodrome

La Terrasse

ÎLOT SACRÉ

Chez Léon *Belgian* ▯

L'Ogenblik *French* ▥

Taverne du Passage
Belgian ▥

Vincent *Belgian* ▥

Chez Toone

Mokafé

Brussels restaurants A to Z

LES ANNÉES FOLLES *French*
Rue Haute 17, B-1000. Map 5F3
☎(02)513.58.58 ▯ ▯ ▯ ▯ *Closed
Sat lunch; Sun. Metro to Porte de Hal, then
a 10min walk.*
A charming restaurant with a turn-of-
the-century decor. It has come into and
gone out of fashion with the in-crowd,
but the faithful are still there in numbers. If you happen to know Belgian
celebrities, it is a place to come to spot
them. Unfortunately they do not have
numbers like trains or aircraft so you
will have to do your homework before
you go. The lunch menu is excellent
value. Try the lamb's sweetbread with
mustard sauce or the fillet of beef. The
braised salmon with honey and lime is
a very good marriage of flavors.

BRASSERIE DE LA ROUE D'OR *Belgian*
Rue des Chapeliers 26, B-1000. Map 3E3
☎(02)514.25.54 ▯ ▯ ▯ ▯ *Closed
Sat; Sun; last 2wks July; 1st wk Aug. Tram
52, 55, 58, 81 to Bourse.*
This is considered by most restaurant
critics to be the best bistro in Brussels.
Although just off Grand'Place, this bas-
tion of Belgian cooking has not been
swallowed up by tourists. Wood-paneling, large mirrors and floating Magritte-
like figures add a Surrealist touch to
walls that have a comfortable patina
from countless steaming dishes. There
are steak, lamb and many fish dishes as
well as the numerous traditional recipes
served. Try warm pig's foot with a sharp
vinaigrette or a gigantic *jambonneau*
(ham knuckle).

LES BRASSERIES GEORGES *French*
*Av. Winston Churchill 259, B-1180. Map
1D3* ☎(02)347.21.00 ▥ ▯ ▯ ▯
Closed Sun. Tram 23, 90 to Longchamp.
Owner Georges Neef has taken all the
ingredients that make for a bistro atmosphere — marble-topped tables,
bentwood chairs, paneled and mirrored
walls, brass fittings, good lighting, and
added atmosphere, hustle and bustle,
the clinking and chinking of glasses,
waiters in long white aprons and a well-
thought-out-menu with Parisian-type
dishes such as *saucisson chaud aux
pistaches et pommes à l'huile* (hot sausage and potato salad with pistachio nuts
and nut oil). The key to this restaurant's
success is the enormous *plateau de
fruits de mer*.

LE CAFÉ DE PARIS *French/seafood*
*Rue de la Vierge Noire 12, B-1000. Map
3D3* ☎(02)512.39.40 ▥ ▯ ▯ ▯
*Closed Sun. Metro or tram 52, 55, 58, 81
to de Brouckère.*
This is one of those places to see and be
seen. Beautiful people, beautiful decor
and smiling helpful service. By the
same owner as LES BRASSERIES GEORGES,
this bistro also owes its success to the
wonderful *plateau de fruits de mer*,
where the shellfish, some cooked,
some raw, are arranged on a bed of
cracked ice and seaweed. Depending
on how much you want to spend, it will
include oysters, mussels, Dublin Bay
prawns, *praires, palourdes, clovisses*
(different species of clam), cockles,
winkles, crab, lobster and so on.

CHEZ JEAN *Belgian* 🍴

Rue des Chapeliers 6, B-1000. Map 3E3
☎*(02)511.98.15* 🔲 *AE* 🔲 *VISA Closed Sun; Mon; June. Tram 52, 55, 58, 81 to Bourse.*

This should really be called son of Jean. Jean himself looks down from a frame on the wall, overseeing this most traditional of restaurants. Yet nothing much has changed here in years. The central stove is still dual-purpose, acting as a plate-warmer and providing heating. The toilet is outside and the black-uniformed, lace-collared waitresses are still motherly. They have been known to refuse more bread before your meal "as you will not be able to eat what you have ordered." Baked cod, mussels and veal kidneys are all good value.

CHEZ LÉON *Belgian*

Rue des Bouchers 18, B-1000. Map 3D3
☎*(02)511.14.15* 🔲 *AE* 🔲 *VISA Metro to de Brouckère.*

If it's mussels and chips that you're after, look no farther than Chez Léon. This down-to-earth restaurant has been satisfying Belgians and tourists alike for many years. It is reputed that a ton of mussels is served and eaten in this establishment every day of the year. In fact, so successful has it been in serving up large quantities of mussels that the idea has now been franchised and has started a new craze in fast food, with restaurants opening throughout Belgium and branching into Paris, Strasbourg and London.

COMME CHEZ SOI *French* 🍴

Place Rouppe 23, B-1000. Map 5F2.
☎*(02)512.29.21* 🔲 *AE* 🔲 *Closed Sun; Mon; July. Tram 52, 55, 58, 81 to Anneessens.*

Pierre Wynants is the owner/chef of this world-famous restaurant. In the Wynants family for three generations, this one time *estaminet* has reached the heady heights of gastronomic excellence. If you would like to watch exquisite food being prepared, there is a *table d'hôte* in the kitchen. For this bird's eye view, as for the rest of the restaurant, reservations will have to be

made at least a month ahead. It is more than worth the price and the wait. Specialities of the house include diced scallops and Dublin Bay prawns with white truffles (Nov-Dec), hot oysters with *chicons* and diced bacon, local free-range chicken with crayfish *béarnaise*, and fresh strawberry meringue spiked with strawberry *eau-de-vie* (a pure alcohol).

The Art Nouveau interior is a recent expensive addition to this unassuming town house in the place Rouppe.

DUE SIGNORI *Italian*

Blvd. Brandt Whitlock 60, B-1200. Map 2C4
☎*(02)733.59.54* 🔲 *AE* 🔲 *Closed Sun; Mon; mid-July to mid-Aug. Metro or bus to Schuman.*

Giovanni Darnala, the owner and host, is the sort of Italian they make movies about. Nervous, loud, embracing, funny, rude—all these emotions within the first three minutes of your crossing the threshold. The decor has an air of bourgeois solidity, and there is a good garden terrace for summertime eating. Although there is a menu, Giovanni always has a few improvisations up his sleeve, so be sure to ask for his recommendations.

L'ÉCAILLER DU PALAIS ROYAL *Seafood* 🍴

Rue Bodenbroeck 18, B-1000. Map 6F4
☎*(02)512.87.51* 🔲 *AE* 🔲 *VISA* 🔲 🔲
Closed Sun; 1st week Mar; Aug. Tram 91, 92, 93, 94 to Petit Sablon.

L'Écailler is one of the best fish restaurants in Brussels. Situated not far from the Palais du Roi, the Parlement and the headquarters of the main Belgian banks, its clientele tends to hail from the business brigade. The decor is warm wood-paneling, and if you can get yourself invited by a Belgian Minister, you might be allowed to take your meal perched on one of the much-coveted bar stools. In any case, however quick or leisurely your meal, the service will be extremely correct.

Specialities include *blanc de turbot au beurre de foie gras* (fillet of turbot with gooseliver butter), *ragoût de lotte et langoustines* (casserole of monkfish and Dublin Bay prawns) and *homard sauté à la crème d'oseille* (lobster in a sorrel and cream sauce).

LE FRUIT DE MA PASSION *French*
Rue J.B. Meunier 53a, B-1180. Map **1D3**
☎*(02)347.32.94* ▥ ▣ ▥ ▥ ▰
Closed Sat; Sun; 1st 3wks July. Tram 91, 92 to Molière.

One of the originators of the now ubiquitous floral display, Eric Rolin's apricot-colored bistro deluxe, with its flickering candles and green plants, is the place to go if you are seducing or want to be seduced. The menu changes with what is available at the market. The dishes chalked up on the blackboard are mainly a guide to what is on offer. The owner personally steers you through the day's suggestions and the wine, if you so wish. But if you are on a budget, ask for the prices or you may find the bill less than seductive.

L'IDIOT DU VILLAGE *French*
Rue Notre-Seigneur 19, B-1000. Map **5F3**
☎*(02)502.55.82* ▥ ▣ ▣ ▥ *Closed Mon. Tram 91, 92, 93, 94 to Petit Sablon, then a 10min walk.*

The prettiest and most charmingly offbeat bistro to emerge in Brussels in the last few years. A dried herb-and-spice display in what was once an old shop window entice you inside to other curiosities — a wall-hanging of dried roses, a post office counter, an empty picture frame on a midnight blue wall. This is an interior that reflects its location between the antique and flea markets. The food is inventive and bistroesque, and the wine list superlative for such a small (25 seats) restaurant.

JACQUES *Seafood* ▱
Quai aux Briques 44, B-1000. Map **3D3**
☎*(02)513.27.62* ▥ *No cards. Closed Sun; July. Metro to Sainte-Catherine.*

A wooden bench runs down one side of this restaurant, so thigh-to-thigh seating can be achieved. This ever-popular fish restaurant prides itself on the main ingredients, and it really is the only Brussels restaurant where the sauces come as a second thought. Try the

mussels, poached cod or skate — all equally good and equally generous in quantity. Reservations a must.

LA MAISON DU CYGNE *French* ▱
Grand'Place 9, B-1000. Map **3E3**
☎*(02)511.82.44* ▥ ▣ ▣ ▥ ▰ ▰
Closed Sat lunch; Sun; 1st 3wks Aug. Tram 52, 55, 58, 81 to Bourse.

When a restaurant is situated in one of the most beautiful squares in the world, it is difficult to imagine that any food could do it justice. The Maison du Cygne's does. The wood paneling and gilt set the atmosphere for classic French cooking. This must be one of the few restaurants that has not changed in favor of lighter sauces and menus. The food is of the highest quality and the sauces of the richest. Belts have to be loosened on leaving. Try to reserve a table on the first floor near the window, where you will have one of the most spectacular views imaginable. Specialities include *huîtres au champagne* (oysters with champagne) and *turbot braisé aux primeurs* (braised turbot with young vegetables).

LA MANUFACTURE *French*
Rue Notre-Dame du Sommeil 12, B-1000. Map **3D2** ☎*(02)502.25.25* ▥ ▣ ▣ ▥
Closed Sat; Sun. Tram 52, 55, 58, 81 to Bourse, then a 10min walk.

This bistro is worth a visit for the design alone. In former times it was a workshop of Delvaux, the upmarket manufacturer of leather goods. Today, the interior is a large open space with walls of a rich, rusty red color, tables in dark gray marble, and an iron staircase leading to an upper gallery. The food itself is both imaginative and reasonably priced.

The other reason for visiting this restaurant is the *sommelier* (wine waiter) Eric Boschman, who, not yet 30, is one of the most exciting wine buffs around. His wine list is impressive not only for what he has to offer, but for what he has left off. "You don't come to a restaurant to sample a great Burgundy — you do that at home for a tenth of the price." He travels continually and his list reflects this, with a large number of wines from smaller vineyards that normally do not make it onto restaurant wine lists. His appreciation of Australian, American and South African wines is second to none in Belgium.

MONOCHROME French ♣
Rue des Deux Églises 98, B-1040. Map 1C3 ☎*(02)230.35.20* ▨▨ Ⓐ Ⓒ ▨ *Closed Sat lunch; Sun. Metro to Madou, then a 5min walk.*
St Josse is not an area renowned for high quality among its great variety of restaurants, but it now considers itself very happy with the opening of Monochrome. A rather self-consciously arty interior has been ragged, dragged and swagged in cold grays and with just a hint of red. The food is well worth the visit. Try fanned steak with seed mustard sauce, or sea bream with a *meunière* sauce flavored and colored with green celery juice, accompanied by caviar from Iran and shredded deep-fried red cabbage — fine value for money.

L'OCÉAN Belgian
Rue Franz Merjay 165, B-1060. Map 1D3 ☎*(02)344.37.12* ▨▨ Ⓐ Ⓒ ▨ *Closed lunch on Sat and Sun. Tram 91, 92 to Darwin.*
This oh-so-very-Belgian bistro is continually crowded, but knee-to-knee seating, loud music and an even louder clientele do not deter the faithful. A marble-and-cream interior with marble-topped tables and kitchen salt containers on the tables set the tone. The food is new bistro-deluxe style, with an interesting wine list and a bill that veers toward the expensive, considering the lack of comfort. The menu changes regularly.

L'OGENBLIK French
Galerie des Princes 1, B-1000. Map 4D4 ☎*(02)511.61.51* ▨▨ Ⓐ Ⓒ ▨ *Closed Sun. Metro to de Brouckère.*
This restaurant, whose name means a knowing wink, winks knowingly from its green glass lamp shades at the ever-faithfuls who come to sample delicious up-to-the minute flavors — the latest being lavender and rose-petal vinegars

imported from warmer climes, used in salads or for de-glazing the *sauté* pan in which duck or goose liver has been cooked, to enhance the ever-changing menu. Most of the menus include some specialities, such as goose liver, casserole of scallops and large prawns, rack of lamb surrounded by young vegetables, and wild mushrooms, which appear frequently when in season.

LA PORTE DES INDES Indian ⌂
Av. Louise 455, B-1050. Map 1C3 ☎*(02)647.86.51* ▨▨ Ⓐ Ⓒ ▨ *Closed Sun. Tram 23, 90, 93, 94 to Legrand.*
On entering this restaurant, you leave behind a European city to become enveloped in the atmosphere of the East. The attendants are all garbed in exotic costumes of the Raj, the bar is a Moghul tent, and the upstairs dining room is decorated with superb Indian carvings and textiles. The food is delicate and reflects the many different Indian regions from which the owners employ their various chefs. The intricate blending of flavors and spices in this restaurant has become a work of art. Recommended are *Jhinga Malai*, a scampi and vegetable curry, or an unusual Parsee dish *Sali Boti*, a casserole of beef or mutton with apricot. But those who think of Indian food as a cheap way of eating will find the prices rather steep.

EN PROVENCE CHEZ MARIUS Seafood
Place du Petit Sablon 1, B-1000. Map 6F4 ☎*(02)511.12.08* ▨▨ Ⓐ Ⓒ ▨ *Closed Sun. Tram 91, 92, 93, 94 to Petit Sablon.*
This is a small, cozy, excellent restaurant that has been around for a long time. The food and welcome reflect the warmth of its name, and if it is a *bouillabaisse* you need to sustain you, Marius' is the best in Brussels. Specialities include *coquilles St Jacques à l'ail doux* (scallops with sweet garlic).

LA QUINCAILLERIE French
Rue du Page 45, B-1050. Off map 6I4 ☎*(02)538.25.53* ▨▨ Ⓐ Ⓒ ▨ *Closed Sat lunch. Tram 81 to Trinité, or tram 91, 92 to Ma Campagne.*

An old hardware-store-turned-restaurant, which has the unusual decor of floor-to-ceiling drawers (the former repository of screws, nails, bolts and other ironmongers' miscellany) covering the dining room walls. This is very much the hangout of the in-crowd. The food is French-bistro deluxe — try the duck with honey, or be trendy and go for the low-calorie menu.

RESTAURANT SAINT-BONIFACE *French Regional* ✆

Rue Saint-Boniface 9, B-1050. Map 6G5
☎*(02)511.53.66* 🔲 🖅 🔘 🕮 *Closed Sat lunch; Sun. Metro to Porte de Namur, then a 5min walk.*

For pure French regional cooking, head toward the rue Saint-Boniface. Fake wooden panels make the color of dark burgundy, posters of past Brussels exhibitions, brass-ringed half-curtains at the windows, sparkling glasses next to bottles of Calvados, Armagnac and *vieux marc* make just the right setting for this no-holds-barred country cooking. Try the *assiette d'oie Landaise* (thin slices of smoked goose breast, warm slices of stuffed neck and goose brawn served with a sharp, shallot-flavored vinaigrette).

AU STEKERLAPATTE *Belgian*

Rue des Prêtres 4, B-1000. Map 5H3
☎*(02)512.86.81* 🔲 *No cards. Closed lunch; Mon eve. Open until 1am. Metro to Hôtel des Monnaies.*

This restaurant is behind the Palais de Justice, in a rather run-down area of the Marolles. In fact the traveler to Brussels might never even know of its existence. The name says it all — "steak on a plate" — plain Belgian cooking in a lively bistro. Very popular with Belgian celebrities, it serves good food, made using local produce, and seems to have a preference for leggy waitresses.

TAVERNE DU PASSAGE *Belgian*

Galerie de la Reine 30, B-1000. Map 4E4
☎*(02)512.37.31* 🔲 🖅 🔘 🕮 *Closed Wed; Thurs in June and July. Metro to de Brouckère.*

This Art Deco bistro has remained on most foodies' lists, not because of the good Belgian dishes, *waterzooi,* shrimp croquettes and the like, but because the wine list, although not what it was five years ago, still has some excellent, dusty finds. The waiters are an institution, renowned for their brusqueness. But even so, when it comes to food, few Belgians allow such behavior to put them off one of the city's most memorable restaurants. If possible, eat on the terrace in the Galerie de la Reine or the tables on the left as you go in.

LA TOUR D'ARGENT *Vietnamese*

Av. Salomé 1, B-1150. Map 2C4
☎*(02)762.99.80* 🔲 🖅 🔘 *Closed Sat lunch; Wed. Tram 39 to rue au Bois.*

A large white villa with airy rooms, beautifully dressed with green leafy plants, sets the scene for exquisite food. With the first whiff of ginger and citronelle you will be mentally transported to Southeast Asia. Try the grilled monkfish with dill, the Vietnamese *carpaccio* or the peasant stewpot, which marries scampi, chicken and lacquered pork in a perfumed sauce.

LES TROIS CHICONS *Belgian* ✆

Rue des Renards 9, B-1000. Map 5G2
☎*(02)511.55.83* 🔲 🖅 🔘 🕮 *Closed Sun eve; last 2wks Aug; 1st wk Sept. Metro to Porte de Hal, then a 10min walk.*

A stone's throw from the flea market, this bare-brick-walled restaurant, with its bric-à-brac decor, is in the heart of the Marolles area. The food is simple yet savory, and the large open fire is welcoming in this homey restaurant. Here is a little oasis of peace after the crowds of flea market bargain hunters.

AU VIEUX BRUXELLES *Belgian* ✆

Rue St-Boniface 35, B-1050. Map 6G5
☎*(02)513.01.81* 🔲 *No cards. Closed Sun; Mon in June and July. Metro to Porte de Namur, then a 10min walk.*

This restaurant specializes in mussels — in fact it has 25 different ways of offering this humble mollusc. Other Belgian specialities, such as eels in green herb sauce, are also on the menu. Very much a locals' favorite, so either get there early for the first sitting or reserve in advance.

LA VILLA LORRAINE French ⌂
Chaussée de la Hulpe 28, B-1180. Map 1D3 ☎*(02)374.31.63* ▥ ⌷ ⌷ ✪ ➤ ☰ ⌷ *Closed Sun; July. No nearby public transport — travel by car or taxi.*

La Villa Lorraine has charmed the Bruxellois since 1953. This large turn-of-the-century villa on the edge of the Forêt de Soignes has a fairy-tale setting, carried through into the restaurant. The light and airy dining room, with its trellis-covered walls, leads onto a wonderful large terrace where chandeliers suspended over the tables from the branches of the overhanging trees give the impression of being all part of the set of some romantic play. The service is as famous as the restaurant and food itself, neither too stuffy nor too familiar.

Specialities include *selle de chevreuil Cumberland* (saddle of venison with Cumberland sauce), *foie de canard rôti aux reinettes, truffes* (roast duck liver with apple and truffles), *petit rouget aux tomates et basilic* (red mullet with tomatoes and basil) and *soufflé au chocolat amer et au jus de noix verts* (bitter chocolate soufflé with green walnut juice liqueur).

VINCENT Belgian
Rue des Dominicains 8-10, B-1000. Map 3D3 ☎*(02)511.23.03* ▥ ⌷ ⌷ ⌷ *Closed Aug. Metro to de Brouckère.*

The food in this restaurant comes almost second to the marvelous turn-of-century tiled murals. You go through the kitchen to the dining rooms. The food is pure Belgian, with mussels, fish and lots of red meat. The T-bone steak is one of the best in the city.

EATING IN THE EUROPEAN QUARTER

The Berlaymont may be empty now, but over the years numerous restaurants have grown up in its shadow. Even though the European Commission has moved its temporary headquarters across to the other side of the rond-point Schuman, many officials, lobbyists, journalists and others still eat in their old haunts along rue Stévin, rue Archimède and rue Franklin.

This is primarily lunchtime eating, when the ambience and gossip are at their strongest. Be aware that the price categories represented by our symbols reflect the price for **lunch**, rather than dinner, when the set menus are replaced by the *carte* and prices rise accordingly.

Most EC cuisines are represented — Belgian, French, German, Italian, Spanish, Danish, Greek, Portuguese, even British and Irish.

Below is just a sample of the range of eating places on offer in the EC quarter. With a two-hour lunch being the norm, it is perfectly possible to take a cab or drive to the center of town if your dining needs are more upmarket. See recommendations on previous pages.

Reservations for lunch are strongly recommended, although there is less pressure on tables in the evening.

L'ACTE UNIQUE French
Rue Stévin 134, B-1040. Map 1C3 ☎*(02)230.40.37* ▥ ⌷ ⌷ ⌷ ⌷ ⌷. *Closed Sun. Last orders 10.30pm. Metro to Schuman.*

A French-style bistro at the front, with a sidewalk eating in summer, and a more sophisticated restaurant behind, this

friendly establishment caters to most tastes with its varied menu. The combination provides diners with a choice, from basic stomach-fillers through hearty brasserie dishes of *choucroute* or pigs' feet to more refined French fare ranging from *magret de canard aux framboises* to *médaillons de lotte aux deux poivres.* Open throughout the year, even on public holidays, it is possible to have something to eat anytime between 11.30am and 10.30pm. When, after three months, the management could not think of a name for their new venture, they decided to display their EC credentials and adopt the name the "Single European Act" (the Act which, in the mid-1980s, revitalized the EC's drive toward a single market). For people eating on their own, or waiting for a dining companion, the restaurant thoughtfully offers a selection of European newspapers and magazines.

BARBANERA *Italian*
Rue Archimède 69, B-1040. Map 1C3
☎(02)736.14.50 ▯ AE VISA *Closed Sun; mid-Aug to early Sept. Last orders 10.30pm. Metro to Schuman.*
The smart canopy over the entrance and the imposing stairs are early signs of the high standards inside. This restaurant in a former town house is a regular favorite of Italians and senior EC officials, and is renowned especially for its wide selection of pastas and grilled fish. Meat eaters are also generously catered to, with dishes such as *entrecôte gorgonzola.* There is an extensive wine list, and the service is dignified and discreet. The eye-catching decoration and skillful use of mirrors creates a relaxing feel of space.

MYKONOS *Greek* ♧
Rue Archimède 63, B-1040. Map 1C3
☎(02)735.17.59 ▯ ♣ AE ◉ ◎ VISA.
Closed Sat lunch; Sun. Last orders 9.30pm. Metro to Schuman.
There is always a warm welcome in this cozy restaurant. American Lee Better presides over the front of the house, while her Greek husband, Argirios Carananos, prepares his specialities in the kitchen. All the meat is jointed and cut on the premises, and highlights are stuffed rack of lamb, suckling pig and rabbit with cherries. The menu, which includes traditional dishes, is boosted by a regular selection of five types of fresh fish, and, in the evenings, includes grilled squid.

MOMOTARO *Japanese*
Av. d'Auderghem 106, B-1040. Map 1C3
☎(02)734.06.64 ▯ AE ◉ ◎ VISA
Closed Sun. Last orders 10.30pm. Metro to Schuman.
A recent arrival to the Japanese restaurant scene in Brussels, the Momotaro offers a reasonably priced and elegantly served business lunch of *sushi, sashimi* or *tempura.* There is a wide choice of *à la carte* dishes, including grilled fish (*Shioyaki*), and, for the more adventurous, a seafood *fondu (Yosenabe).* A traditional Japanese room on the first floor can be used for banquets, with an extensive ten-course menu ranging from raw fish to grilled dishes.

NORDICA *Danish*
Rue Belliard 220, B-1040. Map 1C3
☎(02)230.14.39 ▯ ◉ ◎ VISA *Metro to Schuman.*
Located on a busy corner, the first-floor restaurant is, however, calm and relaxing. It offers 26 different types of smørrebrød and a selection of warm dishes that can be accompanied by wine, beer or schnapps.

POM NOISETTE *French* ♧
Rue Stévin 124, B-1040. Map 1C3
☎(02)231.07.42 ▯ AE ◉ ◎ VISA
Closed Sat; Sun; eves except Fri; last 2wks Aug. Last orders 3pm. Metro to Schuman.
A spacious, airy restaurant specializing in light foods offers at least ten different types of salad ranging from the *exotique* to the *diététique.* The wide-ranging menu also includes many daily specialities, based on seasonal ingredients like asparagus in May or game in the fall.

AL POMO D'ORO *Italian*
Av. d'Auderghem 48, B-1040. Map 1C3
☎(02)230.04.75 ▯ AE ◉ ◎ VISA *Metro to Schuman.*
This lively restaurant has taken on a new lease on life since the European Commission moved its headquarters to within 50 meters of its front door. Not the place to go if you want to conduct confidential business out of the public gaze. But certainly to be recommended

for its pasta, generous cold buffet and Italian charm, even if the hustle and bustle is quite extreme.

LE ROCHER FLEURI Vietnamese 🍴 ♣
Rue Franklin 19, B-1040. Map 1C3
☎(02)735.00.21 ⅢⅢ 🚗 AE ⊙ ⊙ ⅧⅧ
Closed Sat lunch; Sun; last 2wks Aug. Last orders 11pm. Metro to Schuman.

An ideal venue for a quick and light lunch of tasty food, with efficient, smiling service in bright, colorful surroundings. Especially recommended is the set-price weekday lunchtime eat-as-much-as-you-can hot buffet of crispy deep-fried squid, chicken pieces, vegetable and meat dishes, preceded by a bowl of soup and followed by fruit. More elaborate are the *raviolis aux langoustines* and the *nid de cailles* from the *carte*. Vegetarian food is also available.

ROSTICCERIA FIORENTINA Italian 🍴 ♣
Rue Archimède 45, B-1040. Map 1C3
☎(02)734.92.36 ⬜ AE ⊙ ⅧⅧ Closed Sat; Aug; early Sept. Last orders 10pm. Metro to Schuman.

This friendly, unpretentious Italian family restaurant is known to everyone as Nardi's, after the owner-chef, who is to be found in the kitchen. This is a regular lunchtime haunt for Italian and French journalists and EC officials. The tables are clad with paper tablecloths, and basic Italian fare such as pasta, steak and *osso buco* is served with the minimum of fuss at highly competitive prices.

SOLE DI CAPRI Italian
Rue Archimède 12, B-1040. Map 1C3
☎(02)230.82.08 ⅢⅢ AE ⊙ ⊙ ⅧⅧ
Closed Sat; Aug. Last orders 11pm. Metro to Schuman.

A comfortable, intimate restaurant with a wide range of fine dishes, this is a long-time favorite of senior EC officials. Excellent pasta and *fritto misto* feature alongside steaks and copious meat dishes. With some tables rather close to each other, reserve a table at the window or near the bar if you do not want your conversation overheard.

LE STÉVIN French ♣
Rue St Quentin 29, B-1040. Map 1C3
☎(02)230.98.47 ⅢⅢ 🚗 AE ⊙ ⊙ ⅧⅧ
Closed Sat; Sun; first 3wks Aug. Last orders 10pm. Metro to Schuman.

An elegant little restaurant that has built up a name for itself since it was established in a quiet street just off rue Stévin in 1980. The cooking is adventurous, using fresh ingredients. The Italian owner even smokes his own *magret de canard* on the premises. Try the *roquefort* in puff pastry, kidneys, scampi with Ricard, or scallops and leeks. There is a carefully selected wine list. Le Stévin is a favorite lunchtime venue for European Commissioners and senior officials.

TAKESUSHI Japanese ♣ 🍴
Blvd Charlemagne 21, B-1040. Map 1C3
☎(02)230.56.27 ⬜ 🚗 AE ⊙ ⊙ ⅧⅧ
Closed Sat; Sun lunch; mid-Aug. Last orders 10.15pm. Metro to Schuman.

An extremely popular, efficient restaurant frequented by lovers of *sushi*, *sashimi* and *tempura*. More elaborate dishes are also available. The set lunch is a real bargain, light, tasty and quickly served. Regular customers include many Japanese, as the personal bottles of whiskey behind the bar will testify.

VILLA DE BRUSELAS Spanish
Rue Archimède 65-67, B-1040. Map 1C3
☎(02)735.60.90 ⅢⅢ 🚗 AE ⊙ ⊙ ⅧⅧ
Closed Sat lunch; Sun; Aug. Last orders 10.30pm. Metro to Schuman.

A high-class Spanish restaurant in an immaculate setting with impeccable service. The two set menus are especially good value, but the more adventurous can take *merluza*, *gambas* and *paella* (for two) from the *carte*. It is ideal for small group business lunches, with its two private dining rooms, each capable of seating up to 14. For those wanting just a quick snack, there is a *tapas* bar downstairs.

Belgian beers

Ever so gradually, one of Belgium's best-kept secrets is becoming better known to a wider audience. The country is a veritable paradise for beer drinkers. As elsewhere, local artisanal breweries face stiff competition from their larger brethren, but in Belgium they have survived better than most.

There are between 550 and 600 different brews in the country. Many of them are not available outside their own locality, but it is still possible to taste and buy several hundred of them in Brussels. Beer drinking is a serious ritual, and even pouring many of the bottled beers is an art in itself. Most breweries have their own distinctive glasses, and no barman worth his salt would serve a bottled beer in anything else. Among the most memorable are the burgundy glass used by drinkers of Duvel, a lively top-fermented beer, the thistle-shaped glass into which a bottle of Gordon's sweetish Scotch Ale is poured, and the stirrup-cup, which holds the *Kwak* beer from East Flanders.

Scotch Ale is an interesting phenomenon. Although brewed in Great Britain, it is not on sale there. This is partly because British brewers consider it to be too strong in alcohol and hence too expensive for the domestic market. But it is widely appreciated in Belgium under different brand names like Gordon's, Campbells' and McEwan's. Even stronger versions are brewed for the festive season and sold as Christmas Ales.

There is also a strong tradition of brewing by monks in the country, with a large number of Trappist and abbey beers. There are five families of Trappist beers — *Orval, Chimay, Rochefort, Westvleteren* and *Westmalle,* some of which have varying alcoholic strengths. Chimay, for instance, sells its beers with red, white or blue bottle tops to indicate alcohol contents of 7.0, 8.0 and 9.0 by volume.

Tastes have begun to change in recent years, and beer consumption, possibly influenced by health campaigns or by the ever-widening choice of wines now available, continues to decline. In 1990, the average Belgian drank 118 liters of beer. By the following year, the quantity had fallen to 112 liters.

It is the lager, or *pils,* market that has suffered most, as people turn to the myriad of speciality beers. Brewers may bemoan their lot, but their finances have been somewhat cushioned by the sharp increase in exports, as Belgian beer wins new friends and markets outside the country.

Beer is a common ingredient in Belgian cooking. Perhaps the best-known dish is *carbonnade flamande,* a beef stew cooked with brown beer. But beer is also widely used to cook rabbit, fish and game, and to wash down some of the country's tasty cheeses.

Then there are the names. Who could fail to be tempted to try beers with names like Forbidden Fruit, Judas, Brigand, Carolus, St Paul Triple, Palm and Maredsous?

There are three broad categories of Belgian beer: bottom-fermented beers like *Maes, Stella* and *Jupiler* (which are widely on sale on draft or in bottles), where low temperature causes the yeast to sink to the bottom; top-fermented like the Antwerp beer, *De Koninck* or *Grimbergen,* and most speciality beers and wheat beers, where the yeast rises to the surface during fermentation; and spontaneously-fermented beers like *lambic, gueuze, kriek* and *faro,* which are fermented without using yeast.

Traditionally, *Gueuze* has been the beer associated with Brussels. But where once the city had 50 artisanal breweries, now it has just one, the Cantillon brewery. *Gueuze* is made by mixing different ages of *lambic,* a brew that is obtained from rye and wheat, then left to mature for 3 years.

To make the cherry-flavored *kriek,* 150 kilos (330 pounds) of Schaerbeek cherries are added to 500 liters (110 gallons) of *lambic.* Raspberry is added to produce *framboise,* and sugar and a little water to arrive at *faro,* whose lower alcohol content is much appreciated by children.

Cafés

The wealth of Belgium's brewing tradition is matched by the bewildering range of cafés and bars in the city. In the grandeur of the Grand'Place, one can choose any of almost a dozen establishments to explore the country by beer, while around the Bourse are astonishing Art Nouveau cafés.

Elsewhere, you do not need to go far to find a comfortable café, whether it be simple or more upmarket. What they have in common is respect for beer, which will always be carefully served, and frequently accompanied by some peanuts, small pieces of cheese or a few biscuits. The same care goes into serving coffee, which is invariably brought on an individual tray, complete with a biscuit.

Until recently, few cafés served spirits (liquor), since a post-World War I law made it necessary to have a special license to do so (the government of the day felt that the working class would ruin its health and its finances if given access to beer, wine and spirits in cafés). But spirits are now widely available, although if you ask for a Scotch you will still get a dark beer rather than a whisky.

Beer is not the only alcoholic drink from Belgium. Some wine is produced, although not in large quantities — a gap that does not prevent Belgians from being among the world's greatest connoisseurs of the drink. In the Luxembourg province of Belgium, an aperitif, called *Maitrank,* is made from Moselle wine, cognac and woodruff, while in more recent decades *Mandarine Napoléon,* a sweet, orange-flavored liqueur, has emerged.

Cafés generally welcome children and, while opening hours vary, they are always open until late in the evening. Nearly all those listed in the following pages stay open until at least midnight.

Cafés A to Z

LA BÉCASSE
Rue Tabora 11, B-1000. Map 3D3
☎*(02)511.00.06. Open every day from 10am until at least midnight.*

One of Brussels' nicest cafés, and also one of the hardest to find, as it is hidden away down a narrow alleyway. Look out for the illuminated red bird sign (*bécasse* means woodcock) above the wall, or for the metal outline of a bird, set in the sidewalk in 1977 to commemorate the establishment's 100th birthday. The family Steppé has owned the café for generations, and there is a distinctly home-like feel about the wood paneling and polite service. This is the place to try *lambic doux* or *gueuze*, served in gray and blue pottery jugs, helped along perhaps by a *tartine* (an open cheese or meat sandwich). There is a no-smoking area, ice cream for children, and a 70-seater room upstairs that can be reserved at no charge.

BIERODROME
Place Fernand Cocq 21, B-1050. Map 6H5
☎*(02)512.04.56.*

A must on the itinerary for jazz lovers is the corner café on the edge of a charming square, with a vendor of French fries just opposite for the really hungry. Unashamedly claiming the "Best Jazz in Town," it also offers a good selection of bottled Belgian and foreign beers, interesting bric-à-brac, and impromptu conversation with jazz connoisseurs.

LA BROUETTE
Grand'Place 2-3, B-1000. Map 3E3
☎*(02)511.41.61.*

The Grand'Place must be one of the most spectacular places in which to have a quiet drink. In summer, chairs are out on the terraces, providing vantage points from which to contemplate the world passing by or the evening *son et lumière*. In winter, the cafés, with their artificial flickering gas fires, ooze much-appreciated cozy warmth. La Brouette (which means wheelbarrow), one of the smaller Grand'Place cafés, is housed in a former guild property.

LA CHALOUPE D'OR
Grand'Place 24-25, B-1000. Map 3E3
☎*(02)511.41.61.*

If you want to gaze lazily at the magnificent Hôtel de Ville opposite, supping a cool lager or a rich Scotch ale, this is the place to sit. Waiters in white aprons rush about, expertly carrying heavily laden trays of beers, soft drinks and snacks. Gaze at the discreetly painted ceiling of red and green flowers and try a *croque monsieur*, which comes with all the gherkins and pickled onions you can eat.

LE CIRIO ▥
Rue de la Bourse 18, B-1000. Map 3D3
☎*(02)512.13.95.*

A stunning café that first opened its doors in 1886, it preserves a Brussels turn-of-the-century feel, with occasional dashes of Parisian influence. Beautifully carved windows, wrought iron lampshades, wooden tables and copper-clad pillars all combine to create a climate of luxury, far removed from the bustle of the surrounding streets. It is much frequented by elderly Belgians, who enjoy its wide range of beers.

THE DRUM
Av. d'Auderghem 10, B-1040. Map 1C3
☎*(02)230.94.94.*

During the 1970s, the Drum was *the* bar for British and Irish EC officials and politicians in Brussels. Since then it has moved to new premises, just along the road, and has had to face stiff competition from other English pubs. Still a popular meeting place, it offers a highly successful curry (as well as other dishes) and has plans to offer evening meals with last orders at 9.30pm

LE FALSTAFF ▥
Rue Henri Maus 17-23, B-1000. Map 3D3
☎*(02)511.87.89.*

Founded in 1904, the Falstaff is another architectural gem, blending Art Nouveau and Art Deco influences. The varied clientele is spread among seven rooms of different sizes, or sits outside on the covered terrace. The café is invariably busy, offering not just a wide range of beers and wines, but also a good selection of dishes. It is possible to eat a meal until 11.30pm and then to have a nocturnal snack until 4am.

LA FLEUR EN PAPIER DORÉ
Rue des Alexiens 55, B-1000. Map 5F3
☎*(02)511.16.59. Open daily until 1am.*

A venue for writers, poets and artists, this delightful café just five minutes from Grand'Place has been described as "a temple of Surrealism." Max Ernst exhibited here, René Magritte was a customer, and writers still come to try out their unpublished works on their colleagues. The walls are covered in prints, newspaper articles, photographs and other collectors' pieces that would take several visits to peruse. A café was first founded on the site in 1846, but it was not until the 1920s that it adopted its present name.

LE FOL
Rue de la Violette 22, B-1000. Map 3E3
☎*(02)511.13.96.*

Once you enter this narrow café, you are transported into another world. Books, posters, broken records and various artifacts cover the walls or hang suspended from the low ceiling. There is even a statue of the Virgin in a cage. Candles shed the only light, creating an intimate and romantic setting. Old rasping Piaf, Brel, Brassens and Montand records provide music from the juke box. There is a selection of beers and wine, but most of the regular clientele drink long glasses of peach, cherry, blackcurrant and other fruit-flavored wine.

L'IMAIGE NOSTRE-DAME
Impasse des Cadeaux 3 (off rue du Marché aux Herbes 8), B-1000. Map 3D3
☎*(02)219.42.49.*

Under the same ownership as LA BÉCASSE, this café has many pleasant similarities. It has the same comfy feel with leather and wooden benches, is also located down a narrow passageway,

and has a good selection of beers. Try its speciality *Bourgogne des Flandres*.

KITTY O'SHEA'S
Blvd Charlemagne 42, B-1040. Map 1C3
☎*(02)230.78.16. Open until 2am, and later on Fri.*

A fairly recent arrival on the Brussels' café scene, Kitty O'Shea's has become a regular meeting place for Irish and British EC officials, various journalists and visitors to Brussels. The convivial atmosphere attracts many other nationalities. For those wishing more privacy, there is a "snug" bar. Centrally placed in the heart of the EC area, it looks onto the now empty Berlaymont. Customers can drink excellent draft Guinness or Blanche, or choose from a number of bottled beers, wines and spirits. At lunchtime, or in the evening until 10.30pm, meals of homemade soup, smoked salmon, Irish stew and fish dishes are served. There is a brunch on Sundays.

LA LUNETTE
Place de la Monnaie 3, B-1000. Map 3D3
☎*(02)218.03.78.*

A place to relax on the edge of the beautiful place de la Monnaie, just a stone's throw from the theater where the Belgian revolution, which led to the country's independence, started in 1830. La Lunette sells a wide range of seven draft and more than 20 bottled beers. The café specializes in large half-moon glasses that each hold a liter (2 pints).

LE MÉTROPOLE
Place de Brouckère 31, B-1000. Map 3D3
☎*(02)219.23.84. Open daily until 1am, later on weekends.*

This authentic 19thC bar in a famous hotel is a handy meeting place or haven to relax amid the opulence of the ruby red leather chairs, rich wooden tables and beveled mirrors. Signatures on one of the central pillars testify to the presence among its former customers of Maurice Chevalier, whose mother was from Brussels, and Beurthe Bovy, an actress from Liège who spent more than half a century with the Comédie Française. On offer is the house cocktail, Italiano, various wines and champagnes and more than 20 beers.

MOKAFÉ
Galerie du Roi 9, B-1000. Map 4D4
☎*(02)511.78.70.*
An ideal spot for wet days. Located in Brussels' most elegant glass-covered shopping *galerie*, this café caters to all tastes. Beers, soft drinks, snacks and rich delicious cakes, which can be sampled unhurriedly while gazing at the window shoppers ambling along.

LA MORT SUBITE
Rue Montagne aux Herbes Potagères 7, B-1000. Map 4D4 ☎*(02)512.86.64.*
The Mort Subite, which dates from the 1920s, remains one of Brussels' immovable institutions, standing firm against encroaching office development. Benches line the wall, *gueuze, kriek* and other beers flow steadily, and order is assured by the indomitable waitresses. A quiet corner in the afternoons, it can be difficult to find a seat in the evenings.

The name (meaning Sudden Death) comes from a dice game once played by regular visitors from nearby offices. If forced to leave early, they would change the rules, thus ending the game in "sudden death."

LE ROI D'ESPAGNE
Grand'Place 1, B-1000. Map 3E3
☎*(02)513.08.07.*
The best known of the Grand'Place cafés, Le Roi d'Espagne is now also the headquarters of Interbrew, Belgium's largest brewery and the fifth largest in Europe, who recently launched their Hoegaarden Blanche and Leffe Blonde beers onto the American market. The ground floor offers visitors a feast of sights — white-aproned waiters, a stuffed horse, puppets hanging from the ceiling, aging posters stuck to the wall and, in winter, a warm gas fire. For a good view of Grand'Place, climb the stairs and savor your drink from one of the upper floors.

LA TERRASSE
Av. de Tervuren 11, B-1000. Map 2C4
☎*(02)733.22.96.*
For a brief respite from the rigors of the European Community, walk through the Cinquantenaire Park to this family-owned café, which has graced this corner since the end of the last century. It is an equally handy spot in which to relax after strolling through the nearby rue des Tongres, one of the area's best shopping streets. Time counts for little when supping a Scotch ale or a trappist amid the old-fashioned ambience of La Terrasse.

CHEZ TOONE
Impasse Schuddevelde, B-1000. Map 3D3
☎*(02)513.54.86.*
It is easy to miss the narrow entrance off the Petite rue des Bouchers if your gaze is too fixed on the bewildering displays of fish and shellfish. But it would be a pity. The café is right next door to the TOONE PUPPET THEATER and has its own display of little wooden men, women, and even a pig, hanging from the ceiling. Try a draft *Kwak* served in its distinctive stirrup cup and wooden holder, much like something you would expect to find in a science laboratory, or a draft *De Koninck* from Antwerp. Newspapers are provided to pass the time of day and, if short of an idea for a child's present, small modern puppets are on sale at a reasonable price.

DE ULTIEME HALLUCINATIE
Rue Royale 316, B-1030. Map 4D5
☎*(02)217.06.14.*
A highly popular café, with a separate restaurant, the "Ultimate Hallucination" is a favorite spot of the Flemish and the young. The dour facade gives little hint of the rich Art Nouveau interior, where customers sit on wooden benches in a room laid out much like a railway dining car. The tasty food, wide range of beers and memorable decor all contribute to the café's popularity. But be careful, as the area is noted for thefts. A notice on the establishment's door specifically warns you not to leave valuables in your car.

Entertainments

by Lucy Walker

Brussels by night

Brussels may not have the glitz of New York, the hard-partying of London, the repertoire of Milan or the glamor of Paris, but it is a myth that the city sleeps at night. In fact, bars, restaurants and nightspots are open later than in many other capitals — sometimes right around the clock — and beneath the surface pumps a constant energy.

Naturally, as you must expect of a relatively small city, there is not the breadth of choice found in some larger capitals. But Brussels is far from being a cultural desert, and the Belgians have always known how to have a good time. The influx of foreigners over the past 20 years has also served to increase the choice of entertainment and to add to the ethnic mix.

Performing arts

Brussels' small size belies the depth and breadth of its lively arts culture. This culture stretches from the bourgeois splendor of the Neoclassical Théâtre de la Monnaie, where began the revolution that eventually won Belgium its independence in 1830 and which has seen sparks fly since then, as international stars battle to claim control over it, to the post-industrial venues like the Halles de Schaerbeek, a former covered market. Visitors can follow a historical journey, from the Middle Ages as depicted in the rumbustious performance of the marionnettes at Toone, through the 18thC glory of the Théâtre Royal du Parc, to the aggressively stark and modern, epitomized by the Théâtre Varia.

THEATER

Brussels has such a huge range of theater (sometimes the same play will be on in two places in different languages) that it is impossible to give more than a glimpse here. There is something for every theatrical taste — from the classic repertoire of the Théâtre Royal du Parc (worth a visit just to sample its sumptuous decor) to the avant-garde energy of the Improvisation League at the **Mirano Continental**.

The TOONE MARIONNETTE THEATER (see pages 182 and 142) too is worth a visit for its own sake. It is attached to a bar where antique marionettes dangle above the characteristic Brussels beers.

Others, like the **Théâtre Varia**, also boast chic bars open to non-theatergoers. The "What's On" section of *The Bulletin* has latest details of new shows each Thursday. The following theaters are likely to be of most interest to English-speaking visitors.

ESPACE LEOPOLD SENGHOR
Chaussée de Wavre 366, B-1040
☎*(02)230.29.88. Off map* **6G6.**
This small modern theater is popular with amateur drama companies, and is one of the few that regularly puts on productions in English as well as a standard repertoire in French.

KONINKLIJKE VLAAMSE SCHOUWBURG (K.V.S.)
Rue de Laeken 146, B-1000
☎*(02)217.69.37. Map* **3C3.**
A showcase of 1900s architectural splendor, the interior of this flagship theater of the Flemish community is a curious but appealing blend of early Art Deco with the trace of heaviness remaining from the Belle Époque. The repertoire, which is always in Dutch, ranges from variety shows to the classics.

MIRANO CONTINENTAL
Chaussée de Louvain 3, B-1030. Map **4D6.**
Improvisation on Sun eves.
This converted 1960s cinema in an uninspiring part of town was recently given a much needed facelift. The Mirano is best known as the coolest place in Brussels to dance into the early hours, but it also doubles on Sunday evenings as host to improvisation competitions. The pace is fast and furious, and spectators have an advantage if they have a reasonable grasp of Belgian French.

THÉÂTRE NATIONAL DE LA COMMUNAUTÉ FRANÇAISE DE BELGIQUE
Centre Rogier, pl. Rogier, B-1210
☎*(02)217.03.03. Map* **4B4.**
Do not be put off by the location, in one of Brussels' more desolate tower blocks, of this large and comfortable two-stage theater, which recently underwent a thorough renovation. Recently taken over by a young team whose origins were on the "fringe," the company has successfully tackled the classics and become known for a freshness of style that stretches across a wide repertoire.

THÉÂTRE DU RÉSIDENCE PALACE
Rue de la Loi 155, B-1040
☎*(02)231.03.05. Off map* **6E6.**
The architectural epitome of Brussels' high-life in the 1920s, this lavish theater, like the swimming pool in the same building, was built for the in-house pleasure of a sophisticated younger set during the first wave of postwar euphoria. Taken over by the French-speaking **Théâtre de l'Esprit Frappeur,** the theater is now home to intimate concerts and occasional theatrical productions and, although it is still searching for a modern role to match its former glory, is something of a cultural lucky dip today.

THÉÂTRE DU RIDEAU DE BRUXELLES
Palais des Beaux-Arts, rue Ravenstein 23, B-1000 ☎*(02)507.82.00. Map* **4E4.**
Tucked away in the fine **Beaux-Arts** complex, this small, cozy theater has a family atmosphere, having built up an excellent rapport between a regular company and its faithful audience. The pioneering British director Adrian Brine has worked here for more than 20 years to bring the best of English drama to Brussels' audiences, with imaginative productions staged in French.

THÉÂTRE ROYAL DU PARC
3 rue de la Loi, B-1000 ☎*(02)511.41.47. Map* **4E5.**
An intimate theater in a distinctive setting on the edge of a park in the center of Brussels, this is almost a living theater museum. Built in the late 18thC, as the private theater for the former governor in Brussels, the theater is now the faded jewel box of Brussels before the French Revolution. The French-language repertoire is a time-traveler's delight, frequently offering revivals of long-dead plays.

THÉÂTRE VARIA
Rue du Sceptre 78, B-1040
☎*(02)640.82.58. Map* **1C3.**
An impressive if grimly modern decor disguises the energetic atmosphere of this adventurous theater whose young audience are prepared to sit through

some of the most demanding interpretations of the modern repertoire. Productions are mainly in French but sometimes use subtitles or foreign language "voice overs," although this does not always much aid comprehension by the audience. A well-managed establishment, which manages to draw in people to its distinctive Post-Modern café-bar, it also sometimes offers a cheap babysitting service to visitors who call ahead.

TOONE (Marionnette theater)
Impasse Schuddevelde, Petite rue des
Bouchers 21, B-1000 ☎ *(02)511.71.37.*
Map 3D3.

Toone, with its cast of marionettes, is unique to Brussels. They put on a raucous and irreverent show that harks back to the Middle Ages and evokes the images captured in Bruegel's scenes of peasant life. The company takes the classics, from Greek tragedy to Shakespeare, and portrays them with inimitable *Bruxellois* style and a Belgian-French accent guaranteed to baffle tourists. Large helpings of verve and humor guarantee the show a wide appeal.

CLASSICAL MUSIC

Brussels may not have the range of artistic events associated with major international cities such as New York, London and Paris, but for its size there are a lot of good-quality concerts, and visitors and residents alike are spoiled for choice.

Alongside Belgium's own national orchestras like the **Belgian National** or the **Liège Philharmonic**, Brussels attracts to its 17 concert halls names like Dame Kiri Te Kanawa, Sir Yehudi Menuhin, the Chamber Orchestra of Europe and the National Symphony Orchestra of London.

Widespread use is also made of churches, museums, theaters and even hotels to stage recitals of classical music.

FESTIVALS

Until a few years ago, the main concert season ran from September through June, but increasingly there is artistic activity all year round.

The Brussels-based **Reine Elisabeth Music Festival** *(every May and June)* is one of the world's most prestigious musical events, attracting contestants from round the globe. The competition focuses one year on piano, the next on singing and the following, as in 1993, on violin.

In alternate years, the **Brussels Europalia Festival** also invites another country, whether European or non-European, to present highlights of its music, art and culture.

Two umbrella programs presented through late summer and fall by the Festivals of Flanders and of Wallonia have lately grown in popularity.

FESTIVAL VAN VLAANDEREN
Details from the festival office at pl. Flagey
18, B-1050 ☎ *(02)640.15.25.*
Held every year from April to October, the huge six-month event involves more than 40 cities, including Brussels. Around 100 concerts of ancient and Baroque music take place, as well as dozens of choral and oratorio evenings.

Churches, concert halls and theaters are all used as venues.

FESTIVAL DE WALLONIE
Contact the festival office at rue du Jardin
Botanique 29, B-4000 Liège
☎ *(041)22.32.48.*
A smaller initiative than its Flanders namesake, Wallonia's Festival never-

theless offers a wide series of musical events between July and November in Brussels and many Walloon cities, particularly Liège and Namur.

OPERA

In recent years opera has also enjoyed a renaissance in Brussels, largely under the leadership of Gérard Mortier, director until 1992 of the **Théâtre Royal de la Monnaie**. Many opera fans even travel from as far afield as Paris and Germany. The city also has the good fortune to be the home of José Van Dam, one of the world's greatest baritones.

Unlike many other cities, where operas are performed in repertoire, Brussels stages just one opera at a time, usually for a period of two to three weeks and, in all, about ten productions a year. This concentration on individual operas ensures the productions have an air of freshness and vitality. And given the short distances between Belgium's main cities, opera fans think little of traveling to Ghent, Antwerp or Liège as ways of broadening their choice.

Tickets for the opera are like gold dust, and many of the seats are permanently taken by annual subscriptions. Both the **Belgian Tourist Office** (rue du Marché aux Herbes 61) and **Tourist Information Brussels** (in Grand'Place) will help track down tickets. But one of the best methods is to go to the National Opera House at the Monnaie an hour before a performance and try for returns.

DANCE

Performances of classical ballet and folk dance, by visiting European and American companies, are often staged in venues such as the Théâtre de la Monnaie and the Résidence Palace. But the city's main strength lies in contemporary dance, whose fans are offered an embarrassment of riches in Brussels. There are some 40 different venues used by these companies, and enthusiasts can scour the city in search of the most exciting new works by young Belgian troupes, trekking down dark cobbled streets to dingy halls, or sitting on antiquated seats in converted cinemas. They may sometimes be disappointed, but they press on in the hope of finding a fiery new talent. Look out for performances of startling originality by the internationally-acclaimed Belgian choreographer Anna Teresa De Keersmaeker.

Major modern dance works are performed in the glittering **Théâtre de la Monnaie**. Other venues include the **Palais des Beaux-Arts** and the **Atelier Sainte-Anne** (rue des Tanneurs 75-77 ☎ (02)513.40.50).

VENUES

Brussels has a wide range of major venues for classical music, opera and dance. The most important addresses are given below.

MUSÉE D'ART ANCIEN
Rue de la Régence 3, B-1000
☎(02)512.82.47. Map **6F4**.
Lunchtime concerts take place here on Wednesdays, frequently involving former Reine Elisabeth competition winners. Lunch is also served, in a cheerful cafeteria.

CATHÉDRALE ST-MICHEL
Parvis Ste-Gudule, B-1000. Map 4D4.
Concerts featuring the work of composers like Vivaldi, Bach, Poulenc and Handel are held in the cathedral every Sunday *(12.30pm)*.

CHAPELLE DES MINIMES
Rue des Minimes 62, B-1000. Map 5G3.
This church near the Sablon hosts a music festival in July and August.

CIRQUE ROYAL
Rue de l'Enseignement 81, B-1000
☎*(02)218.20.15. Map 4D5.*
The list of attractions ranges from international touring opera to jazz outfits, with a smattering of light entertainment too — such as those hunky American males, the Chippendales.

CONSERVATOIRE ROYAL
Rue de la Régence 30, B-1000
☎*(02)511.04.27. Map 6G4.*
Noted for fine acoustics, this venue stages a regular program of chamber concerts.

MAISON DE LA RADIO
Place Flagey 18, B-1050. Map 1C3. Details from Info Ticket, rue du Marché aux Herbes 61, B-1000 ☎*(02)512.85.54 or 504.03.99.*
A popular venue for classical concerts. It also holds a contemporary music festival, **Ars Musica**, in March.

PALAIS DES BEAUX-ARTS
Rue Ravenstein 23, B-1000
☎*(02)507.82.00. Map 4E4.*
The main concert venue in Brussels, the Palais des Beaux-Arts hosts international ensembles such as the London Symphony Orchestra as well as such national names as the Belgian National Orchestra. The annual Reine Elisabeth competition also takes place here.

PASSAGE 44
Boulevard du Jardin Botanique 44, B-1000
☎*(02)217.60.54. Map 4C4. Metro to Botanique.*
A soulless facade does little justice to this eclectic cultural center, located in a lively shopping arcade.

HÔTEL PULLMAN ASTORIA
Rue Royale 103, B-1000
☎*(02)217.62.90. Map 4C5.*
The works of Beethoven, Schumann, Bach, Mozart and the like are performed in elegant surroundings on a Sunday morning. Concerts start at 11am all year round and can be followed by a reasonably-priced buffet brunch.

THÉÂTRE ROYAL DE LA MONNAIE
Place de la Monnaie, B-1000
☎*(02)218.12.11. Map 4D4.*
The main venue for opera in Brussels, La Monnaie welcomed a new director in 1992, Bernard Foccroulle. As well as opera, the Monnaie has an extensive concert program offering works ranging across the centuries to Shostakovich and Bernstein. These are performed either by the resident Chamber Music Ensemble or The Monnaie Bassquartet, or by visiting artists.

On Friday lunchtimes *(from 12.30-1.30pm)* you can listen, over a modest lunch, to soloists from the Monnaie Symphony Orchestra, who demonstrate their musical repertoire in more informal surroundings and stay around for a chat afterwards.

OTHER CULTURAL EVENTS
A number of significant cultural and folkloric events take place each year, and it is worth considering planning your visit to coincide with one or more of them. See THE BRUSSELS CALENDAR on page 69.

MORE INFORMATION AND TICKETS
Further information on musical events in Brussels and help with securing tickets can be obtained from:

- **Auditorium 44**   boulevard du Jardin Botanique 44, B-1000
  ☎(02)218.2735
- **Info Ticket**   ☎(02)512.85.54 or 504.03.99
- **Tourist Information Brussels (T.I.B.)**   ☎(02)513.89.40 or
  (02)513.83.20 (which charges 25 BF for each seat reserved)
- For a comprehensive list of concerts and musical events, consult
  the weekly *The Bulletin* or the monthly Brussels-based French-
  language publication *Privilège de la Musique*.

Nightlife

Brussels' nightlife provides for all classes and all ages. With a huge
variety of nightspots within walking distance of the city center, the
streets around Grand'Place are often thronged on a Friday and Saturday night by high-spirited, late-night revelers in noisy but relatively
harmless groups. Dress codes are relaxed, but farther away from the
core toward the Haut de la Ville and avenue Louise area, sharp suits
replace the latest street fashion as regulation attire.

Most venues are relatively safe, but conspicuous wallets or purses are
best left behind. Do not forget to tip the doorman.

CINEMA
English-language cinema in Brussels is excellent, and Belgians and
visitors alike flock to see the latest British and American releases, as
well as the good range of avant-garde and foreign-language films, particularly French, Spanish, German and Japanese. Almost all are shown
in **VO** *(version originale)*, which will have subtitles in French and
Dutch. Keep an eye out, however, for the dubbed French version of
some of the Hollywood releases, which may be on release at the same
time as the original English-language version.

Programs change each Wednesday and cheap seats are usually available on Mondays. Cinema listings can be found in the "What's On" section
of the English-language weekly magazine *The Bulletin*, published on
Thursday, and the "MAD" supplement of *Le Soir* on Wednesday. Many
metro stations also have posters displaying the same information.

ENA or **CNA** indicates children under 16 years of age are not admitted.
Even if you only plan a short stay, it may well be worth investing in a
UGC Privilege card, which offers substantial discounts on normal seat
prices in the UGC cinemas. There's either a four-movie card for one
person or a six-movie card for up to two people a time, and both are valid
for two months.

Do not forget to tip the attendant who tears your ticket (20 BF per
person is usual), as they do not get a separate wage.

In addition to the regular screenings, there are a number of special
events dotted through the calendar. Though a far cry from Berlin or
Cannes, Brussels has its own **International Film Festival**, which runs
for two weeks every February at the **Palais des Beaux-Arts** *(rue Raven-*

stein 23, B-1000 ☎*(02)507.82.00, map 3 E4).* At **Le Botanique** *(rue Royale 236, B-1210* ☎ *(02)217.63.86, map 4 C5)* there are annual festivals of gay and Mediterranean films and sometimes open-air screenings in the summer. **Passage 44** (see below) holds a festival of animation and science fiction in the late fall, usually in November.

You do not even need a car to enjoy the **Drive-In movie**, every Friday, Saturday and Sunday nights in July and August on the esplanade of the Parc du Cinquantenaire, as the organizers will supply headphones and a chair. Throughout August, when new releases are few and far between, the **Arenberg Galeries** offers a feast of viewing ranging from the classics to the unknown.

ACTORS STUDIO
Petite rue des Bouchers 16, B-1000
☎*(02)512.16.96. Map 3D3. Metro to de Brouckère.*
Tucked away in a passage linking rue des Bouchers and rue de la Fourche, this unfortunately rather down-at-heel small two-screen theater has one of the best selections of foreign and non-mainstream films, plus reruns of recent releases you may have missed.

ARENBERG GALERIES
Galerie de la Reine 26, B-1000
☎*(02)512.80.63. Map 4E4. Metro to Gare Centrale.*
This is the flagship of avant-garde cinema — more Peter Greenaway than Stephen Spielberg — run by independent distributors Cinélibre from a recently renovated Art Deco theater in a prize location in the elegant Galeries Saint-Hubert. Thursday evening is **Sneak Preview night**, where film buffs flock to see an early one-off of movies straight from the Berlin or Venice festivals and others, several weeks ahead of general release. The film's identity is a well-kept secret until curtain-up, but there is plenty of time to discuss the performance afterwards over a free glass of something bubbly.

ESPACE DELVAUX
Pl. Keym, B-1170 ☎*(02)660.49.60. Map 1C3. Bus 95 or 96.*
Rather off the beaten track, but **Ciné Apéro** is a good Wednesday night alternative for the late-risers who missed Breakfast Cinema on Sunday at the Acropole. You can catch the same movie as was shown the preceding Sunday, with a cocktail included in the price of the ticket.

KINEPOLIS
Heysel Bruparck, av. du Centenaire 1, B-1020 ☎*(02)479.52.52. Map 1B3. Metro to Heysel.*
Part of the Bruparck development, Europe's largest cinema complex, opened in 1989, holds a massive 7,000 people when full. The building, which rather resembles a reconverted multistory parking garage, has 25 screens, some in 70mm with Dolby stereo, and a crowded bar. It is probably worth the trip to see a blockbuster on the big screen, but some of the smaller auditoria offer nothing in terms of quality over their city-center counterparts. Summer often brings one-off events with special screenings from midnight until dawn.

MOVY CLUB
Rue des Moines 21, B-1060
☎*(02)537.69.54. Map 1C3. Tram 18 to Rochefort.*
A chance to see old classics and not-so-new releases in the spectacular setting of an ornate old music-hall theater.

MUSÉE DU CINÉMA
Rue Baron Horta 9, B-1000. Map 6E4. Metro to Gare Centrale or Parc or tram 92, 93 or 94 to Parc.
Here, you can meet the heroes of the silver screen seven days a week. There are two separate programs, one devoted to the silent era, and the other, consecrated to the "talkies," includes even recent releases that have already

passed into the annals of movie lore. The ticket price is topped up by a 20 BF fee for day membership. The program for the month can be obtained for 20 BF from a slot machine outside.

STUDIO, PASSAGE 44,

Boulevard du Jardin Botanique 44, B-1000 ☎*(02)217.60.54. Map 4C4. Metro to Botanique.*

This 1970s-style cinema, with its orange seats and overall decor in molded white plastic, can be relied on to show *A Clockwork Orange* and *Last Tango in Paris* at least once a year. There are special Saturday morning screenings for children.

STYX

Rue de l'Arbre Bénit 72, B-1050 ☎*(02)512.21.02. Map 6H5. Metro to Porte de Namur, then a 5min walk.*

This small two-screen cinema is rather threadbare. But it is certainly the best place to hunt down cult classics and has a showing after midnight most nights. The order of screenings gets juggled frequently, so check times in advance.

UGC ACROPOLE

Galeries de la Toison d'Or and av. de la Toison d'Or, B-1050 ☎*(02)511.43.28.*

Map 6G4. Metro to Porte de Namur.

This 2,200-seat complex has, confusingly, two entrances, but neon arrows above the cinema posters that stare down from above the shops on avenue de la Toison d'Or should point you in the right direction. Buy your tickets in advance to avoid lining up, and have a drink in one of the nearby cafés before the program starts. Sunday morning *(at 10am)* **Breakfast Cinema** offers the chance to see new and not-so-new releases, with a croissant and cup of coffee thrown in for free.

UGC DE BROUCKÈRE

Pl. de Brouckère 38, B-1000 ☎*(02)218.59.50. Map 3C3. Metro to de Brouckère.*

Totally refurbished in 1992, the 2,250-seat complex has a total of 10 screens, all with Dolby stereo and including two in 70mm. Arranged on three floors, the cinema is a futuristic palace in starkly-lit silver-painted brick and black marble. There are two bars, and a big screen showing live sports events and pop videos. All the films start at the same time, so there can be lines at the cash desk. The usual tipping policy does not apply here, although seats are more expensive than elsewhere.

JAZZ AND FOLK

Brussels is renowned for its live jazz and rightly so. There are dozens of jazz bars and clubs, covering every style from trad to improvisation, and every environment from lunchtime sophistication to late-night smoke-filled dens.

What is more, a number of jazz festivals draw fans from all over Belgium. Some of the events are informal gatherings around a beer tent, but others feature renowned international musicians.

- The **Belga Jazz week** in November is the biggest jazz festival in Belgium, lining up the best names that money can buy. Expect to hear the Modern Jazz Quartet, Al Jarreau or the Count Basie orchestra (☎ *(02)534.22.00 for information).*
- The **Brosella Festival** is a more informal event, held each July in the bosky Théâtre de Verdure near the ATOMIUM. Jazz musicians and folk groups perform in a range of styles (☎ *(02)511.79.90 for information).*
- The annual **Jazz Rally** held in late May is a frenetic event for jazz fans. Concerts are staged in a miscellany of venues throughout the

city, from plush hotel bars to dark dives. A map is essential to find out who is playing where. Special buses are laid on to convey weary nightbirds from one concert to another.

- The **Viva Brasil festival** in July is another regular event to spice up Brussels' nightlife. Open-air concerts (some of them free) feature bands playing the best in Brazilian music (☎ *(02)534.22.00 for information)*.

Perhaps the best known venue, the **Travers** *(rue Traversière 11, B-1030, map 4 C6)*, is under continual threat from lack of funds, but it still keeps going and never ceases to attract bill-topping acts. The Monday night jam sessions are free.

Pol, the owner of the **Bierodrome** *(pl. Fernand Cocq 21, B-1050, jazz every Fri and Sat, map 6 H5)*, is almost as much part of the show as the acts themselves. This bar-cum-venue is always packed, so be prepared to arrive early if you want to get a seat and not to mind the soupy haze of cigarette smoke if you stay late.

At the **Preservation Hall** *(rue de Londres 3, B-1050, map 6 G6)*, New Orleans-style jazz is almost an institution, and the regulars come back week after week. A relatively new venture is the Sunday lunchtime jazz brunch at the **Airport Sheraton** *(opposite Departures at the airport at Zaventem)*, which happens twice a month and seems popular despite the slightly antiseptic environment.

ROCK

Belgium features high on the international tour circuit, often attracting international stars as they kick off their European tours. It also has a wealth of home-grown talent, particularly from Ghent and Antwerp where the Techno-pop scene has boomed.

The biggest venue by far is **Forest National** *(av. du Globe 36, B-1190* ☎ *(02)347.03.55, map 1 D2)*, which nonetheless has terrible acoustics. More manageable is the **Ancienne Belgique** *(rue des Pierres 14, B-1000* ☎ *(02)512.59.86, map 3 E3)*, which miraculously manages to keep a fresh air supply going somehow, even when the place is packed. The **Halles de Schaerbeek** *(rue Royale Sainte-Marie 22a, B-1030* ☎ *(02)218.00.31, map 4 B6)* have been undergoing refurbishment to upgrade their somewhat spartan facilities. The former covered market has two main auditoria, a massive 2,000-seat auditorium for concerts and theater, and a much smaller, cozy room for late-night gigs.

Some bands also play the **Cirque Royale** *(rue de l'Enseignement 81, B-1000* ☎ *(02)218.20.05, map 4 D5)*, but don't expect to see much more than their feet and knees from the top balcony. Ticket agents like **FNAC** *(in City 2 at the top of rue Neuve, B-1000, map 4 C4)* also sell tickets for coach-and-concert tours to places like Antwerp, Paris or Amsterdam.

DISCOS AND DANCING

As in any city, the list of hippest nightspots is in constant flux: what is new one month will be old hat the next. The top spot for admiring Brussels young and beautiful still has to be the **Mirano Continental**.

The hard dancing in this defunct movie theater starts late on Saturday *(from 11pm)*, but the real cool cats don't start rolling in until after 1am. Another interesting locale, the **Vaudeville**, is located in an old theater in the Galeries Saint-Hubert. A favorite with young trainees who come to work for 5 months in the European Community institutions, it is their home, on a Friday and Saturday, while on Sunday nights it becomes the mecca for the campest of glam rockers.

For those more interested in dancing than ogling or posing, there is the **Garage**, opposite the Hotel Windsor and not far from Grand'Place. The Garage may not be the newest place in town, but it has kept the intrusion of thumping house music to a minimum. It is always packed and lively, but with a high proportion of tourists.

Also close to Grand'Place, the **Machado** has caught the city's recent Latin fever with salsa, samba and the ubiquitous lambada interspersing the soul music. Another place for you to lambada the night away on a Friday and Saturday is the **Do Brazil**, during the week a restaurant, which at the weekend sees its vaulted dining room swept away to the Latin rhythms.

In the Haut de la Ville, **La Gioconda** is definitely destined for an older clientele. The atmosphere is extravagant, with prices to match, attracting tourists and businessmen from the nearby hotels.

The area between the avenue Louise and the chaussée d'Ixelles is also the center of Brussels' African quarter. Literally dozens of tiny pulsating nightclubs, boasting the city's sharpest dressers, are tucked down seemingly quiet side streets. The blend of funk, African and Caribbean music draws all sorts to the **Écume des Nuits** in the Galerie Louise, but it is hot and cramped.

And for those who want to sing while they dance there is the **Birdie-Karaoke**, Brussels' answer to the craze for making a fool of yourself in front of a room full of people. Serious budding Sinatras should make their way to **Studio Sinatra**, where there is minimum dancing so as not to detract from the main point of the evening.

- **Birdie-Karaoke**   rue Berckmans 10, B-1060, map 6H4. Open Wednesday, Friday and Saturday from 10pm.
- **Do Brazil**   rue de la Caserne 88, B-1000, map 5F2. Closed Sunday, Monday.
- **Écume des Nuits**   Galerie Louise 122a, B-1050, map 4D4. Open Thursday to Sunday from 10pm.
- **Le Garage**   rue Duquesnoy 16, B-1000, map 6E4. Open nightly from 11pm.
- **La Gioconda**   avenue de la Toison d'Or 44, B-1060, map 6G4. Open Tuesday to Saturday from 9pm.
- **Le Machado**   rue des Chapeliers 14, B-1000, map 5E3.
- **Mirano Continental**   chaussée de Louvain 38, B-1030, map 4D6. Open Saturday from 11pm.
- **Studio Sinatra**   chaussée de Bruxelles 113, B-1410 (Waterloo), map 1D2. Open Friday, Saturday from 10pm.
- **Vaudeville**   Galerie de la Reine 15, B-1000, map 4E4. Open 10pm till the early hours.

RESTAURANTS WITH ENTERTAINMENT

The *Bruxellois* know how to enjoy themselves and, as food is central to many a night out, it seems only natural that the dinner-revue has become a well-established part of the Brussels scene. Top of the list has to be **Chez Flo**, which after many years still manages to keep a touch of humor in its dinner-and-drag revue.

Elsewhere in the city center you will still be able to find traces of authentic Brussels humor and songs. Even if you can't understand the tales, everyone gets swept up amid the thigh-slapping and hilarity in the general good humor.

Belgian cabaret revue is almost music-hall in style and tone. The audience can often find that long anecdotes in thick *Bruxellois* dialect alternately rise and sink above and below waves of laughter and chatter. The most typical spots, all in the city center, combine good traditional food in large portions with a large helping of good humor:

- **Chez Flo**   rue au Beurre 25, B-1000 ☎(02)513.31.52, map **3**E3. Dinner and show every night from Wednesday to Saturday at 8pm.
- **Do Brazil**   rue de la Caserne 88, B-1000, map **5**F2. Brazilian music and dancing Tuesday to Saturday.
- **Le Black Bottom**   rue du Lombard 1, B-1000 ☎(02)511.06.08, map **5**E3. Dinner and cabaret featuring impressionists and comedians from 10.30pm on Friday and Saturday.
- **Le Moustache**   quai au Bois à Brûler 61, B-1000, map **3**C3. Dinner with burlesque shows and heaps of *Bruxellois* atmosphere.
- **Le Pré Salé**   rue de Flandre 20, B-1000 ☎(02)513.43.23, map **3**C2. Dinner and show on Friday evenings, with hearty *Bruxellois* mood.

CABARETS

Brussels also has its share of late-night cabarets in the tradition of the Paris Moulin Rouge, where they use an oft-repeated formula that still seems to satisfy its audience despite a seeming lack of originality.

- **Must**   rue du Cirque 10, B-1000, map **3**C3. Every night from 11pm, "Must show" at midnight.
- **Play-Night**   rue Jean Stas 13, B-1060, map **6**H4. Every night except Sunday at 9pm, big show, featuring feather-clad beauties, at midnight.
- **Show-Point**   place Stéphanie 14, B-1050, map **6**H4. Monday to Saturday from 9.30pm until dawn, with go-go girls from 11pm and the big show at midnight.

CASINOS

There is no casino in Brussels. Belgian law states that all games of chance are illegal — except those that are authorized. Casinos are authorized in vacation areas such as the coast and the Ardennes. The nearest is at **Namur**, about 60km (38 miles) to the s, and the largest at **Knokke**, about 110km (70 miles) to the NW on the coast near Zeebrugge.

Shopping

by Lucy Walker

Where to go

Brussels has two distinct major shopping areas — the **Centre Ville** around Grand'Place, with its dense network of busy streets, and the **Haut de la Ville**, where high-fashion boutiques and designer stores line the main boulevards and covered shopping galleries of the avenue Louise and avenue de la Toison d'Or.

Window shopping is a national pastime, with couples often strolling through one of the covered arcades or galleries on a Saturday afternoon or Sunday morning. *Libre entrée/vrij ingang* simply means "browsers welcome."

Don't be surprised if shops offer you a *carte de fidelité/fidelkaart* if you buy something. These are free, and usually work by offering a small reduction, usually 5 or 10 percent, after you have totted up five, 10 or 12 purchases from the same store or chain. Other traders, including the Mister Minute heel bar chain, also operate this system.

Visitors are exempt from paying Value Added Tax (TVA or BTW) on purchases above a certain amount, on completion of a simple form and presentation of a passport at time of purchase. As this currently represents 19.5 percent of the bill, it is well worth the trouble. See VAT REFUNDS on page 46.

Shopping is also made enjoyable by the existence of literally dozens of decent cafés and small restaurants that throng the city center.

CENTRE VILLE

The downtown (Centre Ville) area has stores selling clothes, shoes, books, newspapers and records, and is bustling and practical. More than 50 stores flank **rue Neuve**, a pedestrian shopping street running from the **place de la Monnaie** to **City 2**, a shopping complex on three floors where you will find everything from tennis racquets to terracotta plant pots.

FNAC, the French entertainment chain, has a huge branch on the second floor of City 2, selling maps, books (in many languages), compact discs, and electronic equipment from cameras to computers. A counter at the entrance sells concert tickets. It has a good foreign-language book section, with novels, guides and technical books in English. City 2 also has a branch of the **GB** supermarket in the basement.

A walkway on the third floor of City 2 takes you straight into **Inno**, Brussels' department store. Inno is not in the same league as Harrods or

Neiman Marcus in terms of luxury, grandeur, size or price, but offers in particular, in a comfortable atmosphere, a good selection of clothes and accessories for women and men, especially in its rue Neuve store. The selection of clothing has something to cater to most tastes and pockets. The women's clothing section also stocks a good assortment of some of the better-known Belgian designers and well-known British names including Jaeger and Alexon. It also has a quick and very reasonably priced in-house alterations service.

The rue Neuve store has an excellent household department with everything from good-quality heavy-duty saucepans to Belgian crystal tableware. This branch also has a popular although unremarkable coffee shop that offers weary shoppers a good vantage point over the bustling street below. The range of goods in the smaller chaussée d'Ixelles and Woluwé Shopping Centre branches is rather more limited.

In the area around **Grand'Place**, mass-market souvenir stores are crowded in alongside bars, restaurants and other shops. Worth a look is the **Boutique de Tintin** *(rue de la Colline 13, B-1000, map3 E3)*, which has cards, T-shirts, watches and collectors' models for fans of the intrepid boy reporter created by cartoonist Hergé.

Except for **Godiva**, the *chocolatier* on Grand'Place, and some of the tourist traps in that area which take foreign notes, Belgian francs are the only practical currency.

THE HAUT DE LA VILLE

If you enjoy a spot of *lèche vitrine* (window-shopping, or, literally, "licking windows"), the **Haut de la Ville** is the place to go. There are a number of mouthwateringly chic boutiques on the avenue Louise, boulevard de Waterloo and avenue de la Toison d'Or (two sides of the same wide street outside the Hilton Hotel), and in the Galerie Louise and Galerie de la Toison d'Or.

The best way to observe those who come to parade their finery is to sip a cappuccino or kir at one of the sidewalk cafés. On Saturday afternoons and even on Sundays, when the shops are shut, you will see well-dressed women discussing the latest fashion arrivals.

THE GALERIES

Within a tiny radius of Grand'Place, you can find a collection of the most eclectic shopping galleries that Brussels has to offer.

The GALERIES ST-HUBERT are the relic of a bygone age where bespoke tailors nestled against hatmakers and silversmiths. Today the Galeries St-Hubert (made up of three galleries: **Galerie du Roi**, **Galerie de la Reine** and **Galerie des Princes**) retains some of its old-world charm and its supreme architectural integrity. A handful of shops still selling nothing but umbrellas or parasols, nail scissors and shaving mirrors, or gloves, are tucked beside their more modern competitors selling women's fashions and high-priced designer furniture.

A stone's throw away, the **Galerie Agora**, with its scent of patchouli oil, draws throngs of young people to its second-hand clothes shops, cheap stalls selling tie-dyed shirts and cheap silver jewelry counters. This is the mecca of "alternative" Brussels, but at first glance looks little more than a shabby arcade.

The GALERIE BORTIER *(rue St-Jean to rue de la Madeleine)*, however, envelops passers-by with its musty charm. History oozes from the peeling paintwork across its low, curved ceiling, and specks of dust seem to escape from case after case of exquisite second-hand and rare books. Brussels' foremost feminist bookstore is a bright and freshly-painted burst at one end of the short right-angled arcade.

The **Galerie de la Toison d'Or** and **Galerie Louise** are functional warrens with more than 60 small shops tucked under a massive office development built during the 1960s. Despite their unprepossessing exterior, the ground-floor shops — which sell everything from clothes to candlesticks — are bright. Sandwiched between the two is the **Espace Louise**, a short two-story arcade linking the avenue de la Toison d'Or and Galerie Louise. It has by comparison unremarkable architecture and, as yet, little out of the ordinary to distinguish it.

What to buy

The fame of Belgian **chocolates** is now legendary worldwide, and few visitors come to Brussels without bringing orders from family and friends. Belgian *pralines* are now available — at a price — elsewhere, but there is still nothing like the real thing, filled with fresh cream or a heavenly combination of finely chopped nuts, chosen piece by mouth-watering piece from the display case of one of Brussels' renowned old-established *chocolatiers* and wrapped at the peak of freshness.

Traditional **cheeses** and **abbey-brewed beers** offer a distinctive reminder of the country's culinary heritage, but can prove harder to transport. Pretty **gift tins** will prevent fragile biscuits like *speculoos* and *pain d'amandes* from being crushed. **Lace** is still a distinctive Belgian product, and although much of the cheaper handmade lace is now imported from the Far East, many items still follow traditional designs.

Other typical products that make good souvenirs include **pewter goods** like candle sticks and jugs, either modern or antique, from the former industrial heartland around Liège, and **crystal tableware**. **Clothes and accessories** for men and women are stylish as well as practical, and represent good value for money when compared with many other European capitals. If the budget will stretch far enough, there are top-quality **leather goods** from the legendary Delvaux workshop. Inno has the widest selection of accessories for men and women, stretching almost the length of the ground floor. And if you can cope with a large piece, there are some interesting plaster casts of Roman and Egyptian deities to be had at the MUSÉES ROYAUX D'ART ET D'HISTOIRE.

The self-proclaimed Capital of Europe has to be *the* place for **Euro-gadgets**, and there is a vast range of watches, umbrellas, pens, towels and even a perfume bearing the twelve gold stars of the European Community.

Clothing sizes chart

LADIES
Suits and dresses

Australia	8	10	12	14	16	18	
France	34	36	38	40	42	44	
Germany	32	34	36	38	40	42	
Italy	38	40	42	44	46		
Japan	7	9	11	13			
UK	6	8	10	12	14	16	18
USA	4	6	8	10	12	14	16

Shoes

USA	6	$6\frac{1}{2}$	7	$7\frac{1}{2}$	8	$8\frac{1}{2}$	
UK	$4\frac{1}{2}$	5	$5\frac{1}{2}$	6	$6\frac{1}{2}$	7	
Europe	38	38	39	39	40	41	

MEN
Shirts

USA, UK Europe, Japan	14	$14\frac{1}{2}$	15	$15\frac{1}{2}$	16	$16\frac{1}{2}$	17
Australia	36	37	38	39.5	41	42	43

Sweaters/T-shirts

Australia, USA, Germany	S	M	L	XL
UK	34	36-38	40	42-44
Italy	44	46-48	50	52
France	1	2-3	4	5
Japan		S-M	L	XL

Suits/Coats

UK, USA	36	38	40	42	44
Australia, Italy, France, Germany	46	48	50	52	54
Japan	S	M	L	XL	

Shoes

UK	7	$7\frac{1}{2}$	$8\frac{1}{2}$	$9\frac{1}{2}$	$10\frac{1}{2}$	11
USA	8	$8\frac{1}{2}$	$9\frac{1}{2}$	$10\frac{1}{2}$	$11\frac{1}{2}$	12
Europe	41	42	43	44	45	46

CHILDREN
Clothing

UK

Height (ins)	43	48	55	60	62	
Age	4-5	6-7	9-10	11	12	13

USA

Age	4	6	8	10	12	14

Europe

Height (cms)	125	135	150	155	160	165
Age	7	9	12	13	14	15

CLOTHING AND ACCESSORIES

Brussels boasts an impressive collection of home-grown talent as well as the major outlets for European *prêt-a-porter* designers, and the Belgian designers have established themselves as a creative force in international fashion.

The best known has to be **Olivier Strelli**. The Belgian-born Italian is renowned for his skill with color, setting distinctive bursts of bright color against more muted tones. His hard work promoting Belgian fashion was rewarded when he was chosen to design the distinctive green-and-purple uniforms for Sabena, the national airline. Strelli's own shop *(av. Louise 72, map 6 H4)* has a wide range of clothes for women and men using linen and natural fibers ranging from the bright and casual to more formal cocktail outfits.

Belgium was put on the map in the mid-1980s by the "Antwerp Six," a group of young avant-garde Belgian designers from the Antwerp Royal Academy of Arts. Their stark designs were praised by the critics as uncompromising; other said they were unwearable. Over the years the designs have mellowed.

The distinctive menswear designs of **Dirk Bikkembergs** and **Dries Van Noten** (who designs both mens and womenswear) are making it into the top fashion stores abroad (try the menswear department at Inno in rue Neuve). **Anne Demeulemeester** has her own shop **Danaqué** *(rue Grétry 22, B-1000, map 3 D3)*. Some of this homegrown talent has fled abroad. **Martin Margiela** left Belgium to work with Jean-Paul Gaultier, fashion's latest *enfant terrible*, to become the latest darling of the Paris critics.

The best selection of avant-garde designs from home and abroad are to be found at one of the three **Stijl** boutiques (specializing in men's clothes, women's clothes, and underwear and swimwear respectively) in rue Antoine Dansaert, B-1000 *(map 3 D2)*, along with another local label, **rue Blanche**.

Hats are coming back into vogue, and for the adventurous there is no better place than **Elvis Pompilio** *(rue du Midi 60, B-1000, map 5 E3)*. Pompilio's hats are not for the fainthearted, as one look at his wacky emporium will tell. But his international standing is growing almost by the minute. There appears to be a huge range of shapes, styles and colors on display at any one time, but Pompilio and his assistants make just 10,000 hats a year. Prices are very reasonable for these wearable and collectible items of designer chic.

The top international fashion designers are clustered in the Haut de la Ville, with **Gianni Versace**, **Chanel**, **Krizia**, **Ralph Lauren** and **Gucci** almost cheek-by-jowl lining the boulevard de Waterloo between rue des Quatre Bras and rue de Namur *(map 6 G4-5)*, where **Kenzo** and **Jil Sander** have boutiques. Also along this stretch lies the misleadingly-named **Scapa of Scotland**, which is Belgian through and through and carries a pleasing line of comfortable casual clothes in linen, wool and other natural fibers for women, men and children.

Bouvy *(av. de la Toison d'Or 52, B-1050, map 6 G4)*, is the shopping mecca for the well-dressed Belgian. It is really three stores in one: fronting avenue de la Toison d'Or is an excellent menswear section, which has a particularly good selection of silk ties and socks in pure wool or cotton; inside Galerie Louise there is a casual women's wear department; and at avenue Louise is the more upmarket women's wear, with top-name designers like Calvin Klein and Natan. All three departments connect inside, and all also sell the whole range of accessories from shoes to bags via scarves and socks.

If you are unsure of your size, check the comparative clothing sizes chart on page 194.

Children's clothes

- **A Little Family** *(rue de la Reinette 3, B-1000, map 6 G5)* is the most chic place to dress one's children. Prices are rather steep, but the clothes are good quality and a far cry from the usual selection of pastel blues and pinks adorned with fluffy bunnies. The shop is popular with new mothers, too, who find it hard to resist its matching mother-and-baby pajamas in fruit-patterned or tartan pure brushed cotton.

- **Dujardin** *(av. Louise 8-10, B-1050, map 6 H4)* carries a wide range of clothes and accessories for babies and children up to the age of 10. The collection concentrates on good-quality classics, and includes well-known brands like Petit Bateau, but can be pricey.

- **Max & Lola** *(rue du Pépin 50, B-1000, map 6 G4)* has fashionably casual clothes in everything from pure knitted cottons to corduroy, in attractively muted tones.

- At the opposite end of the spectrum, **Catamini** *(City 2, rue Neuve, B-1000, map 4 C4, or in the Passage Linthout at the top of rue de Tongres, B-1040, map 2 C4, and branches)* has an original range of brightly-colored and patterned own-label designs.

Shoes and leather goods

In the short stretch of avenue Louise between place Louise and place Stéphanie *(map 6 H4)* can be found **Stephane Kélian** and **Robert Clergerie**, who both offer men's and women's shoes, as well as a small selection of other leather goods including handbags and briefcases, in designer styles and at designer prices.

Kélian in particular has made a name for himself with an elegant and distinctive range in woven leather. Black predominates in his collection, which concentrates on providing wearable designer variations of classic shapes and styles. Clergerie opts for a brighter and more trendy selection, with fun flats in vivid suede and wearable tributes to the latest fashion revivals.

Classic high-quality English-made brogues and Oxford shoes for men can be found at **Church's English Shoes** *(pl. Stéphanie 2, B-1050, map 6 H4, or Galerie du Roi 11, B-1000, map 4 D4)*.

Inno *(rue Neuve, map 4 C4)* and **Bouvy** *(Galerie de la Toison d'Or, map 6 G4, and av. Louise, map 6 H4)* both have a good selection of shoes, particularly for men, and both stock brands that include Docksides and Timberland.

Delvaux *(blvd. Adolphe Max 22, B-1000, map 4 C4, Galerie de la Reine 31, B-1000, map 4 E4; also at av. de la Toison d'Or 24, B-1060, map 6 G4)* reigns supreme. It is said to be every Belgian woman's ambition to own a **Delvaux** handbag, and it is even rumored that in one divorce the wronged wife demanded a new Delvaux handbag every year as part of the settlement. These tales help to explain the almost legendary presence of the distinctive designs embossed or adorned with the distinctive elongated **D** and the plethora of fakes that have emerged.

Every handbag shop in Brussels now sells its version of the trademark Delvaux "nosebag" design, but the master craftsmen who have been following the family tradition since 1829 have moved on and bring out new designs twice a year, synchronized with the new catwalk collections. But be warned: the real thing is not cheap. Prices start at around 6,000 BF for a key fob to 30,000 BF for a large handbag, and more for the range of matching luggage.

Another Belgian range of distinctive luggage, briefcases and handbags come from **Louise Fontaine** *(passage du Nord 14, B-1000, map 4 D4, or av. Louise 5, B-1050, map 6 H4)*. Here, distinctive matching luggage and other leather goods come in bright colors such as fiery orange and pillarbox red, as well as the muted classic shades of brown, navy and black. The new season's collection is often distinguished by a new style of grained or embossed leathers, which enliven perennial styles like the characteristic giant duffle bag.

Jewelry

Antwerp is the undisputed center of Belgium's diamond trade (47 percent of the world's polished diamonds pass through the city). The main hotels and the tourist office hold information on the regular excursions from Brussels to visit the cutting factories, diamond exchanges and diamond museum.

In Brussels, the best jewelry shops are in the Haut de la Ville:

* **Cartier**   avenue Louise 1, B-1050, map 6G4
* **Lascar**   boulevard de Waterloo 57, B-1000 *(by the Hilton)*, map 6G4
* **Leysen Frères**   place du Grand Sablon 36, B-1000, map 6F4
* **Van Cleef & Arpels**   Galerie Louise 39, B-1050, map 6H4
* **Wolfers Frères**   avenue Louise 82, B-1050, map 6H4

ANTIQUES

It is easy to make a day out of browsing for antiques. Many of the small antique stores are clustered, along with galleries specializing in modern and **African art**, and sidewalk cafés, around **place du Grand Sablon**. At the weekends, red-and-green awnings attract passers-by to stalls selling books, prints, fine china and jewelry and other "antiques" such as old-fashioned chocolate molds. These occupy the top of the square next to the Église Notre-Dame du Sablon, with its beautifully-lit stained glass windows.

The **Sablon Shopping Gardens** *(map 6 F4)* contains more than 40 shops specializing in art and antiques. The **Hôtel des Ventes** *(pl. du Grand Sablon 39, B-1000* ☎ *(02)512.97.36, map 6F4)* holds evening auctions every few weeks.

Old furniture and some antiques can be found in one of the many *brocantes* lining rue Haute and rue Blaes, which link the upmarket Sablon to the flea market in place du Jeu de Balle. The *brocantes* are large warehouse-like stores, with few frills, where genuine antiques rub shoulders with the shabby proceeds of house clearance sales. Keep your eyes open for Art Nouveau and Art Deco pieces, tribal art from Zaire and Central Africa, and some lovely 18thC French and British furniture.

Details of auctions, sales and markets can be found in the monthly magazine *Arts, Antiques, Auctions* (in English, French and Dutch). Advance notices of auctions are often to be found in the property pages of the "Eco-Soir" supplement of *Le Soir* on a Thursday.

There are no special formalities for exporting antiques from Belgium.

FINE ART

Brussels has been one of the main centers of European art since the Middle Ages. The chances of finding, or being able to afford, an old Flemish Master may be slender, but the astute collector will find several serious commercial galleries in the city.

Commercial galleries are many and varied, and are clustered in two main areas around the Sablon and, slightly more dispersed, where the avenue Louise meets the chaussée de Charleroi. The main area for Belgian 19thC paintings and sculpture is place du Grand Sablon, while paintings by major 20thC artists are sold in the more upmarket galleries on avenue Louise.

For the weird visions of contemporary Belgian Surrealists, look in at the tiny **Galerie des Beaux-Arts** *(rue Ravenstein 20* ☎ *(02)513.67.77, map 4E4),* run by the daughter of the Belgian Surrealist Marcel Broodthaers. The **Galerie Isy Brachot** *(av. Louise 62A* ☎ *(02)511.05.25, map 6H4)* regularly holds exhibitions by the best contemporary Belgian artists, including the Surrealist Paul Delvaux.

Many galleries change, from one season to another, the type of work that they exhibit, and, if you are interested in buying a work of art, a browsing stroll is the best way to take a look at what's on the market.

LACE

Belgian lace is one of the most popular souvenirs, and there is a huge choice of goods from handkerchiefs and doilies to wedding veils and vast tablecloths, all intricately worked. But today much of the lace on sale is only partly hand-made (and the work sometimes done in the Far East), although it still qualifies as "real" lace.

As in most cases, you get what you pay for, and price is the best guide to quality. The finest and most intricate all-needlepoint designs can be found in some of the long-established lace shops, but the exquisite work demands high prices. A small all-needlepoint lace handkerchief can cost as much as 20,000 BF. Markets and antique stores are a good source of second-hand old Brussels' lace.

In the winter months, there are no opportunities to see lace-making in Brussels. But in the summer it is possible to watch practitioners of the art at the **Maison Belge Dentelles** *(Galerie de la Reine 6-8, B-1000, map 4 E4)*, or, if you are traveling farther afield, in the streets of Bruges.

- **Belgische Kantwerkfabriek**   Galerie de la Reine 6-8, B-1000, map 4E4
- **Brussels Lace Centre**   Grand'Place 38, B-1000, map 3E3
- **Renée Foiret**   place de Brouckère 29, B-1000, map 3D3
- **Lace Palace**   rue de la Violette 1-3, B-1000, map 3E3
- **F. Rubbrecht**   Grand'Place 23, B-1000, map 3E3
- **Louise Verschueren**   (the fourth generation of a real lace manufacturer), rue Watteau 16, B-1000, map 5F3

CHOCOLATES

Forget any attempt at dieting as soon as you arrive in Brussels — few visitors resist the lure of its world-famous chocolates. There are almost as many opinions as to who makes the best Belgian chocolates as there are Belgians. In fact, the chocolates that the country is best known for come as a shock to the purists: they are hand-made *pralines*, huge mouth-watering concoctions filled with fresh cream, liqueur and chocolate nut or truffle paste.

Arguably the best chocolatier, **Mary** *(rue Royale 73, B-1000, map 4 D5)*, supplies hand-made pralines to the royal court, from a very elegantly furnished shop.

If you want to impress Belgian friends, take them chocolates or a cake from **Wittamer** *(pl. du Grand Sablon 12, B-1000, map 6 F4)*, possibly Brussels' most expensive chocolatier. It remains a family-run business, also selling exquisite ice creams and mouth-watering cakes. For special occasions they will arrange champagne, food hampers and even birthday cakes made of ice cream.

Other less-exclusive stores with branches around the city sell excellent hand-made chocolates at less ruinous prices. These include **Neuhaus**, **Corné**, **Godiva** and **Leonidas**. Despite being the least expensive, Leonidas probably has the best selection of fresh-cream pralines, and these tend to be what the Belgians buy for themselves. The open-fronted stores commemorate the sidewalk stall in the boulevard Anspach from which the store's founder started selling his handmade chocolates in 1930. The oldest-established *chocolatier* in Brussels, **Neuhaus**, who have some of the best truffles, first opened shop in the Galerie de la Reine in 1857, and still operate from the same elegant premises.

- **Corné**   Galerie du Roi 24, B-1000, map 4D4, and avenue de la Toison d'Or 12, B-1060, map 6G4.
- **Godiva**   Grand'Place 22, map 3E3 (foreign currency accepted), and inside the Hilton Hotel, blvd. de Waterloo 38, B-1000, map 6G4.
- **Leonidas**   blvd. Anspach 46, B-1000, map 3D3 and chaussée d'Ixelles 5, B-1050, map 6G5.

- **Neuhaus**   Galerie de la Reine 25-27, B-1000, map **4**E4.
- If you waver again on the way home, Neuhaus and Godiva are also on sale at the airport, both landside and in the duty-free stores.

BISCUITS

Speculoos are Belgium's distinctive biscuits, flavored with honey, almonds and spices. You'll usually find one, individually wrapped, on the side of your saucer when you order a cup of coffee, but the best and biggest — shaped like people or animals — come from **Dandoy** near Grand'Place *(rue au Beurre 31, B-1000, map* **3** *E3).*

Established in 1829, this biscuit-maker also sells the typically-Belgian, despite its name, *Pain à la Grecque* and tooth-breaking *Couques de Dinant,* each made with their own characteristic spices.

CHEESE

There is a huge variety of Belgian cheeses. Some, like the stinking *Herve,* sold in airtight plastic containers, do not travel well, and your companions will not thank you if the knockout aroma escapes from your luggage. Many others, like *Chimay,* are made with local beers after which they are named. Specialist cheesemongers will give advice and allow you to taste several before making up your mind.

Try **Langhendries** *(rue de la Fourche 41, B-1000, map* **3** *D3)* or **Fromagerie Duysens** *(chaussée de Wavre 1610, Auderghem, B-1160, map* **2** *C4).*

BEER

Belgium boasts over 500 types of beer, including potent brews made by Trappist monks. Some have fantastic labels, like the Delirium Tremens, whose earthenware bottle is decorated with pink elephants.

Although the main supermarkets have a selection of the most common brews, connoisseurs head for **Bières Artisanales** *(chaussée de Wavre 174, B-1050* ☎ *(02)512.17.88, map* **6** *G6).* Friendly staff will guide you through their stock of more than 100 types of traditionally brewed ales, and can even supply the appropriate glasses to drink them from. They will make up a gift pack of beer and glasses to order.

MARKETS

Brussels boasts more than 100 regular street markets. These lively local events are interesting to visit even if you buy nothing more than a waffle. Most of the 19 communes have a market on one or more days of the week, including a number on Sundays.

The local markets almost always feature a cheery Dutch fishmonger, a Flemish market gardener with mud still on his boots, a van stacked with French and Belgian cheeses, a few stalls selling cut flowers and plants, an Italian stall selling imported pasta and fresh *Mozzarella*, and, perhaps, an elderly Belgian man trying to scrape a living selling dog coats.

The more wealthy communes such as Woluwé and Boitsfort are often visited by tradesmen with an expertise in exotic mushrooms, or smallholders from the Ardennes offering goat cheeses.

You can find markets selling almost anything in Brussels, including cars, bicycles, horses, books, antiques, birds and flowers. The markets listed below are among the more interesting ones to visit, although almost any market in Brussels has its particular charms.

Place du Châtelain *Pl. du Châtelain, map 1C3. Wed 2-7pm. Tram 81, 93 or 94 to Lesbroussart.*
The leafy place du Châtelain hosts the most fashionable market in town. Office workers flock here from avenue Louise to buy homemade lasagna, Italian olive oil, and rare mushrooms from the Forêt de Soignes.

Boitsfort *Pl. Bisschoffsheim, map 2D4. Sun 8am-1pm. Tram 94 to Wiener.*
This is the closest you get in Brussels to a small town market. The square in front of Boitsfort's elegant Art Nouveau town hall is crammed with stalls where you can buy everything to make a solid Belgian Sunday lunch, from spit-roast chickens to Ardennes goats' cheese.

Gare Du Midi *Blvd. de l'Europe and neighboring streets, map 5G1. Sun 5am-1pm. Metro to Gare du Midi.*
A sprawling Mediterranean market fills the normally drab streets around the Gare du Midi every Sunday morning. The stalls are heaped with wooden tubs of oily black olives, packs of coriander and saffron, boxes of Tunisian dates, Italian salamis and crates of Spanish oranges. The atmosphere is friendly, but beware pickpockets, who are apt to take advantage of the crush of people.

Grand'Place *Grand'Place, map 3E3. Flower market daily 8am-6pm; bird market Sun only 7am-2pm. Tram 52, 55, 58, 81 to Bourse; metro to Gare Centrale.*
A flower market is held in the middle of Grand'Place every day of the week. Growers from the Pajottenland unload a few boxes of homegrown geraniums or azaleas, which they display under awnings printed with the red and green stripes of Brussels. The flower stalls are highly photogenic, though the prices charged are somewhat steeper than elsewhere.

On Sunday mornings, Grand'Place is filled with the unexpected sounds of cocks crowing and songbirds twittering. Locals flock to pick up racing pigeons, turtle doves and even swans.

Place du Jeu de Balle (Flea market) *Pl. du Jeu de Balle, map 5G2. Daily 7am-2pm. Metro to Porte de Hal.*
Brussels' biggest and most boisterous flea market takes place every day on a square in the heart of the Marolles district. Dealers arrive at first

light to set up stalls where they hawk things that have turned up in dusty Brussels attics: old oil paintings, scratched recordings of dimly-remembered French singers, boxes of rusty keys, cracked mirrors, single shoes and old dentists' drills.

The traders are born optimists and will try to raise a few francs by selling a tattered 1950 Liège telephone directory cover, or a copy of the city's free newspaper. The best bargains, as every flea market enthusiast will tell you, require an early start and a willingness to haggle. Most of the goods left by mid-morning are pure junk.

Sainte-Catherine   *Pl. Sainte-Catherine, map 3D3. Mon-Sat 7am-5pm. Metro to Sainte-Catherine.*
The last surviving food market in the old town takes place next to the dilapidated Église Sainte-Catherine. The potato stall sells old-fashioned Flemish *bintjes,* while a chic stand nearby offers Zeeland oysters served with a glass of Muscadet.

BOOKS IN ENGLISH
- **W H Smith**   blvd. Adolphe Max 71-75, B-1000 ☎(02)219.50.34, map **4**C4. Has newspapers, maps, guides and a good selection of general interest books, novels and educational material. A bustling Saturday morning meeting place for British expatriates stocking up on favorite magazines.
- **House of Paperbacks**   chaussée de Waterloo 813, B-1180 ☎(02)343.11.22, off map **5**I2. A little off the beaten track, this shop has a good selection and helpful staff.
- **The Strathmore Bookshop**   rue Saint Lambert 110, B-1200 ☎(02)771.92.00, map **2**C4. A good selection of books, ranging from do-it-yourself manuals to Shakespeare, near a suburban shopping center.
- **European Bookshop**   rue de la Loi 244, B-1040 ☎(02)231.04.35, off map **6**E6. The official agent for European Community publications and the best selection of history books and textbooks, as well as recent economic and legal analyses on the EC and European integration.

COMIC BOOKS
Comics are not just cartoons for children. Belgians, like the French, take comic books *(bande dessinées or BDs)* very seriously indeed. Many are adult in content, and their creators are revered as artists in their own right.

The center of BD culture in Brussels stretches down the chaussée de Wavre, from the junction with rue du Trône, to place Fernand Cocq. The **Boutique de Tintin** near Grand'Place sells a range of gifts, from plates and teapots to T-shirts.
- **Jonas**   place Fernand Cocq 4, B-1050, map **6**H5
- **Espace BD**   place Fernand Cocq 2, B-1050, map **6**H5

- **La Bande des Six Nez** (*six nez* means six noses — a pun on *bande dessinée* — *chaussée de Wavre 179, B-1050, map* 6G6). This has an exhibition center on the ground floor and a collection of original drawings and rare books.

TOYS

Belgium does not have a toy-making tradition of its own but can offer the next best thing — a wide range of international brands plus a good selection of lovely, hand-made wooden toys from Germany. Late November is when the shelves will be at their fullest, as stores stock up for the annual present-giving for children that marks the feast of Saint Nicholas on 6 December.

- **Christiaensen** has branches throughout the city (*including rue Neuve 123, B-1000, map* 4C4, *and av. de la Toison d'Or 22A, B-1000, map* 6G4).
- **Brand** (*rue du Marché aux Herbes 60, B-1000, map* 3E3) has a good selection of model trains, boats and accessories, for older children and serious collectors.
- **Serneels** (*Galerie de la Toison d'Or 516, B-1060, map* 6G4) has a good collection of toys, games and books, and colorful Babar The Elephant memorabilia.
- A little out of the city center, **Casse-Noisettes** (*chaussée d'Alsemberg 76, B-1060*), has some attractive wooden toys, many of them from Germany.
- **Boris & Lola** (*av. de la Brise 34, B-1020, map* 1B3), has wooden toys and a small selection of clothes.
- The **Maison Picard** (*rue du Lombard 71-75, B-1000, map* 5E3) is an Aladdin's cave of toys and bizarre nicknacks, although its main role is as a carnival costumier. In addition to the impressive range of theatrical makeup and the sort of unpleasant fly-in-a-sugarlump jokes that older children seem to love, it has a huge selection of masks depicting everything from grimacing gorillas and Halloween witches to top international politicians and members of the British Royal family.
- The **annual Christmas fair** in place du Grand Sablon in early December has a good selection of hand-made toys from all over Europe.

EURO-GIFTS

Brussels' claim to be the "Capital of Europe" has spawned a range of souvenir shops where everything is emblazoned with the European Community's trademark circle of 12 gold stars on a bright blue background. There are watches, towels, tracksuits and pens, as well as posters and car bumper stickers proclaiming *Europe: my country* or *Citizen of Europe*. The souvenir to end all souvenirs has to be the blue-and-gold EC umbrella, which seems to be favored by employees of the EC institutions.

- **Euroline**   boulevard Adolphe Max 55b, B-1000, map **4**C4.
- **Eurotempo**   boulevard Charlemagne 44, B-1040, map **1**C3, or rue du Lombard 39a, B-1000, map **5**E3.

COMPUTER SUPPLIES

Diskettes are generally easy to come by, as they are almost universal, but more specialized supplies are harder to find, and the general suppliers will not keep a large range of peripherals in stock. For a special item such as, for example, the telephone cable you need to plug your modem into the Belgian phone system, currently the best advice is to contact the agent for your particular brand of computer.

- For the dexterous and technically-minded, **Tandy** *(in City 2, map 4C4, and elsewhere)* sells the crocodile clips, plugs and cables you need to make a self-assembly alternative.
- **FNAC**, the French-owned multi-media supplies store in the City 2 shopping complex, has a good selection of basic computer accessories such as diskettes, word-processing programs and games.
- Many photographic stores also sell diskettes, including the **Photo Hall** chain *(branches throughout the city)*.
- **Computerland** *(rue de la Loi 19 ☎ (02)230.05.00, map 6E6)*, is worth a special mention. It has a limited selection of accessories for IBM-compatible machines, but does have a large and helpful team of English-speaking technicians who might be able to save the day if you have a problem.

Recreation

Brussels for children

Children in Brussels are presented with an almost bewildering range of enticing activities to keep their spirits buoyant. The choice becomes particularly diverse during the school vacations, when puppet theaters perform in the parks, and endless group activities are organized. Most, of course, will be in French or Dutch. Everything the parent needs to know about Brussels is listed in the widely available book *Le Grand Bruxelles des Tout-Petits*. For current events, look in *The Bulletin* or under *Jeunes* in the Wednesday supplement of *Le Soir*.

BICYCLES
The scatty habits of drivers in Brussels make cycling a risky venture, so those with a yen for taking to a bicycle are best advised to head into the vast FORÊT DE SOIGNES. You can rent bicycles near the forest at **Vélo Pipette** *(rue de l'Hospice Communal 47 ☎(02)672.16.98, open Tues-Sat from 9.30am, tram 94 to Wiener)*. Ask for a bolt-on back seat to transport your child.

CHALET ROBINSON
If the sun shines, take a trip on the creaking mechanical ferry in the BOIS DE LA CAMBRE to reach an alluring island with a playground and puppet theater. Dedicated parents can rent a rowboat by the hour to circumnavigate the island.

   The Chalet Robinson was a popular restaurant located on the island. It has been destroyed by fire, but may one day be rebuilt.

CINEMAS
Children's films in Brussels tend to be dubbed into French or Dutch, although you might track down English-language versions in the cosmopolitan suburbs of the city. The **City 2** cinema complex *(rue Neuve ☎(02)219.42.46, map 4C4, metro to Rogier)* has come up with an inspired formula for families. On Saturdays at 9.30am, they screen a serious French movie for parents in one cinema, and a children's movie in another room.

EATING
Italian pizzerias are often the easiest to eat in with children. They are found in every quarter of Brussels, but especially in the Îlot Sacré and off Grand'Place. For a more traditional Belgian lunch in a relaxed setting, try the **Horta Brasserie** at the CENTRE BELGE DE LA BANDE DESSINÉE.

FESTIVALS

For children who can follow French, the **Festival du Dessin Animé** in late February to early March reliably screens *Cinderella*, *Babar*, *Astérix* and other cartoon films. In July and August, children are kept amused by afternoon puppet shows and clown acts, held at the iron bandstand in the Parc de Bruxelles. Check the posters at the gates for dates.

MUSEUMS

A rambling old mansion near the Ixelles ponds is home to the inspired **Musée des Enfants** *(rue du Bourgmestre 15 ☎(02)640.01.07, map 1 C3 ▨ open Wed, Sat, Sun, holidays 2.30-5pm; tram 23, 90 to chaussée de Boondael)*. The museum is crammed with objects that children can touch and clutch without being told off, and the rooms are reorganized every couple of years to avoid kids getting bored. Expect tunnels, sticky stuff, pens and paper, modeling clay, play houses, giant games and painted faces.

The genial owner of the **Musée du Jouet** *(rue de l'Association 24, map 4 D5 ☎(02)219.61.68 ▨ open daily 10am-6pm; metro or tram 92, 93, 94 to Botanique)* has gradually assembled a collection of toys that now fills two floors of a handsome former insurance office near the botanical gardens. Lofty rooms with Neoclassical ceilings and slender iron columns are crammed with old Belgian jigsaws, spinning tops, moldering teddy bears, wide-eyed porcelain dolls and gutted television sets converted into puppet theaters. Children can paint at big wooden tables or sprawl on the floor playing with the dollhouses. Spacious rooms contain a mock school, a shop, a dolls' hospital, and a model railway.

At the CENTRE BELGE DE LA BANDE DESSINÉE (full details on page 96) children tend to run around just as they please. They can wander amid mock-ups from Lucky Luke and Tintin cartoons, or loll on the library floor reading their favorite comic magazines. Tiny tots are best kept away, but any child over the age of three is bound to appreciate the atmosphere of artful anarchy.

The name may sound dreary, but the MUSÉE DE L'INSTITUT ROYAL DES SCIENCES NATURELLES (see page 113) has become more child-friendly in recent years. The dinosaur skeletons are impressive and the model bathyscaphe offers hi-tech fun. Take along sandwiches, as the café only sells drinks.

The MUSÉES ROYAUX D'ART ET D'HISTOIRE (see page 115) are accustomed to young visitors. Explain to your children that they mustn't run or touch things, then take them to look at the scale model of Rome and the Egyptian mummies. Treat them to an ice cream afterwards at **Capoue** *(av. des Celtes 5, map 2 C4)*.

PARKS

If your kids need swings and slides in a hurry, head for the playground in the formal PARC DE BRUXELLES, which is just a five-minute uphill hike from Grand'Place. But if they want more to do, take them by tram to the vast BOIS DE LA CAMBRE *(tram 93, 94 to Legrand)*, which is more of a forest than a park. The main roads through the park are mercifully closed to traffic in the summer, and Brussels children go there for their first wobble on a bicycle. Children of a dozen nationalities get along fine in the big playground near the Théâtre du Poche. While parents drink a beer on a café terrace, they slide, swing and, in summer, bounce on an inflated castle.

Children can feed the ducks in the PARC JOSAPHAT. It is well equipped, with an adventure playground, sandpit and miniature golf course. There are rowboats to rent at the PARC DE WOLUWÉ and the PARK VAN TERVUREN.

MARIONNETTE THEATERS

Traditional puppet performances remain an essential part of growing up in Belgium. Several companies in Brussels stage shows on Wednesday afternoons and on weekends. Children dressed in chic clothes can be seen flocking to **Le Perruchet** in Ixelles *(av. de la Forêt 50, map 1 D3 ☎(02)673.87.30; performances in French on Wed, Sat and Sun at 3pm; tram 94 to Brésil)*. The company stages traditional fairy tales in the former stables of a whitewashed Brabantine farmhouse. Free balloons and lollipops are doled out as the kids troop home.

The puppet theater **Le Ratinet** *(av. de Fré 44 ☎(02)512.80.30, map 1 D3)* puts on shows in an old brick farmhouse in Uccle.

ROLLER SKATES

Children twirl and tumble to disco music at the **Patinoire du Bois de la Cambre**, an outdoor roller skating rink in the BOIS DE LA CAMBRE.

ROWBOATS

Rowboats and pedalos are rented out on the island in the BOIS DE LA CAMBRE and in the PARC DE WOLUWÉ at the Étangs Mellaerts.

ZOO

Children who want to spend a day at the zoo have to be taken to **Antwerp** *(30mins by train)*. Happily, the well-run 19thC **Dierentuin** (zoo) stands alongside the railway station *(Koningin Astridplein 26 ☎(03)231.16.40, open daily 8.45am-4.45pm)*. Elephants inhabit a mock Egyptian temple, while owl-faced monkeys prowl around simulated Babylonian ruins. Artificial hills and mock Greek temples add yet more romantic allure.

Sports

For a city that prided itself on its gastronomy and beer, Brussels, until ten years ago, had remarkably few places where one could sweat off the advancing kilos. But the increasing numbers of foreigners has acted as a spur to the arrival of more golf courses, squash and tennis courts and fitness centers in the city.

Expatriate clubs and societies also thrive, and a large number of sports centers have modern facilities. There are sports associations, particularly the splendid **ADEPS** (see below), that now cater to a wide range of interests. Today's sporting activities are now widely practiced alongside Belgian's more traditional pastimes of cycling and pigeon racing.

Almost all of Brussels' 19 communes have sports facilities that are open to casual visitors for a small fee. Details of these can be found in the telephone directory under *Administrations Communales*.

In addition, each language community runs a sport and outdoor leisure department, providing public information, arranging country and forest walks, and listing vacation courses in over 100 sports for schoolchildren. Contact **ADEPS** *(Administration de l'Éducation Physique, des Sports et de la Vie en Plein Air, blvd. Leopold II, B-1080 ☎ (02)413.23.11).*

Details of sports facilities for the disabled can be obtained by contacting the **Belgian Sports Federation for the Handicapped** *(pl. Van Gehuchten 4, B-1020 ☎ (02)478.48.50 ext. 125).*

Spectator sports

For the spectator, Brussels offers an opportunity to watch many first-class sportsmen and women. On the **athletics** front, the highlight is the annual **Ivo Van Damme Memorial**, held in August, in honor of Belgium's greatest Olympic 800-meter runner, who died tragically young in a car crash, just months after winning a gold medal for Belgium at the 1976 Montreal Olympics. The event has brought some of the world's top track-and-field athletes to Brussels.

Spectators may also enjoy watching the 20,000 runners of widely varying ability who regularly participate in the 20-kilometer ($12\frac{1}{2}$-mile) **Brussels Run**, at the end of May, and the several thousand contestants in the September **Brussels Marathon**.

In **tennis**, the **Belgian Indoor Championship**, held either at Forest National or the Heysel Exhibition Hall in February or March, has attracted top-ranking players like Boris Becker, Ivan Lendl and Yannick Noah.

The Belgian capital is home of the country's most successful **soccer** team, **Sporting d'Anderlecht**, which has a strongly international squad, based at Astrid Park in Anderlecht. Brussels also hosts the final of many European soccer championships. It was one such event between the then English and Italian champions, Liverpool and Juventus, at the Heysel in 1985, that went down as one of the blackest days in soccer's history when one British and 39 Italian spectators died after a wall collapsed in pre-match fighting initiated by British fans.

In May or June each year, Brussels hosts the **Eddy Merckx Grand Prix**. Named after one of the world's greatest cyclists, the event pits the fastest international speed racers against each other. Recently, Europe's premier cycle race, the *Tour de France*, expanded its itinerary and included Brussels as one of the many stages of the grueling event.

Horse racing is an increasingly popular spectator sport in Belgium. For details of events in and around Brussels contact **Boitsfort** *(chaussée de la Hulpe, B-1170 ☎ (02)660.28.39, map 2 D4)*, **Sterrebeek** *(du Roy de Blicquylaan 43, B-1933 Sterrebeek ☎ (02)767.54.75)* or **Groenendael** *(Leopold II-laan, B-1560 Hoeilaart ☎ (02)657.03.37).*

Participant sports

AEROBICS
Many of Brussels' local communes offer classes. **Woluwé-St-Pierre Sports Center** (☎(02)762.12.75) sometimes has classes with an English-speaking instructor. Classes are organized by the **British and Commonwealth Women's Club** (☎(02)772.53.13) and the **American Women's Club** (☎(02)358.47.53).

AIKIDO, JUDO, KARATE, YOGA
Classes in English can be found at the **Centre de la Culture Japonaise** (rue des Augustins 44, B-1090 ☎(02)426.50.00, map 3 D3).

BADMINTON
The Brussels British Badminton Club (☎(02)653.74.02) has flourished since early this century. Matches are held in Waterloo and Woluwé-Saint-Lambert.

BOATING
If you fancy a spot of gentle boating on a small, quiet lake surrounded by trees and bushes, try the **Étangs Mellaerts** (Parc de Woluwé, corner of av. de Tervuren and blvd. du Souverain, B-1160, map 2 C4), or the BOIS DE LA CAMBRE (from the island), where small boats for adults and children can be rented.

BOWLING
There are a number of bowling and skittle alleys in the city, some near the center. Try **Crosly Super Bowling** (blvd. de l'Empereur 36, B-1000 ☎(02)512.08.74, map 5 F3), which has 20 lanes, or **Bowlmaster** (rue Van Zande 45, B-1080 ☎(02)465.05.10, map 1 C2).

CHESS
Some of Brussels' cafés keep chess sets on the premises for lovers of the game to test their skills over a quiet drink. There are also a number of clubs. Among the most popular: **Caissa Woluwé** (☎(02)720.17.55), **Cercle Royal des Échecs de Bruxelles** (☎(02)215.20.00) and **Les Fous du Roy** (☎(02)640.07.94).

CRICKET
British soldiers played cricket in the Bois de la Cambre on the eve of the battle of Waterloo, but enthusiasts now play with the **Royal Brussels Cricket Club**. Matches are played on an all-weather pitch at **Ground Fifty-One** (Centre-Ohain, Vieux Chemin de Wavre 117, B-1328 Ohain-Lasne ☎(02)764.75.24 or (02)732.27.45) near Royal Waterloo Golf Club.

CYCLING
Cycling is one of Belgium's national pastimes, and the country is riddled with cycle tracks. Cycling in the city can be a hair-raising experi-

ence, but for safety and scenery try the BOIS DE LA CAMBRE, PARC DE WOLUWÉ on avenue de Tervuren, or ride out from rond-point Montgomery to the KONINKLIJK MUSEUM VOOR MIDDENAFRIKA (Central Africa Museum) in Tervuren on the special cycle track. It is possible to take the train to many rail stations in Belgium, and to rent bicycles of various sizes on the spot.

A leaflet giving information about the *Train-Plus-Vélo* scheme is available from Brussels' mainline rail stations. It lists the stations where bicycles can be rented, and, more importantly, the larger number of places where they can be left.

For information on Belgian cycle clubs contact the **Ligue Velocipédique Belge** *(av. du Globe 49, B-1190 ☎(02)349.19.11, map 1 D2)*.

FISHING
Belgians are keen fishermen, setting up their rods alongside lakes, ponds, rivers and canals. Licenses can be obtained at any of the city's post offices. But permits to fish in either Flanders or Wallonia must be obtained from post offices in those regions. Certain restrictions apply to minimum size and closed seasons.

For details, contact **Service des Ressources Naturelles et des Eaux et Forêts** *(rue de Trèves 49, B-1040 ☎(02)231.12.55)*.

FITNESS CENTERS
These exist in a number of hotels such as the Scandic Crown, SAS Royal and the Sheraton (where the center's rooftop location provides a panoramic view of Brussels). See WHERE TO STAY for details.

Otherwise, try **Winners** *(rue Bonneels 13, B-1040 ☎(02)280.02.70, map 1 C3)*, **American Gym** *(boulevard General Jacques 144, B-1050 ☎(02)640.59.92, map 2 C4)* or **The Health Studio** *(rue R. Van der Weyden 3 ☎(02)513.26.16, map 5 F2)*.

FOOTBALL (SOCCER)
There are numerous teams and many opportunities to play football in Brussels, either friendly games or in amateur Belgian leagues. Among the city's expatriate teams are the **Royal Brussels British Football Club** *(☎(02)672.82.34, evenings)*, founded in 1933, which has more than 120 members and runs five teams, and the **British United Football Club** *(☎(02)252.50.50)*.

GLIDING
Contact **Centre National de Vol à Voile** *(Aérodrome de Saint-Hubert, B-6870 Saint-Hubert ☎(061)61.12.68)*. The center, which is some 3km (2 miles) from the village of Saint-Hubert, offers training courses and is open from April to the end of September.

GOLF
Interest in the game has soared in the past decade. There are now more than 60 courses on varied terrain, and more than 20,000 players in Belgium. But the game is no recent arrival. A Brussels decree of 1360

warned that anyone found playing golf in the city had to pay a fine or leave his coat in pawn. The sport can be seen in the landscapes of Pieter Bruegel or Lucas Van Valckenborch. More recently, the Belgian King Baudouin was a member of the national team that beat the Dutch in 1958. The course at Antwerp is among the oldest on mainland Europe.

A good course some 30km (19 miles) from Brussels is at the **Château de la Bawette** *(chaussée du Château de la Bawette, B-1300 Wavre* ☎ *(010)22.33.32)*. It has a 9-hole course for beginners and an 18-hole course for more experienced golfers. For driving ranges and practice, try **Brussels Golf School Training Centre** *(chaussée de la Hulpe, B-1170* ☎ *(02)672.22.22)* and **Evere Golf Club** *(Av. des Anciens Combattants 350, B-1140* ☎ *(02)241.61.87)*. Information on courses can also be obtained from the **Fédération Royale belge de Golf** (Belgian Royal Golf Federation) *(* ☎ *(067)22.04.40)*.

HUNTING
Hunting is a popular sport in Belgium. Visitors from abroad, if they hold a national hunting license, can obtain a special five-day license. Details are available from **Service des Ressources Naturelles et des Eaux et Forêts** *(rue de Trèves 49, B-1040* ☎ *(02)231.12.55)*.

ICE-SKATING
The two major rinks for ice-skating enthusiasts are at **Poseidon** *(av. des Vaillants 4, B-1200* ☎ *(02)762.16.33, map 2 C4)*, open September to April, and **Forêt National** *(Forêt Patinoire, av. du Globe 36, B-1190* ☎ *(02)347.02.30, map 1 D2)*, open September to May.

PARACHUTE JUMPING
You should contact the **Aérodrome de la Sauvenière** *(B-8900 Spa* ☎ *(087)77.41.83)*. The aerodrome, which is 3.5km (2 miles) from the center of Spa, is open from Easter until early October and can offer training courses.

RUGBY
Rugby is a growing sport in Belgium, with the national side improving year by year. In addition to local Belgian clubs, there is also the **Brussels British Rugby Football Club** *(* ☎ *(02)728.51.59)*.

RUNNING
Despite the supremacy of cars in the city, Brussels is an excellent place for runners. PARC DE WOLUWÉ, the PARC DE BRUXELLES, BOIS DE LA CAMBRE and FORÊT DE SOIGNES all provide varied terrain away from car fumes. For the more energetic, the local clubs frequently organize races ranging from 5km to 30km (3-19 miles), and there is the city's annual 20km $(12\frac{1}{2}$ -mile) Brussels Run *(usually on last Sun in May)* and the Brussels Marathon in September.

For fun runners there's a choice of two groups of **Hash House Harriers** *(* ☎ *(02)734.36.77 or (02)242.93.59)* in Brussels, who run on Saturday afternoons and Monday evenings.

SOCCER
See FOOTBALL

SNOOKER
The exposure given to the game by television has boosted snooker's popularity in the city. The game can be played at the **Pot Black Snooker Club** *(Gallery Manhattan Centre, pl. Rogier, B-1210* ☎*(02)217.12.24, map 4 C4)* and **Fort Jaco Squash and Snooker Club** *(chaussée de Waterloo 1333, boîte 28, B-1180* ☎*(02)375.26.77).*

SPORTS COMPLEXES
Auderghem *(Forêt de Soignes Sports Centre, chaussée de Wavre 2057, B-1160* ☎*(02)672.82.30, map 2 C4)* has a wide range of activities, including indoor soccer, gymnastics, dance, badminton, squash, tennis and martial arts.

Etterbeek *(rue des Champs 71, B-1040* ☎*(02)640.39.12, map2 C4)* has body-building, table tennis, weight-lifting and basketball.

Woluwé-Saint-Pierre *(avenue Salomé 2, B-1150* ☎*(02) 762.12.75, map 2 C4)* has tennis, badminton, basketball, handball, volleyball, weight-lifting, dance, squash and martial arts.

SQUASH
One of the oldest and most popular clubs in the city for English-speakers is the **Castle Club** *(av. de la Bécasse 16, B-1970 Wezembeek-Oppem* ☎*(02)731.68.20).*

Also popular is **Fort Jaco** *(chaussée de Waterloo 1333, B-1180* ☎*(02)375.26.77, map 1 D3)* and **Flanders Gate Squash Club** *(blvd. Barthélémy 17, B-1000* ☎*(02)512.51.33).*

You could also try **Liberty's** *(chaussée de Wavre 1068, B-1160* ☎*(02)734.56.83).*

SWIMMING
The city has a number of swimming pools. Among the most impressive and enjoyable for adults and children alike is the **Océadium** complex *(Parc Aquatique, Bruparck, Blvd du Centenaire 20* ☎*(02)478.43.20, map 1 C3).* It contains a wave-making machine, tanning parlor and other extras.

For a completely different style, try the **Victor Boin** swimming pool in Saint-Gilles *(rue de la Perche 38, B-1060* ☎*(02)539.06.15, map1 C3),* with its Turkish and Russian baths.

For the more energetic, the commune of Woluwé-Saint-Pierre has a fine Olympic-sized swimming pool *(at avenue Salomé 2, B-1150* ☎*(02)762.12.75, map2 C4).*

TENNIS
Most clubs are private, but many communes have courts to rent by the hour. Information can also be obtained from the French-speaking **Association Francophone de Tennis** *(passage International de Rogier, boîte 522, B-1020* ☎*(02)217.22.00).*

A brief guide to French

This glossary looks at a few of the language needs of the traveler: for essential vocabulary and simple conversation, visiting the bank, finding accommodation, using public transport or a car, eating in a restaurant.

Basic communication

Mr   *monsieur/M.*
Mrs   *madame/Mme.*
Miss   *mademoiselle/Mlle.*
Ladies/men   *dames/ hommes*
Gentlemen   *messieurs*
Yes   *oui* (*si*, for emphatic contradiction)
No   *non*
Please   *s'il vous plaît*
Thank you   *merci*
I'm very sorry   *je suis désolé/pardon, excusez-moi*
Excuse me   *pardon/excusez-moi*
Not at all/you're welcome   *de rien*
Hello   *bonjour, salut* (familiar), *allô* (on telephone)
Good morning/afternoon   *bonjour*
Good evening   *bonsoir*
Good night   *bonsoir/bonne nuit*
Goodbye   *au revoir*
Morning   *matin* (m)
Afternoon   *après-midi* (m/f)
Evening/night   *soir* (m) *nuit* (f)
Yesterday   *hier*
Today   *aujourd'hui*
Tomorrow   *demain*
Next week   *la semaine prochaine*
Last week   *la semaine dernière*
. . . days ago   *il y a . . . jours*
Month   *mois* (m)
Year   *an* (m) / *année* (f)
Here/there   *ici/là*
Over there   *là-bas*
Big/small   *grand/petit, -e*
Hot/cold   *chaud/froid, -e*
Good   *bon, bonne*
Bad   *mauvais, -e*
Well/badly   *bien/mal*
With   *avec*
And   *et*
But   *mais*
Very   *très*
All   *tout, -e*
Open/closed   *ouvert/fermé, -e*

Left/right   *gauche/droite*
Straight ahead   *tout droit*
Near   *près/proche*
Far   *loin*
Up/down   *en haut/bas*
Early/late   *tôt/tard*
Quickly   *vite*
Pleased to meet you.   *Enchanté.*
Agreed.   *D'accord.*
How are you?   *Comment ça va?* (Formal: *comment allez vous?*)
Very well, thank you.   *Très bien, merci.*
Do you speak English?   *Parlez-vous anglais?*
I don't understand.   *Je ne comprends pas.*
I don't know.   *Je ne sais pas.*
Please explain.   *Pourriez-vous me l'expliquer?*
Please speak more slowly.   *Parlez plus lentement, s'il vous plaît.*
My name is . . .   *Je m'appelle . . .*
I am American/English/Japanese   *Je suis americain,-e,/ anglais,-e/japonais, -e.*
Where is/are?   *Où est/sont . . . ?*
Is there a . . . ?   *Y a-t-il un . . . ?*
What?   *Comment?*
How much?   *Combien?*
How much does it cost?   *Ça coute combien?*
That's too much.   *C'est trop.*
Expensive   *cher/chère*
Cheap   *pas cher/bon marché*
I would like . . .   *je voudrais . . .*
Do you have . . ?   *Avez-vous . . ?*
Just a minute.   *Attendez une minute.* (On telephone: *ne quittez pas!*)
That's fine/OK.   *Ça va/OK/ça y est/d'accord.*
What time is it?   *Quelle heure est-il?*
I don't feel well.   *Je ne me sens pas bien/j'ai mal.*

At the bank

I would like to change some dollars/pounds/travelers' checks.
Je voudrais changer des dollars/livres/chèques de voyage.
What is the exchange rate?
Quel est le cours du change?
Can you cash a personal check?
Pouvez-vous encaisser un chèque?
Can I obtain cash with this charge/credit card?
Puis-je obtenir de l'argent avec cette carte de crédit?
Do you need to see my passport?
Voulez-vous voir mon passeport?

At the hotel

Do you have a room?
Avez-vous une chambre?
I have a reservation. My name is . . .
J'ai une réservation. Je m'appelle . . .
A quiet room with bath/shower/toilet/wash basin
Une chambre tranquille avec bain/douche/toilette/lavabo
. . . overlooking the park/street/back.
. . . qui donne sur le parc/la rue/la cour.
Does the price include breakfast/service/tax?
Ce prix comprend-il le petit déjeuner/le service/les taxes?
This room is too large/small/cold/hot/noisy.
Cette chambre est trop grande/petite/froide/chaude/bruyante.
That's too expensive. Have you anything cheaper?
C'est trop cher. Avez-vous quelquechose de moins cher?
Where can I park my car?
Où puis-je garer ma voiture?
Is it safe to leave the car on the street?
Est-ce qu'on peut laisser la voiture dans la rue?
Do you have a room? *Avez-vous une chambre?*
What time is breakfast? *À quelle heure est le petit déjeuner?*
Can I drink the tap water? *L'eau du robinet est-elle potable?*
What time does the hotel close? *À quelle heure ferme l'hôtel?*
Will I need a key? *Aurai-je besoin d'une clé?*
Is there a night porter? *Y a-t-il un portier de nuit?*
I am leaving tomorrow morning. *Je partirai demain matin.*
Please give me at call at . . . *Voulez-vous m'appeler à . . .*
Come in! *Entrez!*

Floor/story *étage* (m)
Dining room/restaurant *salle à manger* (f)/*restaurant* (m)
Lounge *salon* (m)
Porter *portier/concierge* (m) *porteur (station)*
Manager *directeur* (m)
Maid *femme de chambre* (f)

Car rental and driving

Is full insurance included? *Est-ce que l'assurance tous-risques est comprise?*
Is it insured for another driver? *Est-elle assurée pour un autre conducteur?*
Unlimited mileage *kilométrage illimité*
Deposit *caution* (f)

By what time must I return it? *À quelle heure devrais-je la ramener?*
Can I return it to another depot? *Puis-je la ramener à une autre agence?*
Is the gas tank full? *Est-ce que le réservoir est plein?*
Fill it up. *Le plein, s'il vous plaît.*
Give me . . . francs worth. *Donnez m'en pour . . . francs.*

Road signs

Aire (de repos) stopping place/layby
Autres directions other directions
Camion truck
Centre ville town center
Chaussée deformée irregular surface
Essence (sans plomb) (lead-free) gasoline
Ne pas se garer devant la porte keep exit clear
Parking/stationnement interdit no parking
Parking ouvert parking lot
Passage à niveau level crossing

Péage toll point
Piétons pedestrians
Ralentir slow down
Rappel remember that a previous sign still applies
Route barrée road blocked
Sens obligatoire through traffic
Sortie exit
Sortie de secours emergency exit
Stationnement toléré literally, parking tolerated
Toutes directions all directions
Verglas (black) ice on road
Vitesse speed
Voie sans issue no through road

Other means of transport

Aircraft *avion* (m)
Airport *aéroport* (m)
Bus *autobus/car* (m)
Bus stop *arrêt d'autobus* (m)
Couchette/sleeper *wagon-lit* (m)
Ferry/boat *ferry/bateau/bac* (m)
Ferry port *port du ferry/bateau/bac* (m)

Hovercraft *hovercraft/aéroglisseur* (m)
Station *gare* (m)
Train *train* (m)
Ticket *billet* (m)
Ticket office *guichet* (m)
One-way *billet simple*
Round-trip *billet aller-retour*

When is the next . . for . . ? *À quelle heure est le prochain . . pour . . . ?*
What time does it arrive? *À quelle heure arrive-t-il?*
What time does the last . . . for . . . leave? *À quelle heure part le dernier . . . pour . . . ?*

Which platform/quay/gate? *Quel quai/port?*
Is this the . . . for . . . ? *Est-ce que c'est bien le . . . pour . . . ?*
Is it direct? Where does it stop? *C'est direct? Où est-ce qu'il s'arrête?*
Do I need to change anywhere? *Est-ce que je dois changer?*
Please tell me where to get off? *Pourrez-vous me dire ou descendre?*
Is there a buffet car? *Y a-t-il un wagon-restaurant?*

In the restaurant

Have you a table for . . . ? *Avez-vous une table pour . . . ?*
I want to reserve a table. *Je voudrais réserver une table.*
A quiet table. *Une table bien tranquille.*
A table near the window. *Une table près de la fenêtre.*
Could we have another table? *Est-ce que nous pourrions avoir une autre table?*

Set menu   *Menu prix-fixe*, or, simply *Menu*
I did not order this   *Je n'ai pas commandé cela*
Bring me another . . .   *Apportez-moi encore un* . . .
The bill please   *L'addition, s'il vous plaît*
Is service included?   *Le service est compris?*

Some essential words

Breakfast   *petit déjeuner* (m)
Lunch   *déjeuner* (m)
Dinner   *dîner* (m)
Hot/cold   *chaud/froid*
Glass   *verre* (m)
Bottle   *bouteille* (f)
Half-bottle   *demi-bouteille*
Beer/lager   *bière* (f)/*lager* (m)
Draft beer   *bière (à la) pression*
Mineral water   *eau minérale* (f)
Fizzy/carbonated water   *eau gazeuse* (f)
Still water   *eau non-gazeuse*
Sparkling   *pétillant*
Non-sparkling   *plat*
Fruit juice   *jus de fruit* (m)
Red wine   *vin rouge* (m)
White/rosé wine   *vin blanc/rosé*
Vintage   *année* (f)

Dry   *sec*
Sweet   *doux* (of wine)
    sucré (of food)
Plain   *nature*
Salt/pepper   *sel/poivre* (m)
Mustard   *moutarde* (f)
Vinegar/oil   *vinaigre/huile* (m)
Bread/butter   *pain/beurre* (m)
Cheese   *fromage* (m)
Milk   *lait* (m)
Coffee/tea   *café/thé* (m)
Decaffeinated   *décaféiné*
Herbal tea   *infusion* (f)
Chocolate   *chocolat* (m)
Sugar   *sucre* (m)
    well done   *bien cuit*
    medium   *cuit à point*
    very/rare   *bleu/saignant*
Kosher   *Cachir*
vegetarian   *végétarien*

Useful words from the menu

à l'Alsacienne   food cooked Alsace-style is served with *choucroute*, ham and frankfurter-style sausages
Ail   garlic
Anguilles au vert   eels in creamy herb sauce
Béarnaise   sauce made mayonnaise-style, with tarragon
Béchamel   white sauce flavored with onion or bay leaf
Blanquette   white meat cooked in a white sauce
Boudin   black or white sausage pudding
Boulette   meatball
Canard or *caneton*   duck
Chasseur   cooked hunter-style, with wine, mushrooms and shallots
Coucou de Malines   Mechelen chicken
Coulis   thick purée, served as a sauce

Couque   sweet pastry
Court-bouillon   stock made with herbs, vegetables and white wine
Darne   thick slice, usually of fish
Daube   meat braised in wine stock
Fraises   strawberries
Framboises   raspberries
Julienne   thin vegetable strips poached in butter
Moules marinière   mussels cooked with white wine and shallots
Pistolet   bread roll
Poireaux   leeks
Potage Crécy   carrot soup
Primeurs   young vegetables
à la Reine   with chicken
Tranche   slice/rasher
Volaille   poultry
Witlof   Belgian endive
Waterzooi   stew made with cream, eggs, vegetable and main ingredient e.g. fish or chicken

Index

- **Bold** page numbers indicate main entries.
- *Italic* page numbers indicate illustrations and maps.

Abbatoirs d'Anderlecht, 35
Abbaye de la Cambre, 89, 92, 125, **126**, 145
Abbaye de Forest, 129
Abbaye du Rouge-Cloître, 39, 125, **126-7**, 145
Académie Royale des Beaux-Arts, 42
Accidents, automobile, 64
Addresses and telephone numbers, **29**, **59-61**
Aerobics, **209**
Africa Museum *see* Koninklijk Museum voor Middenafrika
Aikido, **209**
Air travel/airlines, 47, 60
Airport, Zaventem, 12, 45, 46, 47, 48, 52, 54
Alba, Duke of, 17
Albert I, King, 19, 95, 97-8, 136, 139
Albrecht, Archduke of Austria, 17, 41
Alcohol:
  driving laws, 52
  duty-free allowances, 45
Alechinsky, Pierre, 43
All Saints' Day, 71
Alma station, 142
Ambulances, 64
American Express:
  cashpoint machines, 55
  general delivery, 48
  MoneyGram®, 45
  Travel Service, 55
  travelers checks, 45, 65
Anderlecht, 16, **73**, 100, 208
Anneessens, François, 17, **21**, 142
Anneessens Tower, 15
Anspach, Jules, 80, 140
Anspach fountain, 80

Antiques, **197-8**
Antonello da Messina, 38
Antwerp, 38, 40, 41, 53, 150, 183, 211
Antwerp Mannerists, 40
Antwerp Zoo, **207**
Apartment hotels, **163**
Architecture, **32-7**
Archives Générales du Royaume, 83, 121, 139
Ardennes, 53, 150, 190
Arman, 109
Art, **38-43**, 68
Art Deco, **36**, 37, 68, 74
Art galleries, **91**, **198**
Art Nouveau, 12, 13, 19, 34, **35-6**, 68, 74, 113
  Ixelles, **84-6**
Athletics, 208
Atomium, 19, 32, 36, 73, 91, 93, **95**, *95*, 100, 144
Auber, Daniel, 18
Aumale station, 142
Autoworld, 94, **95**, *96*, *97*
Avenue Louise, **72**, 85, 86, 89, **130-1**
  hotels, 155, 158
  nightlife, 185
  restaurants and cafés, 166
  shops, 191, 192

Badminton, **209**
Balat, Alphonse, 35, 101, 124
Ballet of the 20thC, 20
Ballet, **183-4**
Banks, 54-5
Baroque architecture, **33**
Baroque painting, **40-1**
Bas de la Ville *see* Lower Town
Basilique du Sacré-Coeur, 84, **127**

Baudouin, King, 19, 20, 211
Baudouyn, Jean, 118
Beaudouin, Paul, 141
Beaulieu, 28
Beer, **175-6**, 193
  Brasserie Wielemans, **139**
  in cafés, 176
  Musée de la Brasserie, 110
  Musée de la Gueuze, **112**
  Pajottenland, 152
  shops, **200**
Beersel, Kasteel van, 51, **151**
Beguines, 80
Béjart, Maurice, 20
Belga Jazz Festival, 71, 187
Belgian National Day, 70
Belgian Revolt, 18, 80, 96, 180
Bennett, James Gordon, 99
Bériot, Charles de, 74
Berlaymont building, 20, **27-8**, *28*, 29, 36, 72, 172
Bernhardt, Sarah, 160
Bibliotheca Wittockiana, **139**
Bibliothèque Royale, 18, 84, 91, 121, 136, **139**
Bicycles, 53, **209-10**
  for children, **205**
  races, 208
Biogenium, 95
Biographies, **20-5**
Biscuits, **200**
Bizet, Georges, 142
Bizet station, 142
Blérot, Ernest, 86
Blücher, Marshal, 153
Boats:
  boating, **209**
  ferries, 47-8, 60-1
  rowboats, **207**

Bois de la Cambre, 66, 67, 72, 89, 130, **143**, 205, 206-7, 209, 210, 211
Boitsfort, 15, 145, 149 market, **201**
Bollée, Léon, 95
Bommer, Charles, 145
Bonnard, Pierre, 107
Bookstores, 61, **202**
Bordiau, Gédéon, 138
Bornoy, Jan, 123
Borreman, Jan, 117
Bosch, Hieronymus, **39**, 40, 104, 105
Bosquet, Yves, 142
Botanical Garden see Jardin Botanique
Boucher, François, 111
Bouillon, Godefroid de, **21**
Bourse, 76, **121**, *121*, 176
Bourse station, 142
Bouts, Dirk, 16, **39**, 104
Bovy, Beurthe, 178-9
Bowling, **209**
Brabant, 151
Brabant, dukes of, 15, 128, 135, 138
Brabant Kermis, 70
Brabantine Fauvists, **108**
Brant, Isabella, 41
Brasserie Wielemans, **139**
Breakfasts, 156
Brel, Jacques, **21**
Breweries see Beer
Brocantes, 198
Brontë, Charlotte, **21**, 25, 81, 147
Broodthaers, Marcel, 81, 91, 109
Broodthaers, Marie-Puck, 81, 91
Brosella Festival, 70, 187
La Brouette, **134**
Bruegel, Jan, **40**, 105
Bruegel, Pieter the Elder, 38, **40**, 59, 68, 70, 83, 90, 105-6, 110, 111, 129, 135, 151, 152, 164, 211
Bruegel, Pieter the Younger, **40**, 59, 105
Bruegel Festival, 70
Bruges, 38, 39, 53, 66, 150
hotels, 157
Brunfaut, Jules, 141
Bruparck, **144**
Brussels Air Museum, 96, *97*, **101**
Brussels City Museum see Musée Communal

Brussels commune, **72**, 88
Brussels Conservatory, 19
Brussels environs, **151**
Brussels Europalia Festival, 182
Brussels Exhibition Centre, 49, 73, 154
Brussels Marathon, 70, 208, 211
Brussels Public Transport Museum see Musée du Transport Urbain Bruxellois
Brussels Run, 69, 208, 211
Bruyn, G. de, 134, 135
Budget holidays, 59
Buls, Charles, 35, 134, 140, 141
Bureaux de change, 45, 54
Burgundy, dukes of, 16, 31, 38, 139, 146
Bus tours, 60
Buses, 49-50, 51
Business services, **62-3**
Buyssens, Jules, 126
Byron, Lord George Gordon, **21-2**

Cabarets, **190**
Cafés, 166-7, **176-9**
Calendar of events, **69-71**
Campin, Robert, 38, 39, 103
Cantillon, Paul, 112
Caravaggio, 40
Carriage Museum, 118
Cars:
  accidents, 64
  breakdowns, 64
  documents required, 44
  driving in Brussels, 51-2
  ferries, 47
  gasoline, 52
  parking, 52
  renting, 52
  speed limits, 52
Cartoons, **90**
  Centre Belge de la Bande Dessinée, 68, 90, 92, **96**, 120, 205, 206
  Festival du Dessin Animé, 69, 206
  shops, **202-3**
Cashpoint machines, 54-5
Casinos, **190**
Cathédrale Saint-Michel, 32, 33, 59, 68, 73, 81, 125, **127-8**, 184
Cavell, Edith, **22**, 141
Cemeteries, 138
  Cimetière de Bruxelles,

74, 107, **140**, 144
  Cimetière de Laeken, **140-1**, 144
Central Africa Museum see Koninklijk Museum voor Middenafrika
Centre Belge de la Bande Dessinée, 68, 90, 92, **96**, 120, 205, 206
Centre Culturel le Botanique, 92, **140**, 146
Centre Ville, shops, **191-2**
Cercle Gaulois, 146
Cézanne, Paul, 41
Chalet Robinson, **205**
Chaloupe d'Or, **135**
Chambon, Alban, 160
Channel Tunnel, 47
Chapelle de la Madeleine, 84, 91, 125
Chapelle de Marie la Misérable, 125
Chapelle de Nassau, 84, 91, 113, 121, 125, **128**, 136, 139
Chapelle Sainte-Anne, 91
Charge cards, 45, 65
Charlemagne building, *28*
Charles II of Spain, 134
Charles V, Emperor, 16, 40, 69, 97-8, 111, 118, 126
Charles VI, Emperor, 17
Charles of France, 15
Charles of Lorraine, 84, 128, 135, 149
Charles the Bold, 16, 38
Charlier, Guillaume, 110
Charlotte, Empress, 149
Cheese, 166, 193, **200**
Chess, **209**
Chevalier, Maurice, 178
Children, **205-7**
  Bois de la Cambre, 144
  clothes stores, **196**
  in hotels, 157
  Musée des Enfants, **112**, **206**
  Musée du Jouet, 114, **206**
  Parc de Bruxelles, 146-7
  toy stores, **203**
Chirico, Giorgio de, 42, 109
Chocolates, 193, **199-200**
Christmas, 71
Christus, Petrus, **39**, 104
Churches, 59, 61, 92, **125-30**
  listed, 126
  see also individual churches

Churchill, Winston, 161
Ciamberlani, 85
Cimetière de Bruxelles, 74, 107, **140**, 144
Cimetière de Laeken, **140-1**, 144
Cinema, 66-7, **185-7**
  for children, **205**
  International Film Festival, 69, 185-6
  Musée du Cinéma, 81, **110-11**
  tipping ushers, 57
Cinquantenaire Museums, 75, **96-7**, 97, 101
Cinquantenaire Park, 12, 19, 29, 34, 71, 72, 97
Claudel, Paul, **22**
Claus, Emile, 107, 110
Climate, 54, 66
Clothes, 48
  shops, 193, **195-6**
  sizes chart, 194
Cluysenaar, Jean-Pierre, 34, 121-2
Coach services, 61
Cobra, **43**, 109
Cock, Hieronymus, 40
Cocteau, Jean, 12
Coecke, Maria, 129
Coecke Van Aelst, Pieter, 40
Colonne du Congrès, 88
Comic books, **202-3**
Comic Strip Museum see Centre Belge de la Bande Dessinée
Communes, **72-4**
Computer supplies, **204**
Comte de Flandre station, 142
Constable, John, 41, 106
Consulates, 61
Corneille, 109
Coronelli, Vincentius, 117
Cosyns, Jean, 133, 134, 141
Coudenberg, palace of, 15, 139
Council of Ministers, 11, 19, 27, **28-9**
Courier services, 63
Credit cards, 45, 65
Crespin, Adolphe, 85
Cricket, **209**
Curiosities, **90-1**
Currency, 44-5
Currency exchange, 45, 54-5
Customs and excise, 45-6
Cycling see Bicycles

Dalí, Salvador, 104, 109
Dance, **183-4**, **188-9**
David, Gerard, **39**, 104
David, Jacques-Louis, **22**, 80, 106-7, 140
De Smet, Gustave, **42**, 108
Delacroix, Eugène, 41, 106, 111
Delporte, Dr Franz, 105
Delporte Bequest, 105
Delune, Léon, 86
Delvaux, Paul, **42**, 68, 91, 108, 109, 112, 142
Dentists, 64
Devos, Raymond, 20
Dialing codes, 55-6
Diamonds, 197
Dinant, 150
Disabled visitors, 58
Discos, **188-9**
Doctors, 64
Documents required, 44
Dollo, Louis, 113
Driver's licenses, 44
Duden, Willem, 148
Dürer, Albrecht, 100, 111
Duty-free allowances, 45

Ecclesiastical buildings, **125-30**
  listed, 126
Église Notre-Dame de la Chapelle, 33, 40, 70, 83, **128-9**, 135
Église Notre-Dame de Finistère, 33, 92, **128**
Église Notre-Dame du Sablon, 33, 83, 89, 92, 111, 125, **129**, 136
Église Orthodox Russe, 125
Église Saint-Denis, **129**
Église Saint-Jean Baptiste, 80
Église Saint-Nicolas, 81, 92, **129-30**
Egmont, Count, 17, 111, 128, 150
Egmont family, 147
Einstein, Albert, 160
Eisenhower, Dwight D., 161
Electric current, 57
Elisabeth, Queen, 142
Embassies, 61
Emergency information, **64-5**
Empain, Edouard, 20, **22**
L'Enclos des Fusillés, 138, **141**
Engelbert II of Nassau, 128
Engels, Friedrich, 18

English-language bookstores, 61
Ensor, James, **41**, 68, 107, 110
Entertainments, **180-90**
Erasmus, Desiderius, 16, **22**, **100**
  Maison Erasme, **100**
Ernst, Max, 178
Escalier des Juifs, 91
Espace Louise, 193
Espace Photographique Contretype, 120, **141**
Étang des Enfants Noyés, 88
Étangs Mellaerts, 209
Etiquette, 57
L'Étoile, **134**
Euratom, 19, 20
Euro-gifts, **203-4**
Eurocheques, 45
Eurocontrol, 26
Europalia, 70-1
European Christmas Market, 71
European Coal and Steel Community (ECSC), 20, 26
European Commission, 11, 19, 20, 27, 28, 154
European Community (EC), 11, **26-9**, 36, 54, 72, 193, 203-4
European Currency Units (ECU), 45
European Economic Community (EEC), 19, 20, 26
European Free Trade Association, 26
European Parliament, 27, **29**, 148
European Quarter, **72**, **77**
  hotels, 155, 158
  map, 73
  restaurants and cafés, 166, 172-4
Evenpoel, Henri, 107
Evere, 28, **74**
Excursions, **150-3**
Expressionism, 42, 43, 107, 108

Farnese, Alexander, 17
Fax services, 56
Fayd'herbe, Lucas, 129
Ferries, 47-8, 60-1
Festival du Dessin Animé, 69, 206
Festival of Flanders, 70
Festivals, **182-3**, **206**

Film see Cinema
Fire services, 64
First Latem Group, **42**
Fisco, Claude, 136
Fishing, **210**
Fitness centers, **210**
Flamboyant Gothic, 33
Flanders, 30, 31
Flea markets, **201-2**
Flemish Primitives, 38, 67, 117
Floral tapestry, 70, 132
Foire du Midi, 70
Folk music, **187-8**
Fondation pour l'Architecture, **97**, 120
Food and drink:
  beer, 110
  biscuits, **200**
  cafés, **176-9**
  cheese, 166, 193, **200**
  for children, **205**
  chocolates, 193, **199-200**
  in hotels, 156
  markets, **201-2**
  see also Beer; Restaurants
Football (soccer), 208, **210**
Forêt de Soignes, 12, 31, 50, 74, 78, **87-8**, 89, 127, 143, **145**, 146, 148, 151, 152, 205, 211
  map, 87
Fountains, 90
  Anspach, 80
  Manneken Pis, 78, 90, **92-3**, 93
Fourment, Hélène, 41
Francken, Hieronymus the Younger, 106
Free sightseeing, 59
Free University of Brussels, 18, 20, 89

Gainsborough, Thomas, 41, 106
Galerie Agora, 192-3
Galerie Bortier, 34, 84, **121-2**, 193
Galerie de la Reine, 81, 122, 192, 199
Galerie de la Toison d'Or, 193
Galerie des Beaux-Arts, 81, 91
Galerie des Princes, 80, 122, 192
Galerie du Commerce, 34
Galerie du Roi, 80, 122, 192

Galerie Louise, 193
Galeries, **192-3**
Galeries Saint-Hubert, 18, 34, 59, 67, 73, 80, 92, **122**, 192
Galland, Jacques, 120
Gardens see Parks and gardens
Gare Centrale, 36, 48-9
Gare du Midi, 49
  market, **201**
Gare du Nord, 48
Gare Quartier Leopold, 49
Gare Schuman, 49
Gasoline, 52
Gauchier, Paul, 147
Gauguin, Paul, 107
De Gaulle, Général, 12
Geefs, Guillaume, 136, 140
General delivery, 48
Geografisch Arboretum te Tervuren, **145-6**, 152
Géry, St, Bishop of Cambrai, 15, 138
Ghent, 38, 53, 150, 183
Ghirlandaio, 39
Gide, André, 20
Girault, Charles, 96, 98
Gliding, **210**
Gobert, Paul de, 142
Golf, **210-11**
Gonzaga, Ferrante, 118
Gossaert, Jan, **40**, 105
Gothic architecture, **33**
Grand'Place, 17, 32, 33, 35, 66, 67, 73, 78, 81, 91, 92, 110, 120, 130, **131-5**, 131
  cafés, 176
  hotels, 154-5, 158
  map, 133
  market, **201**
  nightlife, 185
  restaurants and cafés, 166, 205
  shops, 191, 192
Grétry, André, 136
Grévisse, Maurice, 20
Grimbergen, 51, **151-2**
Groeningemuseum, Bruges, 39
Grupello, Gabriel, 107
Gudule, St, 127-8
Gueuze Museum see Musée de la Gueuze
Guild houses, Grand'Place, **132-5**
Guimard, Barnabé, 34, 109, 114, 137, 146

Hairdressers, tipping, 58
Halles de Schaerbeek, 35, 180
Halles Saint-Géry, 79
Hallyday, Johnny, 20
Hamesse, Paul, 68
Hankar, Paul, **22**, 35, 84-6, 88
Hannon, Edouard, 41, 141
Hapsburg Empire, 16-17, 40
Hats, 195
Haut de la Ville see Upper Town
Help lines, 65
Henri I, Duke of Brabant, 15, 127, 141
Hepburn, Audrey, **22**
Herbosch, Pieter, 134
Hergé, **24**, 90, 96, 142, 192
Heritage Day, 59, 70, 121
Heysel, **73**
Heysel stadium, 73, 95, 208
Hirohito, Emperor, 161
Historium, **97-8**
History, **15-20**
Hitchhiking, 57
Hoffman, Josef, 89, 124-5
Holbein, Hans, 100
Holidays, public, 54
Hoorn, Count, 17, 111, 128, 150
Hôpital Saint-Luc, 91
Horse-racing, 208
Horta, Victor, **22-3**, 35-6, 48-9, 68, 83, 84-6, 89, 96, 110, **113**, 120, 138, 147
Hôtel de Nassau, 139
Hôtel de Ville, 32, 33, 72, 76, 84, 88, 90, 93, 94, 111, **123-4**, 131, 132
Hôtel Solvay, 35, 86
Hôtel Tassel, 35, 85
Hôtel Van Eetvelde, 35
Hotels, **154-63**
  A-Z list, 158-63
  apartment hotels, 163
  bargains, 156
  children in, 157
  classified by area, 158
  facilities, 155
  food, 156
  location, 154-5
  reservations, 156-7
  tipping, 58, 157
  viewpoints, 94
  weekend rates, 67
Hugo, Victor, 21, **23**, 123, 164
Hunting, **211**

IAMAT (International Association for Medical Assistance to Travelers), 44
Ice-skating, **211**
Identity cards, 44, 57
Îlot Sacré, 80, **135**, 142
    restaurants and cafés, 167, 205
Impressionism, **41**, 67, 68, 106-7, 111
Inquisition, 17
Insurance:
    medical, 44
    travel, 44
Interludes, **91-2**
International Book Fair, 69
International Film Festival, 69, 185-6
International institutions, **26-9**
Isabella, Archduchess, 17, 41
Itterbeek, 152
Ixelles, 68, **74**, **84-6**, 88, 111, 148
    map, 85

Jabbeke, 42
Jacqmain, André, 37
Jamaer, Victor, 111
Janssens, René, 85
Japanese Pagoda see Tour Japonaise
Jardin Botanique, 91-2, 140, **146**
Jardin des Sculptures, 83-4, 92, 107
Jazz, 70, 71, **187-8**
Jazz Rally, 69, 187-8
Jean II, Duke, 16
Jeanne of Aragon and Castile, 16
Jeune Peinture Belge movement, 109
Jewelry, **197**
Jezus-Eik, 145, 152
John, Count of Holland, 38
John the Fearless, 16
Jordaens, Jacob, 106, 164
Jorn, Asger, 43
Joseph II, Emperor, 17
Judo, **209**

Karate, **209**
Kasteel van Beersel, 51, **151**
Keilig, Edmond, 143
Keldermans, Antoon, 111
Keldermans, Rombout, 111
Kelly, Grace, 161

Kennedy, John F., 95
Kienholz, Edward, 109
Kinépolis, 73, 144, 186
Klimt, Gustav, 125
Knokke, 42, 53, 150, 190
Koninklijk Museum voor Middenafrika, 34, 50, 89, 90, 94, **98-9**, 149, 152, 210
Krol, Lucien, 91, 120

Lace, 193, **198-9**
Lace Museum see Musée du Costume et de la Dentelle
Laeken, 17, 69, **73**
Laenen, Jean-Paul, 142
Lainé, 149
Lambeaux, Jef, 147
Lambert II, 15
Landmark buildings, **120-5**
    listed, 121
Language, **30-1**
Latem Painters, **42**, 110
Lavatories, public, 57, 58
Law Courts see Palais de Justice
Laws and regulations, 57
Leather goods, 193, **196-7**
Leonardo da Vinci, 40
Leopold I, King, 18, 19
Leopold II, King, 12, 19, 34, 35, 70, 73, 86, 89, 95, 98, 99, 101, 113, 114, 119-20, 124, 127, 130, 145, 147, 149, 152
Leopold III, King, 19
Libraries:
    Bibliotheca Wittockiana, **139**
    Bibliothèque Royale, 18, 84, 91, **121**, 136, **139**
Licas, Antoine, 95
Liège, 53, 150, 183, 193
Lion de Waterloo, 153
Livingstone, David, 99
Local publications, 58
Lorraine, Dukes of, 138
Lost property, 65
Lost travelers checks, 45, 65
Louis XIV of France, 17
Louvain, counts of, 15
Louvain-la-Neuve, 42
Lower Town (Bas de la Ville), 72, **73**, **78-81**, 88, 93
    hotels, 155, 158
    map, 79
    restaurants and cafés, 166
    sights, 76

Magritte, René, **23**, 38, **42**, 59, 68, 91, 109, 112, 136, 178
Maison Ciamberlani, 85
Maison de la Bellone, 138, **141**
Maison de Saint-Cyr, 35, 35, 138
Maison d'Erasme, 33, 73
Maison des Brasseurs, 110, **134-5**
Maison des Ducs de Brabant, **135**
Maison du Cornet, **134**
Maison du Cygne, **134**
Maison du Louve, **134**
Maison du Peuple, 83
Maison du Renard, **134**
Maison du Roi, 17, 111
Maison du Roi d'Espagne, **133-4**
Maison du Sac, **134**
Maison Émile Vinck, 86
Maison Erasme, **100**
Maison Hankar, 85
Maison José Ciamberlani, 86
Malibran, Maria, 140
Man of Spy, 113
Manet, Edouard, 149
Manhattan Quarter, 36-7
Manneken Pis, 78, 90, **92-3**, 93, 134
Maps:
    European Quarter, 73
    Grand'Place, 133
    Ixelles, 85
    Lower Town, 79
    Upper Town, 82
    walks, 79, 82, 85, 87
Maquet, Henri, 124
Marathons, 69, 70, 208, 211
Margaret of Austria, 105
Maria-Theresa, Empress, 17
Marionnette theaters, **207**
Markets, 67, 73, **200-2**
    Marché du Vieux Papier, 101
    Marolles, 135
    Place du Grand Sablon, 137
    Place Sainte-Catherine, 79-80, 137
Marolles, 93, 120, 124, 130, **135**
    market, **201-2**
Marx, Karl, 11, 18, **23**, 134
Mary of Burgundy, 16, 118
Master of Flémalle, 38, 103, 117

Master of 1473, 104
Master of Mérode, 38
Master of Sainte-Gudule, 104, 127
Maus, Octave, 41, 107, 111
Max, Adolphe, **23**, 123-4, 140
Maximilian, Archduke of Austria, 16, 126
Maximilian, Emperor of Mexico, 149
Maximilian I, Emperor of Austria, 118
Maximilian Emmanuel of Bavaria, 93, 134-5
Medical emergencies, 64
Medical insurance, 44
Medieval wall, 138, **141-2**
Memling, Hans, 16, **39**, 104
Mendelson, Marc, 142
Mercator, Gerhardus, 150
Metro, 49-50
  stations, 138, **142**
Metsys, Quentin, **40**, 105
Metternich, Prince, 21, **23**
Meunier, Constantin, 110, **114**, 146
Meyboom, planting the, 70
Michelangelo, 41
Mini Europe, 73, 93, 95, **100**, 144
Monet, Claude, 107
Money, 44-5
  banks and currency exchange, 54-5
Mont des Arts, 84, 93, 121, **136**, 139
Monument du Pigeon Soldat, 90-1
Moreel, Willem, 104
Moser, Koloman, 124-5
Mosque, 147
Mostaert, Jan, **40**
Mot, Jean de, 116
Movies see Cinema
Murals, metro stations, 142
Musée d'Art Ancien, 38, 39, 40, 41, 59, 67, 68, 84, 88, 91, 92, 94, **101-7**, 118, 127, 146, 183
  plan, *102*
Musée de l'Art Funéraire, 140-1
Musée d'Art Moderne, 38, 42, 43, 59, 68, 81, 84, 88, 91, 94, **107-9**, 118, 137
Musée des Beaux-Arts, 50, 73
Musée Bellevue, 59, 94, **109**, 137

Musée de la Brasserie, **110**, 133, 135
Musée Charlier, **110**
Musée du Cinéma, 81, **110-11**, 187
Musées du Cinquantenaire, 34
Musée Communal, 93, **111**, 131, 132, 145
Musée Communal d'Ixelles, 41, **111-12**
Musée Constantin Meunier, 86, 92, 94, **114**
Musée du Costume et de la Dentelle, **112**
Musée David et Alice van Buuren, **110**
Musée de la Dynastie, 124
Musée des Égouts, **112**
Musée des Enfants, **112**, **206**
Musée de la Gueuze, **112**
Musée Horta, 35, 68, 85, **113**, 120
Musée de l'Imprimerie, 121, 139
Musée de l'Institut Royal des Sciences Naturelles, **113**, 148, 206
Musée Instrumental, 67, 68, 84, 93, 94, **114**, 137
Musée du Jouet, 114, **206**
Musée des Postes et Télécommunications, 83, **114**, 136
Musée Royal de l'Armée et d'Histoire Militaire, 59, 67, 94, 96, *97*, **101**
Musées Royaux d'Art et d'Histoire, 59, 67, 68, 94, 96-7, *97*, 112, **115-18**, 147, 193, 206
Musées Royaux des Beaux-Arts, 84, 91, 92, **118**
Musée du Transport Urbain Bruxellois, 89, 90, **118**, 142
Musée Wiertz, 59, 91, 94, **118-19**
Museum of Brewing see Musée de la Brasserie
Museum of Costume and Lace see Musée du Costume et de la Dentelle
Museum of Country Crafts, Grimbergen, 152
Museum of Modern Art see Musée d'Art Moderne
Museum of Musical Instruments see Musée Instrumental

Museum voor Schone Kunsten, Antwerp, 40, 41
Museums, 67, **94-120**
  for children, **206**
  listed, 94
  opening hours, 59, 75
  see also individual museums
Music:
  classical, **182**
  dance, **183-4**
  discos, **188-9**
  folk, **187-8**
  jazz, 69, 70, 71, **187-8**
  Musée Instrumental, 67, 68, 84, 93, 94, **114**, 137
  opera, **183**
  rock, **188**

Namur, 53, 150, 190
Napoleon I, 18, 69, 153, 158
Napoleon III, 21
Natural Science Museum see Musée de l'Institut Royal des Sciences Naturelles
Neighborhoods, **130-8**
  listed, 130
Neoclassical architecture, **33-4**
Nerval, Gérard de, 21
New Year's Eve, 71
Newspapers, 58
Nightlife, **185-90**
North Atlantic Treaty Organization (Nato), 12, 20, 26, 74, 154
North Sea, 150
Notre-Dame du Bon Secours, 33, 78
Notre-Dame aux Riches Claires, 78

Océadium, 144
Off the beaten track, **138-43**
Old city, 72
Ommegang, 13, 33, 69-70, 129, 132
Opening hours:
  museums, 59, 75
  shops, 55
Opera, **183**
Order of the Golden Fleece, 33
Orientation, **72-4**
Ostend, 41, 108
Otbert, Abbé, 15
Outer Districts, sights, 77
Overijse, 27

Paintings, **38-43**, 68, **198**
Pajottenland, 40, 105, 106, 151, **152**
Palace, Royal see Palais Royal
Palais des Beaux-Arts, 19, 36, 81, 185-6
Palais du Centenaire, 36, 36
Palais de Charles de Lorraine, 34, 84
Palais des Congrès, 42, 136
Palais d'Egmont, 83
Palais de la Folle Chanson, 36, 89
Palais de Justice, 19, 32, 34, 73, 79, 82, 89, 120, **124**, 148
Palais de la Nation, 34, 82
Palais du Roi, 70, 82, 88, **124**
Palais Royal, 17, 73, 77
Palais Stoclet, 89, **124-5**
Parachute jumping, **211**
Parc de Bruxelles, 34, 50, 59, 66, 67, 82, 88, 91, 92, 107, 124, 143, **145-6**, 150, 206, 211
Parc du Cinquantenaire, 71, 72, 94, 96, 97, 115, 120, **147**
Parc Duden, 93, **147-8**
Parc d'Egmont, 83, 91, **147**
Parc Josaphat, **148**, 207
Parc Leopold, 92, 93, 113, **148**
Parc du Roi, 86
Parc station, 142
Parc Tenbosch, 86, **148**
Park van Tervuren, **149-50**, 152, 207
Parc Tournay-Solvay, 88, **148-9**
Parc de Woluwé, 90, **149**, 150, 207, 210, 211
Parc de Wolvendael, **149**
Parking, 52
Parks and gardens, **143-50**
for children, **206-7**
listed, 143
see also individual parks
Passage du Nord, 80
Passports, 44, 57
lost, 65
Pastorana, Anthonis, 129, 134
Pavillon Chinois, **119**
Pavillon des Passions Humaines, 147
Performing arts, **180-5**
Perfume, duty-free allowances, 45

Permeke, Constant, **42**, 108, 110
Petit, Gabrielle, **23**, 84, 141
Petite Ceinture, 72
Pharmacies, 24-hour, 64
Philip II of Spain, 16-17, 39, 69, 126, 128
Philip the Bold, 16
Philip the Fair, 16, 128
Philip the Good, 16, 38, 136
Picton, Lord, 153
Piqué, Charles, 11
Pissoirs, 57
Place des Martyrs, 80, 91, 120, 130, **136**
Place du Châtelain market, **201**
Place du Grand Sablon, 50, 66, 67, 73, 83, 89, **136-7**
Place du Jeu de Balle, market, **201-2**
Place du Petit Sablon, 83, 89, 92, 136, 150
Place Royale, 82, 88, 94, 109, 130, **137**, 146
Place Sainte-Catherine, 79, 130, **137**
Place Saint-Géry, 78, **137-8**
Planetarium, 144
Planting the Meyboom, 70
Plastic Bertrand, 20
Poelaert, Joseph, 34, 79, 124, 140
Police, 64
Porte de Hal, 16, 70, **119**, **125**, 125, 141
Post-Impressionism, 41
Post offices, 48, 55, 60
Poste restante, 48
Prigogine, Ilya, **23-4**
Public holidays, 54
Public lavatories, 57, 58
Public transport, 49-50
Public Transport Weekend, 49, 71
Publications, local and foreign, 58
Puppet theaters, **207**
Théâtre Toone, **142-3**

Quakers, 61

Racing:
cycling, 208
horse, 208
Rail travel, 47, 48-9, 53, 210
Rainy days, 67
Raphael, 40

Recreation, **205-12**
Reiff, Gaston, **24**
Reine Elisabeth Music Festival, 69, 182
Rembrandt, 106, 131
Rémy, George (Hergé), **24**, 90, 96, 142, 192
Renaissance architecture, **33**
Renaissance art, **40**
Renoir, Pierre Auguste, 107
Renting:
bicycles, 205
cars, 52
rowboats, 207
Résidence Palace, 36
Rest rooms, 57
Restaurants, **164-74**
A-Z list, 167-72
cabaret revue, **190**
for children, 205
classified by area, 166-7
European Quarter, 172-4
in hotels, 156
menus, 165-6
tipping, 58
see also Food and drink
Reynolds, Sir Joshua, 41
Richard the Lionheart, 15
Rimbaud, Arthur, 21
Rock music, **188**
Rodin, Auguste, 111, 121
Roller skating, **207**
Romanticism, **41**, 106-7
Roosenboom, Albert, 86
Rowboats, **207**
Royal Fine Arts Museum see Musées Royaux des Beaux-Arts
Royal Greenhouses, Laeken, 69
Royal Library see Bibliothèque Royale
Royal Museum of the Army and Military History see Musée Royal de l'Armée et d'Histoire Militaire
Royal Museums of Art and History see Musées Royaux d'Art et d'Histoire
Royal Palace see Palais Royal
Rubens, Pieter Paul, 33, 38, **40-1**, 68, 101, 103, 105, 106, 132, 136
Rugby, **211**
Running, **211**
Rush hours, 55

Sabena building, 36

Sablon *see* Place du Grand Sablon
Saedeleer, Valerius de, 42
Safety, 185
Sainte-Catherine, 79
  market, **202**
Saint-Gilles, **74**
Saint-Guidon, 73
St-Jacques sur Coudenberg, 137
Saint-Josse-ten-Noode, 21, **74**
St Nicholas' Day, 71
St Nicholas' Eve, 71
Saintenoy, Paul, 84, 114
Salu, Ernest, 140
Sax, Adolphe, **24**
Schaerbeek, 15, **74**
Schultz, George, 12
Schuman, Robert, 28, 54
Sculpture, 90-1, **92-4**
  Jardin des Sculptures, 83-4, 92, 107
  metro stations, 142
  Musée d'Art Ancien, 107
Sea travel, 47-8, 60-1
Second Latem Group, **42**, 110
Senne, River, 16, 78, 80, 111, 112, 124, 138, 151
Sentier du Chemin de Fer, **150**
Serclaes, Everard 't, 78
Serres Royales, 35
Servaes, Albert, 42
Seurat, Georges, 107
Sewers Museum *see* Musée des Égouts
Shoe stores, **196**
Shops, **191-204**
  antiques, **197-8**
  beer, **200**
  biscuits, **200**
  books, 61, **202**
  cheese, **200**
  chocolates, **199-200**
  clothes, 193, **195-6**
  comic books, **202-3**
  computer supplies, **204**
  Euro-gifts, **203-4**
  fine art, **198**
  galeries, **192-3**
  jewelry, **197**
  lace, **198-9**
  leather goods, 193, **196-7**
  markets, **200-2**
  opening hours, 55
  shoes, **196**
  toys, **203**
  what to buy, **193**

Simenon, Georges, 20
Sint-Anna-Pede, 152
Sint-Hubertus-Kapel, Tervuren, 152
Sint-Idesbald, 42
Sint-Martens-Latem, 42
Sisley, Alfred, 107
Snooker, **212**
Snyders, Frans, 106
Soccer, 208, **210**
Solvay, Ernest, **24**, 41
Solvay family, 148
Somville, Roger, 142, 161
Souvenirs, **203-4**
Spa, 150
Spaak, Paul-Henri, **24**
Spaanse Huis, Tervuren, 152
Speed limits, 52
Spilliaert, Léon, 108, 111
Sports, **207-12**
Sports complexes, **212**
Square Marie-Louise, **138**
Squash, **212**
Stanley, Henry Morton, 19, 99
Statues *see* Sculpture
Stephenson, George, 18
Stib, 49-50
Stock Exchange *see* Bourse
Stockel station, 142
Stoclet, Mons, 124
Strauven, Gustave, 35, 86, 138
Street names, 91
Streetscapes, **130-8**
  listed, 130
Stuyvenbergh station, 142
Suburbs:
  hotels, 155, 158
  restaurants and cafés, 166-7
Sundays in Brussels, 66-7
Surrealism, **42**, 68, 81, 91, **108-9**, 111, 198
Suys, Léon-Pierre, *121*
Swimming, **212**
Synagogues, 61

Tassel, 41
Tassis, François de, 129
Tax, value-added (VAT), 46, 191
Taxis, 48, 51
  tipping, 57
  tours, 60
Telegrams, 56
Telephone services, 55-6, 60, 62
Television, 58
  in hotels, 155

Tennis, 208, **212**
Tervuren, 27, 50, 59, 66, 146, **152**
  Geografisch Arboretum te Tervuren, **145-6**, 152
  Park van Tervuren, **149-50**
  tram rides, **89-90**
Theaters, **180-2**
  marionnette, **207**
  tipping, 57
Théâtre du Poche, 144
Théâtre Royal de la Monnaie, 18, 80, 180, 183, 184
Théâtre Royal du Parc, 146, 180, 181
Théâtre Toone, **142-3**, 180, 182
Théâtre Varia, 180, 181-2
Theme parks, Mini Europe, 73, 93, 95, **100**, 144
Thielemans, Jean (Toots), **24**
Tickets:
  entertainments, 184-5
  public transport, 49-50
Time zones, 53-4
Tingueley, Jean, 109
Tintin, 24, 90, 96, 192, 206
Tipping, 57-8
  in cinemas, 57, 185
  in hotels, 58, 157
  taxis, 57
Titian, 40
Tobacco, duty-free allowances, 45
Toone puppet theater, **142-3**, 180, 182
Toulouse-Lautrec, Henri de, 41, 112
Tour d'Anneessens, 142
Tour et Tassis family, 16, 83, 114, 129, 146
Tour Japonaise, 59, 91, 94, **119-20**
Tour Noire, 141-2
Tourist information, **44-65**
  addresses and telephone numbers, **59-61**
  before you go, **44-8**
  calendar of events, **69-71**
  emergencies, **64-5**
  on-the-spot, **53-9**
Tourist offices, 46-7, 59
Town Hall *see* Hôtel de Ville
Toys:
  Musée du Jouet, 114, **206**
  shops, **203**
Trains, 47, 48-9, 53, 210

Trams, 49-50, **88-90**
  Musée du Transport
    Urbain Bruxellois, 118
Translation agencies, 62-3
Travel:
  air, 47, 60
  from airport to city, 48
  bicycles, 53, 205, 209-10
  buses, 49-50, 51, 60
  cars, 51-2
  coaches, 61
  insurance, 44
  metro, 49-50
  rush hours, 55
  sea, 47-8, 60-1
  taxis, 48, 51, 57, 60
  trains, 47, 48-9, 53, 210
  trams, 49-50, **88-90**
  walking, 53, 60
Travelers checks, 45
  lost, 45, 65
Triumphal arch, 34, *34*, 97,
  147

Uccle, 15, **74**
Université Catholique du
  Louvain-la-Neuve, 120
Université Libre de
  Bruxelles (Free
  University), 18, 20, 89
Upper Town (Haut de la
  Ville), 72, **73**, **81-4**, 93
  hotels, 155, 158
  map, *82*
  nightlife, 185
  restaurants and cafés,
    166
  shops, 191, **192**
  sights, 76-7
  tram rides, 88

Value Added Tax (VAT),
  46, 191
Van Buuren, Alice, 110

Van Buuren, David, 110
Van Coninxloo, Jan, 105
Van de Woestijne, Gustave,
  42
Van den Berghe, Fritz, **42**
Van der Goes, Hugo, **39**,
  126, 145
Van der Weyden, Roger,
  16, 38, **39**, 68, 103,
  104, 128, 136
Van Dyck, Anthony, 40, 106
Van Eetevelde, Baron, 138
Van Eyck, Hubert, **38**
Van Eyck, Jan, 16, **38**, 39
Van Gogh, Vincent, 41
Van Hoeydonck, Paul, 142
Van Orley, Bernard, 105
Van Rode, Martin, 123
Van Ruysbroeck, Jan, 33,
  123, 127, 145
Van Rysselberghe,
  Théodore, 107
Van Thienen, Jacob, 123,
  127
Van Valckenborch, Lucas,
  211
Van Vlaenderberch,
  Barbara, 104
Van Zelle, Dr Joris, 105
Vandervelde station, 142
Verlaine, Paul, 21
Vesalius, Andreas, **24-5**
Victoria, Queen, 18
Viewpoints, **93-4**
Villeroy, Marshal de, 17,
  132
Les XX (Les Vingt), **41**,
  107, 111
Viva Brasil festival, 188
Voltaire, 21

Walking in Brussels, 53,
  60, **78-88**
  maps, *79*, *82*, *85*, *87*

Wallonia, 30, 31
Waterloo, battle of, 69, 74,
  101, 140, 158, 209
  battlefield, 51, **153**
Watermael-Boitsfort, **74**,
  88
Watteau, Antoine, 41, 106
Waux Hall, 146
Waxworks, **97-8**
Weather, 54, 66
Wellington, Duke of, 153,
  158
Western European Union,
  12, 26
Wiener Werkstätte, 89,
  124-5
Wiertz, Antoine, **41**,
  118-19
Wiertz Museum, 41
Willebroek canal, 16
William of Orange (16thC),
  17, 128, 150
William of Orange (19thC),
  18
Wine, 176
Woluwé, 150, 201
Woluwé-Saint-Lambert,
  74
Woluwé-Saint-Pierre, **74**,
  125
Words and phrases, 213-6
  emergencies, 65
Wouters, Rik, 108
Wychman, Pieter, 100
Wynants, Pierre, **25**

Yoga, **209**
Yourcenar, Marguerite, **25**

Zaventem airport, 12, 45,
  46, 47, 48, 52, 54
Zero group, 109
Zoo, Antwerp, **207**
Het Zwin, 150

List of street names

- All streets mentioned in this book that fall within the area covered by our city maps **3** to **6** are listed below. Major streets named on the Brussels Environs maps (**1** and **2**) are also listed.
- Map numbers are printed in **bold** type. Some smaller streets are not named on the maps, but the map reference given below will help you locate the correct neighborhood.

Abattoir, bd. de l', **5**D1-E1
Alexiens, rue des, **5**E3-F3
Allard, rue Ernest, **5**G3-6F4
Alsemberg, ch. d', **1**F3-C3
Amigo, rue de l', **3**E3
Anderlecht, rue d', **5**E1-2
Anneessens, pl., **5**E2
Anspach, bd., **3**E2-D3
Anvers, ch. d', **3**B3-4A4
Anvers, bd. d', **3**B3-4B4
Arbre Bénit, rue de l', **6**I5-H5
Arenberg, rue d', **4**D4
Argent, rue d', **4**D4
Arts, av. des, **6**F5-D6
Association, rue de l', **4**C5-D5
Ateliers, rue des, **3**B2
Augustins, rue des, **3**D3
Avenir, rue de l', **3**B1-C2
Aviation, sq. de l', **5**F1

Barricades, pl. des, **4**D6
Barthélémy, bd., **3**D1-C2
Baudouin, bd., **3**B3-4B4
Belliard, rue, **6**F6
Berckmans, rue, **5**H3-6H4
Berlaimont, bd. de, **4**D4-5
Beurre, rue au, **3**D3-E3
Bischoffsheim, bd., **4**C5-D6
Blaes, rue, **5**H2-F3
Blanchisserie, rue de la, **4**C4-5
Blindés, sq. des, **3**C2
Bodenbroeck, rue, **6**F4

Bois à Brûler, quai au, **3**C2-D3
Bois Sauvage, rue du, **4**D4
Boiteux, rue des, **4**D4
Bolivar, bd. Simon, **4**A4
Bouchers, Petite rue des, **3**E3-4D4
Bouchers, rue des, **3**D3-4E4
Boulevard, av. du, **4**B4-C4
Bourse, rue de la, **3**D3
Brabant, rue de, **4**C4-A5
Brasseurs, rue des, **3**E3
Brigittines, rue des, **5**F2-3
Briques, quai aux, **3**C2-D3
Brogniez, rue, **5**F1
Brouckère, pl. de, **3**C3-D3

Cadeaux, impasse des, **3**D3
Camusel, rue, **5**E1-2
Canal, rue du, **3**C2-3
Capucines, rue des, **5**G2-3
Caserne, rue de la, **5**F1-2
Chair et Pain, rue, **3**E3
Champ de Mars, rue du, **6**G5
Champs-Élysées, rue des, **6**H5-I6
Chancellerie, rue de la, **4**E4
Chapeliers, rue des, **3**E3
Chapelle, pl. de la, **5**F3
Charbonnages, quai des, **3**C2-B2
Charleroi, ch. de, **1**C3-D3
Charles Buls, rue, **3**E3

Chartreux, rue des, **5**D2-3
Chêne, rue du, **3**E3
Chevaliers, rue des, **6**G4-5
Cirque, rue du, **3**C3
Cocq, pl. Fernand, **6**H5
Collège, rue du, **6**H6
Colline, rue de la, **3**E3
Colonies, rue des, **4**E4-5
Comédiens, rue des, **4**D4
Commerçants, rue des, **3**B3-4C4
Commerce, quai du, **3**B2-3
Commerce, rue du , **6**E6-F6
Communale, pl., **3**C1
Comte de Flandre, rue du, **3**C1-B1
Concorde, rue de la, **6**H4-5
Congrès, rue des, **4**D5-6
Constitution, pl. de la, **5**G1
Couronne, av. de la, **1**C3
Courtois, rue, **3**B2
Crespel, rue Capitaine, **6**G4-H4
Croix, rue de la, **6**I5-H6
Croix de Fer, rue de la, **4**D5-6

Dansaert, rue Antoine, **3**C2-3
Defacqz, rue, **6**I4-5
Dejoncker, rue de, **5**H3-6H4
Dinant, pl. de, **5**F3
Dixmude, bd. de, **3**B2-3

Dominicains, rue des, **3D3**
Douze (12) Apôtres, rue des, **4E4**
Drapiers, rue des, **6G4-H4**
Ducale, rue, **4F5-E6**
Dupont, rue, **4B5-6**
Duquesnoy, rue, **3E3-4E4**

Ecuyer, rue de l', **3D3-4D4**
Empereur, bd. de l', **5F3-6E4**
Enseignement, rue de l', **4D5**
Éperonniers, rue des, **3E3-4E4**
Ermitage, rue de l', **6I5-6**
Étuve, rue de l', **3E3**
Evêque, rue de l', **3D3**

Fabriques, rue des, **3D1-2**
Féron, rue Émile, **5H1-2**
Fiancée, rue de la, **4C4**
Flandre, rue de, **3C2**
Foin, quai au, **3C2-3**
Fonsny, av., **5H1-G1**
Fontainas, pl., **3E2**
Forest, ch. de, **5I1-H2**
Fossé aux Loups, rue du, **3D3-4D4**
Fourche, rue de la, **3D3**
Frère-Orban, sq., **6E6-F6**
Frick, sq. Henri, **4C6-D6**
Fripiers, rue des, **3D3**

Galerie Agora, **3E3**
Galerie Bortier, **4E4**
Galerie de la Reine, **4E4**
Galerie de la Toison d'Or, **6G4-5**
Galerie des Princes, **4D4**
Galerie du Roi, **4D4**
Galerie Louise, **6G4-H4**
Galerie Ravenstein, **4E4**
Galeries St-Hubert, **4E4-D4**
Galilée, av., **4C5-6**
Gand, ch. de, **1B1-C3**
Gineste, rue, **4C5**
Grand Cerf, rue du, **6G4**
Grand-Hospice, rue du, **3C2-3**
Grand'Place, **3E3**
Grand Sablon, pl. du, **5F3-6F4**
Grand-Serment, rue du, **3D2**

Grande Île, rue de la, **3E2-D2**
Grands Carmes, rue des, **3E3**
Grétry, rue, **3D3**
Grosse Tour, rue de la, **6H4**

Haecht, ch. de, **1C3-2A5**
Hainaut, quai du, **3D1-C1**
Harengs, rue des, **3E3**
Haute, rue, **5H2-F3**
Héliport, av. de l', **3B3-A3**
Héros, pl. des, **5H1**
Hôpital, rue de l', **3E3**
Horta, rue Baron, **4E4-5**
Hôtel des Monnaies, rue de l', **5I2-H3**

Impératrice, bd. de l', **4E4-D4**
Intendant, rue de l', **3A1-2**
Ixelles, ch. d', **6G5-I6**

Jacobs, pl. Jean, **5G3-4G4**
Jacqmain, bd. Émile, **3C3-4A4**
Jamar, bd., **5G1**
Jardin aux Fleurs, pl. du, **3D2**
Jardin Botanique, bd. du, **4B4-C5**
Jardin des Olives, rue du, **3E3**
Jardinier, rue du, **3A1-B1**
Jaspar, av. Henri, **5H2-3**
Jeu de Balle, pl. du, **5G2**
Jourdan, rue, **5I2-6H4**

Keyenveld, rue, **6G5-H5**

Laeken, rue de, **3D3-B3**
Laines, rue aux, **6G4**
Lavallée, rue Adolphe, **3B1-2**
Lebeau, rue, **6F4**
Lemonnier, bd. Maurice, **5F1-E2**
Leopold, rue, **4D4**
Leopold II, bd., **1B2-3**
Lepage, rue Léon, **3D2-C2**
Liberté, pl. de la, **4D5**
Ligne, bd. du 9e de, **3C2-B2**
Livourne, rue de, **6H4-I4**
Loi, rue de la, **1C3**
Lombard, rue du, **5E3**

Londres, pl. de, **6G6**
Londres, rue de, **6G6**
Longue Haie, rue de la, **6H4-I5**
Louise, av., **1C3-D3**
Louise, pl., **6G4**
Louvain, ch. de, **1C3-2B6**
Louvain, rue de, **4E4-D6**
Loxum, rue de, **4D4-E4**
Luxembourg, rue du, **6F5-6**

Madeleine, rue de la, **4E4**
Madou, pl., **4D6**
Marais, rue du, **4D4-C5**
Marché au Charbon, rue du, **3E2-3**
Marché aux Fromages, rue du, **3E3**
Marché aux Herbes, rue du, **3D3-4E4**
Marché aux Poulets, rue du, **3D3**
Marnix, av., **6G5-F5**
Martyrs, pl. des, **4C4-D4**
Maus, rue Henri, **3D3-E3**
Max, bd. Adolphe, **3C3-4C4**
Meeus, sq. de, **6F6-G6**
Mercelis, rue, **6I5-H5**
Mercier, rue du Cardinal, **4E4**
Méridien, rue du, **4B6-C6**
Mérode, rue de, **5H1-G2**
Midi, bd. du, **5E1-F1**
Midi, rue du, **3E3-D3**
Minimes, Petite rue des, **3F3**
Minimes, rue des, **5G3-F3**
Miroir, rue du, **5E3**
Monnaie, pl. de la, **3D3**
Mons, ch. de, **1E2-C2**
Montagne, rue de la, **4E4-D4**
Montagne aux Herbes Potagères, rue, **4D4**
Montagne de la Cour, rue, **6F4**
Moulin, rue du, **4C6**
Musée, rue du, **6F4**

Namur, rue de, **6F4-G5**
Neuve, rue, **3D3-4C4**
9e (Neuvième) de Ligne, bd. du, **3C2-B2**
Nieuport, bd. de, **3C2**
Nord, pge. du, **3C3-4D4**

Nord, rue du, 4C6-D6
Notre-Dame du Sommeil, rue, 3D1-2
Notre-Seigneur, rue, 5F3
Nouveau Marché au Grain, pl. du, 3D2

Orts, rue Auguste, 3D3

Pachéco, bd., 4D5-C5
Paix, rue de la, 6H5-G6
Palais, pl. des, 6F5
Palais, rue des, 4A6-B6
Parvis St-Gilles, 5I2
Parvis Ste-Gudule, 4D4
Parvis St-Jean Baptiste, 3B1
Péniches, quai des, 3B2-A3
Pépin, rue du, 6F4-G5
Persil, rue du, 4D4
Petit Sablon, pl. du, 6F4-G4
Petite rue des Minimes, 3F3
Petite rue des Bouchers, 3E3-4D4
Peuplier, rue du, 3C3
Pierres, rue des, 3E3
Pierres-de-Tailles, quai aux, 3C2-3
Piers, rue, 3B1-A2
Plantes, rue des, 4C5-B5
Poelaert, pl., 5G3
Poincare, bd., 5E1-F1
Pont de la Carpe, rue du, 3D3
Pont Neuf, rue du, 3C3-4C4
Port, av. du, 3B2-A3
Porte de Hal, av. de la, 5G1-H2
Poste, rue de la, 4C5-A6
Prêtres, rue des, 5G3-H3
Prince Royal, rue du, 6H4-G5
Princes, rue des, 3D3-4D4
Progrès, rue du, 4C4-B4

Quatre (4) Bras, rue des, 5G3-6G4
Quint, av. Charles, 1B2

Ravenstein, rue, 4F4-E4
Régence, rue de la, 5G3-6F4
Régent, bd. du, 6G5-E6
Reine, pl. de la, 4B6
Reine, rue de la, 3D3-4D4
Reinette, rue de la, 6G5
Rempart des Moines, rue du, 3D2-C2
Renards, rue des, 5G2-3
Riches Claires, rue des, 3E2
Ring O, 1E2-2C5
Rogier, pl., 4B4-C4
Rollebeek, rue de, 5F3
Rouppe, pl., 5F2
Royale, pl., 6F4
Royale, rue, 4F5-A6
Royale Sainte-Marie, rue, 4B6-A6
Ruysbroeck, rue de, 6F4

Sables, rue des, 4D4
Sablonnière, rue de la, 4C5-D6
Sainctelette, pl., 3B2
Sainctelette, sq., 3B2-3
Ste-Anne, rue, 6F4
St-Boniface, rue, 6G5
Ste-Catherine, pl., 3D2-3
St-Géry, pl., 3D2
Ste-Gudule, pl., 4D4
St-Jacques, impasse, 6F5
St-Jean, pl., 3E3
St-Jean, rue, 3E3-4E4
St-Lazare, bd., 4B5-C5
St-Michel, rue, 4C4
Samedi, pl. du, 3D3
Sans-Souci, rue, 6G5-H6
Scailquin, rue, 4D6
Schuddeveld, impasse, 3D3
Senne, rue de la, 3E1-D2
Six Jetons, rue des, 3D2-E2
Source, rue de la, 5H3-6I4
Stalingrad, av. de, 5G2-F2
Stas, rue Jean, 6H4
Stassart, rue du, 6G5-H4
Stéphanie, pl., 6H4
Stevens, rue Joseph, 5F3
Suisse, rue de, 5H3-I3

Tabora, rue de, 3D3
Tanneurs, rue des, 5G2-F2
Terre-Neuve, rue, 5G2-F3
Tervuren, av. de, 2C4-6
Tervuren, ch. de, 2F4-D4
Toison d'Or, av. de la, 5H3-6G5
Traversière, rue, 4C5-6
Trône, pl. du, 6F5
Trône, rue du, 6F5-G6
Tulipe, rue de la, 6H5-G6

Ulens, rue, 3A2
Une (1) Personne, rue d', 4E4-D4
Ursulines, rue des, 5F2-3

Van Aa, rue, 6H5-6
Van Artevelde, rue, 3E2-D3
Van der Weyden, rue Roger, 5F2
Van Volsem, rue Jean, 6I6
Vanderschrick, rue, 5I1-H2
Vandervelde, pl. Émile, 3F3
Verte, rue, 4C5-A5
Victoire, rue de la, 5H2-I3
Victoria Regina, av., 4C5
Vieille Halle aux Blés, pl. de la, 3E3-F3
Vierge Noire, rue de la, 3D3
Vieux Marché aux Grains, rue du, 3D2
Villers, rue de, 3E3-F3
Violette, rue de la, 3E3

Waterloo, bd. de, 5H2-6G5
Waterloo, ch. de, 1C3-2E4
Watteau, rue, 5F3
Wavre, ch. de, 1C3-2E6
Willebroeck, quai de, 3B3-A3
Woluwé, av. de la, 2C4-B4

Ypres, bd. d', 3B2-C2

KEY TO MAP PAGES

1-2 BRUSSELS ENVIRONS
3-6 BRUSSELS CITY
BRUSSELS TRAM & METRO

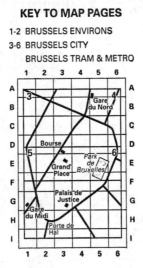

KEY TO MAP SYMBOLS

Area Maps

=O= Motorway / Superhighway
(with access point)

▬ Main Road

▬ Secondary Road

.... Minor Road

A201 Road Number

▬ Railway

✈ Airport

⛪ Church, Abbey

🏛 Chateau

■ Other Place of Interest

🌲 Forested Area

City Maps

▨ Place of Interest or
Important Building

▨ Built-up Area

▨ Park

🕇🕇 Cemetery

† Church

✡ Synagogue

⊞ Hospital

ℹ Information Office

✉ Post Office

✋ Police Station

🚗 Garage / Parking Lot

Ⓜ Metro Station

→ One-way Street

⊥⊥⊥ Stepped Street

╪╪╪ No Entry

3 Adjoining Page No.

```
0      100      200      300m
├───────┼────────┼────────┤
0      100      200      300yds
```

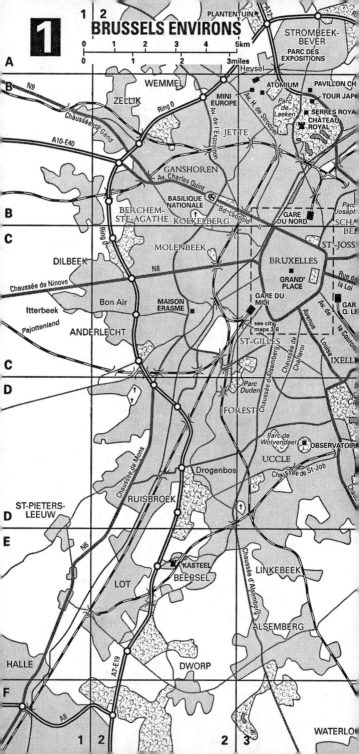

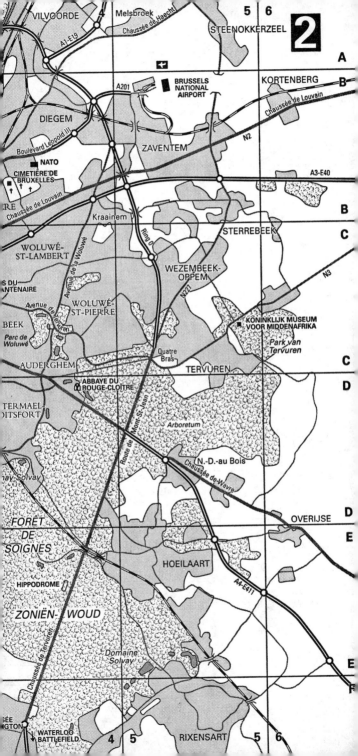

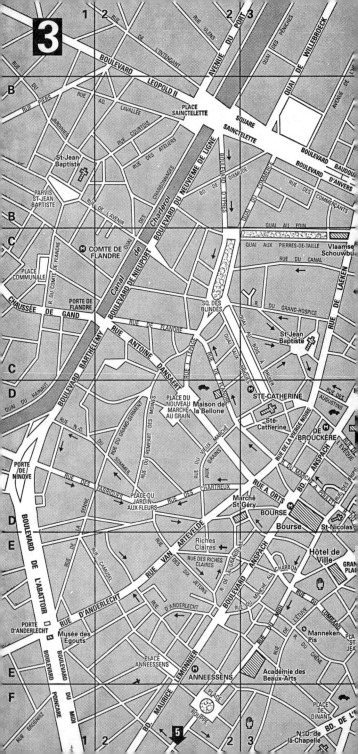

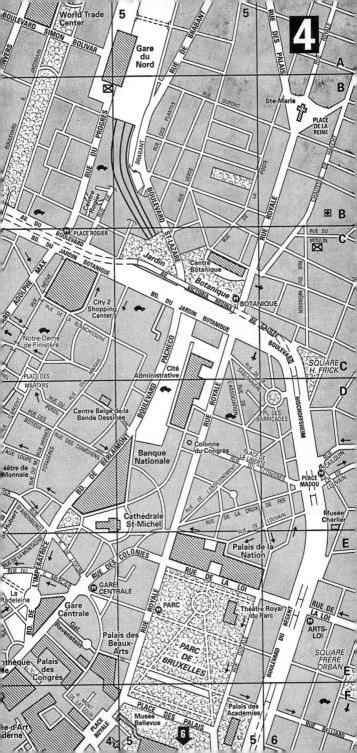

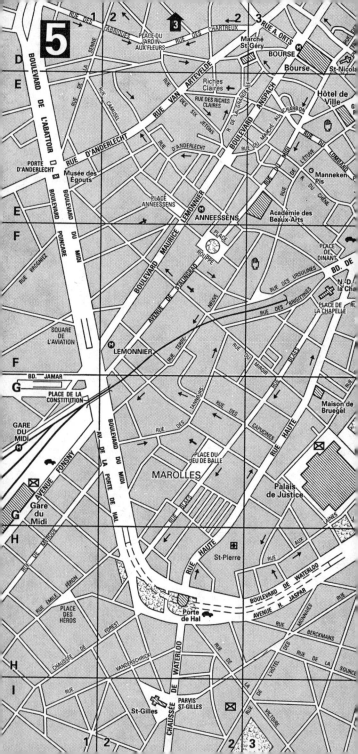

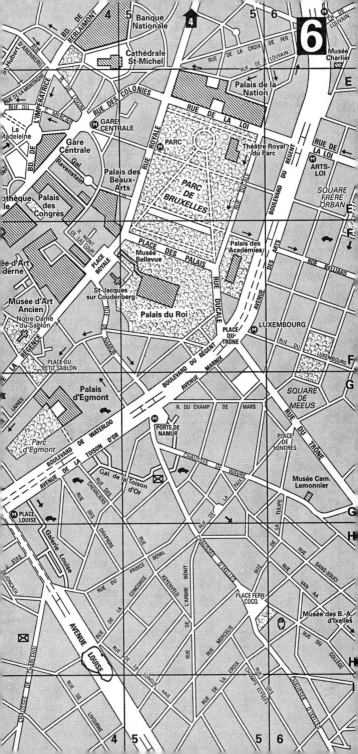

BRUSSELS tram & metro systems

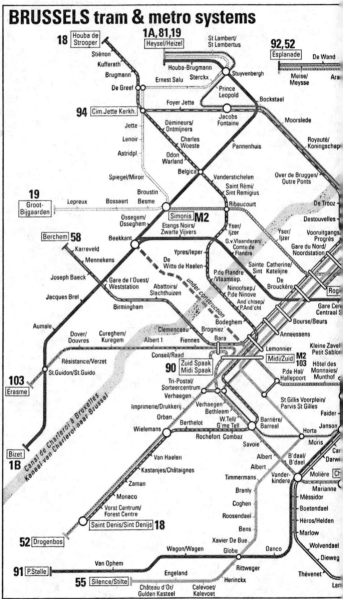

©TCS Designed by R.Woods

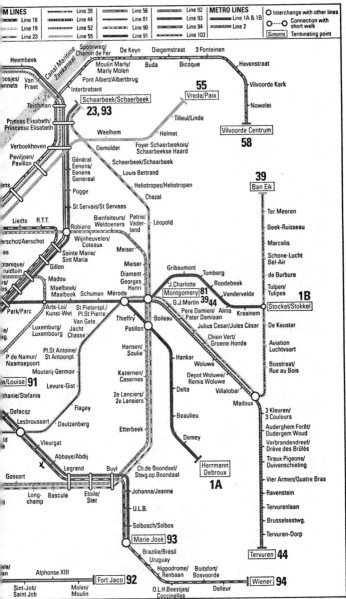

CONVERSION FORMULAE

To convert	Multiply by
Inches to Centimeters	2.540
Centimeters to Inches	0.39370
Feet to Meters	0.3048
Meters to feet	3.2808
Yards to Meters	0.9144
Meters to Yards	1.09361
Miles to Kilometers	1.60934
Kilometers to Miles	0.621371
Sq Meters to Sq Feet	10.7638
Sq Feet to Sq Meters	0.092903
Sq Yards to Sq Meters	0.83612
Sq Meters to Sq Yards	1.19599
Sq Miles to Sq Kilometers	2.5899
Sq Kilometers to Sq Miles	0.386103
Acres to Hectares	0.40468
Hectares to Acres	2.47105
Gallons to Liters	4.545
Liters to Gallons	0.22
Ounces to Grams	28.3495
Grams to Ounces	0.03528
Pounds to Grams	453.592
Grams to Pounds	0.00220
Pounds to Kilograms	0.4536
Kilograms to Pounds	2.2046
Tons (UK) to Kilograms	1016.05
Kilograms to Tons (UK)	0.0009842
Tons (US) to Kilograms	746.483
Kilograms to Tons (US)	0.0013396

Quick conversions

Kilometers to Miles	Divide by 8, multiply by 5
Miles to Kilometers	Divide by 5, multiply by 8
1 meter =	Approximately 3 feet 3 inches
2 centimeters =	Approximately 1 inch
1 pound (weight) =	475 grams (nearly $\frac{1}{2}$ kilogram)
Celsius to Fahrenheit	Divide by 5, multiply by 9, add 32
Fahrenheit to Celsius	Subtract 32, divide by 9, multiply by 5